SECRETS OF
THE BALLOT BOX

HOW THE IRISH VOTING SYSTEM **REALLY** WORKS

By
BRENDAN HENEGHAN

Foreword by Enda Kenny, TD

First Published 2018 by Brendan Heneghan

ISBN 978-1-5272-1819-2

Designed & Printed by Turners Printing Co. Ltd., Longford, Ireland.

FOREWORD
by Enda Kenny, TD

This book is a valuable addition to Irish Politics. Brendan Heneghan has quite literally done the State a service.

The Irish electorate is fascinated with elections, not just about the issues of the day, not just about the mood of the time, but about the parties, personalities, and individuals involved. They are all subject to the system of elections that we have adopted, and that the Irish people have stood by, ie the Proportional Representation System.

Candidates stand or fall, survive or vanish, emerge or decline by electoral outcomes.

That's where this book thrives.

I don't see it as a book just about elections, or just a book about issues. I see the persons involved, the stories around each type of election for over 40 years, the talks, the internal machinations being attempted to bring particular results and the human reaction that in virtually all cases becomes 'every one for themselves'.

There are six parts to the book, but about two fundamental issues. These issues are;

A. Transfers are critical to the individuals receiving them but not critical to the overall outcome, and

B. Very distinct patterns emerge in four seat constituencies when viewed together and similarly for five and six seat areas and so on.

Every public representative, and every aspiring candidate to any office should read this book. There are lessons there for all to learn.

Ireland continues to move on. Our economy, now in a much stronger position will require careful and constant management. Brexit, post Brexit, and a changing Europe present new challenges. Issues emerge constantly, some are dealt with some are not. One hundred years on from the first votes being cast by women, legislation requires political parties to comply with the worthy intention of having a greater balance of gender equality in politics. Social issues, long ignored have been dealt with or are being considered. The new digital world of connection and communications supplies tidal waves of comment and information, and carries with it unprecedented challenges.

One issue that has not changed however is the sovereignty of the Irish people.

On two occasions in the past they rejected a change to the Proportional Representation System. Nor do I see a return to experimenting with electronic voting given that fact, and international investigations into alleged interference with numerous other country electoral systems.

Another General Election will be called, or caused in due course. When that process is eventually concluded, then and only then will the title of this book become reality for all as 'the Secrets of the Ballot Box' tumble forth.

Read it. It provides and provokes really worthy discussion, irrespective of your point of view.

Enda Kenny

Enda Kenny, T.D.

by Brendan Heneghan

I have always been fascinated by the numbers in the Irish political system and understanding how they so often operate to provide either excellent or poor results. My political initiation in this was at the hands of the late Dr Garret Fitzgerald, a man who seemed equally fascinated by them and whom I well recollect leaning in wonder over ballot boxes in the 2011 general election, a short time prior to his death.

The Irish proportional representation is perhaps the most fascinating political system in the world, regardless of one's view as to its efficacy in producing governments and oppositions. It is therefore a privilege to complete a work which attempts to explain the intricacies of the system, particularly the idiosyncracies which arise with different types of multi-seat constituencies. I hope that readers will find a number of the issues which I explore, of interest. I have confined my examination to the period since 1981, over which Irish politics evolved from an essentially two and a half party system to a multi party and complex democracy. The book is intended to be factually correct as of end February 2018.

I am greatly indebted to Enda Kenny T.D. for his foreword to this book. He is one of the very few political figures who spans the period covered by this work and is without a doubt the most eminent. His family have also featured strongly in the unusual results thrown up by the system, most notably his own leadership of the unprecedented four seats of five in Mayo in 2011.

I would also like to acknowledge the invaluable assistance of Michael O'Mahony on those parts of the book which deal with the operation of the system. He is without doubt one of the foremost returning officers, who have ensured the smooth running of quite a complex system. I acknowledge also the assistance of Olga Barry, John Gannon, Gerard James and Noel Rock T.D. who had a number of useful thoughts. While I have never met him, I salute the contribution of Seán Donnelly to making material on Irish elections readily accessible over so many years. I am also most grateful to Turners of Longford, particularly Elizabeth and Roisín, who have done an excellent job in design and printing. There are undoubtedly errors in this book, for which I alone am and accept responsibility.

ABOUT THE AUTHOR
Brendan Heneghan

Brendan Heneghan, while a lawyer by profession, has been a political activist and seasoned political observer for almost 40 years. He has attended numerous counts, been involved in recounts and been a constituency and local area director of elections.

He has also served on the governing body of one of Ireland's leading parties and has in this role been involved in setting the framework for the selection of candidates. He has extensive experience on the analysis of tallies and on the analysis of population trends from census to census. He therefore has very extensive experience of how the Irish electoral system works in practice and the key issues that impact on it.

In memory of Maura and of Uncle Tom

CONTENTS

GLOSSARY
OF TERMS

The following is an explanation of some of the terms used in this book. Some are terms commonly used in politics to describe something. Others are terms used by the author to illustrate points raised in this book.

"addition" the term used to describe a candidate added by a party to its team of candidates for a particular constituency or LEA

"contamination" describes circumstances where for example a Fianna Fáil candidate gets 2,500 first preference votes, but by the time of his elimination has 2,850 votes based on 350 transfers derived from other non-Fianna Fáil candidates, his vote is "contaminated" by 350 votes. Nevertheless almost 88% of his vote represents first preferences, so the sample transferred still substantially reflects those first preferences

"cumann" the term used by Fianna Fáil and Sinn Féin to indicate a branch of the party's organization

"DED" is the abbreviation for District Electoral Division. Every county is divided into numerous DEDs and this is the basic geographic unit for electoral purposes. All voters resident in a DED usually vote at the same polling station and with good tallies it is usually possible to assess how strong or weak a candidate or party is in that DED. The census of population conducted every five years also sets out lots of statistical information by DED. A map of DEDs per county is usually included in the boundary report, when local government boundaries are reviewed

"directive" describes instructions issued by a party as to the number of candidates to be selected to run in a particular constituency or LEA

"dynasties" describes the political phenomenon where several members of the same family are elected to Dáil Eireann. An example is the election for

Fianna Fáil to the Dáil at different times of P.J.Lenihan, his son and daughter Brian Lenihan and Mary O'Rourke and his grandchildren Brian Junior and Conor

"first preference vote" this is a vote recording a number one for a particular candidate

"gene pool" this is a term coined for Independent (or occasionally smaller party) candidates that previously had a close connection with one of the major parties, but had a disagreement. For example in the Tipperary constituency in the 2016 general election, two elected candidates, Michael Lowry and Mattie McGrath had previously served Tipperary as Fine Gael and Fianna Fáil deputies respectively. Thus Lowry is regarded as Fine Gael gene pool and McGrath as Fianna Fáil gene pool

"internal coherence" describes the rate at which transfers from a candidate of a party accrue to other candidates of the same party. Thus for example if a Fianna Fáil candidate is eliminated and 60% of his transfers accrue to other Fianna Fáil candidates, that would represent a 60% rate of internal coherence. The opposite concept is "leakage"

"last man standing" this is a term used by the author for a candidate who is not eliminated on or before the last count in a constituency or LEA, but is not successful. Every count in a three seat constituency will ultimately come down to four candidates and the fourth placed one is deemed "not elected". Very occasionally the mechanics of a particular constituency or LEA mean that two candidates remain at the end of the count without being eliminated

"leaders' enclosure" this is a term used by the author as a label for the three leading candidates after the first count in an election in a three seat constituency or LEA or the leading four candidates in a four seat constituency or LEA and so on for five to ten seats respectively. As can be seen in this book, generally those candidates are the successful candidates

"leakage" this is a term used to describe votes accrued by a party candidate, which do not on transfer of that candidate's votes accrue to his or her party but benefit someone else. For example if a Fine Gael candidate is eliminated and 42% of his vote transfers to other Fine Gael candidates and 10% is non-transferable, there is said to be leakage of 48%. This represents the percentage of the vote transferring to all the other candidates

"LEA" this is an abbreviation of Local Electoral Area which is the equivalent to a constituency for local elections. They can sometimes be referred to as "wards" in large urban areas or "districts" in rural areas

"non-transferable vote" this is a vote which at the point it is examined for purposes of transferring it, shows no preference for a candidate who continues to be part of the contest. Such votes (except in case of surpluses) are credited to a bundle known as the non-transferable votes

"OMOV" this denotes one man one vote, a system used in some political parties to select candidates, which gives every member a single vote for purposes of choosing candidates in a particular area

"plumper" this is a colloquial term often used for a voter who just marks a first preference vote on a ballot paper and does not give a further preference to any other candidate

"quota" this is the number of votes usually required to be elected in a constituency or LEA. This is ascertained by dividing the valid vote by the number of seats plus one and then adding one

"recovery of expenses" this is how Irish law allows candidates to be re-imbursed some of their electoral expenditure, if they are elected or reach at the point they are eliminated a threshold of votes, usually a quarter or a third of a quota

"running mate" this is a term used to describe other candidates from a political party

"seat bonus" this is a term used to describe the phenomenon where a party gets seats greater than it is entitled to as a strict percentage of its overall first preference vote

"surplus" this is the number of votes which a candidate has which exceed the quota for a particular constituency or LEA

"sweeper" this term denotes a candidate run by a party with the expectation that the candidate will gain votes in an area which will transfer to other party candidates, but is unlikely to be elected

"tally" this is a spreadsheet, usually put together after an election, which shows how many first preference votes a candidate got in each ballot box in a constituency or LEA

"tallyman" this is a term used to describe a person working for a candidate who helps to compile the tally by observing votes at a count

"TD" this is short for Teachta Dála, the Irish term for member of parliament (lower house). They are referred to also as "deputy"

"transfer friendly" an expression used to describe an independent or party who seems to receive particularly good transfers from other parties or independents. The opposite is "transfer repellent"

"two traditional large parties" this is a term used by the author to refer to collectively Fianna Fáil and Fine Gael, who have tended to monopolise Irish politics often getting up to 80% of the vote in aggregate. They are referred to using this expression for convenience in this work.

Common abbreviations for Parties are set out in Chapter 1.

PART 1
General

CHAPTER 1
Key features of Irish Electoral System

Certain features must be appreciated to understand how the Irish electoral system works in electing members to Dáil, Seanad and local authorities. The system operated is often called *proportional representation*, but its outcome is not wholly proportionate.

The voters in a constituency each mark a ballot paper with a number of candidates, whom they can rank in order of choice, for example with Mary B as this voter's first choice or *"first preference"*.

BALLOT PAPER CONSTITUENCY OF DUBLIN

John A	3
Mary B	1
Vincent C	4
James D	2

At the election count, the candidates are ranked in order of the number of first preference votes they receive and a *quota* is established. This is known as the first count. Lower ranking candidates are eliminated during following counts and their votes transferred to other continuing candidates (i.e. a candidate not already elected or eliminated); those who exceed a quota usually have their excess votes re-distributed. Voters can express second and lower preferences in numerical order for all or some of the candidates.

Proportional representation

There is a specific requirement of the Irish *Constitution* of 1937 that elections be carried out by a method, probably misleadingly referred to there as proportional representation. For Dáil Eireann, the requirement is set out in

Leabharlanna Poibli Chathair Baile Átha Cliath

Dublin City Public Libraries

Article 16.2.5 which provides that the members shall be elected "on the system of proportional representation by means of the single transferable vote". A similar provision in Article 18.5 so provides for the elected members of the Seanad. This means that the voting system for those elections is constitutionally embedded and therefore is difficult to change.

Technically the expression "*transferable vote*" is defined in legislation as "a vote (a) capable of being given so as to indicate the voter's preference for the candidates in order; and (b) capable of being transferred to the next choice when the vote is not required to give a prior choice the necessary quota of votes, or when, owing to the deficiency in the number of votes given for a prior choice, that choice is eliminated from the list of candidates".

Whatever the electoral system may be called, it is not proportionate in terms of overall outcome. It is fairly usual in Dáil elections that parties with a large percentage of the national vote get a significantly greater percentage of the seats, colloquially called a "*seat bonus*". The highest beneficiaries in the last twelve general elections were the following:

Election	Party	Percentage vote	Percentage seats
1977	FF	50.6	56.8
1981	FG	36.5	39.2
1982 (Feb)	FF	47.3	48.8
1982 (Nov)	FG	39.2	42.2
1987	FF	44.1	48.8
1989	FG	29.3	33.1
1992	FG	24.5	27.1
1997	FF	39.3	46.4
2002	FF	41.5	48.8
2007	FF	41.6	47.0
2011	FG	36.1	45.8
2016	FG	25.5	31.6

By contrast, parties gaining less than 10% of the national vote usually gain less seats than their percentage vote, in many cases 0%. There are isolated examples where the trend is different. For example in the 1992 general election, the Progressive Democrats got 4.7% of the first preference vote, but got 6% of the seats (whereas in the previous general election in 1989 they got 5.5% of the first preference vote and 3.6% of the seats).

In practice the transferable vote requires a voter to give preference 1 to his or her most favoured candidate, preference 2 to his or her second choice and so on until at maximum the number of candidates on the ballot. So if there are 16 candidates on a ballot paper, a votes can choose to vote for one only (referred to colloquially as a *"plumper"*) or can choose to vote say 1 to 8 or can choose to go right down to a 16th preference. Sometimes a very low preference can turn out to be significant. For example in the European election in Ireland East in 2004, discussed in chapter 8, many of the preferences picked up by Avril Doyle, the candidate last elected, might have been as low as 9 or 10.

The quota

A key number to ascertain for any Irish election is the quota. This is in practice the total valid vote ascertained at the end of the first count divided by the number of seats being contested plus one. This is subject to the small issue of adding 1 to the mathematical result and discarding any fraction. Thus in practice for a 3 seat constituency or LEA (local electoral area), the quota is 25% of the first preference vote, in a 4 seat constituency or LEA, 20%, in a 5 seat constituency or LEA, 16.66%, in a 6 seat LEA, 14.28%, in a 7 seat LEA, 12.5%, in an 8 seat LEA, 11.11%, in a 9 seat LEA, 10% and in a 10 seat LEA, 9.09%. In all cases 1 vote is added.

It is easy to see the logic of this in an election for 3 seats with 4,000 valid votes cast. The quota in that instance is 1,001 that is (4,000/4) + 1. If three candidates get to 1,001 votes, the maximum aggregate votes which the other candidates can have is 997, so only three people can attain the quota. Even if the quota were exactly 1,000, it would be an extraordinary fluke were 4 candidates to end up with exactly 1,000 votes each, but the addition of one rules out that possibility.

What happens when someone exceeds the quota?

When a candidate exceeds the quota, usually that part of their vote in excess of the quota needs to be redistributed to other candidates. The excess votes are called the *surplus*. The precise votes to be examined to allocate the surplus depend on whether the quota is exceeded on the first count or on a later count.

If the quota is 1,001 and a candidate "A" has 1,400 number 1 votes on the first count, 399 of these votes are not required to elect him/her and these votes (the surplus) will be redistributed to other candidates. This involves looking at all 1,400 votes cast for A (called a "parcel" or "Sub-parcel"). They are sorted into separate bundles according to the second preference shown and reallocated according to preference 2. Preference 3 is looked at if preference 2 is for another candidate elected on the first count. Each second preference is worth 399/total number of votes that show a second preference. The resultant addition is rounded up or down to the nearest whole number. Votes that do not show any second preference are disregarded except in the unlikely event that less than 399 votes show a preference. So if in the example above candidate B gets 300 second preferences from A, candidate C gets 600 second preferences, candidate D gets 250 second preferences and candidate E gets 200 second preferences, they are allocated an extra 89 votes, 177 votes, 74 votes and 59 votes respectively (or a total of 399). The 50 votes that showed no further preference are disregarded, so because 50 of them are plumpers for candidate A, the total of ballot papers capable of being redistributed is 1,350 (1,400 minus 50) and the value of each is 399/1350. As a practical matter 89 votes showing a preference for B are then *lifted* from the pile of votes allocated to A and added to B's pile and so on. A's remaining vote will be 1,001 which is enough to elect him. The lifted papers are stamped so as to enable them be identified in the event of a recount or petition.

If a candidate exceeds a quota on a subsequent count, the principle is the same, but only those votes that took the candidate through the quota are looked at. So if candidate C had 900 first preference votes on the first count (with a quota of 1,001) and the addition of 177 votes from the surplus took them to 1,077, only those 177 votes are looked at in deciding where C's surplus of 76 votes are allocated. In principle here all 76 surplus votes are re-allocated, but it is not wholly unusual that at a late stage in the count less than 76 votes are actually transferred to another remaining candidate. Thus it is possible that only 65 of the 177 votes express a preference for continuing candidates, in which event they receive an aggregate credit of 65 with 11 votes being deemed non transferable. When transferring a surplus, the highest preference for a continuing candidate needs to be identified. At a late stage in a count, this could for example be preference 5 as the candidates who got preference 2, 3 and 4 have already been elected or excluded.

In all cases on a transfer of a surplus, the appropriate number of votes are lifted from the top of a bundle credited to the elected candidate and are added to the bundles for the other candidates. The extensive sorting and mixing done to reach the first count result ensures the sample is random. Obviously the further preferences on these "transferred votes" may not be exactly representative of the entire vote of the elected candidate. It is quite possible therefore, in a contest with an ultimate gap of less than 10 votes that a different selection from the pile might have produced a different result. For example in the 1987 general election in Kerry North, Dick Spring, the then Labour leader had 8,380 votes on the last count, 4 ahead of Tom McEllistrim of Fianna Fáil. Jimmy Deenihan of Fine Gael had a surplus of 1,396 on the first count and from his votes 180 were lifted and randomly allocated to Kiely (FF), 84 to Finucane (SF) and 17 to Leen (SF). Each of these three were then eliminated and among their votes to transfer on were a number which indicated Deenihan 1 and them 2. These votes would likely have had slightly different patterns of later preferences than the average of Deenihan's votes and with a difference of 4, a different sample of votes lifted and given to each of them could have produced a different result. All of these random votes would have been re-allocated based on the third preferences expressed in them. If electronic voting had been introduced as was mooted in the early 2000's, apparently the system could detect the absolute pattern of lower preferences and allocate transfers more in line with the actual pattern. In the 1997 general election in Dublin South East, there was a close contest between Michael McDowell and John Gormley. This was determined by the votes of Joe Doyle of Fine Gael. In a seven day recount, there was a minute examination of those votes which accumulated into several surpluses. The parties generally felt that the transfers resulting from lifted votes reflected the overall pattern.

Elimination of candidates

Where no candidate exceeds the quota on the first count and therefore there are no surpluses available to redistribute after the first count, the candidate with the lowest number of first preferences is eliminated and this will constitute "count 2". Each of his/her votes needs to be examined for the second preference. On later counts, if the second preference is for a candidate already elected or eliminated, the highest preference to a continuing candidate needs to be ascertained. Inevitably this process will result in some votes which cannot be transferred as they show no preference. There appears to be no example where every single vote of an eliminated candidate falls to be transferred. These votes are assigned to a category of "non-transferable". At a late stage in a count, there can be very significant numbers of non-transferable votes. This particularly arises where the last continuing candidate for a party is eliminated and the only remaining continuing candidates are representing other parties or independents. So for example in Sligo- North Leitrim (3 seats) in the 2007 general election, with the four leading candidates from Fianna Fáil and Fine Gael all needing votes to be elected, the elimination of McManus (SF) with 5,769 votes, resulted in 1,482 non transferable votes or over 25% of his vote. Clearly lots of Sinn Féin voters chose either to vote just for McManus or to just give preferences to independents and minor parties. The result of there being a lot of non transferable votes is that a candidate is likely to be elected without actually reaching the quota.[1]

The ongoing count process involves eliminating the lowest candidates one by one in successive counts until someone reaches the quota. It is possible to eliminate two or more candidates at the one time. When a quota is exceeded, the returning officer has to decide if the surplus is material, in which event the next count consists of its distribution. Eliminations continue until the field is down to the number of seats plus one. For example, in an election for three seats, this is the first count

Candidate	First Preference Votes
A	800
B	700
C	600
D	500
E	400 eliminated count 5
F	350 eliminated count 4
G	300 eliminated count 3
H	150 eliminated count 2
Total	3,800
Quota	**951**

Assuming no one reaches quota and no candidate catches the next, the various counts will be as indicated. After count 5 it is likely to be possible to declare a result, although if by that stage, there is a surplus, it may be necessary to distribute that, likely to decide between C and D. If a voter who gives F preference 1, gives preference 2 to G and preference 3 to A, the 2 to G is ignored when F's votes are being transferred and the vote transfers to A. If by that stage A has reached quota, the 3 to him will also be ignored.

What happens if two candidates are level on votes?

If during a count, two candidates are level on votes, the one to be eliminated is determined by which of them has the higher first preference vote. The lower one is eliminated. This worked to the benefit of Padraig Conneely, a former chairman of the governing body of Fine Gael, in the Galway City no 2 LEA in 2004. Mr Conneely is the ultimate "cat with 9 lives" candidate. On the first count he had 620 first preference votes as opposed to 611 first preference votes for Martin Quinn, the second Fianna Fáil candidate. By count 3, both Conneely and Quinn were on 746 votes. No doubt at that stage there was a bevy of lawyers involved and the count was delayed for some time. Because Mr Conneely had more first preferences he was allowed continue and Mr Quinn was eliminated, but still faced the obstacle of being 91 votes behind the Sinn Féin candidate in the battle for the last seat.

Happily for Mr Conneely he received directly or indirectly from Mr Quinn, the candidate he had just pipped, a transfer of 154 votes, resulting in a lead of 8 votes over the Sinn Féin candidate and his election. Indeed another possible piece of luck for Mr Conneely was the fact, disclosed by the Irish Independent in February 2007 (12 February) that 15 houses in the Cappagh area of Galway had been inadvertently included in the No 2 LEA in 2004, when they actually should have been in a different area. If those 15 houses had given more first preferences to Conneely than to Quinn, the outcome might have been different. If it is not possible to separate the candidates by reference to first preferences, lots are drawn. Candidates being level at an elimination in local elections is not unusual.[2]

A more stark example is when two candidates are level on the final count. The same principle applies and the candidate with the higher first preference vote is elected. This actually happened in Borris in Ossory LEA (Laois) in the 1999 local elections where John Bonham of Fine Gael, a newcomer, prevailed over outgoing Labour councillor Larry Kavanagh. The progress of the counts were as follows

	Bonham	Kavanagh
First count	648	599
FF surplus	657	615
Another FF surplus	664	639
Third FF surplus	666	639
FG elimination	696	663
Independent elimination	748	776
FG surplus	777	781
FG surplus (ex Ind)	794	793
FF surplus (ex FG)	795	795

Despite a petition to the Circuit Court, the result stood and Bonham with 49 more first preferences on the first count prevailed.

Adjudication of votes

At every count in an election, there will be a need to go through a process of adjudication of votes. The purpose of this is to include or exclude votes of doubtful validity, such as where a clear first preference is not shown. This seems to be a great focus of interest for the tallymen, albeit generally irrelevant, except where a tight outcome can be foreseen. There is a discussion elsewhere (chapter 9) as to the main reason why votes on the first count are deemed spoilt. A feature which is more prevalent on subsequent counts is where the order of preferences is not clear. A voter may for example vote 1, 2, 3, 5, 6 (leaving out 4) or may include a 5 crossing the boxes against the names of two candidates. In the former case, the vote is deemed non transferable after the third preference, as the sequence is broken. In the latter case, the vote is liable to be deemed unclear after the fourth preference, if there is a significant crossing into both boxes. The practice of returning officers generally seems to be that once these votes are ruled on, the preferences deemed valid are marked on the side margin of the particular ballot paper, so that it is clear to the count staff what preferences are to be counted. In the court case regarding Borris LEA (Laois) in 1999, there was unfavourable mention of a situation where a particular returning officer marking was directly over the original marking, as this made it difficult for the court to re-assess the ballot paper as it had originally presented. The process of ruling on spoilt votes at first count and ruling on transfers at subsequent stages is referred to as adjudication.

Discretion of returning officer on surpluses and elimination

Generally the rule in all counts is that surpluses must be distributed first and only then should the lowest candidate be eliminated. However returning officers have a discretion to postpone distributing a particular surplus, if it cannot in its totality make a difference in terms of who is next to be eliminated or cannot elect a candidate or allow recovery of expenses. If a small surplus arises on the first count, it can take a couple of hours to examine every single vote, so a returning officer can postpone distributing it until such time as it would or might become relevant as between the then lesser number of continuing candidates; frequently the surplus is not looked at all. Further returning officers have a discretion to eliminate two or more candidates at the one time if the aggregate of all their votes is not enough to overtake the next continuing candidate or to enable one of them claim electoral expenses. Two examples might suffice.

Mr Orange reaches the quota on the fourth count with a surplus of 94, having received 2,394 transfers. All the remaining candidates have gaps between them of more than 94 and no one is within 94 votes of the quota or the level for recovery of expenses. In those circumstances, the returning officer may postpone dealing with the small surplus and proceed instead to eliminate the lowest candidate. If he has to deal with the surplus, he will need to look at all of the 2,394 transfers to Orange.

In an election Mr Blue has 100 votes, Mr Green has 500 votes and Mr Purple has 700 votes. The next lowest candidate, Ms Yellow has 1600 votes. No one has reached the quota. It is mathematically clear that the highest vote Purple can have after Blue and Green are eliminated is 1300 votes (this will not qualify to recover expenses), so it is impossible to overtake Ms Yellow. In these circumstances the returning officer can decide to eliminate all three in the one count. This frequently happens.

Alphabetti spaghetti

At elections, ballot papers are produced with the candidates listed in alphabetical order by surname. In more recent elections, there is a photograph of the candidate opposite their name. The ballot paper can be quite long. In the Wicklow constituency in 2011 there were 24 candidates and the ballot paper was produced with two parallel columns of 12 names each. In Ennis LEA (Clare) in the local elections of 2014, there was a record breaking 27 candidates. In the 2016 general election, there were 21 candidates in Dublin South West and the ballot paper was felt to be quite unwieldy.

There is a perception that Irish politics is very biased in favour of candidates whose surnames appear in the first half of the alphabet. But is this true? For purposes of assessing this, the alphabet has been divided into two parts, A to L and M to Z. This seems a more instructive approach, given the lack of surnames that begin with the letters X or Z. Indeed, although this may change with the advent of the "new Irish", it is doubtful many people with surnames beginning with those letters are entitled to vote or to stand for election, although the 2016 general election saw the return of Deputy Zappone. If the Dublin telephone directory (2008 and 2014/5) residential listings can be taken as indicative of the distribution of Irish surnames, they suggest that about 53.5% of surnames begin with the letters A to L and about 46.5% begin with the letters M to Z.[3]

Further there is perceived to be an excess of surnames represented in the Dáil which begin with the letters A and B. The telephone directory suggests about 10% of surnames begin with those letters.

The following is the pattern over 11 general elections (all with 166 seats except 2016 (with 158)

Election	Number of elected M to Z	Percentage M to Z	Number A -B
1981	55	33%	30
Feb 1982	53	32%	33
Nov 1982	61	37%	31
1987	60	36%	28
1989	64	39%	27
1992	67	40%	29
1997	69	42%	30
2002	76	46%	20
2007	71	43%	25
2011	73	44%	14
2016	72	46%	20

On the basis that the appropriate percentage of persons with the surnames M to Z is about 46.5%, it can be seen that recent elections show a very small deviation from the level of representation appropriate. However in the last century, there was certainly a material variance to the detriment of M-Z. Therefore the suggestion of a serious disadvantage is almost certainly now overstated.

It would also seem that the under-representation of surnames beginning M to Z has something to do with the major parties and latterly Fine Gael. If a sub analysis is done on the candidates elected for Fianna Fáil and Fine Gael in 2007 to 2016 by reference to surnames, the following pattern appears

Election	Party	Number of elected M to Z	Percentage M to Z
2007	FF	31/78	39.7%
2007	FG	21/51	41.2%
2011	FG	29/76	38.2%
2011	FF	10/20	50%
2016	FF	22/44	50%
2016	FG	17/50	34%

If the elected candidates for the two main parties are stripped out, the M to Z group is over represented within the rest of the successful candidates. They consist of 19/37 of the rest in 2007 (or 51.35%), 34/70 of the rest in 2011 (or 48.57%) and 33/64 of the rest in 2016 (or 51.56%)

Why is this so? It is certainly not the case that parties' selection processes are in some way biased against candidates whose surnames start with M to Z. Perhaps the best explanation is the family "dynasties". It is common in Irish politics that several members of the same family have been elected to the Dáil. There was undoubtedly over representation of the A to L group in the past and this has possibly allowed the growth of dynasty brand names over a succession of elections. It is clear that the distortion in favour of A to L remains in recent elections, where a major party has done well. However an examination of the names elected shows a clear representation of the dynasties in the "A to L" range with names such as Ahern, Andrews, Aylward, Blaney, Browne, Calleary, Collins, Coughlan, Cowen, Haughey, Kenneally, Kitt and Lenihan on the Fianna Fáil side and Bruton, Carey, Connaughton, Coveney, Creed, D'Arcy, Deasy, Enright, Flanagan and Kenny on the Fine Gael side. These dynasties just do not seem to occur with such frequency in the M to Z group. It is possibly the case that when the "dynasties" were founded, the alphabetical advantage gave an edge to the founder and thereafter the presence has been maintained through goodwill towards the name. For example former Taoiseach, Bertie Ahern was first elected to the Dáil in Dublin Finglas in 1977 beating a man called Bell by about 3,700 votes to 2,600 votes to take a second seat; it is possible that being first on the ballot paper advantaged him over Bell and enabled the founding of a dynasty. There may also be some issue of alphabetical voting by supporters of the two traditional largest parties.

It is also clear from the above table that historically surnames beginning with the letters A and B were vastly over represented, representing at one point 19% of the members. However they became underrepresented following the 2011 general election. Indeed in the 2011 Dáil, the letter "A" was represented by just one surname, Gerry Adams the Sinn Féin leader and T.D. for Louth. Happily this grotesque under representation was addressed by the election of Bobby Aylward in a bye-election in Carlow Kilkenny in 2015. Generally they are somewhat over-represented.

The pattern of representation of names seems to be quite similar in local elections based on an analysis of the 2009 and 2014 results. In 2014, 418 of the 949 candidates elected (44.05%) had surnames beginning with M to Z. In 2009, 369 of 883 candidates elected (41.79%) had names beginning with the letters M to Z. The pattern is quite random with M to Z representing a majority in Cork City and County, Donegal, Kildare and Wicklow in 2014, but being quite low in Clare, South Dublin, Galway City and County, Kilkenny, Leitrim, Offaly, Roscommon, Tipperary and Westmeath.

While the issues associated with alphabetical order are probably somewhat overstated, it can be evident, particularly while tallying, that a few voters have a tendency to mark ballot papers alphabetically. Occasionally a paper is encountered where candidates are for example marked 1 through 14, exactly as the ballot paper is laid out. More significantly at late stages in a count, you often encounter a pattern where voters seem to have a liking for candidates A to E, but don't have much preference as between the other candidates. Such voters sometimes seem to fill in the balance of the boxes in alphabetical sequence. So if at the end of a long count, voters have to decide between Brown, Green and Orange, there can seem to be a bias in terms of highest of 11th, 12th and 13th preferences in favour of Brown. Further voters who are voting for a party can seem to be influenced by alphabetical order. It is quite notable how parties seem to have two elected representatives whose names are together on a ballot paper such as Breen, Carey (Fine Gael, Clare), Collins, Cregan (Fianna Fáil, Limerick West), McGrath, Martin (Fianna Fáil, Cork SC), Clune, Coveney (Fine Gael, Cork SC), Cannon, Connaughton (Fine Gael, Galway E), Ó'Feargháil, Power (Kildare South) and Collins, Creed (Fine Gael, Cork North West).

It is quite difficult to address this issue. One possible solution is to draw lots for positions on the ballot paper. However this could make it more difficult for voters to find candidates on a ballot paper. Another possibility is that a constituency has half its papers starting with A and half starting with Z; however this would add to the complexity of a count, particularly when count staff are very tired at the end of a long count. On the basis that it is very much a declining issue, it seems that there is no real need for any measures to address it.

The parties

A brief explanation of the parties that have contested recent elections is needed. Irish parties don't readily fit into the right/left framework familiar in other countries. The following is however what would be the broadly perceived positioning of parties on a right to left scale (with the solid line representing the mid point)

Renua	right
Progressive Democrats (defunct) ("PD")	right
Christian Solidarity	right
Fine Gael ("FG")	centre right
Fianna Fáil ("FF")	slightly centre left
Labour	centre left
Social Democrats	centre left
Green	centre left
Sinn Féin ("SF")	left
Anti Austerity ("AAA")	left
Democratic Left (defunct) ("DL")	left
People Before Profit ("PBP")	left
Socialist	left
Solidarity	left
United Left Alliance ("ULA")	left
Workers Party ("WP")	left

References in Chapter 1

[1]   One slight nuance on eliminations is encountered in elections to the Seanad. If a candidate is being eliminated in a Seanad election, their first preference vote is re-distributed first (on the basis that it is all in units of 1,000; in a Seanad election, each first preference vote is treated as being 1,000 to facilitate the process of distributing transfers of surpluses). If that results in an election of a candidate, that elected candidate is not included when the preferences on the votes transferred to the eliminated candidate are being redistributed. So if Mr A who is being eliminated in a Seanad election, had 15 first preferences (or 15,000 votes) and 3,246 transfers, the first operation is to look at the 15,000 votes which will transfer at a value of 1,000 each. If the net effect of those transfers is to elect B, then B will be disregarded, when redistributing the 3,246.

[2]   A more recent example of candidates being level on votes was in the 2014 local elections in Tramore-Waterford West LEA. At the end of count 9, both David Lane of Sinn Féin and Davy Walsh of the Workers Party had 567 votes. However Lane had received 472 first preferences and Walsh had received 409 first preferences. Hence in the battle of the two Dave's, Walsh fell to be eliminated. This was all much ado about nothing, as Lane was himself eliminated on the next count. Further examples of equality of votes between the lowest continuing candidates were seen in the 1991 local elections in each of Kilmacthomas LEA (Waterford) and Coole LEA (Westmeath) and in the 1999 local elections in Dublin North Inner City LEA where both Stafford (FF) and Fogarty (Green) had 937 votes each at the tenth count.

An interesting variant on this issue occurred in Nenagh LEA (North Tipperary) in 2009. After the third count the two lowest continuing candidates were Michael Comerford (FF) with 720 and Tom Harrington (FF) with 707. There was a surplus of 13 still to be distributed arising from the election of Jim Casey another Fianna Fáil candidate. Even if Mr Harrington had got all 13 votes, he would still have fallen to be eliminated as he had less first preferences on the first count. However if he had drawn level, a recount would certainly have been demanded and this could have shown a discrepancy; therefore the returning officer sensibly decided that the 13 votes required to be redistributed but this exercise only required 32 transferred papers to be looked at. In the event, both candidates got two votes so the margin was not altered.

[3]   The percentages are virtually the same across the two directories reviewed (53.5% and 53.8% respectively for A to L).

CHAPTER 2

The Constituencies
– A Description

Since 1981, nearly 60 different constituencies have been fought in general elections, although the actual number in each election varied between 40 and 43. Some constituencies have existed pretty well at all elections since 1923. Others were created by the boundary review prior to the 1981 election and thus have been consistent features of the landscape only since then and are referred to as "modern" below. The following is a brief description of each constituency and of any notable feature associated with it.

Carlow Kilkenny (five seats)

This constituency has been a feature of all modern general elections and comprises the counties of Carlow and Kilkenny. However since 1997, a small portion of county Carlow, around Hacketstown and Rathvilly in the north east of the county has been associated with Wicklow. In the 2016 census this area had a population of 4,501. This is somewhat problematic for Carlow in achieving representation, as the proportion of population between the two counties, already imbalanced in favour of Kilkenny is further skewed to Kilkenny 99,232: Carlow 52,431 (65.4% to 34.6%) . This has probably contributed to election results where only one of the elected TDs lives in Carlow, as it is generally a problem for Carlow to have two representatives. Indeed the 2011 result, repeated in 2016, left a situation where no TD is resident in the Carlow part of the constituency, as the only Carlow TD, Pat Deering of Fine Gael is resident in that part of Carlow, which is attached to Wicklow. The boundary report issued in 2017 recommends that this area be returned to Carlow.

The constituency is quite urban as both Carlow town and Kilkenny City have substantial populations. There are however no other large urban centres. The general pattern of representation has been two Fianna Fáil, two Fine Gael and one Labour (always Kilkenny based). However there are quite a few occasions where Fianna Fáil have won three and Fine Gael has dropped to one. Further the Green Party and Sinn Féin have replaced Labour on one occasion and in 2011, Fine Gael won three to Fianna Fáil's one. There is a pattern of county loyalty in voting with relatively low transfers across the boundary. The feat of winning three seats is usually associated with an ability to exploit the two-county issue.

Cavan Monaghan (five seats reduced to four in 2016)

This constituency has been a feature of all modern general elections and comprises the counties of Cavan and Monaghan. In the 2016 general election, a significant proportion of west Cavan (pretty well everything west of Cavan town, excepting Belturbet, with a population in 2016 of 13,150) was removed and the constituency was reduced to four seats. The boundary commission which reported in 2017 recommended that this area be returned to Cavan. Cavan (76,176) has a somewhat bigger population than Monaghan (61,386), but the imbalance is small. The 2016 adjustment made them almost level. There is a tendency for a majority of the TDs to be Monaghan based even though it has historically had the smaller population. Curiously the 2016 election produced two TDs in each county despite the reduced size of Cavan.

The constituency has two relatively large towns in Cavan and Monaghan, but otherwise is largely rural. Traditionally the constituency returned three Fianna Fáil and two Fine Gael TDs, but since 1997, the prevailing pattern has been two Fianna Fáil, one Fine Gael, one Sinn Féin and another. There are elections however where Fianna Fáil or Fine Gael are reduced to one and indeed in 2011, Fine Gael unexpectedly gained three seats.

Clare (four seats)

This constituency has been a feature of all general elections and comprises the geographic county of Clare, with the exception of a small part of it adjacent to Limerick City. It is a relatively urban constituency, containing the substantial towns of Ennis and Shannon. There are often localised issues of having a TD in West Clare (Kilrush/Kilkee), North Clare (Ennistimon and the Burren) and East Clare (Scariff/Killaloe) which can influence voting patterns in those areas. The early pattern was three Fianna Fáil and one Fine Gael, as the constituency was perceived to be a Fianna Fáil heartland. However the constituency once it acquired a fourth seat in 1981, was always marginal and in November 1982, Fine Gael took the second seat, which it has generally managed to retain, apart from its few bad elections. When Labour does very well nationally, it has taken a seat, making the breakthrough in 1992 with the colourful character of Dr Moosajee Bhamjee.

Cork East (four seats)

This constituency has been a feature of all modern general elections and covers the part of Cork County broadly to the east of Cork City. It is based around the towns of Cobh, Midleton and Youghal in the south and Fermoy, Mallow and Mitchelstown in the north, all of which are in the Blackwater valley area. Its boundary has a tendency to shift marginally in the rural area between Cork City and Mallow, but generally it has been very stable.

Voting patterns show a strong north/south split and because the south has the greater population, it can be difficult for the north to have two local representatives. The prevailing pattern has been two Fianna Fáil, one Fine Gael and one left, either Workers Party or Labour. However Fine Gael has held two on occasions and Fianna Fáil has dropped to one. Notably in the 1981 and February 1982 contests, Fianna Fáil dropped to one seat, as their "second seat'" was taken by Joe Sherlock of the Workers Party, largely courtesy of poor Fianna Fáil electoral strategy. This loss was critical in the then very tight Dáil. The constituency has returned different TDs on a party basis on seven occasions and has never returned the same four TDs in modern elections.

Cork North Central (five reduced to four seats in 2007)

This constituency has been a feature of all modern general elections and comprises the north side of Cork City and the rural hinterland, including Blarney. It has in the past gone south of the river in the city centre and in its 2016 manifestation did so again in the south west of the city. Its rural hinterland frequently shifts boundaries with the neighbouring East and North West. Historically it has tended to have two Fianna Fáil, one Fine Gael and one Labour/Workers Party. However there are instances in its five seat form where Fianna Fáil have held either three or one and in a number of elections Fine Gael gained two. In 2011 Sinn Féin gained a seat and it is to be expected that this is likely to remain a feature of the political landscape here.

The number of seats was reduced to 4 in the 2007 general election. Most elections in this constituency have resulted in a change of representation by party, so it is one of the more volatile constituencies.

Cork North West (three seats)

This constituency has been a feature of all modern general elections. It comprises a large rectangular north/south space in the north west of the county, with the southern end focussed on the town of Macroom and the northern end focussed on the towns of Kanturk, Millstreet and Rath Luirc (Charleville). In recent elections its character and population balance has been altered radically by the introduction of the large suburban town of Ballincollig at its southern end. Its boundaries at its southern and eastern fringes are moved from time to time with small pockets shifting constituency. Notwithstanding the Ballincollig addition, it is arguably the most rural constituency in the country.

It has generally returned two Fine Gael TDs and one Fianna Fáil. However Fine Gael lost its second seat to Fianna Fáil in 1997, did not succeed in regaining it until 2011 and lost it again in 2016. Apart from these changes the constituency has never returned different party representation and thus it is one of the most stable constituencies in the country. When Labour contested the constituency, they were capable of getting up to one half of a quota. They were not however competitive for a seat and their votes usually transferred substantially to Fine Gael, thus underpinning their two seats.

Cork South Central (five seats reduced to four in 2016)

This constituency has been a feature of all modern general elections. It comprises the south side of Cork City and the adjacent suburban towns stretching to Carrigaline. It used to include Ballincollig but that was moved to Cork North West in 2007. In some elections, parts of the south city adjacent to the city centre are included with Cork North Central and in 2016, the south west city was also transferred there .

The prevailing pattern of representation here has been two Fianna Fáil, two Fine Gael and one Labour. However Fianna Fáil secured three a number of times and Fine Gael or Labour have been displaced by the Progressive Democrats and the Greens respectively. Even though it is an urban constituency. it has tended to be relatively stable between elections in terms of party representation, with only five elections returning a different selection of TDs by party.

Cork South West (three seats)

This constituency has been a feature of all general elections. It comprises a rectangular east/west space in the south of the county, with a series of small towns including Bandon, Bantry, Clonakilty, Kinsale, Schull and Skibbereen. Its boundaries at its northern and eastern fringes are moved from time to time with small pockets shifting constituency. It is a predominantly rural constituency.

It has nearly always returned two Fine Gael TDs and one Fianna Fáil and is probably one of the most stable constituencies since 1981. However Fine Gael lost its second seat to Fianna Fáil in 2002, Fianna Fáil lost its seat to Labour in 2011 and Fine Gael lost its second seat to an independent in 2016. There have thus been changes in representation by party in each election since 2002. When Labour contested the constituency, they were capable of getting up to one half of a quota. They were not however usually competitive for a seat up to 2011 and similarly to Cork North West, their votes usually transferred substantially to Fine Gael, thus underpinning their two seats.

Donegal (five seats)

This constituency was created for the 2016 general election. It comprises the entire county apart from the area to the south of Donegal town with 8,500 population. Somewhat surprisingly in 2016, Sinn Féin lost its second seat located in the northern end of the constituency.

Donegal North East (three seats)

This constituency was a feature of all modern general elections up to 2011. It comprised Letterkenny and its hinterland and the Inishowen peninsula. Letterkenny has become a very large urban area. There have been minor boundary adjustments in the vicinity of Raphoe and St Johnstown.

Traditionally it returned one Fianna Fáil, one Fine Gael and an Independent Fianna Fáil candidate. However since 1997, Fianna Fáil have generally taken two. Fine Gael lost its seat for a few elections. In 2011 Sinn Féin took a seat and it was envisaged that this was likely to remain, although the constituency has now become part of a five seat Donegal constituency. However surprisingly Sinn Féin lost this seat in 2016.

Donegal South West (three seats)

This constituency was a feature of all modern general elections up to 2011. It comprised west Donegal from Killybegs to Bunbeg, south Donegal and the Finn Valley. The largest town was the conurbation of Ballybofey and Stranorlar and it was predominantly a rural constituency. There have been minor boundary changes in the north east. A portion of this constituency south of Donegal town became part of Sligo-Leitrim for the 2016 election.

The constituency has been politically very stable and usually returned two Fianna Fáil and one Fine Gael. However on one occasion Fianna Fáil lost its second seat to an independent and in the 2011 election Fianna Fáil lost both its seats to Sinn Féin and an independent.

Dublin

There have been numerous boundary changes in Dublin over the years, so it is much more difficult to describe the Dublin constituencies. Further different constituencies have had different number of seats. This has largely arisen because of a relative levelling of population in the Dublin City area and big increases in the county area, particularly in Fingal. The consequence has been that most of the city based constituencies have lost seats, with increases in the number of seats in county based constituencies. Some significant suburban areas of Dublin notably Ballyfermot, Firhouse, Foxrock, Portmarnock and Templeogue have shifted between constituencies over the period covered, but the core of most constituencies has remained the same. The description below is of the key suburbs forming the core of each constituency. A significant development in 2002 was the creation of a new constituency of Dublin Mid West, with corresponding adjustments to Dublin West and Dublin South West, from which it was carved.

There has been a corresponding level of volatility in who holds the seats in various constituencies, so that it is very difficult to give an average description of a particular constituency, although this is attempted in some cases. In the 2002 general election, Fine Gael only won three seats in Dublin and in the 2011 general election, Fianna Fáil won only a single seat, subsequently lost at a bye-election.

Dublin Central (five reduced to four seats in 1992 and three in 2016)

This constituency covers those parts of the city centre immediately north of the Liffey and extends as far as Drumcondra, Phibsborough and Cabra. It was the base of Bertie Ahern, the former Fianna Fáil leader and Taoiseach, is the base of FG Minister Paschal Donohoe and Sinn Féin's president Mary Lou McDonald and also had a strong independent presence in the form of Tony Gregory. For a few elections, the constituency extended south of the river and included Kilmainham, Inchicore and Ballyfermot. It has also included areas around Fairview and Marino.

The constituency has usually had Fianna Fáil and Independent representation. However Fine Gael and Labour have not always held seats there. The constituency was a five seat constituency until 1989 and since then became a four seat constituency reducing further to three in 2016. The 2017 boundary committee recommended the re-instatement of the fourth seat. Usually there was a change in representation by party at each election, so the constituency is comparatively volatile. In 2016, Dublin Central became the first constituency in the proportional representation system to have only a single candidate representing each party contesting the election, with ten different parties (Fianna Fáil, Fine Gael, Labour, Sinn Féin, Green, Workers Party, Social Democrats, Socialist, Renua and Direct Democracy Ireland) represented, supplemented by five independents. This constituency in its 2016 format has an extraordinarily low electorate by reference to population at 51% and this is in turn compounded by very low turnouts of that electorate. This is possibly partly attributable to the fact that only two thirds of the population were born in Ireland or the United Kingdom. This has resulted in it returning deputies who achieved first preference votes of less than 2,000. The constituency also featured the lowest first preference vote in recent times for a successful candidate, the 939 votes recorded by Cyprian Brady of Fianna Fáil in 2007.

Dublin Mid West (three increased to four seats in 2007)

This constituency, formed for the first time in 2002, covers the western suburbs of Lucan and Palmerstown, carved out from Dublin West and Clondalkin carved out from Dublin South West. It also contains the rural towns of Newcastle, Rathcoole and Saggart. It has had quite varied representation in its lifetime including Fianna Fáil, Fine Gael, Labour, Sinn Féin, Progressive Democrats, Greens and Anti-Austerity Alliance. It was the base of former Progressive Democrat leader Mary Harney and former Tánaiste Frances Fitzgerald.

Dublin North (three increased to four seats in 1992 and five in 2016 with the name changed to Dublin Fingal)

This constituency covers the northern part of the county and comprises the towns of Balbriggan, Donabate, Lusk, Malahide, Rush, Skerries and Swords, as well as their rural hinterland. Generally the town of Portmarnock was included but in one election that was transferred to Dublin North East. A portion of south west Swords was controversially removed for the 2011 election too.

This constituency was the base of senior Fianna Fáil figure Ray Burke until his resignation in 1997 and also of Nora Owen, the former Fine Gael Justice Minister and Trevor Sargent former Green leader. Generally both Fianna Fáil and Fine Gael have held a seat, with the other seat or seats switching about a bit. Representation by party has changed at every election since 1987.

Dublin Bay North (five seats)

This constituency was created for the 2016 general election and is in substance an amalgamation of the old Dublin North Central and Dublin North East constituencies. It was contested by 20 candidates in 2016 and was widely regarded as the "group of death". The constituency was so complex that only the first count was concluded on the first day of the count.

Dublin North Central (four reduced to three seats in 2007)

This constituency covered the eastern part of the north city and included Artane, Clontarf, Killester and Marino. It was the base of former Taoiseach

Charles J Haughey and was also represented by senior Fine Gael figure Richard Bruton. Generally Fianna Fáil have held two seats and Fine Gael one and there was usually some left wing representation. It was merged for the 2016 general election with Dublin North East. This constituency had the record low percentage first preference vote for a successful candidate without a running mate, the 6.6% secured by Labour's Derek McDowell in 1997.

Dublin North East (four reduced to three seats in 2002)

This constituency was a narrow east-west strip in the north east of the city and comprised Baldoyle, parts of Coolock, Donaghmede, Howth, Raheny and Sutton. It was the base of former Fianna Fáil Minister Michael Woods. It has tended to return two Fianna Fáil, one Fine Gael and one Labour. It has on occasions elected two Labour T.D.s. It was merged for the 2016 general election with Dublin North Central.

Dublin North West (four reduced to three seats in 2002)

This constituency is a rectangular shaped area in the north west city. It consists of the suburbs of Ballymun, Finglas, Glasnevin and Santry. It has tended to return two Fianna Fáil and one Labour T.D. Fine Gael were not represented here since 1997, but gained a seat in 2016. In 2011, it became the first constituency ever not to return either a Fianna Fáil or Fine Gael TD. It also featured in 1997, the record lowest polling candidate with 13 votes.

Dublin South (five seats reduced to three seats and renamed Rathdown in 2016)

This constituency comprised suburbs in the south county, including Ballinteer, Churchtown, Dundrum, Kilmacud, Knocklyon, Mount Merrion, Rathfarnham and Stillorgan. It was a very volatile constituency, having seen a change in party representation in all elections since 1987 and twice produced a poll topping candidate with over 17,000 votes. The poll topper has frequently struggled and indeed lost their seat in the following election (Anne Colley, Progressive Democrat, Eithne Fitzgerald, Labour). It was the base of former Fianna Fáil Minister, the late Séamus Brennan, former Fine Gael Minister Alan Shatter and of the prominent Fine Gael TD and constitutional lawyer, the late Professor John Kelly. It was abolished for election 2016 and replaced by a three seat constituency comprising parts of Dún Laoghaire Rathdown council. It was the scene of a significant bye-election win by television personality, George Lee representing Fine Gael in 2009.

Dublin South Central (four/five seats)

This constituency stretches south from the city centre to Templeogue. It comprises the suburbs of Ballyfermot, Chapelizod, Crumlin, Drimnagh, Inchicore, Kilmainham, Kimmage, The Liberties, Templeogue (part) and Walkinstown. It has traditionally returned two Fianna Fáil, one Fine Gael and a left representative. In recent elections, it has elected a few candidates from the left and is one of the most left leaning constituencies in the country. It has generally had five seats, but reverted to a four seat constituency in 1992 and 1997 and again in 2016, at which time the adjacent constituency of Dublin South West increased to five seats.

Dublin South East, renamed Dublin Bay South (four seats)

This constituency comprises the south city centre and the suburbs of Ballsbridge, Donnybrook, Ranelagh, Rathgar, Rathmines, Ringsend, Sandymount and Terenure. Its geography has been relatively stable for a Dublin constituency. It has traditionally returned one Fine Gael, one Fianna Fáil and one Labour, with the fourth seat changing hands at pretty well every election. It was the base of former Taoiseach Dr Garret FitzGerald and of Labour Minister and leader Ruairi Quinn. It was also the constituency of former Renua leader Lucinda Creighton and of former Progressive Democrat leader, Michael McDowell. This constituency has returned a Labour T.D. at every election since February 1982 and therefore apart from Kildare was the most favourable constituency for Labour. However the Labour seat was lost in 2016. The constituency has had a change in representation in party terms at every election bar November 1982 and has never returned the same four TDs. It is therefore probably the most volatile constituency in the country.

Dublin South West (four/five seats)

This constituency comprises the south west suburbs, notably Tallaght and also parts of Firhouse and Templeogue. Until 2002, it also comprised Clondalkin. It has traditionally been represented by two Fianna Fáil, one

Labour and a Progressive Democrat. Fine Gael has struggled to hold a seat here at all times, but has generally managed to hold one since 1997. It was the base of prominent Labour Minister and former leader Pat Rabbitte. The constituency is comparatively volatile and has generally shown a change in personnel in party terms each election. It has generally been a four seat constituency, but increased to five seats for the 1992 and 1997 elections and reverted to four for the 2002 to 2011 elections. For 2016, the Rathfarnham and Knocklyon areas of the old Dublin South were added and it became a five seat constituency once more. This constituency holds the five seat record for the lowest percentage of first preferences gained by a successful candidate with no running mate to assist them, the 6.63% recorded by Katherine Zappone in 2016.

Dublin West (three/four/five seats)

This constituency now comprises the south west part of Fingal county, principally Blanchardstown, Castleknock and Mulhuddart. Historically it included Lucan and Palmerstown until they were moved to Dublin Mid-West and Ballyfermot until it was moved to Dublin Central. It was the base of former Fianna Fáil Ministers Brian Lenihan Senior and Junior and of former Fine Gael Minister Jim Mitchell. It is the base of former Labour Leader and Tanaiste, Joan Burton and of Fine Gael Minister and Taoiseach, Leo Varadkar. It has traditionally been represented by two Fianna Fáil and one Fine Gael member, with a range of other people. It is one of only three constituencies that has been a three, four or five seat constituency at some stage of the modern cycle.[1]

Dún Laoghaire (five reduced to four seats in 2011)

This constituency is the south eastern part of county Dublin and comprises the suburbs of Ballybrack, Blackrock, Booterstown, Dalkey, Deans Grange, Dún Laoghaire, Foxrock, Killiney and Shankill. It has been the base of a number of former Ministers including David Andrews and Mary Hanafin of Fianna Fáil, Sean Barrett of Fine Gael and Barry Desmond of Labour. It has traditionally been represented by two Fianna Fáil, two Fine Gael and one Labour TD, but on occasions both Fianna Fáil and Fine Gael have been reduced to one (or no) seat. The constituency has returned different representatives by party at each election since November 1982 and is accordingly very volatile.

Galway East (three increased to four seats in 1997 and reduced to three in 2016)

This constituency has been a feature of all modern general elections. This constituency comprises the eastern part of the county of Galway and includes the towns of Ballinasloe (excluded in 2016), Gort, Loughrea, Portumna and Tuam and their hinterland. Ballinasloe and Tuam are the biggest urban centres. In its three seat form, it was reliably two Fianna Fáil and one Fine Gael. When increased to four seats, it tended to return two Fianna Fáil and two Fine Gael TDs. When the constituency was in three seat form, there were no changes in representation by party. However every election since it became a four seat constituency has seen a change in representation by party.

Galway West (five seats)

This constituency comprises Galway City and Connemara and is largely an urban constituency. It has traditionally returned two Fianna Fáil, one Fine Gael, one Labour and one other. It was the base of former Progressive Democrat Minister Bobby Molloy, Fianna Fáil Minister, Éamon Ó'Cuív and President Michael D Higgins. It has been comparatively stable with only four elections resulting in change of representation by party. In 2016, a sizeable portion of south Mayo around the town of Ballinrobe was added to the constituency.

Kerry (five seats)

This constituency was created for the 2016 general election, merging the Kerry North and Kerry South constituencies. The election produced an outstanding performance by the Healy-Rae family, with the two brothers obtaining 38.3% of the first preference vote.

Kerry North (three seats)

This constituency was a feature of all modern general elections until 2011. This constituency comprised the northern part of the county of Kerry including Tralee and Listowel. It formerly included the town of Castleisland, but in 2011 this was attached to Kerry South. Tralee is a very substantial urban centre and often there are two TDs elected from the town, with the remaining representative normally Listowel based. The constituency traditionally returned one Fianna Fáil, one Fine Gael and one Labour, although it took until 1987 for Fine Gael to get a foothold here. Latterly Martin Ferris of Sinn Féin has tended to occupy the former Labour seat. A portion of west Limerick including Abbeyfeale and Glin was added for the 2011 election and the constituency was named Kerry North-West Limerick. It was the base of former Labour leader and Tánaiste Dick Spring and of senior Fine Gael Minister, Jimmy Deenihan.

Kerry South (three seats)

This constituency was a feature of all modern general elections until 2011. This constituency comprised peninsular Kerry and the towns of Castleisland and Killarney. Killarney was by far the largest urban centre although there was not always a TD based there. The constituency was otherwise quite rural. It would be the constituency most dependent on the tourism industry. In the early days, it tended to return one Fianna Fáil, one Fine Gael and one Labour TD. In more recent times either Fine Gael or Labour have been replaced by independents. It has been quite volatile in terms of party representation, with changes in most elections since 1987. In 2011 it was the first constituency to return two independent TDs. It was the base of former Fianna Fáil Minister and Ceann Comhairle, John O'Donoghue.

Kildare (five seats)

This constituency was contested up to 1992 and tended to return two Fianna Fáil, two Fine Gael and one Labour TD. While it existed, there was only one election where it returned different representation by party. It comprised the entire county of Kildare. Due to significant increase in the population of Kildare, it was divided in two for the 1997 election. It was the home base of former Fine Gael Minister and leader Alan Dukes. This (and its successor constituencies of Kildare North and Kildare South) was the only constituency in the country to have returned a Labour TD in every general election since 1981. However Labour lost both its seats in 2016.

Kildare North (three increased to four seats in 2007)

This constituency created in 1997 comprises the populous suburban towns in north east Kildare, Celbridge, Clane, Leixlip, Maynooth and Naas as well as some rural hinterland to those places. It is substantially an urban constituency with Naas as the largest centre balanced by three sizeable towns in the north east corner. In its three seat form, it has tended to return one Fianna Fáil, one Fine Gael and one Labour, with the fourth seat when added generally between Fianna Fáil and an independent. It was the home base of former Fianna Fáil Minister for Finance, Charlie McCreevy.

Kildare South (three seats)

This constituency created in 1997 comprises the towns of Athy, Kildare and Newbridge as well as the rural southern end of the county. The internal divide of the county between the two constituencies has shifted a bit to the north of Kildare town and Newbridge. Newbridge is by far the largest population centre, although there is often no TD based there. It has tended to return one Fianna Fáil and one Labour. Fine Gael have struggled on some occasions, with former leader Alan Dukes losing his seat here in 2002. It is the electoral base of Ceann Comhairle Seán Ó'Fearghaíl. The 2017 boundary commission recommended that it be increased in size to 4 seats, with the addition of the Portarlington area of Laois.

Laois-Offaly (five seats)

This constituency was a feature of all general elections until 2016. This constituency comprised the counties of Laois and Offaly. The counties are reasonably evenly balanced with the 2016 census showing Laois at 84,697 population and Offaly at 77,961. In elections up to 1992, three of the elected deputies were Offaly based and two were Laois based. This position has been reversed since 1997. There are two large urban centres in the form of Portlaoise and Tullamore, the respective county towns. It has traditionally elected three Fianna Fáil and two Fine Gael TDs, with Fine Gael occasionally losing its second seat. It was the base of former Taoiseach, Brian Cowen. The constituency was split into its constituent counties for the 2016 general election, because of its rapidly escalating population. The 2017 boundary commission however recommended that it be re-constituted, but excluding Portarlington, which will render the two counties virtually equal in population.

Laois (three seats)

This constituency was created for the 2016 general election and was regarded as the most predictable constituency of those contested in that election. It lived up to billing, comfortably returning a Fianna Fáil, Fine Gael and Sinn Féin TD. It also included a portion of the county of Kildare adjacent to Monasterevin. It is the base of Minister Charles Flanagan.

Limerick East (five reduced to four seats in 2011 and renamed Limerick City)

This constituency has been a feature of modern general elections. This constituency comprises the urban area around Limerick City, including one District Electoral Division from Clare as well as some rural areas to the east of Limerick City. It has traditionally returned two Fianna Fáil, one Fine Gael, one Progressive Democrat and one left seat. For a number of elections, the Progressive Democrats displaced the second Fianna Fáil seat. It has been the base of Progressive Democrat leader and founder, Des O'Malley, Fine Gael Minister Michael Noonan and Fianna Fáil Minister, Willie O'Dea. The constituency became Limerick City for the 2011 election.

Limerick West (three seats)

This constituency has been a feature of all modern general elections. This constituency consists of rural county Limerick including Adare, Kilmallock, Newcastle West and Rathkeale. It is a rural constituency with a few small towns. Traditionally it was reliably two Fianna Fáil and one Fine Gael and it was a major shock when Fine Gael took a second seat in 1997. On four occasions only four candidates contested this constituency, so it is probably on average the least competitive constituency. It has however had quite a number of changes in party representation since 1987 and is comparatively volatile for a three seat constituency. The constituency became known as Limerick County for the 2011 and 2016 elections. In 2002, it featured the lowest winning margin of one vote between two Fine Gael candidates.

Longford-Roscommon (four seats)

This constituency existed for three elections from 1992 to 2002 and comprised the two counties of the same name. The largest urban centre was Longford town. As it straddled two provinces, it was regarded as unsatisfactory. It also had a population imbalance between Roscommon at 61% and Longford at 39% (using 2016 census figures), but Longford still managed to return two TDs at each election, excepting 1992. It tended to return two Fianna Fáil, one Fine Gael and one other. It was the home base of former Taoiseach Albert Reynolds.

Longford-Westmeath (four seats)

This is the traditional arrangement for these two counties outside the 1992 to 2002 elections. There is a significant population imbalance between the two counties with Longford having 40,873 population and the Westmeath portion 80,089 according to the 2016 census. As the population is 2:1 in favour of Westmeath, it has sometimes proved difficult for Longford to have more than one seat. Indeed the outcome of the 2016 election was that Longford was not represented at all, a fact greatly lamented by the losing Fine Gael TD, James Bannon. Traditionally a portion of east Westmeath (with population of 8,681 according to the 2016 census) has been included in a Meath constituency. The constituency is quite urban as it has three large towns, Athlone, Longford and Mullingar. The constituency has tended to return two Fianna Fáil and two Fine Gael TDs, but in recent elections, Labour have tended to take a seat at the expense of Fine Gael. It was the home base of Albert Reynolds, former Taoiseach and of Mary O'Rourke, former Fianna Fáil Minister.

Louth (four increased to five seats in 2011)

This constituency has been a feature of all general elections. This seat comprises the county of Louth, largely the substantial towns of Drogheda and Dundalk. It displays a strong north south political split based on those towns. It has tended to return two Fianna Fáil, one Fine Gael and one Labour. It was the base of former Fianna Fáil Minister, Dermot Ahern and is the base of former Sinn Féin leader Gerry Adams. In 2011, areas of Meath adjacent to Drogheda were added to it to make it a five seat constituency. It has been comparatively stable between elections with only five elections showing a change by party representation.

Mayo (five seats reduced to four in 2016)

This constituency comprises the county of Mayo, its principal towns being Ballina, Castlebar and Westport. Since its creation in 1997, it has been a strong Fine Gael bastion generally returning three Fine Gael TDs and two Fianna Fáil. This is in contrast to its predecessor constituencies, being reliably each 2:1 to Fianna Fáil. There has been a change of representation by party on each of the occasions it has been contested. It is the base of former Taoiseach Enda Kenny. In 2016, a sizeable portion of the county around Ballinrobe was transferred to Galway West, although the 2017 boundary commission recommended the return of Ballinrobe town.

Mayo East (three seats)

This constituency existed from 1981 to 1992 and consisted of Ballina, Ballyhaunis, Claremorris and Swinford and their hinterlands. It was a reliable two for Fianna Fáil and one Fine Gael and never changed in terms of party representation.

Mayo West (three seats)

This constituency also existed from 1981 to 1992 and consisted of Achill, Ballinrobe, Belmullet, Castlebar and Westport. It was a reliable two for Fianna Fáil and one Fine Gael and never changed in terms of party representation, save for the loss of the second Fianna Fáil seat in a bye-election in 1994. It was the base of former Fianna Fáil Ministers Pádraig Flynn and Denis Gallagher as well as former Taoiseach Enda Kenny.

Meath (five seats)

This constituency existed until 2002. It consisted of the county of Meath and also of a portion of Westmeath around Delvin. It had one large urban centre in Navan, the county town, as well as a quasi urban area adjacent to Dublin in the south east of the county. It traditionally returned three Fianna Fáil and two Fine Gael. From time to time, Labour would displace either the third Fianna Fáil or second Fine Gael seat. The constituency often returned different representation by party in an election and was therefore comparatively volatile. It was the base of former Taoiseach and Fine Gael leader, John Bruton and of former Fianna Fáil Minister Noel Dempsey.

Meath East (three seats)

This constituency was created in 2007. It consists of the towns of Ashbourne, Dunboyne, Dunshaughlin and Ratoath in south Meath as well as the smaller towns of Kells and Slane and their hinterlands. In 2011 the coastal areas of east Meath were removed to the Louth constituency. There is no established pattern of representation save that Fine Gael have always held at least one seat. It is the base of Minister Regina Doherty.

Meath West (three seats)

This constituency was created in 2007. It consists of the towns of Athboy, Navan, Oldcastle and Trim as well as a portion of Westmeath adjacent to Delvin. Navan is by far the largest urban centre, although Trim always aspires to have its own TD. There is no established pattern of representation save that Fine Gael have always held one seat.

Offaly (three seats)

This constituency was created for the 2016 general election and consists of the county of Offaly, as well as that portion of Tipperary to the north of Nenagh. In 2016 it returned a Fianna Fáil, Fine Gael and Sinn Féin TD, similar to its former partner Laois. Offaly will be re-united with Laois under the recommendations of the 2017 boundary commission.

Roscommon (three seats)

This constituency existed until 1989 and was re-formatted for the 2016 general election. It consisted of the county of Roscommon and a portion of north east Galway around Glenamaddy. It is a predominantly rural constituency with a number of small towns. It traditionally returned two Fianna Fáil and one Fine Gael TD. It was the base of controversial former Justice Minister, Sean Doherty. Roscommon was associated with Longford for elections 1992 to 2002 and with South Leitrim for elections 2007 and 2011. It became a stand alone constituency again in 2016 renamed Roscommon-Galway, with the addition of a large portion of east Galway, including Ballinasloe. The encroachment into Galway will become greater when the report of the 2017 boundary commission is implemented and a portion of north Roscommon will be transferred to Sligo-Leitrim.

Roscommon-South Leitrim (three seats)

This constituency was controversially created in 2007, as it split Leitrim. It is substantially rural. It consisted of the county of Roscommon and that portion of Leitrim to the south of Lough Allen, including the largest town Carrick on Shannon. On both occasions it returned two Fine Gael TDs.

Sligo-Leitrim (four seats)

This constituency existed from 1981 to 2002. Due to declining population levels relative to other areas, the counties could not sustain four seats after 2002 and the controversial decision was taken to split Leitrim, with its population of just over 30,000. This resulted over two elections in no Leitrim TD being elected, although one of the TDs elected in 2011 had strong Leitrim connections. The population between the two counties is imbalanced with Sligo at 65,535 and Leitrim at 32,044 according to the 2016 census, a ratio of 67.2:32.8. The constituency has one large urban area in Sligo town. The constituency was traditionally two Fianna Fáil and two Fine Gael, but the second Fine Gael seat was lost on various occasions to either Fianna Fáil, Labour or an Independent. The constituency was extremely volatile as there was a change in representation by party at every election contested there. The constituency was re-created for election 2016, but with portions of South Donegal (population 8,535 per census 2016) and West Cavan (population 13,150 per census 2016) added. The inclusion of four counties (across two provinces) was controversial, as is illustrated by the spoiling of a Cavan originating ballot paper in the 2016 general election by the words "I live in Cavan" The 2017 boundary commission recommended that the west Cavan portion be switched for north Roscommon. These additions radically altered the constituency, as Sligo only represented 55% of the enlarged constituency by way of population. However it still returned three of the four TDs in the 2016 general election. It was the base of former Fianna Fáil Minister for Finance, Ray McSharry. It is the only constituency where a first count poll topper, John Ellis from Leitrim, has failed to be elected.

Sligo-North Leitrim (three seats)

This constituency was created in 2007. It consisted of the county of Sligo and that part of Leitrim to the north of Lough Allen, but adding Drumshanbo for 2011. There was no established pattern of representation save that Fine Gael have always held one seat. It was subsumed back into Sligo-Leitrim for the 2016 general election.

Tipperary (five seats)

This constituency was created for the 2016 general election. It comprises the entire county save for a portion to the north of Nenagh, which formed part of Offaly. It returned three independents in 2016 and surprisingly failed to return a single Fine Gael TD. The 2017 boundary commission recommended the return of the areas north of Nenagh, but also the transfer of areas adjacent to Newport to a Limerick constituency.

Tipperary North (three seats)

This constituency was a feature of all modern general elections until 2011. It consisted of the county of North Tipperary with the addition from 1997 of the first five to ten kilometres of South Tipperary county adjacent to Thurles. It had two fairly sizeable towns in Nenagh and Thurles, both of which traditionally elected a TD. Traditionally it was very marginal as to whether Fianna Fáil would take two seats or whether Fine Gael and Labour would each take one and it was regarded as the "bellweather" equivalent of Ohio in Irish politics. However following the controversial departure of former Fine Gael Minister, Michael Lowry to the independent benches, both Fine Gael and Labour have struggled here, although both re-established themselves in 2011. There was a change in personnel in party terms in most elections since 1992; prior to that the constituency was relatively stable. It was the base of former Fianna Fáil Ministers, Michael O'Kennedy and Michael Smith and of the ex-Fine Gael Minister, Michael Lowry.

Tipperary South (four reduced to three seats in 1997)

This constituency was a feature of all modern general elections until 2011. It consisted of the county of South Tipperary with the subtraction since 1997 of the first five to ten kilometres of South Tipperary county adjacent to Thurles. Sometimes a small portion of Waterford, adjacent to Clonmel was included in it. It had one substantial town, Clonmel. In its four seat form it was traditionally two Fianna Fáil, one Fine Gael and one left. In its three seat form, Fianna Fáil have tended to be reduced to one seat. Generally it was one of the more predictable constituencies in elections. For 2016, it and North Tipperary were amalgamated into a single Tipperary constituency.

Waterford (four seats)

This constituency has been a feature of all general elections. It consists of the county of Waterford with the occasional subtraction of a small portion, adjacent to Clonmel. Waterford City is by far the biggest population centre, although Dungarvan is a fairly large town in the western end. The western end has been represented throughout the period by a member of the Deasy family and sometimes has a second representative. Traditionally it has tended to return two Fianna Fáil, one Fine Gael and one Labour. The second Fianna Fáil seat has been taken by smaller parties from time to time. It was the base of former Fianna Fáil Minister and sometime Progressive Democrat, Martin Cullen and of Austin Deasy, former Fine Gael Minister.

Westmeath (three seats)

This constituency existed from 1992 to 2002. It consisted of the county of Westmeath. It was quite urban, as both Athlone and Mullingar are substantial towns. Athlone usually had one representative. In each election it returned one Fianna Fáil, one Fine Gael and one Labour, although the margins could be tight. It was the base of Mary O'Rourke, former Fianna Fáil Minister.

Wexford (five seats)

This constituency has been a feature of all general elections. It consists of the county of Wexford and is unique in the modern era in that it has never suffered county boundary breaches. It traditionally returned two Fianna Fáil, two Fine Gael and one Labour TD. It has one large town, Wexford and three other substantial towns, Enniscorthy, Gorey and New Ross. Wexford town usually elects a deputy, if not two as does Enniscorthy. Gorey and New Ross can struggle to elect someone locally. It is one of the more predictable constituencies although on some occasions the second Fianna Fáil or Fine Gael seat have been taken by an independent and in its early life, both Fianna Fáil and Fine Gael took three seats at the expense of the

Labour party. Because of this shifting pattern, it has been relatively volatile returning a different group of parties in six elections since 1981. It was the base of former Fine Gael Minister Ivan Yates and is the base of Labour leader and former Minister Brendan Howlin.

Wicklow (four increased to five seats in 1992)

This constituency has been a feature of all general elections. This constituency consists of the county of Wicklow with the addition in 1992 of parts of Kildare and since 1997 of a small portion of north east Carlow around Hacketstown and Rathvilly. The constituency became a five seat constituency in 1992. The north east portion of the constituency, centred on Bray and Greystones is highly urban and usually returns two TDs. There are two other substantial towns in Arklow and Wicklow. The western side of the county is quite detached from the rest by a mountain barrier but usually manages to secure representation (although not in 2016), possibly helped by the Carlow addition. Its traditional representation has tended to be two Fianna Fáil, one Fine Gael, one Labour and one other. It was in the early days the base of Labour Minister, Liam Kavanagh and Fine Gael Minister Gemma Hussey. Both Fianna Fáil and Fine Gael usually get a percentage vote below their national average in this constituency. The constituency has a tendency towards a large number of candidates and holds the record at 24 candidates in the 2011 election. It managed a relatively lowly 16 candidates in 2016.

References in Chapter 2

[1] It had five seats until 1989, four seats in the 1992 and 1997 elections, three seats in 2002 and 2007 and four seats in 2011 and 2016. The others are Dublin Central and Dublin North.

CHAPTER 3

Outcome Of Elections

This chapter considers the percentage votes and seats obtained by the various parties in elections from 1981 to 2016. It also considers patterns as to the votes likely to be obtained by each party. There is some degree of predictability by constituency, if the national percentage obtained by a party is known or can be estimated from polls.

Over the period covered by this work, generally Fianna Fáil has been the most successful party in terms of numbers of seats gained and percentage of the first preference vote. However they were overtaken by Fine Gael in elections in both 2009 and 2011 and in the local election of 2014, the two were broadly level in terms of vote share, although Fianna Fáil won rather more seats. Fine Gael remained the largest party following the 2016 general election but only marginally so. Labour has done well on isolated occasions, the general election of 1992, the local elections of 2009 and the general election of 2011. In most elections the two traditional large parties got rather more seats than their strict percentage of the vote would suggest.

Further in many constituencies and councils there is a fairly predictable pattern as to how the two traditional large parties will fare in percentage terms in a particular election by comparison with their national overall performance in that election.

General elections

The following is a summary of the performance of the three main parties and others by seats won (total 166 seats; 158 seats 2016) at each general election since 1981 (including the Ceann Comhairle)

Election	Fianna Fáil	Fine Gael	Labour	Others
1981	78	65	15	8
Feb 1982	81	63	15	7
Nov 1982	75	70	16	5
1987	81	51	12	22
1989	77	55	15	19
1992	68	45	33	20
1997	77	54	17	18
2002	81	31	21	33
2007	78	51	20	17
2011	20	76	37	33
2016	44	50	7	57

Bar the elections of 2011 and 2016 and the blip in 1992, the performance of Fianna Fáil was remarkably consistent, with a range from 75 to 81 seats. This is why Fianna Fáil has generally ended up in government. However often Fianna Fáil have struggled to find a stable partner to get to 84, the number of seats required for a majority up to 2011. Up to 1989 they refused to contemplate coalition. Since then they have tried to govern in coalition, but a number of the partnerships have been quite rocky.

The following is a breakdown of the seats attributed in the last table to "Others" and won by minor parties, none of whom won seats prior to 1987

Election	Democratic Left [1]	Greens	Progressive Democrat	Sinn Féin
1987	4	-	14	-
1989	7	1	6	-
1992	4	1	10	-
1997	4	2	4	1
2002	-	6	8	5
2007	-	6	2	4
2011	-	-	-	14
2016	-	2	-	23

Local elections

The following is a summary of the performance of the three main parties and of others by seats won (total 883 seats; 949 in 2014) at each local election since 1985

Election	Fianna Fáil	Fine Gael	Labour	Others
1985	437	283	58	105
1991	357	270	90	166
1999	382	277	83	141
2004	302	293	101	187
2009	218	340	132	193
2014	267	235	51	396

The aggregate number of seats obtained in local elections by parties is a key indicator of the number of seats taken by each party at any subsequent Seanad election. [2]

The following is a breakdown of the seats attributed to others in the above table and won by the larger minor parties or independents

Election	Independents	Greens	Prog Democrats	Sinn Féin	Other groups
1985	75	-	-	10	20
1991	84	13	37	7	25
1999	81	8	25	21	6
2004	87	18	19	54	9
2009	121	3	-	54	15
2014	192	12	-	159	33

Percentage votes obtained by the two traditional large parties

The following in descending order is the percentage (and number for general elections) of votes obtained by the two traditional large parties and the percentage of seats obtained since 1981. L denotes a local election. Generally those parties get a seat bonus discussed below and the percentage level is indicated in brackets.

Fianna Fáil

Election	Percentage vote	Percentage seats
Feb 1982	47.3 (786,951)	48.8 (+1.5)
1985 L	45.5	49.5 (+4)
1981	45.3 (777,616)	47.0 (+1.7)
Nov 1982	45.2 (763,313)	45.2 (nil)
1987	44.1 (784,547)	48.8 (+4.7)
1989	44.1 (731,472)	46.4 (+2.3)
2007	41.6 (858,565)	47.0 (+5.4)
2002	41.5 (770,846)	48.8 **(+7.3)**
1997	39.3 (703,682)	46.4 (+7.1)
1992	39.1 (674,650)	41.0 (+1.9)
1999 L	38.9	43.3 (+4.4)
1991 L	37.9	40.4 (+2.5)
2004 L	31.8	34.2 (+2.4)
2009 L	25.4	24.7 (-0.7)
2014 L	25.3	28.1 (+2.8)
2016	24.3 (519,356)	27.8 (+3.5)
2011	17.4 (387,358)	12.0 **(-5.4)**

Fine Gael

Election	Percentage vote	Percentage seats
Nov 1982	39.2 (662,284)	42.2 (+3.0)
Feb 1982	37.3 (621,088)	38.0 (+0.7)
1981	36.5 (626,376)	39.2 (+2.7)
2011	36.1 (801,628)	45.8 **(+9.7)**
2009L	32.2	38.5 (+6.3)
1985L	29.8	32.0 (+2.2)
1989	29.3 (485,307)	33.1 (+3.8)
1999L	28.1	31.4 (+3.3)
1997	27.9 (499,936)	32.5 (+4.6)
2004 L	27.6	33.2 (+5.6)
2007	27.3 (564,428)	30.7 (+3.4)
1987	27.1 (481,127)	30.7 (+3.6)
1991 L	26.4	30.6 (+4.2)
2016	25.5 (544,240)	31.6 (+6.1)
1992	24.5 (422,106)	27.1 (+2.6)
2014 L	24	24.8 (+0.8)
2002	22.5 (417,653)	18.7 **(-3.8)**

It can broadly be seen from these tables that these two parties who almost always each obtain over 20% of the vote tend to win a greater percentage of the seats than their strict vote percentage would entitle them to, often known as the seat bonus. However at some point around the low 20's this can disappear and become a deficit. Thus in the 2002 general election, with 22.5% of the vote, Fine Gael got less than 19% of the seats. In the next general election in 2007 its vote increased by about 5% to 27% but this increase delivered almost 31% of the seats.

As a general principle parties securing less than 20% of the vote get less seats than their percentage seems to entitle them to. There are some exceptions though. The Spring Tide of 1992 and the Gilmore Gale of 2011 in both of which Labour got around 19.4% of the vote delivered 19.9% and 22.3% of the seats respectively and otherwise Labour seem to be about equivalent in terms of seats and percentage vote. In the 2014 local elections, Sinn Féin got 15.3% of the vote but got 16.8% of the seats and a similar pattern obtained in the 2016 general election (13.8% votes:14.6% seats). However there is a general pattern that the seat bonus for the major parties is paid for by a seat deficit for others, most notably the independents.

The reasons for seat bonuses of this type are not entirely clear. They are certainly influenced by parties' ability to position their candidates in the "leaders' enclosure" and by picking up transfers. They also seem to be influenced by the relative positioning of parties to each other. So in 2002 the 41.5% plays 22.5% scenario as between the two main parties undoubtedly had an influence in the big seat bonus for Fianna Fáil and the deficit for Fine Gael. Similarly with the 36.1% plays 17.4% scenario in the 2011 election. There is sometimes a view expressed that the seat bonus is largely attributable to transfers. While transfers are undoubtedly a contributing factor, the author does not consider them to be a predominant factor leading to a seat bonus.

The national Labour vote has ranged from 6.4% to 19.4% in general elections since 1981. Sinn Féin's national vote has ranged from 1.2% to 13.8% in general elections since 1981. These parties tend to be strong in particular constituencies.

Labour have tended to win seats in most general elections in 18 constituencies, Carlow Kilkenny, Cork North Central, Cork South Central, Dublin Central, Dublin South Central, Dublin South East, Dublin South West, Dún Laoghaire, Galway West, Kerry North, Kildare, Kildare North, Kildare South, Limerick East, Louth, Westmeath, Wexford and Wicklow. They have generally been competitive to the extent of winning seats from time to time in many other Dublin constituencies and in Cork East, Kerry South, Longford-Westmeath, Tipperary North, Tipperary South and Waterford.

Sinn Féin have established positions in Cavan-Monaghan, Dublin South

Central, Dublin South West, Kerry North and Louth and may over time become established in other constituencies.

Predictability of party votes in particular constituencies

There are some patterns to the level of the Fianna Fáil and Fine Gael votes in particular constituencies. As can be seen from the tables above, the Fianna Fáil vote over the period covered has ranged from 47.3% down to 17.4%. The Fine Gael range is rather less dramatic being from 39.2% down to 22.5%. The exact level of vote for a party will vary from election to election. However, in the case of the two main parties, some constituencies and councils show a general pattern of always being ahead (in percentage terms) of what the party vote is or similar to the party vote or behind the party vote. This pattern has broadly held firm, even in very bad elections for Fianna Fáil and Fine Gael. In some cases therefore it is possible to estimate that if for example the national first preference vote for Fianna Fáil is 30%, constituency A will likely be in or around 35% of the first preference votes, constituency B will be in or around the party's 30% and constituency C will be in or around 25%. There are other constituencies and councils that are wholly unpredictable. However it is possible, assuming an overall level of votes for a party which can be deduced from opinion polls, to predict, in most cases, the likely level of vote that party will secure in a constituency and from that, it should be possible to estimate the number of seats that will be won.

For example, Fianna Fáil always underperforms in elections in Wicklow, be it at constituency or council level. The deviation below its national vote ranges from minus 3.6% (38% v 41.6% national) in the 2007 general election to minus 13.8% in the 1992 general election. Fine Gael also underperforms its national vote there, the only exception being the 2011 and 2016 general elections where it was 3.5% and 2% respectively ahead of its national vote. The pattern for some constituencies seems surprising. Dublin South East may well be seen as Fine Gael heartland, but the percentage vote for Fine Gael there has been below the overall national percentage for Fine Gael in every general election between 1989 and 2011 (but not 2016). Not surprisingly, as Dublin is the most competitive place politically, the two traditional large parties tend at best to be level with their national vote in Dublin constituencies and councils.

Fianna Fáil pattern

The following constituencies and councils have generally recorded first preference percentage vote levels more than 5% ahead of the overall Fianna Fáil vote (in other words, if the Fianna Fáil national vote is at 35%, one would expect these constituencies and councils to be at 40% of the first preferences or more):

Constituencies - Carlow Kilkenny (since 2002), Clare, Cork North West (since 1997), Cork South Central, Donegal South West, Galway East, Kildare South, Laois-Offaly*, Limerick West, Longford-Westmeath, Mayo East*, Mayo West*,
Councils - Co Cavan, Co Clare*, Co Kilkenny, Co Laois, Co Leitrim, Co Limerick, Co Mayo, Co Meath, Co Tipperary North, Co Westmeath

The following constituencies and councils have generally recorded first preference percentage vote levels at about the same percentage level as the overall Fianna Fáil vote:

Constituencies - Carlow Kilkenny (to 1997), Cork South West, Dublin Central, Dublin North, Louth, Mayo, Meath (including East and West), Roscommon-South Leitrim, Sligo-North Leitrim, Tipperary South, Wexford
Councils - Co Carlow, Cork City, Cork County, Co Kildare, Co Longford, Co Louth, Co Monaghan, Co Sligo, Co Tipperary South, Co Waterford, Co Wexford.

The following constituencies and councils have generally recorded first preference percentage vote levels more than 5% behind the overall percentage Fianna Fáil vote:

Constituencies - Cork East, Cork North Central, Dublin Mid West, Dublin South, Dublin South Central, Dublin South East*, Dublin South West, Dublin West, Dún Laoghaire, Kerry North (since 1992), Waterford, Wicklow
Councils - Dublin City, Dún Laoghaire Rathdown County, Fingal County, South Dublin County, Galway City, Limerick City*, Waterford City*, Co Wicklow

*denotes about a 10% or more deviation

Fine Gael pattern

The following constituencies and councils have generally recorded first preference percentage vote levels more than 5% ahead of the overall Fine Gael percentage vote:

Constituencies - Cavan-Monaghan, Cork East, Cork North West*, Cork South West*, Galway East, Longford-Roscommon, Mayo East*, Mayo West*, Mayo*, Roscommon
Councils - Co Cavan*, Cork County, Co Kilkenny, Co Laois, Co Leitrim, Co Limerick, Co Longford*, Co Mayo*, Co Roscommon, Co Sligo, Co Waterford.

The following constituencies and councils have generally recorded first preference percentage vote levels at about the same percentage level as the overall Fine Gael vote:

Constituencies - Carlow Kilkenny, Cork North Central, Dublin North Central, Dublin South (since 1987), Dublin South East (since 1989), Dún Laoghaire (since 1987), Kerry North, Kildare (including North and South), Laois-Offaly, Longford-Westmeath, Meath, Waterford, Wexford
Councils - Co Carlow, Dún Laoghaire Rathdown County, Co Galway, Limerick City, Co Meath, Co Tipperary South Riding, Co Westmeath, Co Wexford.

The following constituencies and councils have generally recorded first preference percentage vote levels more than 5% behind the overall Fine Gael percentage vote:

Constituencies - Dublin Central*, Dublin Mid West, Dublin North East, Dublin North West*, Dublin South West, Galway West, Kerry South, Tipperary North,
Councils - Cork City, Co Donegal, Dublin City*, Fingal County, South Dublin County, Galway City, Co Kerry, Co Kildare, Waterford City*, Co Wicklow.

*denotes about a 10% or more deviation

A number of constituencies and councils are not mentioned, because they have no standard pattern. However there are often patterns in consecutive elections. For example in Limerick East (now Limerick City), the Fianna Fáil vote was similar to the general party vote in 1981 and 1982, it was about

10% below the general party vote when the Progressive Democrats were strong locally, it recovered to levels similar to the general party vote in 1997 and 2002 and in the 2007 to 2016 elections, it was somewhat ahead of the general party vote. The Fine Gael vote in Clare lagged behind the national vote up to and including the election in 1982, when Fine Gael first took a second seat there. At all subsequent elections, it has been ahead of the national vote, sometimes to a substantial extent.

Because most of the other parties only contested a limited number of constituencies in a meaningful way, it is difficult to compare their share of the vote in particular constituencies with the prevailing level of party vote in this way. The Labour vote tends to move in particular constituencies in an erratic way. Sinn Féin may be beginning to develop a pattern, but there are too few elections to draw meaningful conclusions.

References in Chapter 3

[1]   The Democratic Left TDs were elected under the banner of the Workers Party in 1987 and 1989 (indeed the Workers Party had representation in the earlier elections). Democratic Left merged into the Labour Party after the 1997 election.

[2]   Local authority members represent approximately 80% of the Seanad electorate in the panel aspect of that election and in practice the other 20% will not deviate to such an extent in its composition as to be likely to make a material difference. Because the "Others" group is far more disparate, it generally does not result in the election of many senators, but a number of independent senators were elected in 2016.

PART 2
Key Issues In System

CHAPTER 4

Fixing the Constituencies

This chapter deals with the rules for and the process around drawing up the constituencies and LEAs. This is a critical issue in every election.

From 1981 to 2011, the Dáil consisted of 166 seats, divided into approximately 40 constituencies. Since and including the 1981 general election the Dáil constituencies have been fixed by an independent commission. There was relative consistency in the constituencies between 1981 and 2011, but there was a greater change in the 2016 election in connection with the reduction of the size of the Dáil to 158. The fixing of the constituencies is radically affected by a number of provisions of the 1937 Constitution of Ireland.

Constitutional provisions

20,000 to 30,000 level of representation

A number of provisions of the constitution affect the number of seats and the drawing of constituencies. Unlike other countries, such as the United Kingdom, constituencies are fixed by reference to populations, not electorates. These key provisions are contained in Article 16.2 of the Constitution. The number of seats overall cannot be fixed at less than one member for each 30,000 of population or at more than one member for each 20,000 of population. This issue has had to be considered twice in detail.

In July 1961, following a 1959 constituency review declared by the courts to be unconstitutional for different reasons, the Supreme Court was asked to consider a 1961 review. The court's involvement arose out of the power of the Irish President to refer a Bill to the Supreme Court to decide whether it is constitutionally sound, called an Article 26 referral. The review being considered was based on the 1956 census, which indicated a state population of 2,898,264, and proposed a Dáil of 144 seats, an average of 20,126 per member based on that census. However if the population as reckoned for the purposes of the constitutional provision, was in fact a figure lower than 2,880,000, then the lower limit would have been breached. There had in fact been a census completed earlier in April 1961 but the results were being compiled, not apparently becoming available until 1963. However the statistics office suggested the population was in fact 2.834 million and an extrapolation of the electoral register suggested a figure of 2.737 million. The Supreme Court however decided that it was appropriate to look at the 1956 census only, even though the provision in the constitution did not expressly refer to the previous completed census. In actual fact when the 1961 census was eventually finalized, it showed the then population as 2,818,341. Even by the time of the 1966 census, the increase in population only barely passed through the threshold of 2.88 million justifying the maintenance of 144 seats.

A second time where the matter became relevant was the Fine Gael five point plan proposal prior to the February 2011 general election to cut the number of politicians by one third, which implied a reduction in the size of the Dáil by twenty members to 146. This was part of a plan to radically reduce the number of politicians and also proposed the abolition of the Seanad and of town councils. It is not clear that detailed thought was given to this manifesto proposal, in the light of what was known about population. By this stage practice for setting constituencies had evolved so that the size of the Dáil was closer to the maximum of 30,000 average population per Dáil seat. A census took place shortly after the 2011 general election in April 2011. If any such proposal was to be implemented within the limit set by the constitution, the maximum population allowable would have been 4,380,000. As the population in the 2006 census was 4,239,848, this only allowed for a population increase of 140,152 or 3.3%. In fact when the 2011 census was finalized the population was 4.588 million, leaving scope for a minimum of 153 seats, seven more than implied by Fine Gael. It certainly seemed that the authorities were not expecting the level of increase that actually happened, given the extreme recession over the 2006-2011 period. However a cursory examination of excess of births over deaths between 2006 and 2010 would seem to have given grounds for concern.

It is clear, not least because the 1961 legal case considered it, that individual constituencies can be above the 30,000 or below the 20,000 threshold. Thus in 2016, five constituencies had more than 30,000 population (based on the 2011 census) per Dáil seat.

The seat provision for the 2016 Dáil was fixed at 158. This allowed for a maximum population of 4,740,000 as established by the 2016 census. It was probably debatable whether any increase would reach that level. However if that figure were to be exceeded, an increase consequently required of 1 or 2 seats could give rise to an extensive revision. In fact the provisional figures for the 2016 census published in July 2016 showed that the population had reached 4,757,976, meaning that revision was necessary.

As the 2016 census showed an excess over that figure, it was in theory debatable whether it was open to the government to defer a further review until 2024, being 12 years after the 2012 review which gave rise to the 158 seat Dáil. It is arguable that the constitution allows a deferral, as it is at the time of fixing that account needs to be taken of population trends. However the late Professor John Kelly in his monumental work on the Irish constitution ventured the opinion that there would be a duty on the part of the Oireachtas to revise the constituencies to reflect changes in the pattern of population and that an election conducted on unrevised boundaries might well be declared invalid in constituencies not properly represented. According to Professor Kelly, the then Taoiseach sought advice on that issue from the Attorney General in 1973, presumably based on patterns evident from the results of census 1971. It would probably therefore have been foolhardy for a government not to review constituency boundaries once the 2016 census was finalized, so a new boundary review was to be anticipated. In fact steps were taken based on provisional figures to do this and a boundary commission was established. This view was confirmed by the Murphy case discussed below.

There is a school of thought that the Dáil at 150 plus members is simply too large and that for a country of Ireland's size, a Dáil of 100 to 120 people would be more appropriate. Obviously if this line of thought were to be pursued, there would need to be a referendum to alter Article 16.2.2 to broaden the population bands. The current minimum permissible number is 159 and any material rise in population is going to require additional members and substantial revision. Possible alternatives would be to set a ceiling at 50,000 population per member or to simply fix a range of number of members. It is foreseeable that any proposal to change this aspect of the constitution is likely to be contentious, particularly in rural areas, where any dilution in representation level might well be unacceptable.

Equivalent ratio in each constituency

The Constitution also provides in Article 16.2.3 that the ratio between the number of members to be elected at any time for each constituency and the population of each constituency, as ascertained at the last preceding census, shall, so far as is practicable, be the same throughout the country. The Irish version, which prevails if there is a conflict between the two, uses the phrase "sa mhéid gur féidir é" to correspond to "so far as is practicable" and it is believed that the Irish phrase may be more restrictive on what can be done, a matter not really teased out in the 1961 Article 26 referral.

This issue was aired in the 1961 case of O'Donovan v Attorney General and also in the Article 26 reference of the Electoral (Amendment) Bill 1961. Interestingly the solicitor acting for those counsel arguing the case in the 1961 reference was one Richard Ryan, the then serving Fine Gael T.D.

In 1961, the review undertaken in the Electoral (Amendment) Act 1959 was challenged in the High Court case of O'Donovan v Attorney General (legal citation 1961 IR 114). Mr O'Donovan was in fact a Fine Gael member of the 9th Seanad elected in 1957, having previously been elected in 1954 to the Dáil as John A Costello's running mate. The scheme proposed in the 1959 Act had much lesser ratios in western areas than obtained in Dublin. The maximum disparity was Galway South at 16,575 people per deputy whereas Dublin South West had 23,128 people per deputy. The state argued that it was entitled to have wider disparity in rural areas to have regard to the problem of contact and representation between deputies and people which would be of quite a different order in a built up area on the one hand and a thinly population heavily indented area on the other hand. Mr Justice Budd rejected this out of hand, saying that if the people who wrote the constitution had intended this, it was scarcely credible that they would not have written down such a criterion. The constitution also provides that a review was to have due regard to changes in the distribution of population, a fact manifestly ignored in the 1959 review which was done against a background of increasing population in Dublin and other urban areas and declining population in the west. Mr Justice Budd therefore declared the 1959 review unconstitutional.

In the 1961 reference however, the scheme of division had been amended so that the highest population per member was 20,916 in Dublin South Central as against 19,294 in Clare (note this is below the constitutionally specified 20,000). An argument was made that Dublin with a higher population had in aggregate the same number of seats (34) as Connacht plus Clare/Limerick. However Chief Justice Maguire in delivering the court verdict said that the courts would only interfere where there is manifest infringement of the constitution. He indicated that adherence to well known boundaries or to divisions created by physical features would be seen as acceptable features to be taken into account in terms of what was practicable. Interestingly the court was advised that the 1923 and 1935 revisions provided for far higher divergences between the best represented and least represented constituency. This begs the question as to whether those provisions might have been invalid under the similar provision of the 1922 constitution. The 1961 revision was only sanctioned in July of that year, just in time for the general election which took place in October 1961. An attempt was made by a Fianna Fáil government in an October 1968 referendum to allow for much greater deviation in representation of up to one sixth from the average, but this was resoundingly defeated by 61% to 39%, passing narrowly in only 4 western seaboard constituencies.

The matter was further aired in 2007 before Judge Clarke in the case of Murphy v Minister for the Environment. This case seems to have been focussed on the issue of substantial under representation in the constituency of Kildare North. Over time since the 1961 cases the impression had got abroad that a 5% variation upwards or downwards was the maximum permissible. However Judge Clarke said this was not necessarily the case and that the matter needed to be ruled upon having regard to all of the relevant factors.

Revisions to happen at least every 12 years

The Constitution also provides in Article 16.2.4 that revisions take place at least every 12 years, with reference to changes in distribution of population in the interim. Thus historically there were revisions done in 1935, 1947 and 1959, with the last one being declared unconstitutional. This necessitated an emergency revision in 1961. Subsequent revisions were done in 1969 and 1974. Revisions have been somewhat more frequent under the independent commissions first established in 1980, with eight revisions in 1980, 1983, 1990, 1995, 1998, 2005, 2009 and 2013. In practice it seems boundary commissions are now established once preliminary census figures are available so a new commission was formed and reported in 2017. This follows the clear view of the court expressed in the Murphy case.

Minimum size of constituency is three

Article 16.2.6 of the Constitution provides that the minimum number of members in a constituency is to be three. This is the only constitutional provision on size of constituency. In practice since the 1948 general election, the maximum size of constituency has been five. Up to and including the 1944 general election, there were a number of 7 and 8 seat constituencies, with 7 seat constituencies surviving in Dublin City South, Limerick and Tipperary up until then. Where five seat constituencies are used, they tend to be confined to large urban centres and to traditional combinations of two counties, such as Carlow/Kilkenny, Laois/Offaly and Cavan/Monaghan. Sometimes terms of reference for a boundary commission lean towards there being more 5 seat constituencies and at other times lean towards smaller constituencies.

Electorates

Every resident person aged eighteen and upwards is generally entitled to be a registered voter, although entitlement to vote varies by type of election. As is noted above, the allocation of seats to constituencies is based by virtue of the constitution on population and not on registered voters or electorates. This is important as there are for example quite significant variances in electorates when the number of 2016 registered electors is compared with the 2011 census (on which the 2016 boundaries were based). It is appreciated that there is an element of "apples and oranges" here, but this is not considered material. The range in proportion of electorate to population is from 51.38% in Dublin Central to 80.67% in Limerick County. While most constituencies have electorates in the 70% to 80% of population range, constituencies with large urban areas tend to be in the high 60% range and four, Dublin Bay South (62.77%), Dublin Central (51.38%), Dublin Mid West (62.84%) and Dublin West (57.11%) stand out as exceptionally low. If it were permissible to set constituencies by reference to electorates, the cities and in particular Inner City and west Dublin would be less well represented.

The level of electorate per constituency is somewhat mysterious. Both the 2006 and the 2011 census indicate the population aged 17 and under, who would not be entitled to vote, is about 25% of the population (24.4% and 25.3%) respectively. Therefore the national electorate should be about 75% of the population. Electorates materially above this level suggest that people who do not live in the constituency are registered there. The under 18 population in Sligo-Leitrim in 2011 was 24.47%, suggesting that the electorate should not be more than 75.5% of the population. However the 2016 electorate was 80.49% of population. By contrast applying the same principles to Dublin Central, the population aged 17 and under in 2011 was 13.8%, suggesting a possible electorate of 86% as against an actual in 2016 of a mere 51.38%. The statistics however for Dublin Central suggest that one third of the population was born outside of Ireland and the UK; while these people are possibly entitled to be registered, in practice, it is likely that many of them do not do so. However even ignoring all of these factors, there seems to be clear evidence of over registration in some constituencies, predominantly rural and under registration in others. It is therefore entirely appropriate that the issue should be dealt with by reference to population.

Background to independent boundary commission

Up to and including the 1977 general election, the constituency boundaries were set by the Minister for Local Government. On one occasion, in 1959, as noted above, this resulted in a complete overturn of the redraw by the courts. On a second occasion, the 1974 "Tullymander", the exercise spectacularly backfired. This turned out to be the last Ministerial re-draw of constituencies.

The "Tullymander"

The Tullymander was the exercise conducted by the Labour Minister and Meath TD, Jim Tully and set out in the Electoral (Amendment) Act 1974. This exercise was done early in the Dáil term, so it obviously gave full warning to the opposition of the new landscape. The key to the exercise was creating a lot of three seat constituencies. The thinking obviously was that Fianna Fáil would get a seat, Fine Gael would get a seat and that the third seat would in most cases be won by Labour or failing that another anti Fianna Fáil TD. Thus the Tullymander proposed 42 constituencies, 26 being three seats, 10 being 4 seats and 6 being 5 seats (Carlow Kilkenny, Cavan-Monaghan, Cork City, Mid Cork, Donegal and Laois-Offaly). Elections in the sixties had been associated with the notion that the "seventies would be socialist" and this seemed to be an attempt to start to create it by appropriately configured constituencies.

Notably every single constituency in Dublin, bar Dún Laoghaire, the constituency of the then Taoiseach, Liam Cosgrave, became a three seat constituency, so Dublin consisted of 13 three seat constituencies and one four seat constituency. The adjacent constituencies of Kildare and Wicklow were also three seat constituencies, interestingly with the Celbridge, Leixlip and Maynooth areas of Kildare removed to the Dublin West constituency and the Blessington and part of Bray area of Wicklow removed to Dublin Mid/South County. The immediately previous pattern in Dublin had been predominantly four seat constituencies. Curiously in a map designed to create three seat constituencies, a five seat Donegal, Cavan-Monaghan and Cork City were formed, each out of two existing three seat constituencies, but presumably that was perceived as possibly resulting in Fianna Fáil only taking two seats in each of them. The reason for creating these as five seat constituencies was undoubtedly population related.

In the event, the exercise was a spectacular failure. Fianna Fáil won three seats in all of the 6 five seat constituencies bar Donegal, with more than 50% of the vote. The "swing seat" in Donegal was taken by Neil Blaney, the long standing Independent Fianna Fáil deputy, who was probably a certainty to get elected. In the thirteen Dublin three seat constituencies, Fianna Fáil won the second seat in eight and the strategy really only worked on the southside of the city. Spectacular Labour casualties included two outgoing Ministers, Conor Cruise O'Brien in Dublin (Clontarf) and Justin Keating in Dublin West County and the well known broadcaster, David Thornley in Dublin (Cabra). Indeed another unsuccessful Labour candidate on this occasion in Dublin (Rathmines West) was one M Robinson.

Constitution of Independent Commission

It has been the tradition (now enshrined in the law) that the boundary commission is chaired by a judge, in the case of the most recent one that being Mr Justice Robert Haughton. Membership often includes the clerks of the Dáil and Seanad, the Ombudsman and a senior official of the Department of Environment. The terms of reference usually stipulate a range of seat numbers (for example that the number of members will be between 164 and 168) and invariably a stipulation that each constituency has between three and five seats.

Public Submissions

It is usual for the commission to invite public submissions. With the advent of electronic media those submissions are readily available electronically. If a person intends to make a submission, it is useful to consider any related submissions that may already be on the commission's website. In the 2017 boundary review of Dáil constituencies, the submissions numbered 407 and included many political parties, Oireachtas members and councillors. There is a tendency for repetitive submissions on the same point. For example the review prior to the 2011 general election detached south west Swords in Fingal from the rest of the town and included it with Dublin West. This was very unpopular and resulted in numerous submissions seeking the re-uniting of the town, a request which was duly granted. The severing of Leitrim in the 2007 and 2011 general elections also resulted in numerous submissions to the subsequent boundary commissions. Certainly some of their recommendations have been highly controversial but there is no scope to accept any variation once they have pronounced. This contrasts somewhat with other jurisdictions where draft revisions are proposed and there is an opportunity to comment on them before they are finalized. Further their recommendations can be "life threatening" for some serving TDs, by moving core territory to a different constituency.

Consistency since 1981

The constituencies remained relatively stable from 1981 to 2011, despite significant shifts in population. The shifts have usually been accommodated by adjusting the number of seats in a constituency, rather than a wholescale re-draw. Significant changes that took place over the period 1981 to 2011 were

1. the creation of a new Dublin Mid West constituency based on Lucan and Clondalkin, with these areas being removed from Dublin West and Dublin South West respectively. This reflected large population increases.

2. the inclusion for a few elections of Ballyfermot and Kilmainham from Dublin's southside in the otherwise northside Dublin Central

3. differing combinations of Longford, Roscommon and Westmeath, with the latter two at some times being constituencies in their own right

4. the controversial splitting of Leitrim, felt by Leitrim residents to prevent the county from being represented at all

5. the splitting of Meath and Kildare, both originally five seat constituencies into two parts to reflect significant population increase

6. the consolidation of Mayo into a single 5 seat constituency reflecting a declining population.

Boundary breaches

One rather regrettable feature of reviews, that has arisen increasingly since 1981, is the inclusion of small parts of other counties in adjacent constituencies. Breaches were also a significant feature of the Tullymander. The independent committees tend to be over sensitive to the arguments about population reflected in the court decisions of 1959 and 1961 discussed above and seem to think that numerical equality is a major objective. This has resulted in the following anomalies:

- the Rathvilly/Hacketstown area of east Carlow being included in Wicklow

- the Ballyglass area of Clare adjacent to Limerick city being included in a Limerick city based constituency

- small portions of north east Galway adjacent to Roscommon being included with that county

- portions of east Kildare included in Wicklow for the 1992 election

- portions of west Limerick being included in Kerry in 2011

- portions of Meath around Bettystown/Laytown being included in Louth

- portions of south Offaly being included in Tipperary (not part of 2013 review)

- portions of west Waterford adjacent to Clonmel being included in Tipperary (discontinued for some years)

- portions of east Westmeath around Delvin being in Meath

The review which took effect in 2016 added Cavan, Donegal, Galway, Kildare, Mayo and Tipperary to the counties that are partly dismembered. The 2017 proposals will add Laois, Meath, Offaly and Roscommon to the mix.

The 2013 review

The 2013 review was quite radical and reduced the size of the Dáil to 158. This was on foot of government policy to reduce the number of politicians. It occurred on foot of a boundary commission recommendation issued in June 2012 and reflected population trends shown by the completion of the census taken in 2011. The most regrettable feature of the commission's deliberations is that every county outside of Cork, Dublin, Kerry, Waterford and Wexford is part of a constituency affected by county boundary breaches. The review created a position where the average population per member was just over 29,000 with the minimum being 27,607 in Dublin Mid West and the maximum 30,472 in Donegal. The most extreme example of boundary issues was the new four seat constituency of Sligo Leitrim, which consisted of the entire of those two counties but also substantial chunks of Donegal and Cavan producing an area stretching east west from Ballina to Cavan town and north south from Donegal town to Longford town (not including though any of those towns).

The loss of eight seats from the previous 166 was at the expense of Dublin (3), Cork (1), Kerry (1), Tipperary (1), Mayo (1), Donegal (1) and Cavan/Monaghan (1), with an additional seat being allocated to Laois/Offaly). This has meant that the traditional two constituency arrangements in Donegal, Kerry and Tipperary was abolished, with each now constituted as single 5 seat constituencies. By contrast the traditional five seats of Laois and Offaly, a fixture since 1923, has been divided into two county constituencies, each with a sizeable chunk of a neighbouring county.

2017 review

This review is fairly minimal, although it adds a seat to each of Cavan-Monaghan, Dublin Central and Kildare South (the latter case at the expense of Laois and Offaly). Broadly most county boundary breaches are to be retained, except for those in Carlow, Cavan and Clare, but with new ones in Laois, Meath, Offaly and Roscommon.

Local government boundaries

There are no constitutional requirements affecting the fixing of local government boundaries. Local government boundaries have also in recent times been fixed by a boundary committee. Until local elections 2014, the numbers of seats per county was fixed at the same number for many years with anomalous levels of representation. For example County Leitrim had 22 seats, whereas County Wexford with almost five times the population had 21 seats. However an extensive local government reform in 2013 fixed representation at one member per 4,830 population, with a lower limit of 18 and a higher limit of 40. This means that more populous counties have 40 member councils whereas the eight least populated have 18 members each. Dublin City and Cork County have special provision made for them and effectively have more population per member.

The most common variant in terms of reference for local government election boundaries relates to the size of areas. Traditionally local electoral areas had between three and seven members. The terms of reference prior to the 2009 local elections precluded the creation of three seat LEAs except in exceptional circumstances. More controversially the terms of reference prior to the 2014 elections provided for a minimum of six members and a maximum of ten members per LEA. Seemingly this was to facilitate a concern of the then smaller government party, Labour that their chances of winning seats was diminished in LEAs with low numbers of seats. This term of reference of course created great mathematical inflexibility in the counties with 18 seats and also resulted in very large districts in sparsely populated areas. It is to be hoped that some of the more extreme features will be eliminated in time for local elections 2019.

CHAPTER 5

Selection Of Candidates/Gender

This chapter considers how candidates put before the voters at general or local elections come to be candidates.

In the case of independent candidates, the answer is simple, as they themselves decide so to do. There are some procedural issues such as the collecting of signatures or the payment of a deposit, but largely the matter is simple.

In the case of parties, the process of becoming a candidate involves some form of internal process within the party. In some cases this is not competitive, because the party wants two candidates in a constituency or LEA and there are only two contenders. Further it is not unusual that persons indicate an intention to compete for a party nomination, only to withdraw on or before the day the process is to be finalized. However in certain cases there are more potential candidates than the party is prepared to run and there is a need for internal competition, referred to as a "selection convention".

Internal competitions are governed by the rules of the particular party. However two systems are popular, one member one vote (OMOV) and a delegate system. OMOV is the system operated by Fine Gael and latterly by Fianna Fáil. Every member in the relevant constituency or LEA has a single vote and the candidates are chosen in that way. The delegate system works on the basis that every branch or cumann in a constituency or LEA is allocated a number of votes and it is a matter for the branch or cumann to choose delegates to exercise those votes. The delegate system potentially allows a fairer representation of the constituency or LEA by reference to the population in particular areas. However a very significant flaw in a delegate system is that it allows for "paper" branches or cumainn. These are branches that have no substantive political existence, but can be peopled with say 6 members loyal to a particular candidate. In practice, experience has shown that OMOV is possibly more democratic. On the basis that the electoral system in Ireland is by alternative vote (i.e. 1, 2, 3, etc), this is also usually deployed for internal selection processes.

Generally parties set a "directive" as to the number of candidates to be selected in a constituency or LEA. The directive is usually set by a central organizational body such as a candidate committee or executive council, with input from the local area. Sometimes, even if a party envisages for example having three candidates in a constituency, the directive will be to the effect that the constituency is to select two. Further parties usually have power in their own rules to put further limits on the directive. For example in a constituency such as Longford-Westmeath, a directive might be that the party selection convention select two, one of whom will be from Longford and one of whom will be from Westmeath. This will address a situation where internally 80% of those having a say in selection are from Westmeath, but it is clearly desirable to have a Longford candidate. Sometimes the further limit will be to the effect that one of the candidates must be female, an increasing issue with the introduction of gender criteria in legislation. These further limits have the potential to generate enormous controversy, as happened in a few constituencies prior to the 2016 general election.

As noted above, sometimes a party lets a convention select less candidates than the party intends to run. This allows for "additions" by the party, usually heavily influenced by the party leader and professional staff. Additions are not particularly common. In a general election for example, the selection process may select over 90% of the final candidates, with the remaining 10% being "added". Persons added are also often the loser at the party selection convention. The delay in adding them is often due to an uncertainty as to the correct number of candidates to run in an area; this is often only capable of being judged close to election time. For example in Longford-Westmeath in the 2016 general election, Fine Gael selected outgoing TDs James Bannon (from Longford) and Gabrielle MacFadden (from Athlone) at its convention, but there was considerable soul searching as to whether it was desirable to have three candidates. In due course a third candidate Peter Burke from

Mullingar was added. In the actual election there was only one seat for Fine Gael, duly won by Burke, the "added" candidate.

Therefore for parties, it is fair to say that the number of candidates per constituency or LEA is largely determined by the party centrally. The precise candidates who fill the places available are largely determined locally, but the party centrally will have some ability to influence that.

A particular difficulty arises where a party is only going to have one candidate, as in that instance the local members have much greater influence, there being no real issue about a directive. This creates quite significant succession issues when a long standing deputy or councillor from a party retires, as sometimes the "right" successor is not selected and a seat is lost.

A further problem created by selection conventions is a tendency for candidates, who were unsuccessful at convention, to then run as independents or sometimes for smaller parties. This gives rise to the phenomenon of some being seen as Fianna Fáil "gene pool" and others being Fine Gael "gene pool" independents. A significant number of independent candidates run as independents, because they failed to get a nomination through the party machinery. When a party is doing badly, often these candidates can do well, as they may be attractive to disillusioned party supporters. For example in Longford-Westmeath, a successful Independent Alliance candidate in 2016, Kevin "Boxer" Moran had previously been a Fianna Fáil councillor but had possibly been overlooked for a nomination given the Lenihan/O'Rourke domination in Athlone. Most local authorities have a significant stock of gene pool members and seven of the independents elected in the 2016 general election are arguably gene pool Fianna Fáil or Fine Gael.

Gender Issues

For the first time, the 2016 general election had legislative requirements in place that resulted in a requirement for a minimum numbers of candidates of each sex. The legislation is only directed at parties and does not force them to have a minimum number of each sex. However if they decide not to do so, they will be denied one half of certain significant State funding to which they would be otherwise entitled. Needless to say this focussed party minds on fulfilling the criterion. The criterion is that at least 30% of a party's candidates must be men and at least 30% must be women. While framed in a gender neutral way, the substance of the provision is that parties must at least equal a 30% threshold in terms of the numbers of women they run.

The gender legislation is very controversial. It is sometimes argued that it is facilitating better qualified men being displaced by lesser qualified women. This of course involves a qualitative judgment, to which there can be no definite answer. While in individual circumstances that may well be the case, in some instances the only better qualification the man seems to have is a better ability to work the selection system within the party. In practice it seems that every jurisdiction, with any serious intent to increase the participation level of women, has had to alter parties' selection processes to achieve this. For example in the United Kingdom, the Labour party and to a lesser extent the Conservative Party use "all women short lists" to select candidates in safe seats, which will almost certainly be won by the party.

The history of electing women up to 2016, particularly in general elections, was abysmal. While all bar one election since 1981 have resulted in a figure in double digits of female Dáil deputies, the aggregate over ten elections to 2011 was 169 or just over 10% of the deputies. The record number was 25, elected to the 31st Dáil after the 2011 election. Despite generally having smaller numbers of TDs than Fianna Fáil, Fine Gael has produced the greatest number at 60 (up to 2011) and is also the only party (including its forebears) to have elected a woman at every general election since 1923. The Labour Party has probably consistently shown the highest percentage. However the Progressive Democrats, in the six elections they contested, elected female deputies on 17 occasions and probably were the party making the greatest overall contribution, relative to the size of the party. There are appallingly few independent female deputies. They have been elected on 12 occasions since the 1992 general election, but prior to that there was no independent women deputies (some works list one for the 1954 election but this seems to refer to the daughter of a Clann na Poblachta deputy, elected at a bye-election in 1956). [1]

There are also typically very few female independent candidates in general elections. In both general elections 2007 and 2011 in or about 10% of the candidates indicated as having no affiliation to any party or grouping were women. The trend was also downwards. In 2007, 12.5% of these candidates were women. By 2011, despite a near doubling of the number of independent candidates, the percentage level for women candidates had dropped below 10%. Indeed in the politically volatile Dublin area, there was a single independent female candidate in the form of Maureen O'Sullivan, duly elected as a deputy in Dublin Central. As most of the independent candidates tend to do very poorly, a possible explanation is that women simply won't waste their time chasing 200 votes in a general election. The participation level for women as candidates for parties was rather better, particularly in the various left groupings and this contributed to the overall percentage elected being somewhat higher.

Women tend to fare somewhat better in local elections and indeed there are a few examples of a party delegation from a particular LEA being entirely female. For example in the Rathfarnham LEA in South Dublin, the Fine Gael delegation from 2009 to 2017 was all female. As an example of representation levels, the 1999 local elections produced a 15% complement of women and a woman was elected to every council. Women fared possibly even better in the now defunct town councils.

The 2016 election

The 2016 election radically changed the representation of women in the Dáil. Despite the reduction of the size of the Dáil to 158, 35 women were elected, representing just over 22% of the Dáil membership. All parties represented in the Dáil have at least one female TD (Fine Gael 11, Fianna Fáil 6, Sinn Féin 6, Labour 2, Social Democrat 2, Green 1 and People before Profit 2). There are also five independent female deputies.

All bar one (Limerick County) of the 40 constituencies had at least 1 female candidate and 17 of them[2] had five or more female candidates. Women represented 20% of the independent candidates.

Women represent a majority of the TDs elected in quite a number of three seat constituencies: Dublin Central, Dublin Rathdown, Dún Laoghaire (effectively a three seat constituency), Meath East and Offaly and three of the four TDs in Dublin South Central are women. In both Dún Laoghaire and Dublin South Central four of the top five first preference vote getters were female. Every Dublin constituency has a female TD and most constituencies in the northern half of the country have female representation. However Munster is still a "black spot", there being only a single female TD in Cork and three in the entire of Munster (43 seats). Clearly some work is required to increase female representation in that part of the country. While Fine Gael had a poorer election, it vastly increased its percentage of female deputies to 22%. Fianna Fáil remain "underweight" at 13.6% but this is a vast improvement on the 0% outcome in 2011. Other parties and the independent grouping are generally above average.

It is very difficult to say that gender quotas were responsible for securing the election of any of the 35 women elected in 2016. The issue is very sensitive as there appears to be a wholly incorrect perception that "gender quota" females are in some way "less worthy". It is however clear that Fianna Fáil was likely to be in a position to win a single seat in each of Cork South West and Waterford and the fact that the single candidate was a woman made it quite likely that there would be additional female representation there. Equally with Sinn Féin, the gender quota may have influenced the placing of a single female candidate in Dublin Fingal and Offaly, both of whom were duly elected. There also seems to some evidence that a second Fianna Fáil candidate in each of Cavan-Monaghan, Galway East, Kildare South and Mayo was "directed" to be a woman, as was effectively the second Fine Gael candidate in Dún Laoghaire and the second Sinn Féin candidate in Louth. This almost certainly influenced the election of a(n) (eminently capable) woman in each of those constituencies.

There is some evidence also of women who polled badly and were likely to have been selected simply to fill the gender quota. This is particularly evident with Fine Gael and Labour, both of whom had too many male incumbents, who were realistically the only people likely to hold seats, in the prevailing circumstances in 2016. It was indeed quite a feat for those parties to finish the 2016 general election with a reasonable percentage of female TDs. There is also some evidence with Fianna Fáil and Sinn Féin of the placing of women in "no hope" situations and some of the minor parties had a number of poorly polling women. However this was always likely to be part of the introduction of the system and generally it seems to have been successful, perhaps beyond expectations.

References in Chapter 5

[1] This was 21 year old Kathleen O'Connor elected at a bye-election in Kerry North on 29 February 1956 following the death of her father.

[2] The 17 constituencies were Cavan-Monaghan, Clare, Cork South West, Dublin Bay North, Dublin Central, Dublin Mid West, Dublin South Central, Dublin South West, Dún Laoghaire, Galway West, Kildare North, Kildare South, Longford-Westmeath, Meath East, Waterford, Wexford and Wicklow.

CHAPTER 6

Turnout

A significant factor affecting the outcome of Irish elections is who actually comes out to vote on election day. There are quite significant divergences in percentage turnouts between different elections. It is however difficult to establish a pattern which correlates outcome to turnout. This chapter discusses some of the key facts about turnout and comes to some tentative conclusions as to the consequences. The issue of turnout in referenda is dealt with in chapter 30.

The turnouts in Irish elections vary very significantly. However it can be difficult to draw conclusions as to why a particular election has a high or a low turnout. The following are general issues pertinent to turnout

- Turnout in Irish elections is generally far lower as a percentage in urban areas than in rural areas. Particularly turnout in Dublin is very low in political elections (contests electing candidates as opposed to referenda) even by reference to other urban areas. However the gap between Dublin and rural areas has narrowed very considerably in recent general elections.

- Turnout is measured by reference to the register, which is compiled by the relevant local authority. There is little doubt that low turnouts in parts of urban Ireland are somewhat attributable to inaccuracy in registers. For example the inner city, Pembroke and Rathmines areas of Dublin (located in the Dublin Bay South constituency) have some of the lowest turnouts in the country. As noted in chapter 4, this constituency has also got a low percentage electorate. These areas have a high transient population, which is just living there short term. While many of these people are never included in a register, it is clear that there are many people who are included in the register, but are gone away by the time voting occurs on that register. This factor possibly contributes 3 or 4 percentage points to a lesser turnout in areas with a highly transient population.

- There is a tendency for voters who originate from rural Ireland to continue to vote in their "home" constituency, although they may be living in a large urban centre. Some of these people will be registered in both places; some will stay on the register only for the "home" constituency. This again probably contributes at the margins to higher turnout in rural Ireland and lower turnout in urban Ireland.

- There is a perception that higher turnout favours Labour and to a lesser extent Fine Gael, whereas lower turnout favours Fianna Fáil. It is difficult to say that this is completely supported by the data. However the 2004 local elections in which both Fine Gael and Labour did well saw turnout increase from 50% to near 60% and this trend continued into 2009. There was also a somewhat higher turnout in the 2011 general election where both parties achieved record results. The thinking behind the perception is that Fine Gael and particularly Labour supporters are less committed, but are inclined to vote in greater numbers where those parties are improving their electoral position. By contrast there were low turnouts in the 2002 general election and 2014 local election, when Fianna Fáil did comparatively well. The lower turnout in the 2016 general election also happened in an election where Fine Gael and Labour lost many seats.

Turnout in General Elections

National turnout in the 11 general elections being reviewed were

Election	Turnout (%)	Votes (in millions)
1981	76.2	1.73
1982 Feb	73.81	1.68
1982 Nov	72.86	1.7
1987	73.33	1.79
1989	68.51	1.68
1992	68.49	1.75
1997	65.92	1.81
2002	62.73	1.88
2007	67.03	2.08
2011	69.9	2.24
2016	65.21	2.15

It can be seen there are four phases

- a phase in the 1980's where national turnout was around 75%

- a phase from 1987 to 2002 where national turnout dropped by over 10%, co-inciding with elections following which Fianna Fáil formed the government. There were pretty well no extra votes against a background of bigger numbers of electors

- a phase from 2002 to 2011 where turnout increased back towards 70% with about 200,000 extra votes each time

- a possible phase of decline commencing in 2016 with turnout back to less than two thirds and the second lowest percentage turnout of modern times recorded.

If the 76.2% turnout in 1981 is compared with the 70% recorded in 2011, it is notable that the percentage declines in Dublin are marginal. Indeed Dublin South East (59.71% v 60.54%) and Dún Laoghaire (70.48% v 71.34%) recorded slight increases in turnout by 2011, as had Wicklow (73.78% v 74.76%). However the percentage turnout in quite a number of rural constituencies had fallen by more than 10%.[1] These falls were accentuated in 2016 with further declines. Indeed only four constituencies recorded a percentage turnout of 70% plus in 2016.[2] Thus in 1981, turnout in Dublin was in the high 60s and by a circuitous route it is back to about the low to mid 60s%. However the rest of the country has moved from a figure close to the 80% level to the mid 60s%. There is thus a pattern over time of a higher decline in tendency to vote in rural Ireland as compared with Dublin, although rural turnout still exceeds that in Dublin and other urban areas. In 2016 all bar three constituencies were in the range of 60% to 72%, so there is a tendency for turnouts to converge.

Some constituencies seem to produce consistently high turnout

Constituency	Range 1981-2016 (percentages)
Cavan-Monaghan	66.48 to 82.87
Cork North West	70.06 to 85.12
Cork South West	68.55 to 82.99
Galway East	66.66 to 80.1
Kerry North	70.23 to 80.68
Kerry South	71.37 to 81.22
Laois Offaly	66.99 to 80.19
Limerick West (now County)	66.16 to 81.7
Longford-Roscommon	71.21 to 75.21
Longford-Westmeath	62.55 to 80.4
Mayo (incl E & W)	67.76 to 78.16
Roscommon (incl S Leitrim)	71.6 to 83.13
Sligo-Leitrim	65.58 to 82.17
Tipperary North	69.68 to 82.31

While the higher end of these ranges is frequently in the 80's, this percentage was only obtained in most of them in the 1981 general election. However Cork North West and Tipperary North continued to score in the 80's until the 1987 general election and Roscommon exceeded 80% once again in the November 1982 general election. In many of the cases, the lower end of the range was the turnout in 2016.

Cork North West recorded the highest percentage turnout in every election until and including 2002, apart from 1997, when it was narrowly beaten by Longford-Roscommon. However in 2007 and 2011, it was augmented by the addition of the urban area of Ballincollig and while still recording a respectable 73% had drifted behind a few other constituencies including Dublin North Central and Wicklow on the east coast. In 2007 Tipperary North at 78.45% was the champion; the honour fell to Roscommon-South Leitrim at 78.75% in 2011 and to Roscommon-Galway at 71.6% in 2016.

By contrast there are a few noted turnout laggards, nearly all in Dublin

Constituency	Range (percentages)
Cork North Central	57.79 to 74.64
Dublin Central	52.44 to 64.16
Dublin Mid West	52 to 66.57
Dublin North West	55.71 to 68.42
Dublin South Central	51.96 to 66.97
Dublin South East	53.78 to 60.54
Dublin South West	55.91 to 71.91
Kildare	56.07 to 74.35

Dublin South East (now called Bay South) nearly always has the lowest turnout. However it graduated to third last in 1997 (with Dublin South West at the bottom) and third last in 2002 (ahead of Dublin South Central and Dublin Mid West). It even managed to break 60% for the first time in the 2011 election. Dublin Central recorded the lowest turnout in 2016 at 52.44%, no doubt aided by the redrawing of the constituency back to the core of the north inner city. There is as yet no constituency which has registered a turnout of less than 50% in a general election.

Turnout in local elections

Turnout in local elections is always less than it would be in a general election. The following is the position over the six local elections reviewed

Election	National Turnout	Variances in LEAs
1985	58.98	33.53 to 86.4
1991	55.65	36.55 to 78.66
1999	50.26	28.31 to 81.15
2004	58.64	42.27 to 76.31
2009	57.77	37.65 to 77.05
2014	51.7	31.24 to 71.92

As can be seen, turnout dropped by about 10% over the elections from 1985 to 1999. The 2004 election saw a significant rise to levels similar to 1985, but it has since again fallen back to close to 50%. In the 1985 election, 60 of the LEAs saw turnout of in excess of 70%, whereas 39 LEAs had turnout of less than 50%. By 2014, only one LEA, Ballinamore in Co Leitrim, showed a turnout in excess of 70%. By contrast 50 LEAs had turnout of less than 50%. Elections since 1999 have co-incided with elections to the European Parliament, although it is doubtful that that drives turnout.

Dublin City and County show consistently low turnout.[3] The lowest turnout ever seen was the 28.31% in Clondalkin LEA in 1999. The low turnout syndrome is also beginning to affect neighbouring Kildare and Meath, where only Kells LEA (Meath) exceeded 50% in 2014, although all LEAs in Wicklow remained above 50% in the 2014 election. Failing to cross the 50% barrier was also a feature of Limerick City, whereas Cork City and Galway City seem to be at around a 50% level.

Other large urban areas have tended over a number of elections to be at around the 50% turnout level including Carlow, Carrigaline LEA (Cork), Drogheda (Louth), the north east Kildare towns and Wexford.

Certain LEAs (predominantly in Connacht)[4] have tended to remain at above two thirds turnout for most local elections.

Generally outside the areas mentioned which tend to have high or low turnouts, the rest of the country tends to be in the range between the low 50's and 65%.

It is worth noting that on two occasions, Roscommon LEA in 2004 and Ballybay Clones LEA (Monaghan) 2014, voting was deferred for a week or two, due to the death of a candidate during the campaign. In both instances this did not seem to impact materially on turnout, as the turnouts in the special elections seemed commensurate with others in the same county.

Why does local election turnout rise and fall?

It is not clear why there has been this pattern of a fall 1985 to 1999 and then a second fall 2004 to 2014. Certainly a desire by the electorate to make a statement at a particular election, possibly against the then government, seems to be a factor.

In the 2014 local elections, there was a significant drop in turnout. However this decline seemed to be particularly pronounced, where hitherto small separate areas were amalgamated wholly or partly into unwieldy districts.[5] It can be surmised that these amalgamations generally led to an exceptionally high fall in voter participation, often from very high levels before. This is perhaps because there is a lot less identification with candidates in very large areas. It is notable that the smallest decline seen in turnout in the 2014 local elections in Galway city and county was against a background of very little change in areas. This pattern may suggest that the amalgamations effected in 2014, largely to achieve areas with six seats or more, were a very bad idea and ought to be reversed for the 2019 elections.

Over the period under review the decline in local election turnout is far more pronounced in rural Ireland than in the cities. This of course mirrors a pattern also found in general elections. Turnout in Bray/Greystones, Carrigaline LEA (Cork) , Cork City, Dublin City, Dún Laoghaire-Rathdown, Galway City and Waterford City has generally gone up slightly when 2014 is compared with 1985. This may be because those areas have been very settled for many years and the population may have aged and accordingly is more inclined to vote. There are declines in the other urban areas of Fingal, Kildare and South Dublin but rather less than the national trend. The real declines are seen in the rest of Ireland with some figures close to a 20% level of decline over time.[6]

References in Chapter 6

[1] Constituencies with a large fall in percentage turnout between 1981 and 2011 include Cavan-Monaghan (10.13%), Cork East (13.26%), Cork North West (11.65%), Donegal NE (15.25%), Donegal SW (10.61%), Laois-Offaly (10.64%), Limerick West (11.77%), Longford-Westmeath (12.68%), Louth (10.58%), Meath (12.84%) and probably Sligo-Leitrim.

[2] The four constituencies with turnout over 70% in 2016 were Cork North West (70.06%), Kerry (70.73%), Roscommon Galway (71.6%) and Wicklow (70.92%).

[3] There have been 175 local contests in Dublin LEAs and there has never been a turnout of 60% or more. Indeed only two Dublin LEAs, Clontarf and Templeogue-Terenure exceeded 50% in local election 2014. A number of Dublin LEAs often show turnouts in the 30 - 40% range including Clondalkin, Mulhuddart, North Inner City, Pembroke, Rathmines, South Inner City, Swords and Tallaght South.

[4] These are the LEAs which feature relatively high turnout of about two thirds

LEA	County	Range
Killarney	Kerry	64.17 to 77.48
Ballinamore	Leitrim	71.92 to 86.4
Dromahaire	Leitrim	67.81 to 82.3
Manorhamilton	Leitrim	67.81 to 79.92
Ballymahon	Longford	63.65 to 74.92
Drumlish	Longford	66.85 to 77.73
Granard	Longford	66.85 to 77.58
Westport	Mayo	60.93 to 78.42
Athlone	Roscommon	66.53 to 78.67
Boyle	Roscommon	65.91 to 77.64
Ballymote	Sligo	67.00 to 77.44
Dromore	Sligo	67.00 to 74.12
Tobercurry	Sligo	67.00 to 82.96
Templemore	Tipperary N	62.57 to 75.57

[5] Examples of severe turnout decline between 2009 and 2014 in amalgamated LEAs (percentages are 2009 and 2014 percentage turnout respectively) included Belturbet (69.55%) and Cavan (62.63%) amalgamated into Cavan-Belturbet (52.71%)

Kilrush (68.01%) and Ennistimon (69.26%) amalgamated into West Clare (59.69%)

Bantry (65.54%) and Skibbereen (66.74%) amalgamated into West Cork (59.8%)

Dingle (71.01%) and Killorglin (70.3%) amalgamated into South West Kerry (63.74%)

Manorhamilton (74.17%) and Dromahair (77.05%) amalgamated into Manorhamilton (67.81%) (Leitrim)

Castleconnell part (57.31%) and Kilmallock (66.85%) amalgamated into Cappamore-Kilmallock (54.43%) (Limerick)

Belmullet (67.01%) and Westport (67.28%) amalgamated into West Mayo (61.53%)

Carrickmacross (73.42%) and Castleblayney part (69.43%) amalgamated into Carrickmacross-Castleblayney (61.21%) (Monaghan)

Clones (71.31%) and Castleblayney part (69.43%) amalgamated into Ballybay-Clones (58.49%) (Monaghan)

Birr (68.39%) and Ferbane (67.98%) amalgamated into Birr (58.75%) (Offaly)

Boyle (75.29%) and Strokestown (74.48%) amalgamated into Boyle (65.91%) (Roscommon)

Castlerea (73.81%) and Roscommon (73.83%) amalgamated into Roscommon (62.95%)

Nenagh (74.12%) and Newport (73%) amalgamated into Nenagh (64.41%) (Tipperary)

Templemore (75.57%) and Thurles (73.45%) amalgamated into Templemore-Thurles (66.51%) (Tipperary)

Cashel (63.49%) and Tipperary (67.37%) amalgamated into Cashel-Tipperary (58.31%)

Dungarvan (61.91%) and Lismore (61.81%) amalgamated into Dungarvan-Lismore (52.49%) (Waterford)

Coole (61.75%) and Mullingar East (58.96%) amalgamated into Mullingar-Coole (51.72%) (Westmeath)

Kilbeggan (65.24%) and Mullingar West (55.51%) amalgamated into Mullingar-Kilbeggan (49.99%) (Westmeath).

There were also other rural amalgamations in south Carlow, north Cork, east and west Laois, east Longford and west Sligo which had a lesser effect.

[6] Examples of decline of the order of 20% include Dungarvan LEA and Lismore LEA (Waterford) which had respectively 71.12% and 76.78% turnout in 1985 as opposed to 52.49% in 2014, Belturbet LEA and Cavan LEA which had respectively 76.23% and 69.79% in 1985 as opposed to 52.71% in 2014 and Piltown LEA (Kilkenny) which has declined from 70.15% in 1985 to 54.94% in 2014. Dungarvan-Lismore LEA as it existed in 2014 was substantially similar to the LEAs of Dungarvan and Lismore in 1985. A mere 100 more votes were cast in 2014 than in 1985, despite an increase in the electorate of 6,500.

CHAPTER 7

Polling

This chapter deals with polling, which has been an established tool in Irish politics throughout the period covered by this work. There are two types of political polling. One is polling done at a national level which is aimed at assessing national support for the various parties or in the case of a referendum, the proposal. The second type is constituency level polling, generally carried out with a sample ballot paper with named candidates. This work is not intended to be an extensive treatise on polling and hence the comments will be confined to a few key issues.

National polls tend to be carried out on average on a monthly basis and are usually published in one of the national newspapers. They show support for a particular party as if an election was taking place at that time. Because they are wholly hypothetical, they generally do not reflect what is actually going to happen in an election some years or months in the future. But they are useful guides to trends. The most useful regular poll is that conducted by Red C, which appears on a monthly basis in the Sunday Business Post. The regularity with which that poll is conducted is perceived as giving it an authority greater than any other. Occasional polls are carried out by Ipsos MRBI, Millward Brown Lansdowne and Behaviour and Attitude, but these are conducted at best at quarterly intervals and consequently can miss gradual trends in the forming of opinions. The figures shown by the different polls tend to be somewhat divergent, even when conducted at about the same time. There are issues in the methodology of each, which possibly account for some of the differences. Different polling companies can use different sample sizes, different ways of contacting people (such as by landline, mobile phone or internet) and different criteria for assessing the likelihood of a respondent actually voting. There is also the vexed question of how to deal with the undecided voters and frequently national polls state the core vote and then adjust the vote to exclude the undecided voters.

Constituency level polling is largely carried out for political parties. The sample size tends to be considerably lower than a national poll, typically somewhere between 300 and 500 people. They are often carried out by the parties themselves or by some of the less established (in brand name terms) polling companies. They invariably consist of a sample ballot paper and a request to the voter as to the party he/she supported in the last general election and currently supports. It is not at all unusual in a constituency poll to find for example that Fianna Fáil have 25% declared support but that its candidates get 30% of the votes (or vice versa), suggesting the candidates are personally popular but the brand is poor (or good). The results of these polls tend to be a closely held secret, although there are frequent leaks about them, not all of which can be relied upon to be accurate. While these polls frequently ask respondents to mark ballot papers 2, 3 etc, the reliability of that element of a poll is particularly suspect. They are more useful in predicting the general order of candidates on the first count and thus who is likely to be in the "leaders' enclosure". If a poll shows that one candidate for a party is leading the field by a considerable distance and another is a bit behind the "leaders' enclosure", it is likely that the party will make some effort to divert votes from the leader to the candidate who is behind.

Accuracy issues

National polls can sometimes be wildly misleading, particularly more than six months before elections. For example a Millward Brown Lansdowne poll of 1,000 people for the Irish Independent in September 2010 indicated a position of Fine Gael 30%, Labour 35%, Fianna Fáil 22%, Sinn Féin 4%, Greens 2% and Independents 8%. In the election almost exactly five months later the actual result was Fine Gael 36% (+6), Labour 19% (-16), Fianna Fáil 17% (-5), Sinn Féin 10% (+6), Greens 2% (-) and Others 17% (+9). Curiously the previous poll in the same series in February 2010 which showed Fine Gael 34%, Fianna Fáil 27%, Labour 19%, Sinn Féin 8%, Greens 2% and Others 10% was almost spot on the result from a year later, save that the trend of Fianna Fáil support falling off a cliff and independents and other on the rise continued on the same path from February 2010.

Some of the commentary around polls can be accurate and some quite misleading. For example on the above poll, Aine Kerr, Political

Correspondent commented that "The Greens have seen their support fall to just 2%, from almost 5% in the last election. That puts it in Progressive Democrats-territory and facing a wipeout at the next general election. The junior coalition partners stand to lose over half their seats and may only get two TDs returned". That proved to be largely accurate, except that the Greens lost all of their seats. By contrast there was some panic at the September 2010 poll on the Fine Gael side leading to Ms Kerr reporting in an unattributed quote "If there's a contest between Enda Kenny and Eamon Gilmore, Eamon Gilmore will win hands down...if we keep drifting along, people in Fine Gael are going to wake up to Eamon Gilmore as Taoiseach". This comment turned out to be very wide of the mark as did related analysis suggesting Labour gaining 58 seats at a minimum. Seasoned observers of polls could have predicted that the poll was somewhat "rogue". It was clear that Labour simply did not have the infrastructure across 40+ constituencies to capitalize on or maintain the 35% vote share indicated and equally the Sinn Féin figure seemed seriously out of line with the then reality. However a seasoned observer of polls would have been able to exclude the "noise" and come to a sensible conclusion on that poll, so notwithstanding obvious issues, it was helpful. This poll is a fairly extreme example and it is fair to say that the collapse of the Fianna Fáil vote from 40% to below 20% over the 2008 to 2010 period created a huge level of volatility in terms of voters looking for a home.

National polls frequently survey satisfaction with the government and the popularity of various party leaders. While the reporting of these may generate controversy, it is somewhat doubtful that they provide any really useful information. The leaders of the major parties tend to have a high aggregate of positive and negative views, with relatively few "don't knows". Leaders of minor parties are frequently the most popular, but also register a rather higher level of don't knows. For example in a TNS/mrbi poll in May 2008, voters with no opinion on the then leader of the Progressive Democrats, Ciarán Cannon, amounted to 72%. High levels of dissatisfaction with the government do tend to translate into poor poll ratings for the government parties and poor results. There can be a tendency at some times, most notably around the summer, for satisfaction levels with leaders and government to rise across the board. This is probably a phenomenon of voters being in better humour for seasonal reasons rather than any significant trend.

Constituency level polls also need to be treated with a great degree of caution. They are rarely published in the national media, so public examples are difficult to source. One which was, was a poll for Laois Offaly, conducted in March 2002 about two months before the 2002 general election on a sample of about 400 voters and published in the Irish Independent. This showed the following votes for the lead candidates

Candidate	Party	Poll percent	Actual percent
Cowen	FF	28	20
Flanagan	FG	17	10
Enright	FG	13	13
Parlon	PD	9	14
Fleming	FF	9	11
Moloney	FF	7	13
Buckley	FG	5	3
Killaly	FF	4	7
Stanley	SF	4	4
Others		4	4

As seems to be quite usual with this type of poll in the author's experience, the "brand names" are completely overstated. Cowen and Flanagan got 45% of the vote, whereas on the day their actual combined share was 30%. Indeed Charlie Flanagan lost his seat. The vote shares for most of the parties are relatively accurate, with the exception of Fine Gael and the Progressive Democrats. However between then and polling day, there were clearly trends against Fine Gael, which would benefit a well known Progressive Democrat candidate, such as Tom Parlon. The Fianna Fáil vote in the poll showed 32% of the vote accruing to Offaly candidates and 16% to Laois candidates. This was clearly never going to be replicated on the ground. On the whole, the poll would have been useful if read against the background of prevailing trends. One interesting indication of the prevailing trends at the time was an ICM Research poll reported in Ireland on Sunday on March 3 2002, just before the Laois Offaly poll. This poll was quite accurate as to the level of votes secured by each party in the May general election. However exactly the same trends were not picked up in the constituency poll.

In the Laois Offaly poll, transfer trends were also analysed. They showed 59% of Cowen's surplus transferring to his fellow party candidates, whereas the actual percentage was 64%. However the pattern of how they were distributed as between the three other candidates was wholly wrong. Otherwise the pattern of every other transfer was wholly wrong and this concluded in the unreliable result of the poll of an apparent loss of a Fianna Fáil seat. The application of a realistic transfer rate would have shown Fianna Fáil holding their three seats with Tom Parlon losing out. In effect between then and the general election, a change in first preferences (perhaps anticipated in early March) allowed Parlon to displace Flanagan.

Polls during campaigns

Polls during campaigns over the years have tended to be quite accurate, if a reader follows trends shown over the course of the campaign. There were however in 2015 a number of examples outside Ireland where the polls are seen to have got it badly wrong most notably in Canada, Greece and the United Kingdom. In those countries, polls late in campaigns seem to have considerably underestimated support for the respective winners being the Canadian Liberals, Syriza and the British Conservatives. This trend continued in Ireland in the 2016 general election, with most polls showing Fine Gael at levels close to 30%, whereas the final outturn for Fine Gael was just over 25% and also underestimating Fianna Fáil. There was also an impression that polls in the 2016 Brexit referendum were quite inaccurate. This was possibly unfair as Brexit polls sometimes indicated remain would win and sometimes indicated leave would win. Similar considerations apply to the 2016 US presidential election. Recent trends are casting a lot of doubt over political polling worldwide. There is in any event a margin of error in polls and the enormous sensitivity of the Irish electoral system to relatively small percentage vote movements complicates things.

One area where national campaign polls need to be treated with caution is those done during the course of a local election campaign. Because of the tendency for very localised voting and a tendency to elect independents in those campaigns, polling which is more focussed on national trends has a particular deficiency in the context of local elections. Again however, it is usually possible for a skilled observer to make appropriate adjustments to those polls to arrive at an underlying position.

One type of polling, which is useless in a practical sense for the then current election, has turned out to be very accurate. Exit polling has been used in Ireland for general elections 2007 to 2016 and in the United Kingdom for general elections including those of 2015 and 2017. In each case the percentages indicated for parties were almost spot on, although the precise forecasting of how it might translate into seats was not. In the 2011 general election in Ireland, expectations were that Fine Gael would do rather better than its actual 36.1% first preference vote share and the exit poll was the first indication that Fine Gael had not done as well as expected. In practice the seat bonus that Fine Gael got more than made up for any perceived downside in terms of the level of vote. The same could possibly be said of 2016, where a disappointing vote share for Fine Gael, first indicated by exit polls, translated into a rather better performance in terms of seats. Prior to the 2015 UK general election, there was virtual certainty among commentators that parliament would be hung, with the Conservatives as the largest party with 280-300 seats. The exit poll came as a complete surprise and was the first indication that the Conservatives would do far better, but even it did not forecast the overall majority eventually attained. The exit polling for the 2017 UK general election seemed to be the first indication that Labour was doing well. Exit polling is however practically useless for outcome, as it is only telling a party what it is going to find out officially in a number of hours anyhow. For obvious reasons, it does not enable anyone to refine strategy, which is the primary use of polls. However they are useful in establishing the profile of those who voted and issues which might have influenced the way they voted and they merit thorough analysis for that reason.

CHAPTER 8
Tallying

Tallying is a feature of the Irish electoral system that does not seem to be prevalent elsewhere. It involves observing a count and compiling an accurate record of the first preference vote in every ballot box. It is therefore an indispensible tool in planning for future elections, as it breaks down a candidate's votes into meaningful parts.

The art of tallying is seen as one of the very mysterious aspects of the Irish electoral system. It is seen as the province of a strange breed of nerdy political animal, involving some Macbethian black art and witchcraft. In fact it is a very simple process carried out at the count centre when the ballot boxes are opened. It gives a very accurate picture of what the first count result will look like. This picture is accurate to small fractions of a percent in many cases and is usually available a few hours before the first count result is officially declared. Complete tallying of an election count simply involves having enough people in the count centre to record the first preference vote on most if not all of the ballot papers being counted there. The records completed by these people are then added together at a central location in the count centre, thus producing a "tally" for the constituency or LEA.

How is tallying done?
The art of doing a good tally invariably involves co-operation among the representatives of all the candidates in the election and having a sufficient number of people in the count centre to tally all ballot boxes. Counts invariably start at 9am the morning after election day. The count staff sit on one side of a row of rectangular tables set out on two or three sides of a large corral perhaps 10 x 20 metres. There may be thirty count staff sitting on the inside of a rectangle made of these tables. At the other side of the tables, there is a metal crowd control barrier and the party workers stand outside this. There is usually enough space for four people to stand opposite two count staff. Each of these people has printed tally sheets. These list the

candidates in alphabetical order on the left, with plenty of space to record votes for each of them.

At 9am, the count staff start tipping out the content of ballot boxes in front of teams of two count officials. At the start, the people tallying that box need to note the box number and the polling station or area to which it relates. For example it could be box number 100, Dublin Bay South, Cambridge Road, Ringsend. It is usually best that two people "shadow" each count staff member, one verbally calling out the name of the candidate getting the first preference vote and the other recording it in writing on a tally sheet. For example if a candidate is called Walsh, one person calls out "Walsh" on seeing a number 1 vote for Walsh and the other marks it on a sheet of paper called the tally sheet. A team of two record roughly half the votes in the box as they are "shadowing" one count staff member. A neighbouring team of two people shadowing the other staff member, equally record the other half of the votes in the box. The person writing usually records first preference votes in units of 5, so that it is easy to count the entire number at the end. The count staff will often open the ballot paper facing out towards the count observers, so the skill of reading upside down is not usually required.

Generally calling out the recipient of the number 1 vote requires the greater experience; it also requires decent eyesight. For that reason it is best that more experienced people are put on the job of watching the ballot paper and calling out the first preference. At the end of the opening of all votes in a ballot box, it is critical that the two teams tallying that box swap their information, so that the result for the full box is known. Once this is done, there is an accurate record of the first preference votes by candidate cast in the box being tallied. It is also helpful, although not always general practice, to verify with the count staff the number of votes officially recorded as being cast in that ballot box and to note any significant discrepancy between the tally total and the actual votes.

In the author's experience at count centres, it is practice to open between 8 and 15 ballot boxes each time (with 16 to 30 count staff respectively). There is usually a gap of about 10 minutes for a breather after two count staff have opened a box and before they are given another one. Therefore an effective tally requires 32 to 60 tally people (two per count staff) between all the candidates. It is frequently the case at general elections that there are more people than really required and often the surplus people are a complete nuisance. If there are not enough people, frequently an experienced person can both watch and call, so that only one person is needed per count staff member. So if 8 boxes are being opened at the same time, a team of 16 experienced people can cover the entire count. If numbers are very low, the best option is to tally half of a box (although it is often the case that the other half has a somewhat different pattern). Generally there is a "runner" on the floor who brings the completed tally sheets back to a central base, usually operated by all parties in co-operation.

One pattern which is notable is that the people who vote in the evening (presumably younger working people) tend to have their votes at the bottom of the pile when the ballot papers are tipped onto the table. By contrast the top of the pile probably represents the morning voters. This can manifest itself as a different trend in voting towards the end of the tally of the box. The first count tally is solely focussed on where the number one vote is cast. No attempt should be made to record preferences. An experienced tallyman will however mentally observe patterns of transfer.

Inaccuracies in tallies

While people at an election count can and do fret enormously about missing boxes and incomplete tallies of a particular ballot box, the reality is that a very large sample of tallies has usually so randomized the votes that it will give an accurate picture in percentage terms of the entire election. This is shown by the example of a partial tally set out below. In general elections, sometimes there are a couple of boxes missed entirely and some where only a half box tally is available. Generally if 200 ballot papers are opened by the count staff, the tally may only cover 198 votes, because two could not be seen properly. It is more difficult to see the first preference where the voter has ordered every candidate on the ballot paper, which perhaps typically affects about a quarter of the papers. Another common error is where there are two candidates of the same name.[1] The discrepancies in these types of cases tend to be greater than would otherwise be the case. In producing tallies, it is a cardinal sin to guess what might be the picture in any missing box as part of the official tallies. However if there is a missing box in an area known from other related boxes to be strong for a particular candidate, any

101

assessment of those tallies should include some additional notional figure for that candidate.

Where a tally is partial only, it is still, provided it is random enough, a very good guide to the likely first count outcome. So even if only 6 people are available to tally and 10 boxes are being opened at the same time, good tallies on 6 half boxes spread across a range of polling stations is likely to give a guide as to the outcome. Lack of people is not usually an issue in general or local elections. It tends to be more of an issue with European elections and referenda. However partial tallies were done for example in many Dublin constituencies in the European elections 2014 and these were quite good in coming to a guess as to the final outcome.

A good example of a partial tally, which still comes close to the final position is a 79.9% (in other words only 79.9% of the votes were actually captured by the tally people) tally in Carlow Kilkenny for General Election 2011. This suggested the following outcome.

Candidate	party	tally	tally percent	actual	actual percent	variance (%)
Phelan JP	FG	9,041	15.35	10,929	14.82	(0.53)
Hogan P	FG	8,503	14.44	10,525	14.27	(0.17)
McGuinness J	FF	7,415	12.59	9,531	12.92	0.33
Phelan A	Lab	6,534	11.09	8,072	10.95	(0.16)
Deering P	FG	6,243	10.60	7,470	10.13	(0.47)
Aylward B	FF	5,463	9.27	6,762	9.17	(0.10)
Murnane O'C J	FF	3,598	6.11	4,428	6.00	(0.11)
Funchion K	SF	3,120	5.30	4,075	5.53	0.23
Hurley D	Lab	2,896	4.92	3,908	5.30	0.38
Cassin J	SF	2,337	3.97	2,958	4.01	0.04
White M	G	1,653	2.81	2,072	2.81	-
MacLiam C	Soc	674	1.14	1,135	1.54	0.40

Kelly S	NP	379	0.64	601	0.81	0.17
Couchman J	NP	281	0.48	384	0.52	0.04
O'Hara J	NP	213	0.36	253	0.34	(0.02)
Murphy D	NP	198	0.34	195	0.26	(0.08)
Leahy R	NP	177	0.30	256	0.35	0.05
Walsh N	NP	111	0.19	119	0.16	(0.03)
Dalton J	NP	67	0.11	70	0.09	(0.02)
Totals		**58,903**		**73,743**		

The highest negative variance is for JP Phelan. If he had got the percent indicated by the tallies he would have received 11,319 votes, 390 more than he actually did. By contrast, the Socialist MacLiam was under-recorded and if he had received a percentage of votes as predicted by the tally, he would have received 841 votes as opposed to an actual 1,135, a difference of 294 votes. However even these maximum variances would not cause there to be a different outcome. The tallies therefore were reliable in terms of predicting the outcome, which was the election of the leading five candidates. Indeed they also seem reliable in assessing the level of votes in perhaps as many as 75% of the ballot boxes in the constituency and in assessing the overall vote in the bigger urban centres. This is all despite one in every five votes not being recorded in the tally.

It is quite difficult to see how the differences occurred in that particular tally. However there seemed to be a pattern of poorer tallies in urban areas, which may have affected the lower ranking candidates, who were generally urban based, more. The tally people also tend to be from the major parties and sometimes do not "see" votes for minor parties and independents, most of whom in that case did slightly better than tallies indicated. As this was an election where Fine Gael were very successful, it is possible that Fine Gael tally people were in the predominance and that they tended to "see" Fine Gael votes more readily than votes for others, thus giving rise to an aggregate overstatement of the first preference vote for Fine Gael of over 1%. It is also notoriously difficult on a long ballot paper to see preferences for those near the middle of the ballot paper and it is notable that nearly all of these are under-recorded.

The Carlow Kilkenny 2011 tally also recorded 236 spoilt votes, whereas actually there were 821 spoilt votes. This is an unusually high level of almost 3.5 times under-recording. This is difficult to understand. It probably results from a lot of the individual tally sheets failing to record any spoilt votes, even though they were in the box. It is also quite difficult to spot spoilt votes if they lack an official mark or have a 1 and 7 that look similar. Even a very good quality tally will under-record the spoilt votes for that reason.

However the Carlow Kilkenny partial tally demonstrates that for all practical purposes, partial tallies are pretty accurate in terms of assessing the result.

Tallying for multiple elections

It is not unusual that two elections are held at the one time. Since 1999 local and European elections have been held on the same day. Two referenda or a referendum and an election can also take place on the same day. Where two elections are combined, the ballot papers are of two colours, say white and blue. Thus for example a ballot paper for local election candidates might be white and a referendum held at the same time might have a blue ballot paper. This causes a difficulty in that the blue papers (being say a referendum) merit little interest from the tally people and that the people monitoring blue, instead get involved in an unhelpful way in the counting of the whites. Ideally the blues should be tallied fully if there are enough volunteers. However the central tally operation will have to put the subsidiary election returns to one side and prioritize the "white" ballot paper for the purpose of getting to a final tally.

The central tally area

It has been the practice for many years that the main parties co-operate in producing a central tally, relying on the field work done by the actual tally people. The central tally area in the count centre needs to have a good access to power as inevitably there will be a requirement to plug in computers, printers and the like. Usually each party has a key person for each constituency or LEA. Generally these people will be the same election to election and can work well together.

It is practice that once about 10 percent of the boxes are inputted, that the tally area starts to issue ongoing "state of the count" spreadsheet reports. While these are generally wholly accurate as to the votes in those areas, they are completely unreliable guides as to the outcome of the election as a whole. This is because boxes tend to be opened in a geographical sequence so the first boxes tend to favour local candidates from that area.[2] None of this stops the national and local media reporting sensational outcomes, such as Fianna Fáil taking four out of five seats, based on the actual outcome of the first 20 boxes. So when a listener hears anything on the news at 11am, it needs to be treated with a considerable degree of scepticism. Reliance on partial tallies between about 11am and 4pm on polling day is a common source of misleading information. It is correct that a very experienced tally person can give a prognosis based on the first 20% to 30% of boxes, but that needs to be given somewhat of a health warning. It is really only when things are heading towards 70% to 80% tally complete that a sensible read can be made and even that needs to factor in candidates who are likely to be very strong in areas yet to be tallied.

The final tally

This tends to become available in urban constituencies about 1 or 2 pm on the day of the count, assuming that counting started at 9am. In rural constituencies it can take longer, as there are a lot more boxes. The final tally (unlike the interim ones) is in the author's view a reliable guide to the likely first preferences secured by each candidate. Further it is usually possible in at least 80% of cases to be certain about the final destination of all of the seats and the likely order of eliminations. The author has always covered the Dublin City counts which cover 6 constituencies in Dáil elections and anything from 8 to 11 LEAs in local elections. Usually in Dáil elections, it is fairly clear from the complete tallies what is going to happen in 5 of the 6 and in local elections there are probably at most three LEAs that are in doubt. Therefore the focus of attention should ideally switch to trying to refine a prediction as to the outcome for those doubtful constituencies and LEAs. This is a task that requires advanced tallying skills.

The following are a few examples of full tallies which show how relatively accurate they are. These samples are fairly representative of a number of tallies in the possession of the author.

Dublin South Central General Election 2011

Candidate	Tally total	Percent	Actual vote	Percent (variation)
Eric Byrne	8,197	16.15	8,357	16.41 (+0.26)
Aengus Ó'Snodaigh	6,810	13.41	6,804	13.36 (-0.05)
Joan Collins	6,553	12.91	6,574	12.91 (nil)
Catherine Byrne	5,649	11.13	5,604	11.00 (-0.13)
Michael Conaghan	5,465	10.76	5,492	10.78 (+0.02)
Michael Mulcahy	4,788	9.43	4,837	9.50 (+0.07)
Henry Upton	4,155	8.18	4,183	8.21 (+0.03)
Colm Brophy	3,397	6.69	3,376	6.63 (-0.06)
Ruairi McGinley	3,031	5.97	2,976	5.84 (-0.13)
Oisin Ó'hAlmháin	1,008	1.99	1,015	1.99 (nil)
Peter O'Neill	440	0.87	456	0.90 (+0.03)
Neville Bradley	315	0.62	323	0.63 (+0.01)
Colm Callanan	246	0.48	239	0.47 (-0.01)
Sean C Farrell	191	0.38	178	0.35 (-0.03)
Paul King	146	0.29	146	0.29 (nil)
Gerry Kelly	132	0.26	137	0.27 (+0.01)
Noel Bennett	130	0.26	128	0.25 (-0.01)
Dominic Mooney	116	0.23	102	0.20 (-0.03)
Totals	**50,769**		**50,927**	

So there was a discrepancy of 158 votes between those tallied and the actual valid vote or about 0.31% of the actual vote. As noted above, there was probably a tendency to confuse votes for Catherine Byrne and Eric Byrne, both sharing a surname. These appear to be the greatest deviations in percentage terms and indeed unusually Catherine Byrne got more votes according to the tally than she actually received. Calling out "Eric" for an

Eric Byrne vote and "Catherine" for a Catherine Byrne vote when tallying is probably the best way to avoid this. Notably 13 of the 18 candidates are within 0.05% of their actual first preference vote.

This summary would have been available by about 3pm on the day of the count. It could be predicted from this that the quota would be slightly over 8,462 and that the lower candidates would be eliminated broadly in the order in which they stood. It was also fairly predictable that the first five would be elected. This was because the combined vote of Brophy and McGinley, both Fine Gael, at 6,400 were unlikely to exceed either Catherine Byrne, also Fine Gael or Conaghan Labour. Equally it was difficult for Upton of Labour to close the 1,300 gap on his party colleague Conaghan or for Mulcahy, the sole Fianna Fáil candidate to close the gap of 600 on Conaghan. In practice it took until 5am the following morning, an extraordinary amount of agonizing and 13 counts to formally decide the destination of the five seats.

Clondalkin LEA (South Dublin) Local Election 2009

This is a somewhat more typical example. 15,184 votes were tallied, whereas the actual valid vote was 15,634, so it is a 97% tally. The following are the tallies and actual votes recorded by the main candidates

Candidate	Tallied votes	Actual votes	Variation
Robert Dowds	2,357	2,449	+92
Tony Delaney	1,689	1,725	+36
Therese Ridge	1,478	1,575	+97
Matthew McDonagh	1,444	1,502	+58
Jim Daly	1,239	1,254	+15
Shane O'Connor	1,204	1,221	+17
Gino Kenny	1,080	1,137	+57
Trevor Gilligan	1,006	1,034	+28
Total	**15,184**	**15,634**	

Again as can be seen the discrepancy between the tallied vote and the actual vote per candidate is at worst about 100 short of the actual vote. This probably arises because the tally for a box or boxes in which both Dowds and Ridge were strong somewhat underestimate the real vote. There are indeed a few boxes in this tally where the turnout assessed by reference to votes recorded seems quite low. For all practical purposes however the difference is immaterial. A feature which this tally brings out is a slight over-recording of the candidates who get small numbers of votes. It is not clear why this arises but it is a common distortion in tallies.

Subsequent tallying operations at count

The operation in which the first count tally takes place is the initial unfolding of the ballot papers from each ballot box. Once the count staff are satisfied that the number of votes in each ballot box conforms with other information they have, they then proceed to separate out the votes by candidate. This part of the count process gives an opportunity for subsequent tallying to look at preferences and assess likely transfer patterns. This is an aspect of tallying that has fallen into spectacular disuse in recent years.

Tallying should not finish once the first count tally is available, but should continue to try and ascertain the destination of preferences of candidates likely to be eliminated. The subsequent tallying should be aimed at establishing where transfers are going as between the likely candidates for the seats, for which the outcome is in doubt. This can be quite a difficult thing to do practically, as it is not always the case that the ballot papers are put on public display, in such a way that the preferences of lower candidates can be easily examined. While the number of first preferences for those candidates has to be counted by the count staff, this is sometimes done in a way that makes it difficult to see the preferences one is trying to track. However usually some count staff will oblige, so that a reasonable sample can be got. In practice as the first preferences have to be properly counted to get to an official first count declaration, there is always an opportunity once the first preference tally is available to have a look at votes for lower ranking candidates in the course of their first preference vote being established and counted. There needs to be a firm plan as to the information that needs to be obtained from a subsequent tally. First preferences votes for low polling candidates transferred to other candidates likely to be eliminated are irrelevant to calling the result and frequently one needs to be looking to where the vote will finally end up. In practice if this exercise is done correctly, it is possible to form an accurate view on the likely outcome. Two examples are useful

Dublin North Central 2007

The destiny of the last seat in the three seat Dublin North Central in the 2007 general election was in doubt based on the first count tally. It was evident from the first count tally that Sean Haughey Fianna Fáil, the son of the then late Taoiseach Charles J Haughey and Richard Bruton Fine Gael were going to be elected, both polling a quota or thereabouts on the first count. The real issue was as between Ivor Callely, Fianna Fáil on 7,003 first preference votes and Finian Mc Grath, Independent on 5,169 first preference votes with the gap at about 2,000 votes. It was also clear that all of the three lower candidates would be eliminated and that their transfers would favour McGrath. The national media were calling it confidently for Callely. The remaining candidates (actual result but tallies were similar) were:

Derek McDowell, Lab	2,649
Bronwen Maher, Green	1,891
Peter Lawlor, SF	1,375

There were therefore about 6,000 votes available for transfer. As a minor aside, Haughey needed about 80 more votes to reach quota, which he duly got on the transfers of Lawlor, but this could be ignored for practical purposes. It was pretty likely that McGrath would close the gap but the "informed wisdom", no doubt aided by Fianna Fáil "spinning", was that Callely would be the victor. To anyone versed in the art, it seemed pretty likely that McGrath would win, aided enormously by the exceptionally small field of seven candidates, which increased the likelihood of voters voting the whole way down the ballot paper (unlike the Leinster 2004 election discussed below). However to confirm this as the certain outcome, what was required was a sizeable sampling of the preferences as between Callely and McGrath on the votes of the three lower candidates. For this purpose, when the ballot papers of McDowell, Maher and Lawlor were again brought out to be counted, a sample was taken of about 400 to 500 of the papers of each, importantly ignoring all issues except as to whether the highest preference was for Callely or McGrath. In the alternative, if neither got a preference, the paper would ultimately prove to be non transferable.

The sampling suggested that McGrath would pick up about 66% of the transfers, with about 16% going to each of Callely and Non transferable (slightly more to non transferable). The original tallies and projected transfers suggested broadly the following:

Callely	6,900	+1000	final position	7,900
McGrath	5,100	+3800	final position	8,900
Other candidates	5,800	(-4800)	non transferable	1,000

The tally following sampling thus predicted that McGrath would win the seat by a thousand votes.

In actual fact on transfers of those votes, Mc Grath picked up 4,185 votes, Callely picked up 933 votes and the non transferables were 857. The sampling therefore slightly underestimated McGrath, who got in excess of 70% of the transfers. The notes taken by the author at the time described the pattern of transfers as 4 McGrath:1 Callely:1 NT for convenience and this may be the prime reason for the disparity between the sampling and the actual transfers.

The earlier eliminations affecting the Callely/McGrath competition clearly illustrate how misleading individual eliminations can be in forming the final picture. This is why the sampling exercise is focused on the candidates competing for the doubtful seat. The returning officer in this case eliminated Lawlor first, as he had to do, as if in fact all of his transfers had gone to the two lower candidates, either of them could in theory then have overtaken McGrath. A completely false picture was promulgated based on these transfers as 382 of them went to Fianna Fáil (Haughey still needing 80 votes) and 556 went to McGrath. 390 went to the two other candidates. If subsequent transfers had indeed followed that type of pattern, then Callely would have held on comfortably. However this completely ignored the already known fact that tallying sampling of all three candidates had indicated the overall 4:1:1 pattern and the fact that Sean Haughey as a very popular local candidate with impeccable local pedigree was going to take some votes from Sinn Féin, which would not then transfer on within Fianna Fáil. This was shown to be the case on the next count as only 50% of the small Haughey surplus (which of course only involved a re-examination of the transfers he took from Sinn Féin) went to his party colleague Callely. However even that pattern was taken as suggesting the outcome was very much in doubt. It was only the final count that confirmed the sampling done before the official first count, as on that count McGrath took 5 transfers for every one taken by Callely.

Leinster 2004 European Election

A similar subsequent tally was carried out in the very fraught Leinster (technically Ireland East) European campaign of 2004. It will be recollected that Leinster was a three seat constituency at that time in which both Fianna Fáil and Fine Gael held a seat, with the last seat being marginal. Avril Doyle the sitting Fine Gael MEP had been joined on the ticket by the very well known then television personality Mairéad McGuinness. This it could fairly be said was not entirely welcome to Avril Doyle, as it created the unusual circumstance where a sitting member was being joined by a very formidable candidate, in circumstances where one seat was the more likely outcome. The campaign apparently became quite heated, with the usual type of disputes over infringement of the territory allocated to the other. It was also the case that polling evidence was indicating that McGuinness was somewhat stronger than Doyle. The other major piece of the jigsaw was that this was a time when the Labour Party's fortunes were improving and they had a well known candidate Peter Cassells, with impeccable trade union credentials. Against all of this background, the Doyle/McGuinness tensions were one of the main stories of the campaign that year and the public got a sense of a major battle. There is a suspicion that this "battle" might have been exaggerated to some extent to maximise the Fine Gael vote and more importantly third party transfers.

In the event the first count produced the following results for the lead candidates with a quota of 113,295

McGuinness FG	114,249
Doyle FG	69,511
Aylward FF	68,206
Cassells Lab	59,158
Kirk FF	45,454

McGuinness exceeded quota and took the first seat. It was fairly obvious from this, that Liam Aylward would also take a seat and as he needed virtually all of Kirk's vote to get to the quota, he was unlikely to exceed quota. The real issue was whether the 10,000 margin held by Doyle over Cassells would be eroded by a field of 8 lower ranking candidates, predominantly of the left, who had 96,600 votes between them. The biggest component of these were a Wexford based Sinn Féin candidate, John Dwyer who had 39,356 votes and a south Carlow based Green candidate, subsequent TD Mary White, who had 25,576 votes. Both these candidates were based geographically close to Ms Doyle and rather distant from the Navan, Co Meath based Cassells. However their vote was likely to have come from all across Leinster, which might render the geography irrelevant.

There was huge tension around the count centre, which was the Puddenhill activity centre in the heart of rural Meath. As is usual with European elections, shopping trollies were commandeered from the local branch of Tesco to wheel around ballot papers. The prevailing view in all of this was that Cassells would close the gap and end up with a significant lead. Mrs Doyle was reported to be not best pleased. It was also obvious that the count would go on for some days. In the circumstances what needed to be done was to look at a sample of transfers from each of the 8 lower candidates, who would clearly be eliminated and to look at second preferences from Mr Kirk to either Doyle or Cassells directly and to extrapolate from those samples the likely real number of votes, which would accrue to the two competitors as the count progressed. The sample was about 500 votes for the candidates below 10,000 votes and about 1,000 for the three candidates with higher votes. In the event a distillation of all of this when the official count was at about count 2, suggested that contrary to all speculation, Ms Doyle would eventually win the seat by about 7,500. In fact at the end of the day, the winning margin was 7,065. Therefore sample tallying over 96,600 votes of others and 45,454 votes of Seamus Kirk, the second Fianna Fáil candidate produced a prediction that was within 400 or so votes of the actual position. It was not clear at the time that either the Fine Gael party leader, Enda Kenny or Avril Doyle (or indeed the expert tallymen themselves) believed this prediction, but one could be pretty confident that Doyle would win based on the size of sampling and close correlation in patterns across transfers from various candidates. It should be said that it was somewhat of a fluke to be within 400 votes of the final outcome, as distinct from predicting a win. The focus of this tally was solely on which of Cassells or Doyle or Aylward were getting the highest preference from the first 8 to be eliminated. So if a paper was marked Aylward 10, Cassells 8, Doyle 7 that was treated as a Doyle paper as it would eventually accrue to her. The focus on the Kirk vote was on transfers that would come to Cassells or Doyle before the more likely destination of Aylward. In fact over five counts involving eliminations (there were two collective eliminations), Doyle got more transfers than Cassells on three of these, with Cassells only benefitting more from the Green and Sinn Féin transfers. While the prognosis that Doyle would win was made by the few expert in tally at second count stage, it was only after the Sinn Féin candidate Dwyer was eliminated that the Doyle camp became comfortable that they would win. This was perhaps a whole day after the prediction by a few tallymen that Doyle would hold the lead fairly comfortably. Before the Sinn Féin elimination, the lead was almost exactly 10,000. After the 46,247 papers were distributed, the lead had shrunk towards 6,000.

What became apparent during the count was that while geography probably had some influence on the outcome, a far more significant factor was that those voters who favoured minor parties and candidates, felt a need to have their say in the highly publicized "fight" between the two women. Most of these voters seemed to favour McGuinness and gave her a sixth or seventh preference. However critically they then gave the next preference to Doyle. She therefore picked up 20,990 votes on transfers from left parties and Fianna Fáil that might have been expected to be transfer unfriendly to a Fine Gael candidate. Cassells by contrast picked up 24,717 from what would appear to have been transfer friendlier sources for him. Another material factor was the level of votes from the lowest 8 candidates which proved to be non transferable. These totalled almost 42,000, a factor which was evident enough from any cursory tally where voters who clearly did not like the established parties frequently voted 1 to 8 for the minor parties and independents and then stopped. This suggested that the sheer number of independents militated against the likelihood of voters voting down the ballot paper, a position completely different from the example from Dublin North Central set out above.

Using tallies to predict the order of elimination

The order of elimination of candidates is a key issue, as sometimes the elimination of candidate A before candidate B can lead to the election of B or vice versa. In a tight contest, predicting the order of elimination is difficult. In the 7 seat Ballymun LEA (Dublin City) in 2014, with a projected quota of 2,104, the tally suggested the following:

Noeleen Reilly SF	2,513
Cathleen Carney Boud SF	2,296
Andrew Montague Lab	1,543
Paul McAuliffe FF	1,442
Noel Rock FG	1,219

All of the above were regarded as certain of election. Following this the competitors for the two remaining seats were:

Laura Reid FF	1,112
Áine Clancy Lab	926
Gerry Breen FG	896
Caroline Conroy Green	735
Bill Tormey FG	650
Andrew Keegan PBP	623
Geraldine Gough Ind	594

The question was whether further tallying could predict the order of elimination that would apply to this group. Any two of this group (excepting possibly Tormey) were capable of being elected, as behind them was a bunch of left wing and independent candidates on 458, 403, 353, 339, 273, 163, 149 and 145 votes respectively. There was also the issue of about 600 Sinn Féin transfers arising from surpluses. The likelihood was that one of Clancy, Breen or Conroy would take a seat and that the other would be one of Keegan or Gough. It was also possible that Reid would not be caught by two of the chasing pack. Key issues to assess in the tally were whether Breen with the benefit of 650 Fine Gael votes (to be shared with Rock) could pass out Clancy, as he would likely then benefit from her transfers or whether the opposite would happen. Further if Conroy, Green managed to get ahead of Clancy, Conroy might benefit from her transfers. Further if there were substantial transfers to Gough from other independents, Gough might move ahead of the pack. Substantial transfers from other left parties might also bring Keegan to the front. The gaps were so fine, that the tallies were really unable to predict the order of elimination. In the event Clancy and Keegan filled the last two seats. It should be noted in passing that over 98% of the votes were tallied and that the largest discrepancy understated a candidate's votes by 0.13%, illustrating the extraordinary accuracy of the tally.

Conclusion on second round tallying

It can be concluded that focussed preference tallying is usually quite effective in determining the likely destiny of the seat or seats, where that outcome is not quite clear from the initial tally for the first count. It will not however really help where the margins are down to 100 or 200 votes in a general election or 50 or less votes in a local election, where it is virtually impossible to predict an outcome until a late stage in counting. It is also often difficult to get the necessary people to do an effective second round tally when it is first possible. Often this co-incides with the adjudication of the spoilt votes, a process which is often attended by a cast of thousands, in circumstances where the number of doubtful papers about which there can be any doubt can probably be counted on two hands. It is also a somewhat difficult task to predict the order of eliminations, which can have a dramatic impact on the outturn.

Uses made of tally information after the count

This in practice is the most significant purpose of completing tallies. A comprehensive tally in an Excel type format is nearly always available after every general and local election. In rural Ireland they are sometimes printed in the local media. These are a highly useful source of pretty accurate information as to the voting behaviour of pockets of voters in numbers of anywhere between 50 and 400. These are the numbers of votes routinely found in a single ballot box.

In urban areas, there tends to be more than one ballot box in the base unit of electoral geography, the District Electoral Division (almost invariably referred to as DED). Usually in these areas, the roads are listed in alphabetical order, so box 1 in a four box DED might contain the votes cast by voters living on roads with names beginning with the letters A to F (with inevitably a long road beginning with F split between two boxes). Thus for mapping purposes, it is probably necessary to aggregate the four together and get total figures across the four boxes. It is also not unusual in urban areas that DEDs are split in two for polling purposes on a geographical basis, so that it is possibly to have a micro level of detail within a single DED. This is particularly prevalent in the outer reaches of Dublin where DEDs formerly consisting of farmland and a few houses, now often have populations of over 10,000. It is always possible to obtain accurate figures for the area covered by a polling station.[3]

Immediately after an election, the tallies are useful for candidates to see where they got their votes in a constituency/LEA. Particularly in local elections, there is a tendency for the votes for a candidate to be highly geographic, with a successful candidate often getting 80% of their vote in a very concentrated area and minimal numbers of votes elsewhere. If a candidate is getting a substantial vote everywhere, that is usually indicative of someone who will be easily elected. Obviously then candidates will focus their work on their key area and attempt to build a profile in other areas where they seem to have got more than a minimal number of votes.

So for example in Dublin South Central in the 2011 general election, tallies show Labour TD, Michael Conaghan receiving respectively 91, 150, 108 and 89 votes in the four boxes in the Ballyfermot Carna DED area and it is evident that this was one of his stronger areas. By contrast he got 3, 8, 3 and 6 votes in the four boxes in the Kimmage E DED area of that constituency, suggesting that this was a relatively weak area for him. The tallies are clearly sufficiently accurate that one can work out how many first preference votes Conaghan got per polling area and what percentage they represented.

Tallies are also of strategic significance where parties are running more than one candidate in a constituency and are trying to organize their vote. It is usually the case that parties maximise their chances of getting extra seats by having candidates who poll similar numbers of votes. If for example, a party has 15,000 votes in Wexford according to tallies from the last election, the best prospect of securing two seats, may be to get two candidates of broadly equal merit securing about 7,500 votes each. If the county is split in accordance with historic tally information into two blocks, each of which contain approximately 7,500 votes for the party, the chances are quite high that, with discipline, the two candidates will poll relatively equally. The blocks need to be set by reference to the geographical location of candidates and also areas where candidates might for some other reason poll better. Frequently these types of strategies will not divide the entire county. For example Wexford might be divided into two equal blocks of 6,000 exclusive to each candidate with a common territory of 3,000 votes. Further if candidate Ms A is a well known government Minister, the 3,000 block might be allocated exclusively to the other candidate Mr B, on the basis that the Minister will naturally pick up more votes in the places not allotted to her. If these strategies are implemented, the intent is that candidates confine themselves to the area allotted to them in terms of their posters, literature and canvassing and that the electorate fully understands that if they are voting for that party, who they ought to vote for. The maintenance of discipline in these cases is always problematic; the problems can be eased by a reasonably sized area open to everyone.

In the context of an election, any good candidate or their team will have thoroughly assessed all available tallies. These will tell the candidate the areas where people are most likely to vote for a candidate of that profile.

They will also indicate areas where none of the rival candidates are particularly strong and therefore those areas may merit particular attention as part of a canvassing or literature strategy.

It should be mentioned in this context that apart from tallies showing who voted for whom in a DED, there is a massive amount of other statistical information available about every DED through the website of the Irish Census. This includes analysis of the area by age profile and indications of how many people have cars, television and internet. In urban areas this information can be narrowed down to very small areas consisting of a few roads (although regrettably this cannot be done with the tally figures as well, absent very specific local knowledge).

A major challenge with tallies is communicating the information to candidates. This is not helped by the usual format of tally reports. Tally sheets are traditionally prepared including the name of the polling station and a two digit code, both of which appear on the black ballot box. However for all other purposes, particularly maps, an area will be known by its DED name; this information is rarely included in the basic tally sheet. This means that a person reviewing historic tallies has to know what polling station relates to each area, which can often be difficult to ascertain. The problem for candidates is that the tallies are a mass of detailed numbers in very fine print. There are many ways to present them more effectively. These might include maps showing percentage obtained or maps showing the absolute numbers of votes a candidate or party obtained in an area.

References in Chapter 8

[1]   For example in the 2011 general election in Dublin South Central, Catherine Byrne Fine Gael and Eric Byrne Labour were more likely to have votes for one incorrectly attributed to the other (so that on the tally Catherine Byrne got 5,649 votes per the tallies as opposed to 5,604 in the actual count and Eric Byrne got 8,197 as opposed to 8,357 in the actual count).

[2]   For example in Dublin Bay South constituency, which is approximately square shaped, the process starts in the north east corner (Ringsend), then heads clockwise to the south east corner, then to the south west and finishes in the north west corner (Christchurch area). This means that early tallies tend to massively favour candidates based in the east. It is only as the tally proceeds that the other candidates based in the west begin to catch up.

[3]   The largest polling station covering a single DED, which the author has seen in the country, seems to be the one located at Garryduff Sports Centre in the Douglas/Rochestown area of suburban Cork and that may be the one where the tally information is least specific in the entire country. In general election 2011, 3,814 votes were tallied there and there may be no real meaningful breakdown beyond what individual candidates got there.

CHAPTER 9

Spoilt Votes and
Other Irregularities

For a variety of reasons, a number of votes cast in every Irish election are deemed to be wholly invalid and thus are regarded as spoilt. They are thus disregarded in determining the actual first preference vote for each candidate and ascertaining the quota. However, of more general interest, but irrelevant to the count process, the total vote (including the spoilt votes) determines the percentage of the registered electors who actually voted (the percentage turnout). The number of spoilt votes is typically slightly more than one percent, but for reasons explained below, can "allegedly" reach 2% or more in local elections and referenda. Further, some votes, although valid as to the first preference, prove to be non transferable for error at a later stage. An excellent work on this subject is the 2000 book by Louis Brennan, "Count Recount and Petition" outlining the saga of the Borris-in-Ossory LEA (Laois) count in 1999 and in particular the re-allocation of 19 votes (out of 7,814) at the recount stage and the detailed examination of 21 votes by the Circuit Court in a subsequent election petition hearing. The Borris case illustrates some of the practical problems and is referred to a few times below. Mr Brennan was the returning officer for that election.

On the day of a count, there is usually a large rush for the corner of the polling corral, headed by the assorted lawyers, when the returning officer announces the adjudication of the "doubtful" votes. An enormous huddle of bodies, twice the size of a New Zealand scrum (and sometimes including individuals of a bulk that would qualify them for that scrum) envelops a few count officials. Quite why there is such interest, is difficult to understand. It is probably already evident from the tally how the seats are going to shake out. The vast majority of doubtful votes will be declared rejected for wholly unexciting reasons discussed below. There is always the odd moment of excitement because some witty voter has decided to write something entertaining on the ballot paper or someone has drawn a body part (invariably male) against one or more of the candidates (curiously in the 2015 general election in the UK, this was held to be a valid vote for the Montgomery Conservative candidate). However, the time spent by tally people is a wholescale waste of electoral expertise in ruling out doubtful votes, 95% plus of which are clearly invalid for one of the usual reasons. If a very tight final count is envisaged, there is greater room for vigilance, but it is still relatively unlikely that the returning officer will come to an adverse view at the spoilt votes stage that is hugely material. If it is apprehended that the result will be close, there is merit in seeking to have the few genuinely doubtful papers put aside and looked at by a much smaller sized scrum, ideally inside the corral. An issue which is of concern is that if the margin in an election comes down to a handful of votes, it may be legally more difficult to challenge the decision to reject a vote as spoilt than any other decision possibly material to preserving or overturning that tight margin.

Usually the number of doubtful votes to be adjudicated is rather more than the final number of spoilt votes. This is because members of the count staff engaged in sorting votes by reference to first preferences are instructed to place in the "doubtful" cubby hole any ballot paper they would otherwise have to delay on to ascertain the clear first preference. By way of example, it is reported that in the Listowel LEA (Kerry) in 2014, 230 doubtful votes were set aside to be adjudicated. Apparently 57 (almost 25%) of those votes were admitted, with the balance of 173 being rejected. At the end of that count, Dan Kiely, an independent candidate, lost by a margin of two votes. He subsequently challenged the result, on the basis that he was not permitted to inspect the 173 rejected votes, although the subsequent hearing in the Supreme Court focussed on a different issue. His case was dismissed by Mr Justice Carroll Moran of the Circuit Court, but this decision was reviewed by the Supreme Court in October 2015 on the basis that the issues raised were a matter of public importance and a re-count was ordered with directions as to its conduct.

Frequency of spoilt votes

It is frankly quite shocking to note that in most Irish elections more than 1 in 100 votes cast are treated as spoilt. In the first general election reviewed, that of 1981, the level of spoilt votes ranged from a low of 0.64% in both

Dublin North Central and Longford Westmeath to a high of 1.44% in Dublin North West. The pattern improved somewhat through the two 1982 general elections, presumably because people learnt how to vote correctly with three elections close together. It then reverted to the previous pattern by 1987, with a range in that election of 0.5% to 1.42%. The 1992 general election co-incided with three right to life referenda and this resulted in a spike in spoilt votes with rates of over 2% recorded in Donegal South West, Dublin South Central, Dublin South East and Louth. The rate reverted to norm in the 1997 general election with a range of 0.55% to 1.49%. However it has gone upwards in the 21st century general elections with as many as 30 constituencies recording spoilt votes of over 1% in the 2002 general election. Electronic voting was used in three constituencies in that election and it was impossible to spoil a vote cast electronically, one of the possible advantages of that system. In the 2011 general election 23 of the 43 constituencies recorded spoilt votes in excess of 1% of the total votes cast. The position improved somewhat in 2016 with only 6 of the 40 constituencies recording spoilt votes of in excess of 1%. Therefore it can be said that the general election pattern of spoilt votes is that in most elections close to 1% of the vote overall is spoilt. There was somewhat of an improvement on this in the two 1982 elections and in 2016 and a significant increase in 1992 where the general election was accompanied by referenda.

There is a somewhat uneven pattern as to the constituencies where high or low numbers of spoilt votes are encountered. However the constituencies of Carlow Kilkenny, Dublin Central, Dublin South Central, Dublin North West and Wexford usually record significantly more than 1% of the votes as spoilt. By contrast, lower than average levels of spoilt votes are usually encountered in Clare, Dublin South/Rathdown, Dún Laoghaire, Limerick East/City, Mayo and Tipperary North. Local election patterns also suggest that the Leitrim part of whatever constituency Leitrim happens to be in has a low level of spoilt votes.[1]

The levels of spoilt votes are higher in local elections. This is probably because in each local election 1999 to 2014, a European election was held on the same day and the referendum effect described below comes into play. The earlier local elections of 1985 and 1991 produced 1.3% and 0.9% spoilt votes respectively.

General reasons for spoilt votes

The analysis of the 2009 local elections produced by the Department of the Environment Heritage and Local Government contains an interesting table analysing the 1.3% of the votes treated as spoilt in that election. The following are approximate percentages for the stated reasons:

Want of official mark	10%
First preference not clearly indicated	47%
First preference indicated for more than one candidate	38%
Writing or mark by which voter could be identified	5%

In nearly all counties, the rate of spoilt votes in 2009 was in excess of 1%, with a high of 1.73% in Cork City and a low of 0.94% in Leitrim.

The following are commonly encountered practical reasons for a vote being spoilt.

3 X's for a party

Both Fianna Fáil and Fine Gael to a lesser extent, suffer from voters, who perhaps in a naive fit of enthusiasm for the party's candidates, put an "x" or "1" beside each of them. That vote is invalid as it does not indicate a clear preference for one candidate. Labour, Sinn Féin and other parties do not suffer as much from this. This is probably because they don't tend to run more than one candidate, not the lack of over enthusiastic voters. An occasional "witty" variant on the theme is a 1 against every or several candidates, with the words "as promised" written at the end. This is the "first preference indicated for more than one candidate ground". It is notable that in general election 2016, the major parties frequently ran only one candidate in a constituency, thus mitigating this problem; this may have contributed to a decrease in spoilt votes.

Lacking the official mark

For a ballot paper to be valid it must be impressed at the top with an official perforation. Occasionally this is not done and the vote, through no fault of the voter, is invalid. This is relatively uncommon. If this is noted several times in the one ballot box, it is clearly indicative of poor practice by the presiding officer at the polling station. An extreme example of this is the Ferbane LEA (Offaly) in 1999 where over 7% of the vote was declared spoilt, apparently largely on this ground. Nothing can be done to regularize the vote, but the presiding officer involved presumably will never officiate again. In one Dublin constituency in the 2015 equal marriage referendum, there were over 200 spoilt papers, of which a little more than 10 lacked the official mark. It is therefore reasonable to speculate that where a normal level of spoilt votes is observed, about 5% of the rejected ballot papers are due to this problem, although the 2009 report suggests a figure closer to 10% in a political election. In the recount of the votes in the Borris LEA (Laois) from 1999, the circuit court judge confirmed as correct the rejection of papers where the official mark was placed on the counterfoil but not the ballot paper itself.

A problem occasionally encountered when a count is ongoing is finding a ballot paper lacking the official mark which has managed to escape the earlier detection process and has been counted as a valid first preference. That ballot paper is not taken out at that stage, but it may be tagged and included in an adjustment. In the 1999 Borris-in-Ossory LEA case, 4 ballot papers were found to lack the official mark, causing the quota to reduce by 1.

Marks crossing boxes on the ballot paper
The voter is asked to place a "1, 2, 3 etc" within the boxes beside the name of each candidate, but sometimes the figure straddles the boxes. A minor crossing should not be a problem, but it is sometimes impossible to decide whether a preference is in one box or in another. In that event the vote is treated as non transferable from that preference onwards. On adjudication, these ballot papers are often re-marked by the returning officer in red or green ink to indicate those preferences accepted as clear, a practice also adopted for broken sequences. There seemed to have been a peripheral issue in the Borris case that these green markings were marked over the actual writing on the paper, an issue accepted by the returning officer as an error. These errors are generally an issue with the subsequent ongoing transferability of a vote rather than the vote being invalid from the outset.

Writing on the paper

Writing on the paper is likely to invalidate the paper, but there are widely differing interpretations of this. Before the entry of Sinn Féin into electoral politics, it was quite common to have Republican slogans written on ballot papers. Some voters cannot resist a witty comment. The personal favourite at one time was "If all of the above were on fire, I wouldn't give the steam off me piss to put them out", a ballot paper reproduced on the front of national newspapers some years ago, although arguably reproduced in breach of electoral secrecy laws. It is unusual to find writing on a ballot paper combined with an identifiable first preference.

Blank ballot papers

It is not unusual that no preference at all is indicated on a ballot paper. Such a paper is treated as spoilt. This problem is particularly an issue when two referenda are held at the same time or a referendum is combined with a general or local election. The explanation for this seems to be that the voter is handed an election ballot paper and a referendum paper together but has no interest in or opinion on the referendum (or indeed the election). In October 2011, at the election at which Michael D Higgins was elected president of Ireland, there were also two referenda amending the Constitution, one on judges' pay and the other on Oireachtas inquiries. 37,696 or 2.11% of ballot papers on judges' pay were allegedly spoilt. The level went as high as 3.12% in Donegal South West and 3.01% in Galway East. The level was even higher in the referendum on Oireachtas inquiries. It is almost certain that what happened was that people went to vote in the Presidential election and they were given, without specific request, the two referenda ballot papers, which they then placed in the ballot box blank. Indeed almost 5,000 more votes were cast in the Presidential election, which suggests that some people took a blank referendum ballot paper home. There was a higher than usual level of spoilt ballot papers in the Presidential election too, probably a result of the same syndrome and possibly also influenced by the lack of an official Fianna Fáil candidate in that election. In the Carlow Kilkenny bye-election (May 2015) there was an unusually high level of spoilt ballot papers, 2,066 or almost 3%. Almost certainly the bulk of these were blank, representing people who were keen to vote in the equal marriage referendum held on the same day, but had zero interest in whether tweedledum or tweedledee would represent them in Dáil Eireann for a vacancy with a maximum life of 10 months.

Sequential voting over two elections

For some reason when a local and a European Parliament election are held on the same day, some voters are inclined to mark the local ballot paper 1, 2, 3, 4 and then to proceed to mark the European ballot 5, 6, 7, 8, 9 or vice versa. The former recommended practice on this outlined in a memorandum of guidance seemed to have been to regard the 5 to 9 vote as valid to the extent it had an unbroken sequence. This was because of a bias in favour of allowing a vote where possible in the interests of democracy rather than disallowing it on narrower technical grounds. A more bizarre practice is for a voter to combine the two ballot papers and then mark 1 to 9 sequentially but across the two. This vote was liable to be ineffective apart from the highest preference (in numbers) evident on each. In the 1999 Borris-in-Ossory LEA case, three of the votes reviewed by the court seem clearly to fall into this category and at that time they were allowed. This issue was central to the challenge by former senator and independent candidate, Dan Kiely, to the result of the local elections in Listowel LEA (Kerry) in 2014. This matter was laid before the Supreme Court in October 2015 in Kiely v Kerry County Council and there were apparently potentially up to 57 such ballot papers admitted. The Supreme Court effectively ruled that any ballot paper lacking a number 1 should be treated as invalid, a decision not greatly welcomed by returning officers who have great practical experience of the sometimes confused but likely genuine minds of the voters. The recount that was ordered as a result unhappily produced no joy for Mr Kiely. However guidance has now been revised, which undoubtedly will have an impact in years to come in an increased number of spoilt votes.

Different ranking systems

The ballot paper instructs persons to vote 1, 2, 3 etc in order of choice. While formulations by a voter such as "one, two, three" or "i, ii, iii, iv" are sometimes found, these do not invalidate a vote as clear preferences are shown. Nor is the placing of an X or a tick in a single box invalid. In the Borris-in-Ossory LEA case, an "–" opposite a candidate was held to be a valid vote as was 1 and 2 on top of each other in the same box. Equally in a referendum writing "yes" or "no" or a mark in one box should suffice (although writing "no" in the "I approve" box is likely to cause confusion). The fundamental test is whether the intention of the voter can be ascertained.

It is not a very good idea to put an X anywhere near a ballot paper in a proportional representation election. Quite a number of the votes looked at by the court in the 1999 Borris-in-Ossory LEA case involved Xs. On some there were 2 x's which were marked over 1 and 2. In others the sequence was X, 2, 3. These were all held to be valid, but in the latter case, the judge seemed to believe that the fact that the returning officer allowed them restricted his course of action.

Broken sequences

While this will not cause a vote to be regarded as spoilt, a broken sequence will negative the ongoing transferability of a vote. So if a voter knows who he is giving 1, 2 and 3 to, but then hesitates before making his next choice and inadvertently picks up the sequence as 5, 6, 7, 8, the vote is likely (perhaps somewhat unfairly) to be deemed non transferable beyond preference 3. In very tightly contested last seats, the spotting of broken sequences, where a relevant candidate is getting a low preference, is an art form. If there are 13 candidates on a ballot paper and someone is getting a 14, there is clearly a broken sequence.

Two number 1s

This is quite common and will clearly cause a ballot paper to be rejected. On close re-counts, attention is often paid to whether a 7 or 11 is written in a way that it can be confused with a 1. Some votes will need to be scrutinized for this reason. Obviously if the same number is repeated twice as a lower preference, the preference will not be valid from and including that preference. Two preferences of the same number can be spotted by noting that the lowest preference on a fully marked ballot paper of 15 candidates is 14. In the Borris case three votes, which were allowed, featured a 5, 7 and 9 which looked awfully like a 1. In each case they were adjudged to be the lower preference, thus avoiding the fate of two number 1s. In the Borris case also, one ballot paper showed the lowest preference as 8, whereas 9 candidates are given a preference; this paper was only disallowed for further transfer when the recount took place.

Two boxes marked in a referendum

It is curiously quite common for both the "yes" and "no" boxes to be marked in a referendum. The referendum ballot paper, no matter how confusing it may be alleged to be, directs that an "X" be placed in one box only. It is difficult to understand how a small minority of voters can't follow a simple instruction. However a significant number of voters manage to mark both boxes. Sometimes there is a "tick" in one box and an "x" in the other. Sometimes they write "no" in the box specified for approval and "yes" in the box specified for non approval. With the best will in the world, no one can really be certain what that voter is trying to convey and the vote will inevitably be rejected. Sometimes the mark in the second box is an attempt to correct an error; practice varies between presiding officers where this happens. In that case there is a lot of merit in a voter returning to the voting table and asking for a new ballot paper having surrendered the old one. The incorrectly marked paper is retained and a record of re-issue is made in the ballot paper account which accompanies the ballot box to the count centre. The marking of two boxes in a referendum ballot paper is almost certainly the principal reason for rejection in a referendum.

References in Chapter 9

[1] It is worth noting that the unusual ballot paper layout in Wicklow in general election 2011 where there were two columns of 12 names did not seem to produce an excessive number of spoilt votes.

PART 3
Transfers

CHAPTER 10

Transfers Generally

As the vast majority of elected candidates in Irish elections do not reach the quota on the first count, transfers (on distribution of surpluses and on eliminations) from other candidates are an important feature of the Irish electoral system. It is therefore appropriate that this work should address transfers. However it would be a key conclusion of this work that the importance of transfers is overrated. Instead it is much more important to ensure that candidates finish in the "leaders' enclosure" (the top three in a three seat constituency and so on in terms of first preference votes at the end of the first count), as experience shows that largely these are the candidates who are elected.

Transfers are seen as the key facet of any Irish election. Before the election, there is often speculation about transfer pacts (discussed in chapter 13 - Electoral Pacts). In many elections, there was a form of pact between Fine Gael and Labour. During their period of existence, the Progressive Democrats had pacts with both Fianna Fáil and Fine Gael for different elections. For election 2016, there was a form of a pact between anti-austerity parties as well as the more familiar "pact" between Fine Gael and Labour. These pacts are very much reflected in the media coverage of the election and are occasionally reflected in the fine print of election material circulating in particular constituencies. For example a leaflet issued by Fine Gael may ask voters to vote 1 and 2 for the Fine Gael candidates and then continue their preference to the Labour candidate.

On the count day, it usually takes until the late afternoon or the early evening to produce a first official count. After that however there are many long hours examining surpluses as they arise and eliminating the lowest candidates. There is a lot of attention as to how the preferences are going to be distributed. There is particular focus on the elimination of candidates from the main parties and anticipation of what percentage of their preferences are likely to accrue to fellow candidates from the same party. It should however be appreciated that, ignoring first count and other surpluses, in general only about 30% of the votes cast in any election will be re-examined for preferences in later counts.

A clear distinction needs to be drawn between Fianna Fáil and Fine Gael on the one hand and all other parties on the other hand in analysing transfers. Fianna Fáil and Fine Gael generally run more than one candidate in each constituency. Therefore the predominant feature of Fianna Fáil and Fine Gael transfers is that their votes transfer mainly to other candidates of the same party and the level of that transfer is critical. Other parties infrequently run more than one candidate in an election and therefore the predominant point of interest is to what other parties will their votes transfer, if the candidate is not elected. The outcome of the local elections of 2014 suggests that Sinn Féin could join Fianna Fáil/Fine Gael in concern about internal transfers, at least for local elections. For the 2016 general election, only Fianna Fáil and Fine Gael had multiple candidates to any material extent.

Notwithstanding the arguably peripheral relevance of transfers considered in chapter 11, it is still instructive and very important to analyse them. The analysis starts with a number of technical statutory based rules, which are in some cases capable of producing anomalies. While many analyses produced about particular elections have set out numerous statistics on how transfers worked in those elections, the reality is that the pattern for transfers, particularly between candidates of the same party, is greatly influenced by the range of candidates still in contention at the point a particular transfer takes place.

It is arguable that the best source for the analysis of transfer patterns is to look at the distributions of the surplus of candidates elected on the first count and this is considered in Chapter 14. At this point the maximum possible range of other candidates, is still in the field to receive transfers (apart from another candidate also elected on the first count). Arguably therefore, this should give the best indication of the propensity of supporters of a party to transfer to other candidates of the same party or to transfer elsewhere.

Transfers on later counts are affected by other votes acquired on transfer by a candidate and are therefore "contaminated"; however the level of "contamination" is usually small and it is still instructive to analyse them.

Broad propositions applicable to transfers

The following general propositions seem to apply with transfers.

- there is a strong pattern of transfers between fellow candidates of the two traditional large parties, Fianna Fáil and Fine Gael. Patterns within Fianna Fáil between two or more Fianna Fáil candidates have historically been a little stronger than within Fine Gael, in part due to a tendency of some Fine Gael supporters to transfer with preference 2 to Labour candidates.

- historically transfers between Labour party candidates were much weaker, particularly in earlier local elections in the period covered by this work, when Labour tended to run far too many candidates. Labour have become more disciplined on electoral strategy in the last two decades, most notably by running one candidate in most cases, so that transfers to another Labour candidate are not an issue at all. Where there are patterns of Labour transfers in recent years, they still tend to be weaker than between the two traditional large parties.

- there is very little available evidence on transfers patterns within other parties, as usually they do not run more than one candidate. There are a limited number of examples of transfers between Progressive Democrat, Democratic Left/Workers Party and Sinn Féin candidates, which suggests different patterns within those parties. As a general principle transfers within Sinn Féin and the Workers Party have tended to be at rates similar to the two traditional large parties. Transfer patterns between Progressive Democrat candidates were generally quite poor, except for the first election fought by the Progressive Democrats in 1987. In recent elections where Sinn Féin has had more than one candidate, it has been relatively unusual to have transfers between them, as they generally seem to effectively balance the vote between them and remain in the count until the final stage. The 2014 local elections however show a marked tendency for Sinn Féin candidates to transfer to other Sinn Féin candidates at rates better than that for the two traditional large parties and this feature became even more pronounced in the 2016 general election.

Technical rules related to transfers

There are a few significant statutory based rules that apply on transfers relating to:

- surpluses on a first count

- surpluses on a subsequent count

- the elimination of candidates

- votes being looked at a couple of times

- the discretion to eliminate two or more candidates at the one time

- the discretion not to distribute a surplus

Surpluses on a first count

If a candidate is elected on the first count, in practice all the other candidates (excepting another also elected on the first count) will be credited on transfer with an aggregate number of votes equal to the surplus of the successful candidate. Each continuing candidate on count 2 will be credited with a proportion of the surplus. This means that there are never any non-transferable votes arising from a first count surplus . To illustrate, if a candidate got 12,000 votes in a constituency with a quota of 8,000, that parcel of 12,000 ballot papers would have to consist of more than 8,000 plumpers for that candidate in order to give rise to a non-transferable parcel from that surplus. There is no actual example of a candidate recording non transferable votes after a first count surplus is redistributed, showing that it is in practice impossible. Once there is a second preference on more than 4,000 of those votes, the full 4,000 will be redistributed on transfer, with the elected candidate being noted as minus 4,000, reducing his or her vote for technical count purposes to the exact quota of 8,000 votes. The make up of this physical bundle of 8,000 ballot papers (that will play no further part in the ongoing count) will be the elected candidate's "plumpers" and his other first preference votes (excluding the 4,000 lifted and credited to the other candidates).

The effect of this with candidates who would normally produce a high level of non transferable votes is that continuing candidates get a greater number of votes than would ordinarily be the case on a transfer. An extreme example is the 2014 local election where Sinn Féin accrued quite a number of first count surpluses with no remaining Sinn Féin candidates. This often resulted in relatively big numbers of transfers accruing to independent and smaller party candidates with paltry first preference votes, as these were presumably a more palatable alternative to Sinn Féin voters than the three "establishment" parties.[1]

Surpluses on a subsequent count

Where a continuing candidate reaches quota on a count subsequent to the first count and has a surplus, the only ballot papers that are looked at for purposes of redistributing the surplus are the ballot papers contained in the last "sub-parcel" of votes received by that now successful candidate bringing him or her from under to over the quota. So if the quota is 8,000 and a candidate on 7,750 votes on the fifth count receives 400 votes on transfer bringing him or her to 8,150 votes on the sixth count, the only votes to be looked at in dealing with his or her surplus (of 150) are the sub-parcel of 400 votes received on transfer. This makes the process of distributing the surplus administratively much easier. Further in allocating the surplus, once at least 150 of those votes show a lower preference for a continuing candidate, the surplus of 150 (randomly lifted from transferable papers) will be transferred at full value across the remaining candidates. This also means that in a majority of instances, surpluses on later counts are distributed at full value, with perhaps some 30% of instances with a non-transferable residue of votes following the distribution.

From a sample of general elections, the instances of cases where non transferable votes accrue from a later count surplus seems surprisingly high. Non transferable residues should generally only arise where that surplus is high by comparison with the total number of votes transferred to bring the candidate over quota. For example in Galway West in the 2002 general election, Michael D Higgins, now President, was one vote short of quota on the 13th count and he received 2,336 votes on the 14th count, creating a surplus of 99.9% (2,335) of the votes transferred to him on that count. It was inevitable that there would be non transferable votes when his surplus was distributed on the 15th count, as indeed there were. Generally non transferable votes should not arise where the value of the surplus is less than about half of the votes transferred to the candidate just elected. However a classic exception, from Mayo in the 2002 general election, is the case of Enda Kenny's surplus of 1,341 on the tenth count derived from the elimination of his colleague Jim Higgins and the transfer of 4,615 votes from Higgins. Only 23.7% of those 4,615 votes showed a preference for the three continuing Fianna Fáil candidates, so that there was a very considerable number of non transferable votes. The impact was lessened because the system dis-regarded the first 3,300 or so votes ex Higgins that showed no relevant preference. As a rule of thumb, where there is a later count surplus, one would expect full value to accrue from the surplus where it represents less than 60% of the transferred vote. However there are exceptions to that, particularly where the source of the transfer is known to be "politically unfriendly" to the continuing candidates. [2]

The apparent transfer from the successful candidate will also reflect the political inclinations and location of the voters for the eliminated candidate. So if the 400 votes transferred to the successful centre right candidate in the south of a constituency come from a radical left candidate living in the same geographical area (with neighbours giving high preference to each local candidate irrespective of political difference between them), the distribution of the surplus of the successful centre right candidate is likely to favour other left candidates, as opposed to the successful candidate's running mate at the north end of the constituency. This anomaly was most notably seen in Clare in the general election of November 1982, where 84% of the surplus of Madeleine Taylor-Quinn (Fine Gael) derived from Billy Loughnane, an ex Fianna Fáil independent candidate who by public repute had a political antipathy towards Sile de Valera, transferred to the other Fine Gael candidate, Donal Carey, thus depriving Sile de Valera of Fianna Fáil of a seat. Indeed a Fianna Fáil surplus derived from the same independent only transferred at a rate of 42% to Ms de Valera. This is a significant issue, as transfers "apparently" from a surplus of a large party candidate are distributed to places not expected.

Elimination of candidates

When a candidate is eliminated, their vote consists of their original first preferences and a number of votes accumulated on transfers. It is virtually certain that some non transferable votes will arise on the elimination of a candidate, as invariably there are voters who have just given a number 1 to the unsuccessful candidate or have given preferences only to candidates already elected or eliminated. A ballot paper which shows no preferences for candidates other than those elected or eliminated earlier in the count is called "non-transferable" and is not effective for the rest of the count. In the 2016 general election, the lowest number of non transferable votes seen on the elimination of a candidate was two.[3] Any vote that is transferred on the elimination of one candidate to another candidate is transferred on at full value. Any non transferable votes are credited to a bundle so labelled. In analysing patterns of transfer, particularly when assessing rates of transfers within parties, the fact that some of the votes are "transferred votes" means that the sample being looked at is not pure. In practice this issue has to be ignored as the level of "contamination" is usually quite low.

Votes being looked at a couple of times

It is sometimes the case that a candidate's (A) transfers elect another candidate B. It is often the case that when B's surplus, consisting of transfers from A to B, is distributed, it in turn elects candidate C. The votes which do this originally come from A, so that in effect A's voters' preferences become relevant to the election of both B and C and fall to be scrutinised twice. Further it is possible for a distribution on A's elimination to elect both B and C. An example of this is shown in the November 1982 election in Clare where the votes of Billy Loughnane (independent formerly FF) on his elimination created a surplus for both Daly (FF) and Taylor-Quinn (FG) meaning that some of Loughnane's votes needed to be looked at twice more. Another good example is Joe Doyle of Fine Gael in Dublin South East in 1997, where his 4,886 votes on transfer successively elected Frances Fitzgerald (FG), Ruairi Quinn (Lab) and John Gormley (Green).[4] In any general election there will be a couple of candidates who are eliminated late on, whose votes will be effectively looked at twice or even three times. Preferences from those candidates are especially significant.

Discretion to eliminate two or more candidates at the one time

This happens quite regularly in general elections, although much less so in local elections. If the votes of two or more candidates when added together cannot mathematically overtake the next one of them, it is possible for the returning officer to eliminate both or all of them in a single count. This is provided that the total vote of the lower candidate(s) cannot bring another candidate over quota or cause a candidate to exceed one quarter of the quota (the latter allowing them to claim electoral expenses). This happens quite frequently in elections, particularly with candidates with small numbers of votes. For example in the general elections of both 2011 and 2016 it occurred in all but 2 constituencies.[5] The technical problems for analysis and associated with multiple eliminations are noted later in this chapter.

Discretion not to distribute a surplus

Where a small surplus arises and it is not going to make a material difference to the count or elect anyone, it is quite common that dealing with it is deferred or that the surplus is never dealt with. The returning officer has a discretion to do this. This is quite usual, as many candidates who exceed quota on the first count, do so by marginal amounts and many candidates who exceed quotas on a subsequent count do so, on the receipt of a small bundle of transfers. In the 2011 general election this happened in 12 constituencies and in 2016 it happened in 13. For example in the 2016 general election in Dublin Rathdown, Shane Ross of the Independent Alliance exceeded the quota by 209 votes in an early count. That surplus of 209 was never distributed.

How many votes in a constituency typically are looked at when transferring votes?

It should be borne in mind that only a relatively small percentage of the votes cast in a constituency will be looked at for transfer purposes in an election, particularly where no candidate exceeds the quota on the first count. The transferred votes largely come from lower placed unsuccessful candidates. Within the pool of votes that are looked at, it is usually the last few eliminations that have the potential to create any change.

By way of example, in the 2011 general election, 57,916 valid votes (with a quota of 11,584) were cast in the Clare constituency as follows:

Breen P FG	9,855	elected
McNamara Lab	8,572	elected
Carey FG	7,840	elected
Mulcahy FG	6,829	
Dooley FF	6,789	elected
Breen James Ind	6,491	last man standing
Hillery FF	6,015	
Others (9)	5,525	

As Breen FG, McNamara, Carey and Dooley were elected, their first preference votes did not require to be looked at at any stage after they were counted to arrive at a first count result. Further at the end of the final count James Breen was the "last man standing", so therefore his 6,491 first preference votes did not require to be examined at any stage of the count. Thus 39,547 first preference votes, apart from being counted at the first count stage, did not come into play at any time. This represents over 68% of the valid vote. The only votes therefore looked at for transfer purposes were the 6,829 first preferences cast for Mulcahy, the 6,015 cast for Hillery and the 5,525 cast for the other nine candidates (aggregate 18,369 or 31.72%). In practice because some of these votes transferred within this group some of them needed to be looked at several times. In fact 20,692 votes were èxamined on eliminations. At the last but one count, Breen FG had a surplus of 1,780 votes arising from a transfer of 2,346 votes from Mulcahy. The 2,346 votes transferred by Mulcahy to Breen needed to be looked at to decide where the surplus would be credited. Of the 18,369 actual votes looked at for purposes of transfer on elimination, 1,419 became non transferable at some stage during the count meaning that only 16,950 of the votes cast for the lower ranking candidates were relevant for purposes of deciding the contest. This example is possibly quite typical of the level of votes that need to be re-examined for the purpose of determining transfers.

The size of the pool of transferred votes is typically around a 30% of the entire valid vote. In the 2016 general election (including first count and later surpluses), 19 constituencies had a pool of transferred votes in the range 30% to 40% of the valid vote, 7 had a pool of transferred votes of over 40% and 14 had pools of less than 30%. The two highest were Dublin Bay North and Sligo-Leitrim, among the most competitive constituencies. Laois by contrast had a "transfer pool" of about 14%, mainly a first count surplus. 20 constituencies had to re-examine the entire first preference vote of a candidate to determine the destination of a surplus. Two constituencies, Cork South Central and Dublin Mid West had to do this twice before proceeding with any elimination. First count surpluses are an important delaying factor in completing counts and there is some relationship between them and a constituency being late to declare a result on election day. [6]

It could be assumed that areas with very large numbers of seats should produce a greater number of votes for candidates in the leaders' enclosure and hence a smaller transfer pool. However an examination of the six 10 seat areas in local elections 2014 shows an average pool ex-surpluses of 24%, which is not materially different for pools in general elections with much less seats per constituency. Curiously for nine seat areas, the size of the pool ex-surpluses seems to average about 20%, possibly because these were less competitive. The size of the pool seems to have more to do with the number of candidates than the number of seats available.

The fact that only a small pool of votes of perhaps around 30% is available to be transferred is clearly a factor in explaining why transfers are not in reality that effective in changing the order of candidates in elections. There is somewhat of a correlation between relatively high transfer pools and candidates displacing the "leaders' enclosure", with all of the 13 cases in 2016 being in the group of constituencies with a transfer pool of over 30%.

Issues with analysis of transfers

There are a number of problems inherent in analysis of the benefit of transfers. This book takes a different approach to others in dealing with some of these problems.

In the case of transfers by a candidate, the only instance where the votes being examined are all first preferences for that candidate is where there is a surplus on the first count. In that instance one can tell fairly exactly what proportion of that candidate's second preferences went to each of the other candidates, subject to two minor problems. The first minor problem is that in distributing second preferences, second preferences given to another candidate elected on the first count are ignored and thus it is impossible to tell what percentage of the second preferences went to that candidate. The second problem is that where a vote for the candidate whose preferences are being distributed is a "plumper" i.e. a number one only, that vote is effectively ignored for transfer purposes. However given that all of the other candidates tend to be in the field, the distribution of a surplus on the first count seems to be a reasonable basis on which to examine transfer patterns, as is done in Chapter 14. A suspected complication from analysing transfers from a candidate elected on the first count is the personal vote issue. A candidate who is so successful often has a "personal vote" which may be inclined to transfer more readily to candidates other than the person's running mates.

Where transfers are being examined on the elimination of a candidate, an issue for analysis is that the vote will not be "pure". For example a Labour candidate being eliminated may have got 2,500 votes on the first count, but have picked up 288 votes from various sources on transfers before being eliminated with 2,788 votes. Thus slightly less than 90% of that vote is a "Labour" vote, with a bit more than 10% coming from other sources. In practice provided the extra component is not very large, it is safe to ignore it. However the extra votes can become quite substantial in number when heading towards the later stages of a count and thus the measure of how the transfers divided can be somewhat misleading. The issue of the vote not being "pure" does not arise where no candidate exceeds quota on the first count and the lowest candidate is eliminated; however it is rare that this happens in circumstances where the lowest candidate has a meaningful number of votes and is eliminated just by themselves.

Where the net votes of two or more candidates cannot catch the next candidate or otherwise make any difference to a count, two or more candidates can be collectively eliminated together. In these circumstances, it is impossible to say whose votes went where on transfer. Therefore in any analysis, it is safer (as in this work) to ignore these aggregate transfers, except in the unusual instance where a particular candidate makes up the vast bulk of it. If a particular candidate makes up the bulk of a collective elimination, the position is rather similar to the elimination of a candidate who has picked up some preferences prior to elimination. This multiple elimination happened in nearly every constituency in the 2011 and 2016 general elections.[5] This is an occasional problem in assessing the rate of transfer of Labour and Sinn Féin candidates and a frequent problem with smaller parties and independents. It rarely happens with Fianna Fáil or Fine Gael candidates.

As noted above, where a candidate exceeds the quota on a later count than the first count, the only votes looked at will be the votes that took that candidate from below quota to above quota. This means that the transfer pattern of these types of votes can be quite mixed. Generally these types of transfers are best ignored (as in this work) in analysis, except where they are transfers within the same party, in which event the surplus should have a tendency to travel on to other candidates of the same party.

References in Chapter 10

1. This happened for example in Clondalkin and Tallaght South LEAs in South Dublin where non-party and other left (non-Labour) candidates got over 70% of Sinn Féin transfers from first count surpluses at full value.

2. Where the level of transfers have been analysed for purposes of this book, a different approach to the usual one has been taken where a non-transferable residue occurs on the transfer of a surplus. In that case, the real level of transfer to the continuing candidates is the proportion as between the vote credited to them in the distribution and the entire vote transferred to create the surplus. For example a candidate has a surplus of 200 arising from a transfer of 250 to him. Candidate A gets 75 votes from the surplus and another 75 votes accrue to other candidates. However there are 50 non transferable votes credited as such. The standard approach is to regard A as getting 75/200 or 37.5% of the transfers. However the reality is that of the 250 votes comprising the transfer examined, we know that only 75 gave A the best preference as between continuing candidates, so in practice the "effective" transfer rate was 30%. This approach is adopted in assessing the proportions of transferable and non transferable votes on a transfer.

3. This was a FIS candidate in Donegal, two of whose 70 votes were non transferable.

4. The Dublin South East 1997 election is discussed more fully in chapter 29. Another good example is in 1992 in Wicklow where the votes of Shane Ross (then Fine Gael) elected both Godfrey Timmins (FG) and Liz McManus (Democratic Left) and on their transfer as part of a surplus elected Johnny Fox (Independent).

5. Dublin North and Kildare South were the only constituencies where there were no multiple eliminations in the 2011 general election and Dublin Rathdown and Laois were the only constituencies where there were no multiple eliminations in the 2016 general election. Some constituencies had more than one multiple elimination. In the past it was less common; for example in November 1982 it occurred in 10 of the 41 then constituencies.

6. By way of contrast , in the 2011 general election (ignoring first count surpluses) 31 constituencies had a pool of transferred votes of less than 30%, whereas 12 had pools of greater than 30%. Curiously the two highest were the two Galway constituencies, which were also relatively high in 2016. Limerick City and Tipperary North by contrast each had "transfer pools" of about 10%, although in each case a first count surplus was relevant. 17 constituencies (three twice over) had to re-examine the entire first preference vote of a candidate to determine the destination of a surplus. Kildare South had to re-examine over 61% of its vote before proceeding with any elimination.

CHAPTER 11
Are Transfers Overrated?

It is the considered view of this work that in Irish elections, transfers are generally regarded, particularly by the media, as having a much greater importance than in practice they do have.

The leaders' enclosure phenomenon

A fact that seems little appreciated, is that in practice, it is generally the leading three candidates on first preferences in a three seat constituency, the leading four candidates on first preferences in a four seat constituency and so on for five seats etc, who are elected. A candidate elected from outside this "leaders' enclosure" is very much the exception and tends to occur somewhat less than once in every ten candidates actually elected. In practice in general elections (and also in local elections), it happens in between a third and a half of the constituencies, but rarely affects more than one position.[1] The affected position in about 65% of cases is the last position (eg fifth of 5 on the first count). Therefore it can be said that the impact of transfers in Irish politics is highly overrated. By contrast an underrated issue is the necessity to get a candidate in the "leaders' enclosure" on the first count and how to go about doing that. In a five seat constituency, a party that gets its candidates in positions 4 and 5, both being well clear of the field, has done a good job.[2] In practice the key role of transfers may be re-inforcing the position of those already in the leaders' enclosure, rather than enabling those outside it to catch up.

A good practical forum for appreciating the "leaders' enclosure" in practice is the Dublin City Count Centre in Ballsbridge. This is the count centre where the votes from six (reduced to 5 in 2016) city constituencies have been counted in general elections and where the votes from the ten or so LEAs in Dublin City are counted. It is by far the largest count centre in the country. It usually takes until about 2pm on count day to get an accurate picture from tallies as to what the first count is going to look like. However, for experienced observers, once that point is reached, it is usually fairly obvious based on ranking who will win the seats in about five of the six constituencies and in about eight of the LEAs. This allows for focus on the key races where the outcome might be uncertain. Candidates involved may have a completely different perspective as to outcome, but for those who are in the "leaders' enclosure", it is generally unwarranted pessimism and for those who are not, it is equally unwarranted optimism as to the likely destination of transfers.[3]

While there is a lot of focus on candidates getting transfers, a close examination of the five most recent elections 2007, 2009, 2011, 2014 and 2016 (discussed in the case of general elections in more detail in chapter 12) shows that in each case the vast majority of successful candidates finished in the "leaders' enclosure" in the top three to five respectively (in the case of Dáil elections with three to five seats) and in the top three to ten (in the case of local elections), so that if a first past the post system with no further counts had applied they would have been elected.

Election	No of seats	No of successful cand's in leaders' enclosure	No of successful cand's needing to catch up	Percentage represented by catch up
2007	166	152	14	8.43%
2009	883	813	70	7.93%
2011	166	155	11	6.63%
2014	949	866	83	8.75%
2016	158	145	13	8.23%

This pattern is indeed evident over the eleven general elections being reviewed in this work. In those elections a total 162 seats out of 1,818 were filled by candidates who were not in the first three, four or five in order of first preferences on the first count. This represents less than 9% of the available seats. Further in all general elections since 1981, there are only fifty cases (2.75% of cases) where a gap of more than 1,000 votes was bridged and a mere eleven cases (0.6% of cases) where a gap of 2,000 or more votes was made up. The level of "catch up" varies from a low of 9 cases in the February 1982 election to a high of 19 in the 1981 and 2002 general elections. The pattern is equally evident in local elections. For example in the 2014 local elections only 83 of 949 and in the 2009 local elections, only 70 elected candidates of the 883 elected councillors finished outside the "leaders' enclosure" on the first count.[4]

Level of gap that can be made up

In many cases where a candidate in the original "leaders' enclosure" is displaced, the gap to be closed on that candidate is relatively small, with 40% of the cases involving less than 500 votes. The largest gaps in recent general elections were

Election	Largest	Successful candidate	Unsuccessful candidate	Bridge Gap
2007	2,378	Terence Flanagan (FG)	Martin Brady (FF)	2,751 transfers running mate
2011	2,354	Robert Troy (FF)	Peter Burke (FG)	6,900 votes running mates
2016	2,000	K Zappone (Ind)	AM Dermody (FG)	2,000 independent votes. [5]

Curiously the two biggest deficits ever made up in modern elections of 2,833 and 2,611 votes respectively were made up by the same candidate John Farrelly of Fine Gael in Meath in 1981 and November 1982 respectively. In both cases the candidate displaced was Michael Lynch of Fianna Fáil. In each case, substantial transfers of a surplus from John Bruton, a senior Fine Gael deputy made up some of the deficit and the transfers of a third Fine Gael candidate gave a substantial margin of victory. It is equally the case that where 2,000 votes are made up, it is nearly always based on a large amount of transfers from a fellow party candidate and in most cases that has been more than enough to close the gap.

Equally in local elections the gap to be bridged usually tends to be very small. For example in the 2014 local elections, the gap to be closed exceeded 200 votes in only 19 of the 83 cases where a candidate caught up. Again the most notable catch ups were by independent and left candidates such as Keegan (PBP) in Ballymun LEA (Dublin City), Cullinane (Independent) in Cobh LEA (Cork) and a Sinn Féin and Independent candidate in Ballincollig-Carrigaline (Cork).The highest gaps seen were 489 in Cobh and 486 in Ballymun. This suggests that the maximum gap which is bridgeable in local elections is 500.[6] Notably in the 2014 local elections some of the very big electoral areas saw two displacements from the leaders' enclosure.

In summary a gap of about 2,000 is the maximum that can be bridged in general elections, the local election comparator is about 500.

Who is caught?

In general the party with the greatest experience of having candidates in the "leaders' enclosure" and then being caught is Fianna Fáil. Most often its candidate is passed out by a Fine Gael candidate. Several Fianna Fáil candidates have been serial losers in these battles including Jim Gibbons in Carlow Kilkenny, Mark Killilea in Galway West, Tom Bellew in Louth, Michael Lynch in Meath, Sean Byrne in South Tipperary, Henry Abbott in Westmeath and Lorcan Allen in Wexford. This is why all of those people were occasional TDs. These candidates who have been serially displaced often have a matching nemesis from Fine Gael, Des Governey in Carlow Kilkenny, Brendan McGahon in Louth and the champion in the stakes, John Farrelly in Meath who displaced the hapless Michael Lynch on three occasions and displaced another Fianna Fáil candidate on two further occasions. Many of the candidates who are serially displaced are poorly located geographically in their respective constituencies. For example Michael Lynch was based in Oldcastle in the rural far north west of Meath.

Quite a number of displacements involved rival candidates from the same party. Thus Mark Killilea of Fianna Fáil was regularly displaced by Máire Geoghegan Quinn or another party member in Galway West and Liam

Naughten and John Connor of Fine Gael displaced each other on one occasion each as did Dinny McGinley in Donegal South West in two battles with Jim White.

An extreme example of a candidate being caught happened to John Ellis, the Sligo-Leitrim candidate for Fianna Fáil in the November 1982 general election. In that election he topped the poll on the first count with 8,552 votes, a mere 735 votes short of the quota. As a Leitrim based candidate, he needed a cushion as he was unlikely to pick up too many transfers from other candidates, who were largely based in Sligo. He was 1,870 votes clear of Ted Nealon, a Fine Gael Sligo based candidate in fifth position. However Ellis was not elected, being beaten by almost 1,500 votes by Nealon and being shaded out by his party colleague Ray McSharry by 87 votes. Thus his prediction of being "the most vulnerable deputy in the Dáil", described by others as "poor mouthing" was spectacularly borne out as the truth. It is therefore ironic to see the presence in the same race of a candidate for the "Sligo Leitrim Society for the Prevention of Cruelty to Constituents by Lying and Cheating Politicians". (see Magill Book of Irish Politics 1983). Curiously the phenomenon of a Leitrim candidate being caught was evident yet again in the 2016 general election, with Gerry Reynolds of Fine Gael in second place on the first count being caught by the fifth placed candidate. [7]

There is no very obvious pattern to the types of candidates who tend to be caught or to the types of candidates who catch up. With party candidates, a significant feature of catching up is the availability of transfers from other party candidates. There is somewhat of a trend for independents to close gaps based on being quite transfer friendly in a number of directions. There is also somewhat of a trend for Sinn Féin candidates to be placed in the "leaders' enclosure" only to then be caught by candidates who attract transfers, where the Sinn Féin candidate attracts little or none. [8]

The Green Alliance have been particularly successful in coming from behind to gain seats. They have done so in general elections on nine occasions, which represents half of the aggregate Dáil seats they have obtained in their history. Thus a candidate in a top position needs to be particularly wary of

"Greens bearing transfers", an agony of which ex Fine Gael Minister Alan Shatter in Dublin Rathdown is only too well aware.

All of this suggests that for good electoral planning, it is far more important to focus on getting a candidate placed on the first count in order of first preferences within the number of seats available. Experience shows that it is relatively unlikely that the candidate will be caught. Further the majority of candidates who are caught finish in the last position in the "leaders' enclosure". For example in the 2009 local elections, of the 70 candidates displaced from the leaders' enclosure, 51 of them were in the last "leaders' enclosure" spot on the first count. Only four candidates were three from the bottom, the most notable being the unfortunate Fianna Fáil candidate in Glenties (Donegal), outgoing councillor Joe Kelly, who was third out of five on the first count but ended up not being elected. In the last three general elections, only 17 candidates not in third, fourth or fifth respectively were displaced.[9]

Why are transfers so relatively ineffective?

If the reader looks at the subsequent chapters of this work on transfers by various parties, it becomes readily apparent that there is a tendency for transfers, other than within parties, to be at best at about a 30% level. Further there is a tendency for the other candidates ahead of someone receiving 30% to get a reasonable level of transfers, perhaps up to 10%. This makes gaps quite difficult to close, even when large numbers of votes are to be transferred.

An example will suffice. In this example candidate A is 1,000 votes ahead of candidate B at the end of count 4. There are 8,000 remaining votes to be transferred and co-incidentally (purely to assist illustration) at the point of their elimination every candidate has votes of a multiple of 1,000. B is getting exactly 30% of the transfers and A is getting exactly 20% of the transfers on each elimination. The following is the picture for material candidates as the counts proceed. Candidates with more than 6,000 votes have been ignored.

Candidate	Count 4	Count 5	Count 6	Count 7	Count 8
A	6,000	6,200 (+200)	6,600 (+400)	7,000 (+400)	7,600 (+600)
B	5,000	5,300 (+300)	5,900 (+600)	6,500 (+600)	7,400 (+900)
C	3,000	eliminated count 8			
D	2,000	eliminated count 7			
E	2,000	eliminated count 6			
F	1,000	eliminated count 5			

So the transfer of an aggregate 8,000 votes has only eroded the gap by 800, from a gap of 1,000 at the start to a gap of 200 at the end. If A was only getting 10%, which is the lower end of the range of likely transfers at this stage of a count, he would have got to 6,800 votes by count 8, but this is still only 600 behind. Even at a 15% rate of transfers, A gets to an aggregate of 7,200, so any slippage by B from the 30% rate of benefit is likely to be fatal. Thus to catch a candidate with a margin of as low as 1,000 when all one is receiving is transfers at a 30% rate is a "big ask". There is always the problem that the candidate you are chasing is picking votes up too and these need to be matched before a gap can be closed.

A very good example showing the relative ineffectiveness of transfers is Dublin North Central in the 1997 general election. In that election Derek McDowell of Labour (him again!) got 2,848 first preferences and his ultimate rival for the last seat Sean Dublin Bay Loftus got 2,485 first preferences, a margin of 363. By the last count McDowell had picked up 4,144 transfers to reach 6,992. Mr Loftus had picked up slightly less 4,131 to reach 6,616. Thus the margin changed by 13 in McDowell's favour. There were however very big differentials in individual transfers. Mr McDowell got rather more transfers from Democratic Left and Fine Gael. Mr Loftus took more from Fianna Fáil surpluses and an elimination, from the Progressive Democrats and from the Greens. The picture was fairly even between them on the elimination of independents. This is fairly typical of the ebbs and flows that can happen in a real life transfer scenario.

Additional problem of directing transfers for the two traditional large parties

The problem of closing a gap is compounded for the two traditional large parties by the fact that transfers from another party candidate don't always transfer to the weaker candidate, which the party would like them to do. If a party has three candidates as follows

Mr A	6,000 votes
Ms B	4,500 votes
Mr C	3,000 votes

it seems to be invariably the case that the transfers of Mr C on elimination will favour A over B (often in a ratio of about 4:3, the same as the actual vote). Thus if Ms B is chasing a candidate of another party D with 5,200 votes, the effect of transfers being skewed in favour of Mr A is likely to make it impossible for B to bridge the gap of 700. Further to the extent that D gets any transfers from C, B needs to match that.

For example in Ballymun LEA (Dublin City) in 2014, three Fine Gael candidates were positioned after the tenth count as follows

Cllr Gerry Breen	992
Noel Rock	1,370
Cllr Prof Bill Tormey	754

Tormey was next to be eliminated. Breen needed to catch Aine Clancy of Labour who was on 1,034 or 42 votes ahead to have any chance of election and also needed to be significantly ahead of her. To complicate the position for Clancy, she had a further Labour candidate, Montague on 1,733 available to take transfers.

In the event the material transfers on the 11th count from Tormey were as follows:

Breen	+137	1,129
Clancy	+62	1,096
Montague	+65	1,798
Rock	+174	1,544

Subsequently favourable left transfers meant that Breen was behind Clancy by 93 votes for the critical elimination. He got 18% of Tormey's transfers when he really needed over 30%. From his (and Fine Gael's) point of view it would have been helpful if Rock had only got +74 and he had got +237 (ie a swing of 100 votes to himself from Rock). However as nearly always seems to be the case, the leading candidate got more transfers. It is quite notable that before the Tormey elimination, the proportion of votes as between Rock and Breen was 58:42. The ratio of transfers to them from Tormey was virtually the same at 56:44.

Further Clancy on the Tormey elimination got 62 transfers, which Breen needed to match, before any progress could be made on closing the gap. She also closely matched the level of transfers which accrued to Montague even though he was quite close to twice her vote. The figures are good to illustrate the problem; in practice there were so many left leaning candidates in the field that even if Breen had remained a continuing candidate until after Clancy was eliminated, one would have to doubt whether he would actually have been elected on the day.

References in Chapter 11

[1] The only instances where two candidates came from outside the leaders' enclosure are Cavan-Monaghan, Meath (1981), Carlow Kilkenny (1987) and Cork South Central (1989). Some constituencies feature quite frequently in displacements. Over the last five general elections Carlow Kilkenny, Cavan-Monaghan, Dublin Central, Dublin North East, Galway East, Galway West, Limerick East, Longford Westmeath and Wicklow have featured three times.

[2] Fine Gael managed two candidates being at the bottom of the "leaders' enclosure" in a number of constituencies in 2016 including Clare, Limerick County, Louth, Meath East and Wexford, thus contributing to a seat advantage over Fianna Fáil, who managed it in Kildare South and Mayo.

[3] Strictly speaking in Dublin, only three or four of the five/six constituencies and about five – seven of the LEAs will have all the elected candidates in the "leaders' enclosure" on the final first count tally. However in many of the other constituencies and LEAs, it will be obvious on an intelligent reading of likely transfers that a candidate will catch the field and displace another.

[4] The comparative figures for 1999 and 2004 were 71 and 88 respectively.

[5] Five of the fourteen "catch ups" in the 2007 election were based on a gap of less than 500 to be bridged, as were five of eleven in 2011 and four of thirteen in 2016. It should also be noted that in 2016 in the constituency of Dublin Rathdown the Green Party deputy leader Catherine Martin closed a gap of 1,783 on Alan Shatter of Fine Gael. Other impressive feats of closing a gap were achieved by independents Finian McGrath (Dublin North Central) in 2007 and John Halligan (Waterford) in 2011. In both cases there was a gap approaching 2,000 with a Fianna Fáil candidate and in each case the gap was bridged, primarily with strong transfers from other left candidates.

[6] Further in the 2009 local elections, the gap to be closed exceeded 100 votes in only 33 of the 70 cases where a candidate caught up. Again the most notable catch ups were by independent and left candidates such as Boyle (Independent) in Carrigaline LEA (Cork), Farren (Labour) in Inishowen LEA(Donegal), McKeon (Independent) in Balbriggan LEA (Fingal) and Grehan (Independent) in Dundalk South LEA (Louth). The highest gaps seen were 367 in Cork City South West, 391 in Tallaght Central LEA (South Dublin) and 421 in Dundalk South LEA (Louth). Indeed an earlier local election, that of 1991, confirms the pattern. Less than half of the 83 gaps made up in that election were of more than a 100 vote deficit. 6 were of a deficit of more than 300 and 2 were of a deficit of more than 400, Curiously the highest gap was a 488 deficit made up by Derek McDowell of Labour on Joe Burke of Fianna Fáil in Clontarf LEA (Dublin). Subsequently Mr McDowell had a spectacular escape in the 1997 general election, although that escape was based on very good transfers.

7   Another curiosity is the fate of former Minister Martin Cullen, then Progressive Democrat, in two separate LEAs in Waterford in the 1991 local elections. Mr Cullen contested the Waterford No 1 LEA in the city and the Tramore LEA in the county. In the city area, he finished outside the leaders' enclosure with a deficit of 44 votes on a Fine Gael candidate whom he duly displaced with a winning margin of 63 votes. By contrast in Tramore LEA, he was in the leaders' enclosure with a margin of 47 votes over another Fine Gael candidate. However there he was overhauled on the last count by the Fine Gael candidate, who had a winning margin at the end of 42 votes. Thus a completely contrasting experience for the one individual of the leaders' enclosure phenomenon.

8   This happened to Sinn Féin candidates, MacLochlainn in Donegal North East in 2007, to O'Toole in Dublin North East and Brady in Wicklow in 2011 and to Ó'Clochartaigh in Galway West and Hogan in Longford-Westmeath in 2016 and also happened in the 2014 local elections in Cavan, Cork City, Dublin North Inner City, Dún Laoghaire and Louth.

9   Candidates in general elections 2007 to 2016 displaced from a position higher than the last leaders' enclosure position were
Jennifer Murnane O'Connor (Fianna Fáil) Carlow Kilkenny in fourth place of 5 in 2016,
Paul Bradford (Fine Gael) Cork East in third place of 4 in 2007,
Denis O'Donovan (Fianna Fáil) Cork South West, in second place of 3 in 2007,
Pádraig MacLochlainn (Sinn Féin) Donegal North East in second place of 3 in 2007,
Aodhan O'Riordáin (Labour) Dublin Bay North in fourth place of 5 in 2016,
Frances Fitzgerald (Fine Gael) Dublin Mid West in third place of 4 in 2007,
Martin Brady (Fianna Fáil) Dublin North East in second place of 3 in 2007,
Trevor O'Clochartaigh (Sinn Féin) Galway West in fourth place of 5 in 2016,
Tom Fleming (Fianna Fáil) Kerry South in second place of 3 in 2007,
Kieran O'Donnell (Fine Gael) Limerick City in third place of 4 in 2016,
Peter Burke (Fine Gael) Longford Westmeath in third place of 4 in 2011,
Gerry Reynolds (Fine Gael) Sligo-Leitrim in **second place of 4** in 2016,
Michael Smith (Fianna Fáil) Tipperary North in second place of 3 in 2007,
Ollie Wilkinson (Fianna Fáil) Waterford in third place of 4 in 2007,
Brendan Kenneally (Fianna Fáil) Waterford also in third place of 4 in 2011,
Michael D'Arcy (Fine Gael) Wexford in fourth place of 5 in 2011 and
John Brady (Sinn Féin) Wicklow in fourth place of 5 in 2011.

CHAPTER 12

Catching Up On Transfers

As stated in chapter 11, it is generally the case that in a three seat constituency, the top three candidates on the first count take the seats, with the top four and top five doing so in four and five seat constituencies. In the last five general elections, 817 seats were contested.[1] There were only 75 cases (9.2%) where a candidate outside the top 3, 4 or 5 caught up on transfers. It is instructive to list these, to identify the margin and the position of the successful candidate and to set out the principal reasons it happened.

General Election 1997 (18)

Constituency (no of seats)	Candidate	Margin by which behind (place)	Reason caught up	Party displaced
Carlow Kilkenny (5)	Pattison (Lab)	397 6th	running mate with 2,995 votes and Green transfers	FF (5th)
Cavan Monaghan (5)	Boylan (FG)	1,670 6th	running mates with 9,197 votes	FF (4th)
Cork SC (5)	Clune (FG)	306 6th	running mate with 2,701 votes	Lab (5th)
Donegal SW (3)	Gildea (Ind)	150 4th	better transfers from others	FF (2nd)
Dublin N (4)	Sargent (G)	2 5th	better transfers from others	Lab (4th)
Dublin NE (4)	Broughan (Lab)	947 5th	running mate with 2,986 votes	FF (3rd)

Dublin S (5)	O 'Donnell (PD)	703 6th	strong residual transfers from Fianna Fáil	Lab (5th)
Dublin SC (5)	Upton (Lab)	362 6th	strong residual transfers from Fine Gael	DL (4th)
Dublin SE (4)	Gormley (G)	245 5th	better transfers from others despite strong Fianna Fáil to PD	FG (4th)
Dublin W (4)	Lawlor (FF)	612 5th	running mate with 2,216 votes and PD transfers	Lab (4th)
Galway E (4)	Kitt (FF)	785 5th	better local transfers displacing colleague	FF (4th)
Kerry N (3)	Foley (FF)	315 4th	running mate with 4,036 votes	SF (3rd)
Laois Offaly (5)	Fleming (FF)	1,260 6th	running mate with 4,328 votes	Lab (5th)
Limerick E (5)	Kemmy (Lab)	701 7th	running mate with 1,866 votes and better transfers	DL (5th)
Louth (4)	McGahon (FG)	140 5th	caught party colleague and third FG candidate at his end of constituency	FG (4th)
Mayo (5)	Moffatt (FF)	1,056 6th	good level of transfers in Ballina from FG candidate	FF (5th)
Tipperary S (3)	Ferris (Lab)	133 4th	better local transfers from Fianna Fáil	WUAG (3rd)
Wicklow (5)	Timmins (FG)	120 6th	running mates with 5,137 votes	Lab (4th)

General Election 2002 (19)

Constituency (no of seats)	Candidate	Margin by which behind (place)	Reason caught up	Party displaced
Clare (4)	Breen (FG)	2,176 5th	running mates with 8,139 votes	FF (4th)
Cork E (4)	Sherlock (Lab)	2,261 5th	left transfers at 29.2% and 44.4%	FG (3rd)
Cork SC (5)	Boyle (G)	583 7th	strong left transfers	FG (3rd)
Donegal SW (3)	McGinley (FG)	302 4th	better transfers from others based on geography	FG (3rd)
Dublin C (4)	Fitzpatrick (FF)	2,382 6th	Ahern (FF) surplus and residual Fine Gael votes	SF (4th)
Dublin NC (4)	McGrath (Ind)	1,752 6th	Green and Labour transfers at 34.6% and 33.9%	FF (3rd)
Dublin NW (3)	Shortall (Lab)	390 4th	Independent and Fine Gael transfers	SF (3rd)
Dublin S (5)	Ryan (G)	141 7th	better left transfers	FG (5th)
Galway W (5)	Grealish (PD)	534 6th	running mates with 3,457 votes	FF (5th)
Kerry N (3)	Deenihan (FG)	121 4th	better transfers based on geography	Lab (3rd)
Kerry S (3)	Moynihan (Lab)	1,605 4th	strong residual transfer from Fine Gael	FF (2nd)
Limerick E (5)	Power (FF)	587 6th	running mates with surplus (4,840) and transfers (2,918)	FG (5th)
Longford-Roscommon (4)	Sexton (PD)	1,751 6th	strong transfers from FG based on geography	FF (4th)

161

Mayo (5)	Kenny (FG)	702 7th	running mates with substantial votes and FF transfer based on geography	FF (4th)
Meath (5)	English (FG)	84 6th	running mate with 3,877 votes	SF (4th)
Sligo-Leitrim (4)	Devins (FF)	38 5th	stronger Sligo town transfers	FF (4th)
Westmeath (3)	McGrath (FG)	874 4th	running mate with 3,793 votes	FF (3rd)
Wexford (5)	Twomey (Ind)	1,741 6th	strong transfers from SF and (residual) FG	FF (3rd)
Wicklow (5)	Fox (Ind)	205 6th	better transfers Green and Labour based on geography	Lab (5th)

General Election 2007 (14)

Constituency (no of seats)	Candidate	Margin by which behind (place)	Reason caught up	Party displaced
Carlow Kilkenny (5)	White (G)	1,108 6th	numerous Carlow transfers based on geography	FG (5th)
Cavan Monaghan (4*)	Conlon (FF)	247 5th	running mate with surplus and Monaghan transfers	FG (4th)
Cork E (4)	Sherlock (Lab)	1,621 5th	running mate with 3,954 votes	FG (3rd)
Cork SW (3)	O'Keeffe (FG)	200 4th	Labour transfers	FF (2nd)
Donegal NE (3)	Blaney (FF)	445 5th	running mate with 6,362 votes	SF (2nd)
Dublin C (4)	Brady (FF)	2,363 9th	running mates with surplus of 5,806 and votes of 1,725	FG (4th)

Dublin MW (4)	Gogarty (G)	437 5th	strong independent, left and FF transfers	FG (3rd)
Dublin NC (3)	McGrath (Ind)	1,834 4th	strong left transfers at 40.3% and 70.4% respectively	FF (3rd)
Dublin NE (3)	Flanagan (FG)	2,378 5th	running mate with 3,529 votes	FF (2nd)
Dún Laoghaire (5)	Cuffe (G)	699 6th	transfers from Fine Gael	PBP (5th)
Galway E (4)	Burke (FG)	668 5th	running mates with 9,797 votes	FF (4th)
Kerry S (3)	Sheahan (FG)	1,140 4th	running mate with 4,195 votes	FF (2nd)
Tipperary N (3)	Coonan (FG)	810 4th	Labour transfers	FF (2nd)
Waterford (4)	O'Shea (Lab)	353 5th	left and Fine Gael transfers	FF (3rd)

* effectively a 4 seat constituency as Ceann Comhairle automatically returned

General Election 2011 (11)

Constituency (no of seats)	Candidate	Margin by which behind (place)	Reason caught up	Party displaced
Clare (4)	Dooley (FF)	40 5th	running mate with 6,015 votes	FG (4th)
Cork NC (4)	Murphy (FG)	475 5th	better transfers from Gilroy of Labour	FG (4th)
Dublin NE (3)	Kenny (Lab)	667 5th	better transfers from others particularly Fianna Fáil	SF (3rd)
Dublin SE (4)	Humphreys (Lab)	472 5th	better transfers from all sources	FF (4th)

Galway E (4)	Keaveney (Lab)	1,578 8th	running mate with 3,577 votes and strong independent transfers	FG (4th)
Galway W (5)	Kyne (FG)	474 7th	better transfer from Connemara based candidates	FG (5th)
Longford W'meath (4)	Troy (FF)	2,354 6th	running mates with almost 7,000 votes	FG (3rd)
Meath W (3)	Butler (FG)	170 4th	running mate with 3,898 votes	Lab (3rd)
Waterford (4)	Halligan (Ind)	1,969 5th	strong Labour and Sinn Féin (35%) transfers	FF (3rd)
Wexford (5)	Browne (FF)	1,066 6th	running mate with 6,675 votes	FG (4th)
Wicklow (5)	Ferris (Lab)	1,656 6th	running mates with 6,672 votes	SF (4th)

General Election 2016 (13)

Constituency (no of seats)	Candidate	Margin by which behind (place)	Reason caught up	Party displaced
Carlow Kilkenny (5)	Deering (FG)	1,811 6th	running mate with 5,017 votes	FF (4th)
Cavan - Monaghan (4)	Smyth N (FF)	298 5th	running mate with 2,909 votes	FG (4th)
Dublin Bay N (5)	Mitchell (SF)	636 6th	running mate with 3,527 votes	Lab (4th)
Dublin Central (3)	O'Sullivan (Ind)	518 7th	strong independent and Fianna Fáil transfers	FF (3rd)

Dublin NW (3)	Rock (FG)	108 4th	strong Labour transfers	FF (3rd)
Dublin Rathdown (3)	Martin (G)	1,783 5th	strong transfers from SF and FF	FG (3rd)
Dublin SC (4)	Smith (PBP)	1,067 5th	left transfers	FF(4th)
Dublin S West (5)	Zappone (Ind)	2,000 6th	strong transfers from independents	FG (5th)
Galway W (5)	Naughton (FG)	1,188 7th	running mate with 4,734 votes	SF (4th)
Limerick City (4)	O'Sullivan (Lab)	820 5th	better transfers from other sources	FG (3rd)
Longford Westmeath (4)	Penrose (Lab)	453 5th	Fine Gael transfers	SF (4th)
Offaly (3)	Nolan (SF)	384 4th	better transfers based on geography	Ind (3rd)
Sligo Leitrim (4)	Scanlon (FF)	798 5th	Sligo v Leitrim issue	FG (2nd)

A number of clear principles can be deduced

- 49 of the 75 instances (about two thirds) are cases where the deficit was less than 1,000 votes. By contrast only 7 cases involved a deficit of 2,000 votes or more and five of those cases involve a running mate.

- the predominant reason (33 cases) that a candidate catches up is the availability of votes from a running mate. It is true that in some of those cases, some of those votes were required to elect another candidate. However in nearly every case the votes available, even with a poor level of transfers, would have been enough to elect the candidate.

- a number of the cases show Fine Gael candidates being elected with the benefit of Labour transfers and Labour candidates being elected with the benefit of Fine Gael transfers. This shows the significance of the relationship which generally exists, whether formal or informal, between those parties.

- the Green Party have been significant beneficiaries from the catch up phenomenon, featuring 8 times above. If they get enough votes to be on the tail of the leaders' enclosure, they have a strong track record of picking up transfers from all sources. This is amply illustrated by the way Catherine Martin, the party's deputy leader caught Alan Shatter of Fine Gael in Dublin Rathdown in 2016, picking up 5,299 transfers to beat him by a margin of almost 1,000.
- geography is a factor in many of the cases, particularly where the deficit is very small
- In most case, the candidate displaced is in the last spot. However in almost 40% of cases, someone higher up the order of first preferences is displaced.
- Equally it is pretty standard that the person benefitting from catching up is the "runner up" on the first count. There are only 16 cases where the person catching up is not the first count "runner up"
- Fianna Fáil candidates were displaced on 28 occasions and Fine Gael on 23 occasions . There is an element of swings and roundabouts with both. Sinn Féin however are net losers being displaced nine times and catching up twice.

While looking at the "catch up" situations is a useful illustration of issues with efficacy of transfers, it would be fair criticism to suggest that this is an over simplistic analysis. There are a few cases that illustrate some of the issues.

In Cork South Central in the 2002 general election, Dan Boyle in seventh on the first count caught Deirdre Clune in third, closing a gap of 583 votes. The first count order of a closely bunched group was

Clune FG	5,535
Dennehy FF	5,533 elected
Coveney FG	5,183 elected
Sinnott Ind	4,984 "last woman" standing
Boyle G	4,952 elected

But why did Clune fail and get passed out by three people below her and indeed get eliminated before Sinnott? In the case of Dennehy passing her out, it was simple, as a large surplus of Micheál Martin put him into a comfortable third, although his lead was clawed back to a mere 6 votes by Kathy Sinnott. The success of Boyle in passing her out was driven by transfers from parties of the left, particularly Sinn Féin and Labour as they were eliminated. Quite frankly given known patterns of transfers, where women tend to be more transfer friendly, it is difficult to explain how Coveney closed a gap of 352 votes to end up 41 votes ahead at the critical stage, but over five critical counts he picked up more transfers at each stage bar one. Sinnott also did significantly better than Clune on transfers from others, to the extent of being 622 votes ahead when Clune was eliminated. Thus Clune was passed out by four candidates, which is probably a very unusual thing to happen in any count.

In the 1992 general election, Eric Byrne of Democratic Left made a valiant attempt to close a deficit of 1,395 votes on Ben Briscoe of Fianna Fáil. He managed to pick up a net 1,390, failing at the end by a mere 5 votes, one of the narrowest margins ever. As this was the year of the Spring tide, he started well with 1,031 transfers from Upton, the sole Labour candidate and this narrowed the deficit to 518 votes. There were 6,773 further votes to be transferred, which were liable to be more favourable to him. While 1,005 of these votes were Fine Gael votes, they were to minimal extent needed to elect Gay Mitchell, the successful Fine Gael candidate. There were also 1,684 Fianna Fáil votes but some of these were needed to elect the other Fianna Fáil candidate, Dr John O'Connell. The net impact of all of this was a further narrowing of the deficit by about 500 votes. This shows the relative inefficiency of transfers, given the large number available in that case. Eric Byrne seems to be quite unfortunate with transfers as he was also the Democratic Left candidate caught in 1997 by a lower placed candidate. Undoubtedly there was probably a perception at the time of Democratic Left being somewhat more left than in reality they were.

References in Chapter 12

[1]   That is 165 x 4 and 157 x 1 , as the Ceann Comhairle is automatically elected.

CHAPTER 13
Transfers And Parties

This chapter examines transfer patterns over eleven general elections by reference to each party contesting those elections. In the case of both Fianna Fáil and Fine Gael, there is usually another candidate of the party left when transfers become available. Therefore, as already noted, in the case of those two parties the predominant feature is an internal transfer and generally there are only crumbs for others. It is however the case that over time, the level of internal cohesion has dropped for both parties, so therefore there is greater benefit to other parties in later elections.

For all other parties, it is the exception rather than the rule, that another candidate of the same party is available to take a transfer in a general election. Therefore the key issue is which other party or parties tends to benefit to the greatest extent from transfers of that party.

Every transfer event is unique as there will be usually a completely different line up of candidates and parties available to take transfers in pretty well every transfer event. It is unusual that all the main parties are available and examples of where this has happened are useful in confirming patterns. What this work is trying to identify is patterns suggesting the average destination of transfers. As transfers in recent elections are more significant, they are considered more fully in Chapter 16.

Methodology for examining Transfers
It is quite standard that works on particular elections measure transferability by reference to actual numbers of votes transferred. While these figures are useful, it is my sense that they can be misleading. The calculation method used for figures in this work is to establish the percentage of transfers to each party and then to look for the averages of these numbers. For example if there were four transfers by Fianna Fáil candidates to other Fianna Fáil

candidates as follows:

Transfer 1	to other FF 73.5%
Transfer 2	to other FF 61.6%
Transfer 3	to other FF 59.5%
Transfer 4	to other FF 62.1%

These four figures total 256.7 which when divided by 4 reaches an average of 64.175%. I therefore would conclude that the average rate of transferability is 64.2%.

The appropriateness of this method as opposed to methods involving actual numbers can be debated. However I believe it is the best guide to the average pattern and indeed in some of the samples, the deviation of individual transfers from this average is generally quite modest.

A factor discussed earlier, which can be an issue with analysing transfers from candidates other than Fianna Fáil or Fine Gael candidates, is the tendency to eliminate several candidates in one go. This has happened in virtually every constituency in the past three general elections.[1] This is a huge issue in assessing the transfer patterns from independents and smaller parties, most notably the Workers Party. Where the collective elimination is substantially comprised of the votes of one party, it is all treated as being votes of that party. However where the mixture means that less than about 75% of the aggregate vote is attributable to a party, it is safer to ignore that transfer for statistical purposes (which is not the general approach of many analyses of transfer patterns in individual elections). The problem is somewhat analogous to analysis of transfers on elimination as inevitably the core party vote will have been "contaminated" by votes transferred from other parties. However in many such cases the level of contamination is at worst of the order of 10%, so can be ignored.

Fianna Fáil And Transfers

Over the time covered by this work, there is a strong pattern of Fianna Fáil transfers to other Fianna Fáil candidates. However with limited exceptions, Fianna Fáil voters are relatively agnostic when it comes to other parties.

There are also comparatively few occasions where a Fianna Fáil candidate has transfers to deliver, with no other Fianna Fáil candidate available to receive them. There is a clear pattern where there is no Fianna Fáil candidate available for a transfer, that a high proportion of the votes become non transferable.

Internal Fianna Fáil transfers

For most of the period 1981 to 2016, high levels of Fianna Fáil transfers from one Fianna Fáil candidate to another was one of the key features of a party, which was perhaps the most successful party in western Europe. The party was generally able to outperform Fine Gael on this internal loyalty front, and this combined with the much more important benefit of having more votes, led to great successes. However there has been a very marked decline in the pattern in the elections in the 21st century and this has perhaps not been given as much attention as warranted.

General elections in the early 1980's show that an average of over 80% of Fianna Fáil votes transferred on to other Fianna Fáil candidates and indeed as that series wore on, the percentage headed towards the mid 80's. There were virtually no occasions where a Fianna Fáil candidate was not available to take a transfer. The consequence is that there were only crumbs available for anyone else, predominantly driven by geography. This pattern continued into the late 1980's.

By 1997 however things were beginning to change. In the general election of that year Fianna Fáil transfer rates within the party had declined to an average level of about 67%. There were therefore more votes available for other parties and independents, but these tended to spread over a wide range of candidates. 2002 was a poor election for Labour and particularly poor for Fine Gael. However Fianna Fáil internal cohesion drifted further to about an average 65%. The last three general elections have seen a further decline. 2007 saw an upwards blip, with the average going up to about 69%. The disastrous 2011 election however, despite the fact that the Fianna Fáil reduced performance perhaps meant that it was reduced to the core party vote, saw an internal cohesion rate of about an average 58% with a slight further decline in 2016 to about 55%. There is therefore a general election pattern of decline in cohesion within Fianna Fáil from about 85% to about 55%.[2]

Transfers within Fianna Fáil (indeed either of the two traditional large parties) fall into three categories. The first is transfers arising on elimination of a candidate. The second is transfers from a first count surplus which is discussed in Chapter 14. The third is transfers of surpluses which arise because of an internal Fianna Fáil transfer. In the third case, which involves having at least three candidates, the level of transfer is usually about 10 percentage points ahead of the prevailing level, showing a degree of 1,2,3,4 party support. Generally the level of transfers is similar however whether it arises from a first count surplus or a later count. However in some general elections with meaningful samples, there is a pattern that Fianna Fáil first count surpluses (discussed in chapter 14) transfer at a lesser level than subsequent count transfers. Further the transfer rates of candidates whose first count surpluses are more than 1,000 votes, show an even worse pattern. In 2007, the regular transfer percentage averaged at 69.8%. However first count surpluses only transferred at average 65.4% and those with large surpluses transferred at average 64.8%.[3] This demonstrates the benefit of trying to extract core Fianna Fáil party supporters from the vote accruing to strong candidates so as to reduce them below quota as discussed in chapter 14.

A question may be asked, given the relative decline in Fianna Fáil transfer levels over time from 80% to 55%, as to who has benefitted. While all other parties have received a greater share of Fianna Fáil transfers over time, the substantial beneficiary seems to be Fine Gael, who in recent general elections have often got about 20% of available Fianna Fáil transfers. The converse has equally been the case so that the effect of lower transfers within the two major parties is somewhat cancelled out.

The patterns noted above in relation to general elections are also relevant to local elections, although there internal party cohesion is always significantly lower than would be the case in general elections. In local elections 2009 and 2014, Fianna Fáil internal rates seem to be at a rate somewhere in the 50% and low 40% range respectively.

Transfers Fianna Fáil to other parties

Historically Fianna Fáil has nearly always had other candidates available to take transfers and therefore other parties rarely have the opportunity to benefit substantially. There are some exceptions, usually favouring parties with whom Fianna Fáil have a coalition or support arrangement. Over the period 1992 to 2007 when the Progressive Democrats were potential coalition partners, rates of transfer in general elections to the Progressive Democrats were quite strong, but usually only when no Fianna Fáil candidate was available. They did however result in the election of several Progressive Democrats.

The impact on other parties has otherwise tended to be particular to individual candidates and there are good examples in the 2002 election, one of which proved to be enormously significant to subsequent history. In the 2002 general election in Mayo, Enda Kenny of Fine Gael was 400 votes behind his running mate, Jim Higgins with only Fianna Fáil candidates remaining. The next elimination was Frank Chambers a Newport based candidate, who delivered 600 transfers to Kenny (Castlebar based) enabling him to overtake Higgins and then be elected on the transfer of Higgins' votes. He subsequently became party leader and eventually Taoiseach. If this had not happened, it is likely Jim Higgins would have been a leading contender in the subsequent leadership election.[4]

Non transferable Fianna Fáil votes
There is a strong pattern in general elections in the few historic cases where no Fianna Fáil candidate is available to take transfers, that a large proportion of the votes become non transferable. This reflects a traditional pattern of voters voting 1,2,3,4 Fianna Fáil and then stopping. In the few cases in the 1980's, they are all at over 50% level. The cases become more numerous from 1997 onwards, but still stay at levels close to 50%. In 2007 and 2011, the level drops into the 40% range, but there are a few cases where a Progressive Democrat or Fianna Fáil gene pool candidate reduced the non-transferable vote percentage to the teens. It can however be said that all evidence, absent a candidate to whom Fianna Fáil voters might be sympathetic, points to a large non transferable vote where no Fianna Fáil candidate remains.

Fianna Fáil - transfer friendly
There was a lot of talk in the late nineties and early noughties that Fianna Fáil had become transfer friendly, as opposed to its previous status as "transfer toxic". This seems to be largely a myth. It is true that the 1997 alliance with the Progressive Democrats led to a harvest of votes from a source, likely to have a material number of transfers to deliver. However outside that,

there is little evidence of many extra transfers being delivered to Fianna Fáil to compensate for internal breakdown in transfers. It is probably correct however to conclude that the product of a general breakdown in transfer patterns across all parties meant that it became much harder to catch Fianna Fáil candidates in the "leaders' enclosure". Certainly it is difficult to envisage that John Farrelly, the master of bridging the 2,000 gap with a Fianna Fáil candidate, could possibly have achieved that in recent elections. What was much more important post 1997 was Fianna Fáil managing its vote, as discussed in Chapter 27.

Fianna Fáil Transfers - Conclusion

There is a high rate of internal Fianna Fáil transfers but this has dropped over 35 years from the mid 80's to the mid 50's for general elections. In the relatively few cases of transfers where no Fianna Fáil candidate remains, there is a tendency for votes to become non transferable. But Enda Kenny probably owed his being in a position to become Taoiseach to the vagaries of Fianna Fáil transfers.

Fine Gael And Transfers

Over the time period covered by this work, there is a strong pattern of Fine Gael transfers to other Fine Gael candidates. However, unlike Fianna Fáil, Fine Gael voters are inclined to be somewhat more generous when it comes to other parties, particularly the Labour party. There are also comparatively few occasions where a Fine Gael candidate has transfers to deliver, with no other Fine Gael party candidate available to receive them.

Elections in the early 1980's show that in general elections an average of just less than 80% of Fine Gael votes transferred on within the party and indeed as that series wore on, the percentage headed towards the mid 80s.[5] Like Fianna Fáil, there were virtually no occasions where a Fine Gael candidate was not available to take a transfer. The consequence is that there were only a small number of transfers available for anyone else, mainly the Labour Party.

By 1987 however things were beginning to change and Fine Gael internal transfer rates began to decline. By the general election of 1997, a reasonable election for Fine Gael, Fine Gael transferability had declined to 64% (not however materially worse than Fianna Fáil at the same time). There were therefore more votes available for others, but these tended to spread all over the place, notably towards Labour. 2002 was a disastrous election for Fine Gael and internal cohesion drifted further to about 60%. The subsequent two general elections saw improvements, with 2007 showing an average going up to about 65%, 2011 showing a further improvement in the average to 67% but a decline in 2016 to about 60%. In effect in general elections since 1997, Fine Gael has had a transfer rate to other Fine Gael candidates in the mid to high 60's and by 2011 and 2016 had significantly outpaced Fianna Fáil in its level of transfer efficiency within the party.

A question may also be asked that given the relative decline in Fine Gael transfer levels over time from 80% to 60% as to who has benefitted. While all other parties have received a greater share of Fine Gael transfers over time, the substantial beneficiary seems to be Fianna Fáil, who in recent general elections have often got about 10-15% of available Fine Gael transfers. Labour has also done well when in contention. The converse has equally been the case so that the effect of lower transfers within the two major parties is somewhat cancelled out.

Transfers Fine Gael to other parties

Historically Fine Gael has nearly always had other candidates available to take transfers and therefore other parties rarely have the opportunity to benefit substantially. There is however a notable position where there is no Fine Gael candidate available to take transfers. In those instances, there is a clear pattern of very strong transfers to the Labour Party, at rates often in the 60s% and 70s%.[6] There has been a clear level of Fine Gael and Labour co-operation in a number of constituencies, most notably Carlow Kilkenny, Kerry South, Kildare, Tipperary North, Westmeath and Wexford. While this co-operation is not always manifested in transfers, transfers are a vital component of the relationship and have secured extra seats in many elections for both parties.

Non transferable Fine Gael votes

There is a strong pattern in the few historic cases where no Fine Gael or Labour or another independent candidate is available to take transfers from a Fine Gael candidate, that a large proportion of the votes become non transferable. This reflects a traditional pattern of voters voting 1,2,3,4 Fine Gael and Labour but expressing no view as between the Fianna Fáil candidates. In the few cases in the 1980's they are all at over 50% level. The cases become more numerous from 1997 onwards, but still stay at levels close to 50%. In 2007 and 2011, the level drops into the 40% range. It can however be said that all evidence, absent a Labour or palatable other candidate, points to a large non transferable vote where no Fine Gael candidate remains.

The Labour Party And Transfers

The Labour party has joined government with Fine Gael after the elections of 1981, November 1982, 1992 (albeit only in late 1994) and in 2011. Thus, in four of the general elections reviewed, a partnership with Fine Gael was envisaged and in four more February 1982, 1987, 1997 and 2016, a government with Fine Gael had just ended. There is sometimes also a pact between the parties. There is therefore a perception that Labour votes have a tendency to transfer to Fine Gael. But is this true?

Over the general elections reviewed (apart from the 1981 and 2011 general elections) the tendency of the Labour Party generally has been to run one candidate only in a constituency. This means that if the Labour candidate has a surplus or is eliminated, the votes will all transfer, if they transfer at all, to other parties. It is very much in a minority of situations that there is a further Labour candidate available to take the transfers. In most general elections, Labour transfers become available in about 20 constituencies; however in the "Spring Tide" of 1992 and the "Gilmore Gale" of 2011, both elections where Labour did exceptionally well, Labour votes became available for transfer in close to 30 of the constituencies.

The review summarised here takes account of all Labour transfers over the 1981 to 2016 general election cycle.[7]
The following general principles seem to apply to Labour transfers

- transfers within the party where another Labour candidate is available to take those transfers tend to be at percentages at best in the 60's, so internal coherence falls significantly behind that of other parties. The best ever seen was at 75.3% in Dublin South in November 1982

- there is some tendency to transfer strongly to Fine Gael in contests where the alternative destination is Fianna Fáil. However transfer rates to Fine Gael are relatively poor in elections where Fine Gael is doing poorly
- there is a growing tendency starting in the late 1980's elections for Labour transfers to have a preference for strong left candidates as opposed to Fine Gael
- Labour had a lot of surpluses on the first count in the 1992 Spring Tide but in most cases had no further candidate to benefit. In the 2011 Gilmore Gale, the number of first count surpluses was vastly reduced; more importantly in most cases there was a further Labour candidate to take up some of the surpluses.

Internal Labour transfers

The following is the percentage range of internal transfers from one Labour candidate to another Labour candidate in general elections. The heading "indicative" is the author's assessment of the average level of internal Labour transfers, having regard to factors particular to the constituencies where transfers took place.

Election	number of instances	range (Percentage)	indicative
1981	19 [8]	36 to 75	60
Feb 1982	5	39 to 69	60
Nov 1982	4	55 to 75	65
1987	3	53 to 63	55
1989	5	51 to 69	57
1992	3	60 to 66	63
1997	4	36 to 60	50
2002	3	44 to 66	50
2007	6	34 to 52	45
2011	16	36 to 66	55
2016	2	26 to 40	33

In 2011, the instances of transfers between Labour candidates rose because Labour ran more second candidates, whose elimination sometimes then elected the lead candidate. In some of these instances a second candidate was actually elected. Thus vote management was far better than in the previous general election in 1992, when Labour had done well, but had few second candidates to benefit.

Some of the poorest Labour transfers between fellow candidates are in constituencies where geography is relevant. Labour always need to think hard in Carlow Kilkenny as to whether a second candidate in the other county is required. They have had two candidates there on seven occasions, with transfers within Labour ranging from 44% to 62%.[9]

In general however where Labour have second or third candidates to receive transfers, the trend over time is towards only half of the votes being transferred to other Labour candidates. This improves somewhat where Labour were doing well such as in 1992 and 2011. Thus if Labour candidate A has 6,000 votes and candidate B has 3,000 votes, A can only expect to get about 1,500 votes on transfer, bringing them to 7,500. This is an issue that is hugely relevant to candidate tactics for Labour. It is probable that one of the reasons why Labour has poorer internal transfers than the other major parties is because it infrequently has two candidates who are both seen as competitive for a seat. Labour supporters may simply not be used to having a choice of candidate.

Transfers Labour to Fine Gael

In the majority of cases, where Labour transfers become available, there is no Labour candidate to receive them. Over the eleven general elections reviewed, in these circumstances the greatest share of them usually goes to Fine Gael. However in more recent elections, the benefit to Fine Gael has lessened considerably; in particular where there is a strong candidate from another left party (but not Sinn Féin), that candidate is often the major beneficiary of Labour transfers. The 2016 pattern seemed to move back to favouring Fine Gael, with an average level of transfer of over 50% to Fine Gael.

There is quite a strong pattern of Labour transfers to Fine Gael in constituencies where it is important for Fine Gael in securing a second (or sometimes third) seat. Thus in a range of elections, strong transfers, often in the 60% range, are seen from Labour to Fine Gael in Clare, Cork North West, Cork South West, Kerry North, Limerick West and Wexford. This pattern was also seen in earlier elections where Fine Gael was successful in Dublin North, Dublin North Central, Dublin South and Dublin West. These transfers were in many elections crucial for Fine Gael getting two seats or three seats (or in the case of Kerry North, the single seat held by Jimmy Deenihan). Fine Gael perhaps got greater benefit than Labour in terms of numbers of seats obtained from transfers from the other.

There is however over time a notable pattern of fall off in the level of Labour transfers to Fine Gael, particularly outside the constituencies where there may be some local appreciation as to their value. In the 2011 election most of the transfers where no Labour candidate remained were in the 40% range and this is a pattern that has been evident for a number of elections. The patterns in the early 80's were much more favourable to Fine Gael and indeed there are a number of instances then of transfers in the 70% range, something Labour achieves infrequently between its own candidates. Thus if a Labour candidate has 1000 votes and there is no available other Labour candidate, it is reasonable for Fine Gael to expect to receive about 400 of them.

It should of course be noted that in many cases where a Labour candidate is available to take transfers, Fine Gael usually gets the second biggest share, often of the order of 20%.

Transfers Labour to Other Left

There is a long established pattern of strong Labour transfers to parties such as Democratic Left, the Workers Party, the Greens, Socialists, United Left and a range of left independents. This trend can be seen right back to the three elections of the early 1980's where left candidates got a large share of Labour transfers. Examples from then include Joe Sherlock (WP Cork East 24%, 55%, 36%) and Paddy Gallagher (WP Waterford 13%, 36%, 29%). It is now pretty predictable that the left will take a strong share of Labour transfers where it has a significant presence. Thus in the 2011 general election there were strong Labour to left transfers in Dublin Central (50%) Dublin North (36%

Socialist, 20% Greens), Dún Laoghaire (34% PBPA), Kildare North (45% Catherine Murphy), Roscommon South Leitrim (35% Ming Flanagan) and Tipperary South (35% ULA). Often where there is a significant left presence, transfers to the left will be at a greater rate than to Fine Gael. However in the 2016 general election on a very depleted Labour vote, Fine Gael tended to do better on Labour transfers than other left candidates.

Transfers Labour to Sinn Féin
Labour transfers to Sinn Féin have really only become a feature of Irish politics since the 2007 general election.[10] In 2011, there were far more instances of transfers from Labour to Sinn Féin, most of them at a rate of less than 10% and less than delivered to Fine Gael, with limited exceptions.[11] However it can generally be said that, notwithstanding the high number of votes Labour had available for transfer in 2011, very few of the accrued to Sinn Féin. Much the same pattern was evident in 2016 based on transfers of the reduced Labour vote.

Transfers Labour to Fianna Fáil
Uniformly over the period in question, despite Fianna Fáil candidates often being available to receive transfers, the transfer rate from Labour to Fianna Fáil is poor, often below 10%, although the rate can improve in the later stages of counts where only three or four candidates remain in the field. Rates above 25% are few and far between.[12]

Transfers Labour to others
There is a pattern of reasonably strong Labour transfers to independents and other parties, particularly those of the left. In the 1987 elections when the Progressive Democrats were quite strong, there are quite a few transfers at about a 20% level. This is despite a possible left and right perception as between those parties. This remained a feature of elections through to 2002 (but not 1997) in constituencies where the Progressive Democrats were competitive.

Non transferable Labour votes
Generally where there a number of other parties in the race, the level of non transferable Labour votes is quite low, 10% or less. There is a greater

tendency however in recent elections for Labour votes to be non transferable at rates of 25% or more. This for example happened three times in the 2011 election, in each case involving a material number of votes, a pattern replicated in 2016.

General summary of Labour transfers

Labour is perhaps the most important source of transfers to others in general elections. The Labour party has a poor enough record of transferring between its own candidates as opposed to the record of other established parties, although there are relatively few cases of other Labour candidates being available to take transfers, as Labour generally does not run more than one candidate . In general Labour transfers tend to favour either Fine Gael or other left parties. There is an increasing trend (somewhat bucked in 2016) for other left parties and candidates to get better transfers, where there is competition between them and Fine Gael. Labour transfers generally do not accrue to a significant extent to Fianna Fáil or Sinn Féin. They generally do not end up in the non transferable category either, but this is less so now than would have been the case in the past.

Sinn Féin And Transfers

For the period under review, the general pattern is that Sinn Féin only ran one candidate per constituency or LEA, so that the transfer issue generally focusses on transfers to others on elimination of that candidate. While Sinn Féin have been contesting elections for a considerable length of time, it is probably only in elections since 2009 that there has been a pattern of two or more Sinn Féin candidates, so that one can pick up transfers from the other. There were exceptions, such as both Dublin Central and Dublin West in 1989, where two candidates featured, but this is unusual. It is also only really in the local election of 2014 that there are a significant number of examples of Sinn Féin running two candidates, with numerous examples of transfers from one to the other.

There is perceived to be a pattern of a high rate of non transferability of Sinn Féin votes. However this is more perception than reality. An examination of Sinn Féin transfers in general elections 2007 and 2011 shows that the average level of non transferable votes when no Sinn Féin candidate remains is 15% rising to 25% in 2011.[13]   However there was a significant change in 2016 in that when Sinn Féin transfers became available, they tended to reject all the established parties and by default became non transferable at a high rate. It was only in cases where there was a strong independent or other left candidate that Sinn Féin transfers accrued in any number. In the last two local elections 2009 and 2014, the level of non transferable Sinn Féin votes was on average in the 20% to 30% range.[14]

What seems much more evident with Sinn Féin transfers however is that they tend to spread across a range of candidates and have very little impact on the ordering of position between the other candidates. There are some exceptions. For example in 2011, significant transfers from David Cullinane in Waterford were significant in giving John Halligan (Independent) the last seat against Fianna Fáil. However the general impression is that they don't contribute materially to the order of things in terms of electing other candidates. With the growth in Sinn Féin, it is likely that a future pattern will see part quotas, insufficient to elect a second candidate and in weaker constituencies, a significant parcel of votes to be transferred at a late count. This was very much evident in the 2016 general election.

A very clear pattern with Sinn Féin is running the minimal level of candidates and seeking to aggregate the vote around one candidate. For example in general election 2011, there were two Sinn Féin candidates in only three constituencies Cavan-Monaghan, Carlow Kilkenny and Mayo, with transfers between the two Sinn Féin candidates happening at around 57%. In general election 2016 there were two or more Sinn Féin candidates in nine constituencies and where one was eliminated, there were high transfers to the other. This minimal pattern was also evident in 2007 and 2009. It is only in the 2014 local election that Sinn Féin started to run multiple candidates generally, largely in urban areas.[15]

A very good example of Sinn Féin transfers which shows a typical pattern is seen in Cork City South East LEA in the 2004 local elections. In that case Dermot O'Mahony, the Sinn Féin candidate was eliminated with 946 votes at count 6, with a single Fianna Fáil, Fine Gael, Labour, Progressive Democrat and Green candidate remaining. The Sinn Féin vote split broadly 36 Green: 29 non transferable: 14 Labour: 11 Fianna Fáil: 5 Fine Gael: 5 Progressive

Democrat, electing each of the Green, Labour, Fine Gael and Fianna Fáil candidates. The pattern is consistent with the averages normally seen, save that the non transferable element seems somewhat high.

Transfers from one Sinn Féin candidate to another

There are a small number of examples prior to 2014 where Sinn Féin had two candidates in a constituency or LEA. Generally the transfer rate between two Sinn Féin candidates was impressive, 55% to 60%.[16] The level of internal cohesion however improved very significantly in the 2014 local elections with internal Sinn Féin transfers typically in the 60% plus range. This was a very significant achievement in local elections and rather better than any other party could achieve. Of the 30 instances where Sinn Féin could transfer to another Sinn Féin candidate, 25 were at a rate of over 50%. Internal transfer rates in the 2016 general election at about 75% were also highly impressive.

Transfers Sinn Féin to other Left candidates

There has been a strong pattern over many elections of Sinn Féin transfers in the 20% to 30% range to parties of the Left other than (excepting 2011) Labour. This often reflects which smaller left party is in favour at that election. In election 1989, strong transfers towards the Workers Party are notable. In 2002 and 2007, the Greens seemed to be in favour. In 2007, 2009, 2014 and 2016 the Anti Austerity Alliance, People before Profit and the Socialists were beneficiaries. It is predictable therefore that such parties will be strong beneficiaries of Sinn Féin transfers where they have candidates available to receive them.

Transfers Sinn Féin to Labour

Labour has at times been the beneficiary of Sinn Féin transfers of the order of 20% to 30%. This was particularly noticable in the 2011 election when Labour did well. However even then, they tended to take less transfers than other left or independents, where they are still in the count. However by 2014, when Labour were in government, transfers from Sinn Féin had collapsed generally to at best percentages in the low teens and often behind Fianna Fáil or Fine Gael and this pattern was also evident in 2016. In earlier elections transfers from Sinn Féin to Labour tended to be quite high where they had a candidate available to receive them.

Transfers Sinn Féin to Fianna Fáil

Historically there were quite high rates of transfer between Sinn Féin and Fianna Fáil, perhaps reflecting the "Republican" roots of both. In the earlier elections Fianna Fáil often got up to 30% of Sinn Féin transfers, often a multiple of six times of what accrued to Fine Gael. However in recent elections Fianna Fáil has become significantly less popular with Sinn Féin voters, often registering single digit percentages and being equally as unpopular as Fine Gael. The trend improved for Fianna Fáil in 2016.

Transfers Sinn Féin to Fine Gael

There is a general pattern of Sinn Féin aversion (which is mutual) to transfers to Fine Gael. For example in the 1989 general election, when Sinn Féin voters were asked to sort out the final two seats between three Fine Gael candidates in Cavan Monaghan, 71.66% of the Sinn Féin voters expressed no preference for any of them. There are however some recent examples of levels of transfers in the 20% to 30% range, often dictated by the geography of particular Sinn Féin candidates. This may reflect voters that were historically Fine Gael voters drifting to Sinn Féin and being prepared to come back to Fine Gael with a later preference. One notable trend is that Fine Gael and Fianna Fáil now take similarly low percentages of available Sinn Féin transfers, whereas historically Fianna Fáil beat Fine Gael on such transfers by a substantial margin.

Transfers Sinn Féin to others

There is a clear pattern in recent elections of a high level of Sinn Féin transfers to independent candidates, particularly those competitive for a seat. In the 2014 local elections, Sinn Féin surpluses were particularly generous to independents, even in excess of 50%, where there was no Sinn Féin candidate available, possibly aided by the fact that there cannot in practice be any non transferable votes on a first count surplus. It is notable that the trend to transfer to independents still seems to apply where the independent would probably be of the centre right. It should be noted that in the days of the Progressive Democrats, Sinn Féin transfers were extremely low to that party. They were even behind paltry Fine Gael levels. This would suggest that Sinn Féin will not produce many transfers for any new groupings seen as on the right of politics, such as Renua, an issue not really explored in the 2016 general election due to the poor Renua performance.

Non transferable Sinn Féin votes

As noted above, while Sinn Féin tends to produce a somewhat greater level of non-transferable votes than other parties, the level is nothing like is perceived. This is because of a tendency to transfer to other left, independents and to a lesser extent the Labour party. In the few instances however where the only possible destination for Sinn Féin transfers is either Fianna Fáil or Fine Gael, there is a tendency for the bulk of the vote to become non-transferable. For example in the Carlow Kilkenny bye-election 2015, over 60% of the Sinn Féin vote (albeit supplemented by transfers) proved to be non-transferable. The 2016 general election did however produce a greater level of non-transferable votes.

Summary of Sinn Féin transfers
- While there is only a recent trend for Sinn Féin to have a significant number of second candidates in electoral areas, they have, based on 2014 and 2016 patterns, achieved an excellent rate of internal transfer between their candidates, reaching 75% in 2016
- Contrary to perception, in most instances where there is no available Sinn Féin candidate, most of the Sinn Féin vote will transfer to other parties, with a relatively small percentage proving non transferable
- Sinn Féin transfers tend, not unexpectedly, to favour other left candidates and independents. They tend to a lesser extent to favour Labour. They are generally hostile to Fianna Fáil and Fine Gael, with both parties ranking equally unfavourably.

The Green Party And Transfers

As the Green party is liable to have a reasonable number of votes, but usually will not have many candidates either elected or "last man standing", the destination of its transfers are potentially quite significant, where the margins between candidates in the hunt for seats is tight. It is therefore particularly instructive to examine its transfers, particularly in the 2002, 2007, 2011 and 2016 general elections where it ran candidates in all of the constituencies (2002 majority of constituencies). Indeed in the 2011 general election, every single Green vote was transferred, as all the Green candidates were eliminated at some stage. The party, albeit winning six seats, did moderately well in 2002, very well in 2007 (also winning 6 seats), extremely badly in 2011 (losing all of its seats) and recovered somewhat in 2016 with two seats. In the 2011 general election it had just come out of government with Fianna Fáil, although the government had broken up in very acrimonious circumstances and Fianna Fáil were facing into a nightmare election. A minor technical difficulty in analysing its transfers already alluded to, particularly in the 2011 election, is that in that election many of its candidates were eliminated as part of a "job lot" of candidates. While some of the written material from that election analysed these transfers, they are nearly always an unreliable guide to how Green voters behaved, so they have been ignored.

There is virtually no instance where there is a second Green candidate, so the issue of internal transfers is not really relevant.[17]

The curious fact that emerges from analysis of recent Green transfers is that the percentages of transfer to the major parties, when aggregated, over the three general elections from 2002 to 2011 is remarkably consistent. The average range for Labour is 34% to 35.9%. The average range for Fine Gael is 20% to 29.64% and the average range for Fianna Fáil is 12.6% to 14%. In each case the level of non transferable votes is 9.45% to 10.82%. The only material variation is the lowly 20% average received by Fine Gael in 2002, undoubtedly explained by the dreadful performance by Fine Gael in that election. The 2007 and 2011 elections show 28.6% and 29.64% averages respectively for Fine Gael, which is probably closer to the norm. Sinn Féin are also occasional beneficiaries of Green transfers usually at rates between 8% and 14%, with a rather poorer performance in 2011. Individual independents and smaller party candidates are often beneficiaries in the 20/30% range too.[18] There was somewhat of a change in the 2016 general election, with a greater tendency for Green transfers to scatter widely, but still favouring Fine Gael and Labour with 19% and 21% average respectively..

A very good example of the typical pattern of Green transfers in practice is seen in Cork City South West LEA in the 2004 local elections. In that case Pat Murray, the Green candidate was eliminated with 832 votes at count 4, with a single Fianna Fáil, Fine Gael, Labour and Sinn Féin candidate remaining. The gap between the continuing four was 249 votes. The Green vote split broadly 26 Labour: 22 non transferable: 19 Fine Gael: 18 Fianna Fáil and 14 Sinn Féin, electing each of the Labour, Fine Gael and Fianna Fáil candidates. The precise pattern is not entirely consistent with the averages normally seen.

Transfers Green to Labour

Labour are clearly the main beneficiary of Green transfers. Further as there is nearly always only one Labour candidate, they are the biggest individual beneficiary by far from Green votes. Some more successful Labour candidates also received transfers beyond the usual mid 30% level.[19] So where Green voters have a choice of an electable Labour candidate, they usually opt for that choice in large numbers.

Transfers Green to Fine Gael

A pattern which might not have been expected is that Green voters in a normal election and even with Labour competition, tend to transfer to Fine Gael candidates at rates heading towards 30%. Indeed in the 60 or so constituencies where Green transfers are measurable over the three general elections 2002 to 2011, Fine Gael got a larger share than Labour in about a fifth of the constituencies where the two parties were in competition and in many further instances was a few percentage points behind. The problem for Fine Gael is that these transfers are often spread across two or even three candidates, so it is highly unlikely that an individual Fine Gael candidate will benefit as much as a Labour candidate. However these votes are useful to Fine Gael where it is in competition with either Fianna Fáil or Sinn Féin, given that it gets a significantly greater share of them.

Transfers Green to other parties

As noted, a much smaller number of Green transfers accrue to Fianna Fáil and to Sinn Féin. The pattern is also remarkably consistent across a number of elections. In practice Green voters are relatively adverse to both parties. It is notable that even after four years in alliance with Fianna Fáil, Green voters transferred to Fianna Fáil at a lesser rate in 2011 (12.6%) than they did in 2007 (13.22%). This was almost certainly down to the unpopularity of Fianna Fáil in 2011. In 2016 a number of independent and minor party candidates benefitted strongly from Green transfers.

Non transferable Green votes

There is a strong tendency for Green voters to transfer, with the vast majority of transfer events resulting in a non transferable balance of less than 10%. The average is distorted towards 10% by a number of instances in the 20% range, often at the end of a count or where no Labour candidate is available.

Green Transfers -Conclusion

In a reasonable election, the Greens can have a significant number of transferable votes and therefore they are very important to the issue of transfers. Recent general elections prior to 2016 have suggested a strong tendency of Green voters to transfer and the average pattern seems to be Labour 35: Fine Gael 29: Fianna Fáil 13: Sinn Féin 11: Non transferable 10. However individual Labour candidates are usually the main beneficiary and a Green transfer can sometimes be relevant to their election. The 2016 general election showed a greater tendency for Green transfers to scatter.

Progressive Democrats And Transfers

The Progressive Democrats were founded in 1985 and contested six general elections from 1987 to 2007 inclusive. Following a disastrous performance in the 2007 general election when it was reduced to two seats, it was disbanded and its two surviving TDs, Mary Harney and Noel Grealish became independent deputies.

There are relatively limited examples where the Progressive Democrats had two or more candidates in a general election and where transfers took place. In their first election in 1987, they had two or more candidates in a number of places and the rate of transfer between them was quite high and comparable (if slightly less) to rates obtaining between the two traditional large parties. Generally the rate of internal coherence after that was quite poor by comparison with the other parties, a factor also demonstrated in local elections. For example in Edenderry LEA (Offaly) in 1991, its internal transfer rate was 21.84%.

Progressive Democrat transfers with no remaining Progressive Democrat candidate became available in all elections. In the 1987, 1989 and 1992 elections, its transfers tended to benefit Fine Gael at a very high level. Indeed in 1989, it was in a formal transfer pact with that party and transfers to Fine Gael ranged from 40% to 72%, averaging about 60%. After 1997, it went into government with Fianna Fáil and hence for two of the three remaining general elections in its life, its transfers tended to favour Fianna Fáil, generally at rates over 40%. In 2002 it took a strongly anti-Fianna Fáil stance and its transfers scattered widely. Much more significantly, in later elections the holding of seats by the Progressive Democrats was facilitated by substantial Fianna Fáil transfers.[20]

Workers Party And Transfers

There are relatively few examples over the eleven general elections under review where the Workers Party had transfers available for distribution. The party has rather a colourful history. It started in the 1981 elections as Sinn Féin the Workers Party (SFWP). By November 1982, it had become the Workers Party and by 1987 it had developed serious critical mass. In the early 1990's a critical mass of its people had left the party and become Democratic Left. This left a residual party which failed to make much of an impact in any of the elections after 1992. Further because of the poor performance of the party post 1992, it is quite common that its candidates are eliminated as part of a serial elimination and it is unclear how its voters behaved in terms of transfers.

From the limited clear examples of Workers Party eliminations, it is clear that its voters have a tendency to transfer to other left parties. Usually because it is eliminated early, there are other left candidates available to take transfers. Transfers would typically be at a 25% rate, but there would be examples where two parties each take about 25%. In the elections of the early 1980's the Labour party frequently took about 50% of the Workers Party transfers, but the level of benefit drifted back to the 30% level from the 1987 election onwards. There is little pattern of transfers to the "right wing" parties of Fianna Fáil, Fine Gael and the Progressive Democrats.

Democratic Left And Transfers

Democratic Left was a spin off from the Workers Party in the early 1990's and it fought general elections in 1992 and 1997. At that point it merged into the Labour Party and two subsequent leaders of the Labour Party were former Democratic Left TDs, Pat Rabbitte and Eamon Gilmore.

From the limited examples of Democratic Left eliminations, it is clear that its voters had a tendency to transfer to other left parties. Usually because it was eliminated early, there were other left candidates available to take transfers. Transfers would typically be at a 25% rate, but there would be individual examples with much higher transfers. There was little pattern of transfers to the "right wing" parties of Fianna Fáil and Fine Gael but the Progressive Democrats did a little better.

Smaller Parties And Transfers

A variety of smaller parties and groupings above those specifically discussed have contested general elections, particularly elections since 2002. The parties and groupings include Christian Solidarity, CPPC, Fis Nua, New Vision, Social Democrats, Renua, People before Profit Alliance, Socialists and United Left. The latter three have met with some degree of success and their transfers broadly mirror the pattern of parties such as the Workers Party and Democratic Left, but with strong Sinn Féin leaning in 2016.

Christian Solidarity, CPPC, Fis Nua and New Vision have all fared very badly. Further there is a tendency for their candidates to be eliminated as part of a collective elimination and consequently it is difficult to interpret their transfers. The tendency seems to be to slightly favour other independents and then left parties, possibly more because it is an anti-establishment vote. In the case of Christian Solidarity, the vote tends to favour Fianna Fáil and Fine Gael candidates, particularly individuals known to be themselves socially conservative. As these four groupings rarely get many votes, there is no great significance to their transfers, except where a contest is extremely tight indeed. Renua and the Social Democrats are considered in Chapter 16.

Independents And Transfers

There has always been a tendency for transfers from an independent candidate to favour other independent candidates and this trend can be seen in elections right back to the 1980's. A big difference over time is that there are now far more independents, so the chances that one will be available to take a transfer are much greater. The analysis of independent transfers is particularly hindered by a tendency to eliminate a number of them at once, so there is no picture as to the rate of transfer between them. A superficial look over elections where independents have done well suggests an average transfer rate of the order of 30% as was the case in 2011. This was quite a significant increase on 2007. Independents also transferred well to other independents in the 2016 general election at rates averaging 30%. However closer examination shows that high percentage rates dominate for candidates with low first preferences. It is therefore quite common that a voter who votes for an independent with 100 first preferences has a tendency to give a number 2 to a candidate with 150 first preferences. Once the count comes to independent candidates with a significant first preference vote, the level of transfers declines, often to significantly less than 20%. Therefore while there are undoubtedly cases where transfers to independents from other independents are at material level, such as transfers to the late Tony Gregory in Dublin Central, the prevailing pattern is that they are not hugely relevant to election outcomes.

Electoral Pacts

As noted in the sections dealing with individual parties, electoral pacts have been a feature of the general electoral landscape, usually between Fine Gael and Labour. Further in 1989 there was a pact between Progressive Democrats and Fine Gael and in 1997 and 2007, somewhat of a pact between Progressive Democrats and Fianna Fáil. Electoral pacts are not necessarily all good for the parties involved. The involvement of party A in a pact with party B, may leave some people less inclined to support A or B. However parties obviously judge there to be more upside than downside, given the prevalence of them.

Given that transfers are not in practice overly significant to the outcome in terms of seats, there can be a tendency to overrate the impact of pacts. However all Irish elections (except 1992) up to 2011 resulted in a government with a very slim overall majority, so the ability to win or lose a few seats based on pacts is quite significant. There are probably up to three or four seats in each election where the outcome would have been different in the absence of a pact. A different outcome in those would have changed the course of history, as there could have been a different government. In particular the short lived Fianna Fáil minority government following the February 1982 election could have had a much longer life span, but for the effect of pacts. In February 1982, seats in Carlow Kilkenny, Cork North West and Dublin North were impacted against Fianna Fáil by pacts and if they had fallen the other way, Fianna Fáil would have had a slim overall majority of two as opposed to being a minority of four. Given the various debacles associated with that government, memorably christened as GUBU by the former Labour deputy Conor Cruise O'Brien, that could have proved to be a significant change.

Pacts between Fine Gael and Labour have been helpful in those parties winning a majority of the seats in a number of three and five seat constituencies, most notably Carlow Kilkenny, Cork North West, Cork South West, Kerry South, Tipperary North and Wexford. They have also been relevant from time to time in a number of Dublin constituencies such as Dublin North, Dublin North Central, Dublin North West, Dublin South Central and Dún Laoghaire. The effect of Fine Gael/Labour pacts has probably lessened in elections of the 21st century. The effect of the pact may be more in the sense of restrained competition between the two parties in the relevant constituencies, such that their key candidates finish after the first count in the appropriate positions. While Fine Gael have probably won more seats based on the pact, the pact has been critical for Labour in moving its critical mass of deputies from a figure near 10 to a figure near 15. Therefore its proportional effect on Labour Dáil strength is much greater.

Other pacts tended to involve the Progressive Democrats. Pact or not, the Progessive Democrat voter tended to lean Fine Gael from 1987 through 1992 and tended to lean Fianna Fáil in1997 and 2007. The result was a spectacular level of transfer, often as high as 70% towards the preferred partner when no candidate of the other remained to take transfers.[20] It is quite notable how Progressive Democrat voters were willing radically to shift their voting behaviour as to preferences. This is perhaps because they saw themselves as a party of government and their supporters were willing to back whatever major party they were currently aligned with. It is open to speculate that their latter day alliance with Fianna Fáil led to their demise, perhaps deferred to 2007 by the wretched performance by Fine Gael in the 2002 election.

Electoral pacts involving Fianna Fáil and Fine Gael as one side of the bargain are somewhat unbalanced. In most cases those parties have another candidate on an elimination and therefore on most transfers there is limited benefit to the pact partner. Conversely, where the other smaller party is eliminated, there is often no other candidate, so transfers tend to flow in significant amounts towards Fianna Fáil and Fine Gael. However smaller parties do on the few occasions that there is no further candidate from the major party pick up votes and in many cases this leads to an extra seat, significantly increasing their Dáil presence. There is therefore a symbiotic relationship in the pacts to date. It is less clear what benefit a pact between Sinn Féin and other anti-austerity parties and groups could have for the other parties, which may be why many of them are suspicious of it.

Conclusion

It is clear that there are established patterns of behaviour by supporters of different parties as to how they transfer their votes beyond their first preference. In the case of both Fianna Fáil and Fine Gael, the trend is to transfer to other candidates of the same party and usually there is one available. In the case of other parties and independents, it is unusual that they have a further candidate of the same party and there are individual patterns outlined above. Contrary to general impression, the level of non transferable votes is generally not high after a transfer, with exceptions where one of Fianna Fáil, Fine Gael or Sinn Féin is eliminated and the only further choice is the others of them. Transfer pacts have however had a clear impact on the destiny of a number of seats.

References in Chapter 13

[1]   Multiple eliminations happened in all but 2 constituencies in 2016, all but 2 in 2011 and all but 8 in 2007.

[2]   The percentages are stated after excluding distributions where no Fianna Fáil candidate was available to take transfers. The poor internal cohesion rate in 2011 almost certainly cost Fianna Fáil a couple of seats in constituencies where they had two candidates, with realistically one seat available. For example in Cork East, Kevin O'Keeffe finished 649 votes behind Sandra McLellan of Sinn Féin on the final count. On the internal Fianna Fáil transfer he received 55.56% of the votes (2,666 votes) from his running mate. If instead he had got about 70% (3,358) of the votes he would have closed the gap on McLellan, although this would have had a knock on effect on transfers to others.

[3]   By contrast in 2002, the transfer percentage in later counts averaged at 64.7%. However first count surpluses transferred at average 63.7% and candidates who had large surpluses on the first count transferred at average 62.5%. For reasons associated with the decline of Fianna Fáil, there are no meaningful comparators for 2011 or 2016.

[4]   In the 2002 general election also, Jimmy Deenihan of Fine Gael ousted Dick Spring of Labour on the basis of favourable Fianna Fáil transfers from a candidate local to Deenihan. In Limerick West outgoing Fine Gael deputies Dan Neville and Michael Finucane were separated by 36 votes on the first count. Fianna Fáil surpluses favoured Finucane and put him ahead by 5 , but Neville managed to win by one vote, based on a few extra transfers from the collective elimination of the minor candidates.

An interesting transfer anomaly occurred in Roscommon in both February 1982 and 1987, which shows why raw transfer statistics, as commonly used in works on a particular election, need a health warning. In both of those elections two Fianna Fáil candidates had surpluses and in each case 100% of their transfers went to the two Fine Gael candidates, again determining which of them was to be elected. This seems to be the only case of one party getting 100% of the transfers on all transfer events in a constituency.

[5]   The Fine Gael pattern in the 1981 election was quite ragged, with an average internal transfer rate of 78.3%. However by November 1982, Fine Gael was virtually matching Fianna Fáil rates, with an average rate of internal transfer of 84%.

[6]   Examples of strong general election transfers from Fine Gael to Labour include Carlow Kilkenny 1981 (88.68%), Wexford 1981 (82.05%), Carlow Kilkenny November 1982 (84.03%), Dún Laoghaire November 1982 (84.09%), Kildare November 1982 (79.53%), Tipperary North November 1982 (86.29%), Dublin North Central 1997 (52.4%), Dublin South Central 1997 (51.86%), Dublin South East 1997 (80.24%), Kerry South 1997 (66.35%), Kerry South 2002 (49.5%) Dublin North West 2007 (69.61%) and Dublin North East 2011 (58.49%).

Many of these transfers have enabled Labour to take seats that they would not have taken without the high level of transfers.

[7] In a number of cases, a Labour candidate was eliminated along with another candidate, so it is impossible to tell how the Labour votes were transferred. Further, as noted, eliminated candidates have usually picked up a number of transfers, which means that their transferred vote is a mixture of original Labour first preferences and votes acquired from other sources, often of the left. However usually the "contamination" is minor and it has been ignored for purposes of this analysis.

[8] There were 19 instances of Labour transfers to other Labour candidates in 1981, because the party ran a lot of candidates in that election, many of whom had very small numbers of transfers to give to other Labour candidates. Indeed the party may have lost seats in that election on account of the excessive number of candidates it ran. For example in Dublin North, it had three candidates and lost to Nora Owen(see chapter 18 for detail).

[9] The same problem of poor internal Labour transfers can be seen in Cork East, which tends to have a sharp north south split. They also seem to have issues with low internal transfers in the Limerick East constituency, possibly driven by the somewhat combative history of the separate Labour Party and Democratic Socialist Party, before their merger.

[10] Prior to 2007, there are no recorded instances of Labour/Sinn Féin transfers excepting a transfer of 16% to the H Block candidate in Louth in 1981 (with 41% and 30% respectively to Fine Gael and Fianna Fáil) and a few transfers of small numbers of votes in the 2002 general election. In the 2007 general election, transfers to Sinn Féin ranged between 18% in Meath West to 8% in Louth and were significantly adrift of transfer levels to Fine Gael.

[11] Exceptions included the 31% transfer rate to Sandra McLellan, facilitating her election in Cork East (these being transfers from a "south" candidate to another "south" candidate). Other exceptions were a 26% transfer rate in Cavan Monaghan and a 22% transfer rate in Sligo-North Leitrim.

[12] High rates of transfer from Labour to Fianna Fáil are seen for significant transfers (those where Labour has over 1,000 votes) in Cork SW 1981 (30%), Longford Westmeath 1981 (31%), Louth 1981 (30%), Cork North West February 1982 (28%), Cork South West February 1982 (28%), Cork North West November 1982 (32%), Kerry North 1982 (48%), Dublin North Central 1987 (26%), Dublin North East 1987 (30%), Meath 1987 (34%), Tipperary South 1987 (32%), Carlow Kilkenny 1992 (26%), Donegal NE 1992 (38%), Galway East 1992 (32%), Kerry North 1992 (39%), Cavan Monaghan 1997 (34%), Galway East 1997 (32%), Tipperary North 2002 (43%), Tipperary North 2007 (32%), Tipperary South 2007 (29%) and Wicklow 2007 (29%). It is worth noting however that in two constituencies, Kerry North and Tipperary North, which were marginal in terms of producing an outcome 1 Fianna Fáil, 1 Fine Gael and 1 Labour, that transfers from Labour to Fianna Fáil have been quite high in many of the elections where Labour transfers were available in those constituencies.

Indeed a poor rate of transfer from Spring Labour to Deenihan Fine Gael in November 1982 at 51% cost Jimmy Deenihan a seat on that occasion, a position spectacularly remedied by him in the 1987 election.

[13] The average is elevated by a few cases where the only choice on Sinn Féin transfers was Fianna Fáil and/or Fine Gael. The two general elections were different in that in general election 2007, four Sinn Féin candidates were elected and four were "last man standing". By 2011, the position had improved such that 14 Sinn Féin candidates were elected and a further six were "last man standing". The rise in the level of non transferability of votes in 2011 is probably because on average Sinn Féin candidates were eliminated later in the counts and with less options to choose from, there was inevitably going to be higher non transferable votes.

[14] The two local elections were quite different however as far as Sinn Féin were concerned. In 2009, a significant number of Sinn Féin candidates (heading towards 70) were eliminated, with no other Sinn Féin candidate available. Generally their transfers were spread across a number of parties, principally from the left, including Labour. By 2014, transfers from Sinn Féin often arose from surpluses, generally on the first count and there were fewer examples of Sinn Féin transfers. In many instances other Sinn Féin candidates were available and they took a very high rate of transfer. Where other Sinn Féin candidates were not available, transfers tended to favour the more radical left and independents. The three established parties took very few transfers, with Labour doing particularly badly; where all or any of the three were the only destination for transfers on elimination, a huge proportion of the vote was non transferable. A key issue in 2014 was that often transfers from Sinn Féin arose as a result of a surplus on the first count, which gave rise for technical reasons already explained to no non transferable votes. Any aggregate picture of non transferable votes in that election will therefore distort the picture.

[15] There are a couple of LEAs in Dublin where an extra seat might have been obtained by Sinn Féin in 2014 with a further candidate most notably Ballymun LEA (Dublin), Mulhuddart LEA (Fingal) and Tallaght South LEA (South Dublin).

[16] For example in 1989, the two internal Sinn Féin transfers were at rates in the mid 60s% but with very small numbers of votes. In the limited instances where they occurred in the local elections of 2009 and the general election of 2011, they were in the mid 50s% (2009 average in 11 cases 55%; 2011 average in two cases 57%)

[17] In the 2007 general election, there was a second Green candidate in Dublin North and there were internal transfers at a rate of 61%; one transfer is not reliable to reach a conclusion however.

[18] Candidates who benefitted from Green transfers include Tony Gregory (Dublin Central), Joe Higgins (Dublin West), James Breen (Clare), Catherine Murphy (Kildare North) and Clare Daly (Dublin North).

[19] Labour candidates who benefitted substantially from Green transfers included Michael D Higgins (Galway West) at 61.88% in 2002 and 58.45% in

2007, Emmet Stagg (Kildare North) at 41.87% in 2002 and 28.19% in 2007, Kathleen Lynch (Cork North Central) at 38.67% in 2002 and 34.97% in 2007, Jan O'Sullivan (Limerick East) at 33.33% in 2002 and 42% in 2007 and the Labour candidates in Dublin South Central, Mary Upton and Eric Byrne at 49.85% in 2002 and 57.02% in 2007. Because the Labour party did so well in 2011, the Green transfers were less relevant, but it benefitted in a number of places including Carlow Kilkenny (32.62%), Clare (38.31%), Cork South Central (37.56%), Dublin South East (45.91%) and Louth (41.96%).

[20] The Progressive Democrats took seats such as Pat O'Malley in 1987 in Dublin West (FG transfers), Liz O'Donnell in 1997 in Dublin South (FF transfers) and Mary Harney in 2007 in Dublin Mid-West (FF transfers). There were also some near misses by the Progressive Democrats, notably with Michael McDowell, who missed out in 1997 and 2007 despite strong Fianna Fáil support in the form of transfers. Equally Fine Gael took seats helped by strong Progressive Democrat transfers in the 1987 to 1992 period and Fianna Fáil took seats in 1997 and 2007 helped by strong Progressive Democrat transfers, most notably the three seats taken in both Cork North Central and Cork South Central in 1997 and candidates such as GV Wright (1997, Dublin North).

CHAPTER 14

Persons Elected on the First Count

As this is the purest form of transfer by candidates, it is useful to look separately at this in terms of the three established parties. On a first count transfer, all other candidates (except in the relatively rare circumstances that two or three candidates are elected on the first count) are available to take transfers, so it is the purest measure of transfers. Over the course of eleven general elections 1981 to 2016 the following numbers of candidates were elected on the first count and a number of them had significant surpluses (in excess of 1,000 votes)

Election	No elected on first count	Surplus in excess of 1,000
1981	33	19
February 1982	41	19
November 1982	40	14
1987	24	13
1989	47	13
1992	42	24
1997	26	13
2002	24	8
2007	32	16
2011	21	12
2016	23	11

On average in each of the elections 32 candidates were elected on the first count, just under 20% on the basis of 165 seats (with TD number 166, the Ceann Comhairle being automatically returned). A majority of them represented Fianna Fáil. The number has reduced in the last 20 years. In most elections about a half of those have a substantial surplus, treated for this purpose to be a surplus in excess of 1,000.

It is useful to look at the pattern of transfers from one party candidate to other(s) of first count surpluses for each major party over the last 11 general elections. Where a party had one or two first count surpluses in an election, the evidence is regarded as inconclusive and "no meaningful data" is indicated. Some anomalous positions are disregarded. There are quite a number of cases where a candidate for a party has exceeded quota on the first count, but there are no party colleagues available to take transfers; these cases have also been disregarded. They arose in particular in elections where Labour (1992, 2011) experienced a "surge", but did not have other candidates in place to benefit. The levels of transfer indicated are probably closest to the true level of transfers within a party, without the distortions created by accumulated transfers and a smaller field of candidates to take transfers.

Fianna Fáil

Election	Range of percentage of transfers within party	General average
1981	69 to 95	more than 80
Feb 1982	78 to 95	mid 80's
Nov 1982	67 to 93	mid 80's
1987	74 to 89	high 70's
1989	62 to 93	mid 80's
1992	62 to 84	high 60's
1997	53 to 76	mid 60's
2002	47 to 74	low 60's
2007	45 to 81	mid 60's
2011	no meaningful data	
2016	36 to 66	mid 50's

Fine Gael

Election	Range of percentage of transfers within party	General average
1981	69 to 89	75
Feb 1982	70 to 98	80
Nov 1982	81 to 94	85
1987	no meaningful data	
1989	68 to 85	high 70's
1992	no meaningful data	
1997	55 to 70	Mid 60's
2002	no meaningful data	
2007	no meaningful data	
2011	42 to 70	60
2016	47 to 85	60

Labour

Election	Range of percentage of transfers within party	General average
1992	60 to 66.5	low 60's
2011	36 to 61	low 50's

Thus if there was a Fianna Fáil first count surplus of 1000 in 1981, anywhere between 690 to 950 votes would transfer on to other Fianna Fáil candidates, with an average transfer of more than 800 votes. With a similar Fianna Fáil surplus in 2007, 450 to 810 would transfer within the party, with an average transfer of in or around 650 votes.

There is a very clear pattern of a decline in inter party loyalty among voters who vote for the "star" candidate. This is clearly evident across all of the parties. There is also evidence of a decline in the number of candidates who exceed the quota and who get substantial surpluses. The prevailing reason for this is probably the increase in the number of parties and independents, making it harder for a candidate to exceed the quota; planning by parties to bring "star" candidates' votes a bit lower is also a factor, but possibly a lesser one.

Large first count surpluses and "leakage"

There are quite a number of examples over the years of candidates who had first count surpluses in excess of 4,000 in a general election and these give rise to a significant leakage of votes.[1] Leakage is the phenomenon where votes transfer to candidates from other parties and independents. Prominent examples are

Election	Candidate	Surplus	Percentage transferred within party	Leakage
1981	Haughey FF	9,520	84.92	1,436
1981	Collins G FF	6,478	94.97	326
1982 Feb	Haughey FF	7,983	89.89	807
1982 Nov	Haughey FF	6,421	93.43	422
1989	Ahern B FF	6,700	80.79	1,287
2007	Cowen B FF	7,186	67.04	2,368
2007	O'Dea W FF	10,852	61.30	4,200
2016	Healy-Rae M Ind	7,165	53.52	3,330

This is a loss of votes (the "leakage") to the party right at the start of a count, many of which goes to candidates of rival parties who end up either being elected or being the "last man standing". While in the cases with a 4,000 surplus, the leakage generally hasn't resulted in a loss of a seat, it has left some results closer than they might have been. One case which led to the loss of a seat was the 1992 leakage in Dublin Central by Bertie Ahern of 1,248 votes. Fianna Fáil failed to take a second seat on 1.96 quotas by a margin of 801 votes, which is a margin considerably less than the votes "leaked". This is discussed in terms of management below.

There is an unsophisticated view by some in politics that the easiest route to success is to have a candidate who gets a very big surplus and that candidate will then "drag" one or two more fellow candidates in on his surplus. While in practice large surpluses have not proved to be damaging to parties' prospects, in nearly all cases the party would in any event have got the number of seats it achieved, despite the large surplus. Having candidates accruing large surpluses is in practice an inefficient use of a party vote and any good planning will try and minimise this.

Managing a large surplus

It is sometimes the case that a party will try and manage a candidate anticipated to achieve a large surplus, to manage the surplus down. A good example where management might have delivered an extra seat (two instead of one) is the Fianna Fáil performance in Dublin Central in 1992 where the party had 39.28% or 1.96 quotas. To illustrate this, it is worth trying to estimate the number of second preferences given to each candidate where a number 1 vote was cast for Bertie Ahern in 1992 (ignoring "plumpers" of which there were probably a few). Ahern had 11,374 first preferences over 4,000 above the quota. The estimate of second preferences is based on the number of transfers actually allocated to each candidate out of the surplus

Candidate	Estimated number 2's ex Ahern	Actual transfer
Gregory Ind	1,998	719
Mitchell FG	778	280
Fitzpatrick FF	3,762	1,354
Bennett FF	4,143	1,491
Burke SF	261	94
McKenna Gn	202	73
Others x 4	228	82
Total	**11,372**	

It is possible for very popular candidates to ask the electorate not to give them a number 1 vote and to instead give the number 1 to another party candidate. This was famously done on a few occasions by the late Taoiseach

Dr Garret FitzGerald (Fine Gael) in Dublin South East. This is usually achieved by writing to the electorate in an area where the other party candidate(s) is/are relatively strong and asking electors as a personal favour to give their number 1 to the other candidate. Bennett was based south of the Liffey and Fitzpatrick in the west of the constituency and it could well have been possible to persuade approximately 2,000 Ahern voters in those areas to vote for Bennett and 2,000 for Fitzpatrick. This would have adjusted the first count to the position outlined below and also would have avoided Ahern having any material surplus (so that the lesser number of votes transferring to every other candidate would be immaterial). The adjustments add to the two lower Fianna Fáil candidates' votes the votes notionally diverted from Ahern and then subtract the transfer each of them actually accrued from Ahern, as the adjustment reduces his surplus to virtually nil. The adjusted first count for material candidates would have been:

Ahern FF	7,374 (-4,000)
Costello Lab	7,308
Gregory Ind	5,809
Mitchell FG	5,125
Fitzpatrick FF	3,838 (+2,000)
Bennett FF	3,087 (+2,000)

At the material count when Bennett was eliminated, the following is the projected position

Mitchell	5,909	(this is the 6,189 actual per the count, less 280 actually transferred from Ahern)
Fitzpatrick	4,224	(this is the 3,578 actual per the count plus 2,000 and less 1,354 actually transferred from Ahern)
Bennett	3,592	(this is the 3,083 actual per the count plus 2,000 less 1,491 actually transferred from Ahern)

If the pattern of Bennett's transfers had remained 70.8% FF, 12.1% FG and 17.1% non transferable, the transfers from Bennett would have given

Fitzpatrick +2,543 bringing his total to 6,767 and Mitchell +434 bringing his total to 6,343, thus producing a Fianna Fáil win by 400 votes rather than a loss by a margin of 800.[2]

References in Chapter 14

[1]   Other examples of significant surpluses are:

Election	Candidate	Surplus	Percentage transferred within party	Leakage
1981	Woods M FF	4,122	75.25	1,020
1981	Fitzgerald G FG	5,630	82.04	1,011
1982 Feb	Fitzgerald G FF	4,613	82.31	816
1982 Feb	Collins G FF	4,773	94.72	252
1982 Feb	Bruton J FG	4,094	79.36	845
1982 Nov	Collins G FF	4,770	92.60	353
1987	Ahern B FF	5,725	77.80	1,271
1987	Haughey C FF	4,401	89.07	481
1987	O'Malley D PD	4,089	74.15	1,057
1989	Brennan S FF	4,899	84.24	772
1989	Collins G FF	4,623	87.17	507
1992	Ahern B FF	4,093	69.51	1,248
1997	Ahern B FF	5,026	59.23	2,049
1997	O'Dea W FF	4,297	64.70	1,517
2002	Martin M FF	5,535	61.26	2,144
2002	Ahern B FF	4,075	55.58	1,810
2002	O'Dea W FF	4,840	63.39	1,772
2007	Ahern B FF	5,806	64.85	2,041
2011	Noonan M FG	4,653	62.35	1,752
2011	Kenny E FG	5,112	70.15	1,526

[2] In fact the projected position is probably unfavourable to Fianna Fáil. The 4,000 votes notionally re-directed to the two others are probably Fianna Fáil supporters and more likely to transfer within Fianna Fáil thus increasing the 70.8% rate of transfer on from Bennett to Fitzpatrick and the lack of a surplus from Ahern would have kept Gregory hunting for transferred votes later than in the actual count, thus diluting transfers for others.

CHAPTER 15
Transfers in Local Elections

Transfer patterns in local elections reflect the trends in general elections. However there are two obvious variations. In local elections and there is an obvious clue in the word "local", there is a tendency for many voters to vote for a candidate who is resident in their immediate neighbourhood and then to transfer to other local candidates. This results in strong transfers between candidates based in the same area of an LEA. This trend is most notable in very large rural LEAs such as Glenties LEA in West Donegal and Connemara LEA in Galway; it is much less a feature in large urban areas.[1]

A logical consequence of the stronger local pattern of voting is that transfers within parties between two or more candidates of the same party tend to be at a lesser rate than a general election. The weaker transfer pattern is partly because of the strength of local voting patterns, but it also reflects a greater tendency in local elections to vote for individuals rather than parties. Notwithstanding this, transfers at a significant level within Fianna Fáil (i.e from one Fianna Fáil candidate to another) and Fine Gael are still prevalent in local elections. Further in the 2014 local elections Sinn Féin demonstrated a significant level of internal cohesion, with a very strong rate of transfers where one Sinn Féin candidate had a surplus or was eliminated and another Sinn Féin candidate remained. The Labour party has often run multiple candidates in a LEA, but the internal rate of transfer between Labour candidates has been in too many cases quite abysmal and has led to seats not being gained. Smaller parties, most notably the Progressive Democrats occasionally ran more than one candidate, but again high transfer rates between two candidates of the same smaller party have proved elusive.

As with general elections, when assessing Fianna Fáil and Fine Gael transfers in local elections, there is nearly always another candidate of the same party and the predominant feature of interest is the percentage level of that transfer. For all other parties, there is generally no other party candidate available when one is eliminated, so the pattern to be examined is to which other parties those transfers go.

Other trends common in general elections are also replicated in local elections:

* a tendency for Green voters to transfer to other moderate left parties such as Labour, the Workers Party and independent socialists
* a tendency for voters for left parties other than Labour to transfer to other left parties including Sinn Féin
* a tendency for a high proportion of Fianna Fáil votes to become non transferable when there is no Fianna Fáil candidate left to take transfers .

There appears to be a somewhat higher level of non transferable votes generally on eliminations than would be the case in general elections, particularly where there is no continuing candidate of the same party. Further the general election pattern of relatively strong transfers between Fine Gael and Labour seems to be somewhat weaker in local elections.

1985, 1991 and 1999 local elections

The following is the pattern of transfers[2] within parties in these elections:

	1985	1991	1999
Fianna Fáil	c 70%	low 60%	low 50%
Fine Gael	low to mid 60s%	c 50%	c50%
Labour*	c 45%	c 43%	c 41%
Independents	c 30%	20-30%	20-25%
Prog Democrats*	-	40%	40%
Workers Party*[3]	-	mid 60s	-
Inter left [4]	-	-	20-40%

*relatively few examples

These rates generally are 10% or more less than rates in general elections in the years immediately before or after those elections.

2004 local elections

The 2004 local elections saw a relatively strong performance by Fine Gael and a weaker performance by Fianna Fáil. The Labour Party also did relatively well. Extensive sampling of transfer patterns in the 2004 local elections suggests a further decline in the level of transfers between candidates of the three main parties. Fianna Fáil levels seemed to average in the high 40's%, but they seemed to achieve slightly greater voter loyalty in the major urban centres, particularly Dublin City and Dún Laoghaire. Fine Gael rates of transfer between Fine Gael candidates were slightly lower at around 45%. Labour rates fell to about the high 30% level, but again rather better rates were achieved in the larger urban areas with an average of about 45%, not materially different from the other two major parties . Of course it was far more significant for Labour to achieve much better rates of transfer in urban Ireland, as this was where they tended to be most competitive for seats.

A number of smaller parties and groupings had a small number of second candidates and therefore a level of transfer between two party candidates. The level achieved by Sinn Féin was quite significant, coming out at over 60%. This was significantly better than any of the major parties. The 2004 local elections were the first occasion where a material number of LEAs had two Sinn Féin candidates.[5]

There was a growing tendency in the 2004 local elections for a rise in the volume of non transferable votes on eliminations, a trend also creeping-in in 1999. Even with Fianna Fáil candidates left in the race, in general at least 10% of Fianna Fáil vote transfers proved to be non transferable and from a Fianna Fáil point of view there are a disturbing number of instances where the level of non transferable votes exceed 20%, in cases where a Fianna Fáil candidate was available for transfers. This suggests a tendency to give a first preference to a single Fianna Fáil candidate but then to continue to other lowly placed candidates and not to give a preference to a further Fianna Fáil candidate. There is also a pattern with Fine Gael and Labour of a slightly greater volume of non transferable votes, but this is not as significant as with Fianna Fáil.

Where Fine Gael or Labour transfers were available and a candidate of both parties was still in the race, it was still fairly common in 2004 that the other party got 10% or more of the vote. Indeed there are only a few cases of Labour eliminations where Fine Gael got less than 10% of the transfers, even where a Labour candidate was available to take them. Further in the few cases where a Fine Gael candidate was eliminated with only a Labour candidate left to receive transfers, the Labour party tended to benefit at a rate of 30% and indeed as high as 55% in Dublin's North Inner City LEA. Similarly in the far more numerous cases where Labour was eliminated or elected but there was no Labour candidate available to take transfers, Fine Gael tended to benefit at a rate of around 30% rising to 53% in the Bandon and Mallow LEAS in Cork.

2009 and 2014 local elections

The patterns in these elections are discussed at greater length in chapter 16 "Transfers in Recent Elections". They do however show a levelling out in the ability of parties' candidates on a transfer to deliver transfers to fellow party candidates. A notable exception to this is Fine Gael in 2009, as in that local election Fine Gael managed to achieve an average percentage of transfer from one Fine Gael candidate to another in excess of 50%. Further in the case of Sinn Féin, there has possibly been a slight decline in the average level of transfer of votes as between Sinn Féin candidates. However it is clear that notwithstanding a small decline, the level of transfer achieved by Sinn Féin between party candidates in the 2014 local elections is not far short of 60% and is significantly better than any other party.

A notable feature of both the 2009 and 2014 local elections is that the level of transfers from one Fine Gael candidate to another probably on average exceeded the comparable percentage for Fianna Fáil. This is against a background where Fine Gael did exceptionally well in 2009 and relatively poorly in 2014 and may suggest a modern pattern that Fine Gael are slightly more effective in this regard.

Another notable feature seen widely for the first time in the 2014 local elections is that in very many cases another party did better on the transfers of a party's candidate, than did the party itself. So cases arose where for example on the transfer of votes from a Fine Gael candidate, other Fine Gael candidates accrued 30% of the transfers and Fianna Fáil candidates accrued 40% of the transfers. While this had happened in isolated cases in earlier local elections, 2014 is the first election where it was not automatically predictable that the major beneficiaries of a party's transfers would be other candidates of that party.

Variations in transfer patterns as between counties

In the local elections over the review period, it is evident that transfer patterns for all parties are weaker in some counties and rather stronger in others. Counties which seem to display rather weak patterns of transfers within the same party include Carlow, Cork City, Donegal, Kerry and Limerick City. Coherence within a party seems generally to be stronger in Cork County, Dublin City and Dún Laoghaire Rathdown. This may be an issue that merits somewhat further investigation by the larger parties. The pattern is not uniform for all parties and there are particular parties that don't seem to conform to the norm for a particular county.

References in Chapter 15

[1]   A good example of the apparently illogical effects of local transfer patterns is found in the 2004 local election in the Navan LEA in Co Meath. In that election the last seat was being contested by a Fine Gael and Fianna Fáil candidate, each of whom had a party candidate behind them who was duly eliminated. The Fianna Fáil transfers resulted in FG +170; FF +49 as between the two competitors. The Fine Gael transfers resulted in FF +158; FG +119. In the event the Fine Gael candidate won by roughly the margin by which he did better in those two transfers. This is likely due to local voting patterns.

[2]   As the pattern in local elections in the eighties and nineties is largely an issue only of historic interest, only limited random sampling has been done to reach the conclusions set out in this work. However it is still believed that these conclusions are reliable.

[3]   The (limited example) pattern for Workers Party in 1991 shows itself again in the case of the 2014 local elections where Sinn Féin achieved a high level of discipline. Therefore it seems possible for a more radical left party to achieve a high level of voter discipline between its candidates, but this feat eludes the Labour Party.

[4]   The 1999 local elections were perhaps the first local elections with a sizeable contingent of left wing candidates including Sinn Féin, Green Alliance, Workers Party and Socialist Workers. Candidates for these parties were invariably eliminated with no fellow candidate available to take transfers. There was a tendency in these cases for transfers in the order of 20 - 40% to accrue to other left parties.

[5]   In the 2004 local elections, two other groupings, Independent Fianna Fáil based in Donegal and the Progressive Democrats in their last local elections achieved much poorer transfers between their own candidates at levels of about 35% and 25% respectively.

CHAPTER 16
Transfers in Recent Elections

There is merit in examining the pattern of transfers shown in the five most recent elections, those from 2007 to 2016, as these are more indicative of modern trends. As there is in any event a different transfer pattern in general as opposed to local elections, it is appropriate to deal with these separately. Some of the patterns becoming evident in these five elections are likely to be mirrored in future elections and therefore it is possible to extrapolate some trends as to the likely future impact of transfers.

General Election 2007

Fianna Fáil
- Fianna Fáil performed exceptionally well in this election and consequently more cases of Fianna Fáil transfers arose from first count surpluses, rather than later surpluses or eliminations
- In all types of transfers, the average Fianna Fáil transfers to other Fianna Fáil candidates were in the high 60% range. However notably on average first count Fianna Fáil surpluses transferred on to other Fianna Fáil candidates at about a 65% rate, transfers to other Fianna Fáil candidates on elimination were at almost 70% and transfers on of Fianna Fáil derived surpluses were at 78%. Thus the better polling Fianna Fáil candidates who exceeded quota on the first count had significantly less voter loyalty to Fianna Fáil than lower polling candidates, particularly bearing in mind that there are no non transferable votes on the first count, whereas eliminations involve a "contaminated" vote.
- There were few non-transferable votes in cases where there was a continuing Fianna Fáil candidate. In the few cases where there were none, the levels were usually quite low, but in most of those cases, the Progressive Democrats, then in government with Fianna Fáil, took a sizeable number of transfers.
- There is no clear pattern of where other votes not transferred to Fianna

213

Fáil went. It wasn't however unusual for Fine Gael to get of the order of 20% of Fianna Fáil transfers, thus showing some propensity of Fianna Fáil voters to pass on votes to Fine Gael in rather greater numbers than past patterns demonstrated.

Fine Gael

- Fine Gael performed reasonably well in the 2007 general election, recovering 20 seats from its 2002 general election disaster. The vast majority of Fine Gael transfers arose from eliminations of other Fine Gael candidates with only a few examples of first count surpluses.
- The average transfer rate from a Fine Gael candidate to another Fine Gael candidate seemed to be of the order of 65%, but the average is affected by a few cases where there was substantial leakage to Labour, likely based on geography.[1] In practice the normal average transfer rate seemed to be mid 60's, a couple of percent lower than obtained with Fianna Fáil.
- In the few instances there were surpluses, the rate of transfer was very impressive at over 75%.
- In the few situations where there was no available Fine Gael candidate to take Fine Gael transfers, Labour were strong beneficiaries.
- Non transferable votes on the elimination of a Fine Gael candidate were uniformly low, usually at far less than 10%. In the one instance in Galway West, where neither Labour nor Fine Gael could benefit, non transferable votes reached an effective 60% level with Progressive Democrats and Fianna Fáil splitting the balance 2:1.

Labour

- There were 25 cases in which Labour transfers were relevant in the 2007 general election, all arising from eliminations.
- In the five instances where Labour had a further candidate, an average of 44% transferred to another Labour candidate, considerably lower than the other two main parties.
- In most cases where there was no available Labour candidate, but there was a Fine Gael candidate, transfers accrued to Fine Gael at rates ranging from 21% to 66% and Fine Gael was the key beneficiary of the Labour transfers. The average rate of transfer from Labour to Fine Gael was higher however than transfers within Labour. Thus curiously Fine Gael

did better from Labour transfers where no Labour candidate remained, than the average Labour candidate would have done.

- Where there was a strong other left candidate, particularly a Green candidate, Labour transfers accrued to that candidate, often at a better rate than Fine Gael. This trend was particularly noticeable in places such as Carlow Kilkenny and Dublin South where the Greens won a seat.
- Transfers from Labour to Fianna Fáil were at best in the high teens and there were virtually no Labour transfers to Sinn Féin.
- Non transferable votes on Labour eliminations averaged about 10%.

Sinn Féin
- Sinn Féin probably performed below expectations in the 2007 general election. Sinn Féin ran one candidate per constituency in almost all constituencies in 2007. Four were elected and four were "last man standing".
- In every other case there were transfers on the elimination of a Sinn Féin candidate, where there was no Sinn Féin candidate to benefit. The votes available were mainly in the 1,000 to 2,500 range. The average non transferability level was a lowly 15%, so that the vast majority of the votes transferred on elsewhere, contrary to what might be perceived about Sinn Féin votes.[2] This level of non transferability is consistent with what happened in 2002.
- There were a variety of beneficiaries of Sinn Féin transfers, rarely at a level of greater than 40%. In the majority of cases, where there was a candidate of the left (Green, Labour, People before Profit or Socialist), that candidate was the greatest beneficiary.
- Even where Fianna Fáil or Fine Gael were the only potential material beneficiaries of Sinn Féin transfers, one or other of them got a reasonable number of transfers. Local circumstances influenced which of them got more transfers from Sinn Féin. It is possible that the relative success of stronger Fianna Fáil candidates contributed to a lesser number of transfers from Sinn Féin accruing to Fianna Fáil by way of comparison with Fine Gael, as often the strong Fianna Fáil candidates were already elected before Sinn Féin transfers became available.
- The relatively level nature of transfers from Sinn Féin across a range of parties seemed to result in little relative benefit to any particular candidate.

Green Party

The Green Party did very well in the 2007 general election and secured six seats in Dáil Eireann. They only ran a second candidate in one constituency and secured a credible 61% transfer rate from that candidate to the other Green candidate. In all the other cases, transfers became available on the elimination of the sole Green candidate. The principal beneficiary of these transfers was the Labour Party, often securing in excess of 30% of the vote. Indeed in a number of critical constituencies such as Dublin South Central, Galway West and Kildare South, the Labour Party secured in excess of 50% of Green transfers, assisting it to take seats in those constituencies. Fine Gael was the other major beneficiary, with rates of transfer in the mid to high 20% range quite usual. Neither Fianna Fáil nor Sinn Féin were material beneficiaries of Green votes, each taking about an average 10%. The level of non transferable votes was also somewhat less than 10% in most cases.

Independents

There is some evidence in the 2007 general election of a tendency for independent candidates to transfer to each other. However the average rate of transfer was less than 20%, so the transfers were somewhat meaningless in terms of electing candidates. The highest rate of transfers to other independents when one was eliminated was 39%, this being on the elimination of Cieran Perry in Dublin Central. The independent candidates elected in the 2007 general election in any event finished in the "leaders' enclosure" after the first count, with the exception of Finian McGrath, who closed a significant gap in Dublin North Central, but entirely on the basis of transfers from Sinn Féin, Green Party and Labour.

There were a number of constituencies where the last independent in the race was eliminated and the pattern of transfers when that happened was very mixed. There were cases where each of Fianna Fáil, Fine Gael, Labour, Green Alliance and Sinn Féin were the principal beneficiary.

Smaller parties

A number of smaller parties and groupings contested the 2007 elections including the Progressive Democrats, the Workers Party, the Socialists, the Christian Solidarity Party and Fathers Rights and Responsibilities. In many cases it is difficult to analyse how their votes transferred as they generally fared very badly and their candidates were often eliminated as part of a collective elimination. This was also an issue with independents.

In the case of the Progressive Democrats, the most notable feature was the strength of transfers to Fianna Fáil, their then government partner. Transfers to Fianna Fáil when a Progressive Democrat candidate was eliminated ranged from 35% to 60%. Curiously on the two occasions where a Progressive Democrat was available to receive transfers from another Progressive Democrat candidate, the rates of transfer were respectively a poor 34% and 25%. The party was therefore able to persuade its supporters to transfer to Fianna Fáil at rather better rates than it could achieve between its own candidates. Fine Gael also did relatively well from Progressive Democrat transfers in 2007, generally achieving transfers in the 20% range.

Where there was a visibility on Workers Party and Socialist transfers, there was a strong pattern of them transferring left to Labour, Sinn Féin, the Greens and other left independents. Often there were two such groups left each getting transfers in the 20% or 30% range. Non transferable votes were of the order of 10%.

There was little evidence about Christian Solidarity or Fathers Rights and Responsibilities transfers as their candidates all fared very poorly and were the subject of collective eliminations.

General Election 2011

Fianna Fáil
* This was a disastrous election for Fianna Fáil and this was reflected in unprecedented transfer patterns
* Even on a much reduced and arguably "core" vote, transfer rates from Fianna Fáil to Fianna Fáil, nearly all on eliminations, were in the 50% range, a significant decline. The balance spread across a number of parties without much net benefit to any and there were up to 10% non transferable votes.
* In 10 constituencies, the only or last Fianna Fáil candidate was eliminated. This produced a high level of non transferable votes ranging from 13% to 53%. Fine Gael picked up about 23% of those transfers.

In a few constituencies, such as Kerry South and Tipperary North, there were remaining Fianna Fáil "gene pool" candidates when a Fianna Fáil candidate was eliminated and they got high levels of transfers.

Fine Gael
- This was an exceptionally good election for Fine Gael, but they had surprisingly few transfer events, as they avoided too many surpluses on first count and had relatively few eliminations.
- The transfer rate to other Fine Gael candidates on the relatively few Fine Gael first count surpluses was surprisingly low.[3] On elimination related transfers, the transfer rate within Fine Gael was considerably better, with nearly all being significantly over 60% and averaging 67.5%. Among the highest rates were two separate transfers in Dublin South Central of 80% and 79% respectively; your author was director of elections in that constituency.
- There was a tendency with many Fine Gael transfers for Labour to take a good percentage, generally in the mid to high teens. Labour transfers accounted for much of the Fine Gael leakage.
- Non transferable votes on a Fine Gael elimination were generally very low.

Labour
- Labour did extremely well in 2011 and more interestingly for the first time, there was some degree of vote management by Labour.
- Unlike any previous election, Labour often had a second candidate available to take transfers and percentage transfer rates to other Labour candidates varied from 36% (a north to south transfer in Cork East) to 67%. This was a significantly greater level of internal loyalty than the Labour party would have had in most previous experience. It was still somewhat short of what the other three main parties can achieve.
- Labour had relatively few candidates who exceeded quota on the first count, which meant few votes were wasted on surpluses.
- Generally in the relatively few (by Labour standards) cases where no further Labour candidate was available, Fine Gael were the major beneficiaries at 30% to 40%. However some strong left candidates, including the Sinn Féin deputy elected in Cork East, also got significant Labour transfers. Fianna Fáil generally got single digit percentages.

- There were relatively few non transferable votes where other Labour candidates were available. Where there were no continuing Labour candidates, non transferable votes were sometimes (but not always) quite high, heading towards the 20-30% range.

Sinn Féin

- Sinn Féin also ran a candidate in nearly every constituency in 2011. The success rate improved to 14 elected and six more as "last man standing", resulting in less samples of transfers
- There were only two cases of internal transfers between two Sinn Féin candidates, Carlow Kilkenny and Mayo, at the nearly identical rate of 56.88% and 58.57% respectively with 5% non transferability. This is an impressive rate of transfer and both were in geographically large constituencies
- The level of non transferable votes was somewhat higher than in 2007 at a general level of about 22%. However in three constituencies where the Sinn Féin vote was relevant only to sorting out the election of remaining Fine Gael and Fianna Fáil candidates, the level of non transferable votes was heading towards 50%.
- Labour and left leaning independents were the main beneficiaries of Sinn Féin transfers and the levels received were often in the 40% + bracket, making it more likely that they could be meaningful
- In most cases Fine Gael benefitted a lot more than Fianna Fáil from Sinn Féin transfers, almost certainly reflecting Sinn Féin voters' views on the outgoing government headed by Fianna Fáil.
- The pattern of transfers and non transferable votes from Sinn Féin was therefore somewhat different from what happened in 2007, making projecting future patterns more difficult.

Green Party

The 2011 election was a very traumatic experience for the Green Party as it lost all its Dáil representation. Consequently every single candidate was eliminated and their votes distributed to other parties. The principal beneficiaries of their votes, where the transfers can be analysed, were the Labour Party who got about an average one third of the transfers. Fine Gael did nearly as well with close to an average 30% of the transfers. About 10% of the transfers went to Fianna Fáil, the Greens' then recent government partners, Sinn Féin received about 6% or 7% and about 10% were non transferable. Despite a markedly poorer performance by the Greens, the transfer patterns were remarkably similar to what obtained in 2007.

Independents

A clear pattern beginning to emerge in the 2011 general election was that independents had a propensity to transfer to each other at quite high percentage rates. Indeed quite a number of rates of transfer to other independents at over 40% can be noted. However the average pattern is misleading, as when it came to the elimination of independents, who had a significant number of first preferences, transfer rates to other independents were generally down around the 20% level.[4] Therefore the high rate of transfers between independents in 2011 was mainly from independents who got a couple of hundred votes and those "minor" independents did indeed have a propensity to transfer their votes to other independents. Thus there was clearly a type of voter who was prepared to give a first preference to a "no hope" candidate and then to give further preferences to other similar candidates. However ultimately when all this vote coalesced together as part of the vote of the last independent, the votes dispersed widely on the elimination of that independent.

In two constituencies, Louth and Wicklow there were multiple separate eliminations of independents, which showed the trend of weakening loyalty as the number of independents was whittled down. In Louth, the elimination of the lowest polling independent of a series of eight produced a transfer rate to other independents of 66%. By the time of elimination of the last independent, the rate had dwindled to 22% with a fairly progressive downward trend. Similarly in Wicklow, the elimination of the lowest ranking independent produced transfers of 66% to other independents but successive eliminations reduced these transfer percentages to 52%, 45%, 39%, 27%, 27%, 33%, 36% and 18%.

It is also notable that the fourteen independents elected in 2011 all did so from within the "leaders' enclosure", except for John Halligan. Indeed a number of independents such as Shane Ross (Dublin South), Michael Lowry (Tipperary North) and Mick Wallace (Wexford) achieved a significant surplus on the first count. The perceived success of independents in 2011 was far more due to the strong first preference performance of many of them, than any success due to strong transfer patterns between them.

Smaller Parties

A number of smaller parties and groupings contested the 2011 elections including the People Before Profit Alliance, the Socialists, the Workers Party, the United Left Alliance, the Christian Solidarity Party, People's Candidate CPPC, New Vision and Fis Nua.

The People Before Profit Alliance, Socialists, Workers Party and United Left Alliance were all left leaning groups. Their transfers benefitted Labour, Sinn Féin and independent left candidates. Unlike 2007, the Greens did not benefit from those transfers, possibly because in many cases the Greens were already eliminated. Usually two or more groupings would benefit and usually in the 20% to 30% range. The level of non transferable votes was generally less than 10%.

There are limited examples of Christian Solidarity transfers and these tended to benefit Fianna Fáil and Fine Gael. In cases where Fis Nua transfers can be seen, there is no clear pattern. Generally however Christian Solidarity, People's Candidate CPPC and Fis Nua performed badly and were eliminated as part of a collective elimination.

General election 2016

Fianna Fáil

There were 36 occasions in the 2016 general election where it was possible to measure the destination of Fianna Fáil transfers. Because Fianna Fáil adopted a minimalist candidate strategy and did rather better than expected, there were a significant number of cases where no other Fianna Fáil candidate was available to receive transfers. This included nine first count surpluses with no Fianna Fáil candidate available to take the available transfers.

Where other Fianna Fáil candidates were available, the rate of transfer averaged about 55%, a little less than within Fine Gael and a lot less than within Sinn Féin. Most such transfers were in the 50% to 59% range.[5]

In cases where no other Fianna Fáil candidate remained, a sizeable proportion, averaging 35%, of the available transfers (excepting first count surpluses) were non transferable. A notable beneficiary of Fianna Fáil transfers where no Fianna Fáil candidate was available, was Fine Gael. In all these cases (bar Tipperary where Fine Gael failed to take a seat) it received 20% or more of Fianna Fáil transfers and benefitted at over 40% in Cork South Central and Wexford. Labour and Sinn Féin generally did poorly from Fianna Fáil transfers. Candidates outside the main parties were the other significant beneficiaries of Fianna Fáil transfers.

Fine Gael

There were 28 occasions in the 2016 general election where it was possible to measure the destination of Fine Gael transfers. Unlike Fianna Fáil there were only a few instances where there was no other Fine Gael candidate available to receive transfers.

Where other Fine Gael candidates were available, the rate of transfer within Fine Gael averaged about 59%, a little more than within Fianna Fáil and a lot less than within Sinn Féin. Most such inter Fine Gael transfers were in the 50% to 65% range.[6] Where Labour was available as a beneficiary, it attracted at least 10% of Fine Gael transfers. In both Dublin Bay North and Kildare South, Labour took 58% of Fine Gael transfers; however its first preference vote was not enough to benefit from this in either case. Fianna Fáil was also a significant beneficiary of Fine Gael transfers in cases where no Fine Gael remained to benefit. This mirrored a pattern also seen in favour of Fine Gael, where no Fianna Fáil candidate remained. This seems to be an evolving trend in Irish politics.

Labour

The Labour Party fared very poorly in the 2016 election and therefore there were many instances where its candidate was eliminated and transfers became available. There were only two instances where another Labour party candidate remained to benefit from transfers, Dublin South West and Louth and the average rate of transfer was a poor 33%, typical of many past Labour performances.

In every other case of a Labour elimination, Fine Gael was available to benefit and it did so by an average of 53%[7] of the available transfers, a rate which compared very favourably with its own internal rate of transfer. Other established parties generally did not benefit from Labour transfers. In a number of instances however independents and minor parties took a share of transfers in the 30% range.

Sinn Féin

The most notable feature of Sinn Féin transfers in the 2016 general election was the high level of transfers within the party and the very high level of non transferable votes when no Sinn Féin or other left candidate was available. It is also notable that Sinn Féin were not particularly transfer friendly in 2016 with candidates in Galway West and Longford-Westmeath being displaced from the leaders' enclosure in later counts and candidates in Dublin Bay South, Dublin West, Meath East and Wexford failing to make much progress against candidates for parties to whom there was evident voter resistance.

Where other Sinn Féin candidates were available, the rate of transfer averaged about 76%, far superior to any other party. There is thus an extraordinary internal discipline within Sinn Féin. A number of such transfers were in the 80% range, with poorer levels in Dublin and the two county constituency of Sligo-Leitrim. The highest level was almost 89%, being the transfer of Gary Doherty in Donegal. However the management of that transfer was poor as the bulk of it went to Pearse Doherty causing him to exceed the quota, with very little going to Pádraig MacLochlainn, who ended up losing his seat by a narrow margin.

Where no Sinn Féin candidate was available to receive transfers, there was a notably high level of non transferable votes, averaging about 45% and going as high as an effective 79% in Cork North Central when Sinn Féin voters were asked to choose between two Fine Gael and one Labour candidate. Generally Fianna Fáil, Fine Gael and Labour did poorly from Sinn Féin transfers, with Fianna Fáil faring best followed by Fine Gael and Labour. In the few instances where candidates from other parties of the left remained in contention, they benefitted significantly from Sinn Féin transfers.[8]

Green Party

There were over 20 occasions in the 2016 general election where Green Party transfers could be reviewed. The general pattern was that they transferred in various different ways and were not really relevant to the outcome of any contest. The older patterns where Labour did quite well and Fine Gael moderately well were still evident but to a somewhat lesser degree than previously. Most transfers to Labour were of the order of the low 20% range and Fine Gael tended to average high teens. Fianna Fáil and Sinn Féin did less well on Green transfers. Where there were credible candidates outside the four established parties, they often took the largest share of the Green transfers.

Other Left Parties

There were about thirty instances in the 2016 general election of transfers being available from other left parties, principally the Socialist Party and People before Profit. In nearly every case, Sinn Féin was available to take those transfers and the most striking feature was that most of the transfers to Sinn Féin were at a rate of 33% or less, a seemingly low figure for Sinn Féin transfers from the left. Only three constituencies, Dublin North West, Dublin South West and Limerick City showed higher rates of transfer from other left to Sinn Féin. This may be a material contributing factor to Sinn Féin not being very transfer friendly. It seems evident that supporters of other left parties did not particularly like Sinn Féin.

Where other left parties apart from Sinn Féin were available on a left transfer, they did very well, sometimes at rates over 50%. Generally Fianna Fáil, Fine Gael and Labour did poorly on these transfers. There was a propensity to quite high non-transferable rates from other left candidates with about a third of the cases showing non-transferable votes of 20% or more.

Social Democrats

The Social Democrats ran relatively few candidates, but quite a number of them were eliminated with in excess of 2,000 votes. They were thus in a position to contribute substantially to the transfer pool. The most notable feature of their transfers was that they went in substantial numbers, often around 40% to 50% to parties outside the principal four. The next most significant beneficiary was the Labour Party, who generally benefitted in percentages in the high teens. The three other principal parties generally ranged around the 10% level each, but there are some notable deviations from this pattern. Generally about 10% of their votes proved to be non-transferable.

Renua

There were about 20 instances of transfers from Renua candidates, all of whom (with the exception of Billy Timmins in Wicklow) were eliminated. As all of the prominent Renua personnel were ex Fine Gael, it might have been assumed that Fine Gael would be the main beneficiary of their transfers. However in practice each of Fine Gael and Fianna Fáil benefitted to a similar extent with broadly 20%+ of the transfers each. As with the Social Democrats, other parties (outside the principal 4) were generally the largest beneficiaries. Sinn Féin and Labour fared relatively poorly. On average about 11% of Renua votes proved to be non transferable.

Independents

There were close to 100 instances of independent transfers in the 2016 general election and they show a very clear pattern of transfers to other independents at a rate averaging very close to 30%. Indeed an analysis of transfers from independents who had more than 1,000 votes and those who had less than 1,000 votes shows very little difference in the average percentage rate of transfer. Thus the 2016 election seems to establish a preference for independent voters to transfer to other independents, in the same way as party voters transfer to their own party, but at a somewhat lower rate than might be the case within parties. The rate does however compare quite favourably with the poor cohesion within Labour, although Labour comparator examples in 2016 were scarce. The highest rate of transfer noted from an independent with over 1,000 votes was the 53.8% from Niamh Kennedy in Donegal to other independents (although the inter independent transfers in Kerry from Michael Healy Rae, largely to his brother were at a slightly higher level).

There are by contrast relatively few instances where independent voters transfer to other parties at a rate of greater than 30% and transfers from independents at that level were more to parties of the left, including Sinn Féin. Transfers to Fianna Fáil, Fine Gael and Labour were not favoured by voters for independent candidates and in many cases those parties each received less than 10% of available transfers. The Labour Party did particularly badly with transfers from independent voters.

Local Elections 2009

Fianna Fáil
- Fianna Fáil did poorly in the 2009 local elections, losing 84 seats and falling behind Fine Gael by number of seats for the first time.
- However the rate of transfer between Fianna Fáil candidates levelled off in 2009 and was at a level similar to 2004, despite the drop in the Fianna Fáil vote. Transfer rates in most LEAs between Fianna Fáil candidates were in the range 40% to 59%, with comparatively few instances falling outside that range. The overall average seemed to be in the region of 50%, with somewhat better transfer patterns in urban areas and somewhat worse in rural Ireland.
- Another notable change in 2009 was that relatively few Fianna Fáil candidates achieved a quota on the first count and there were also few examples of quotas on later counts where there was a material surplus available for other Fianna Fáil candidates.

Fine Gael
- Fine Gael did well in the 2009 elections, becoming the largest grouping in a large scale national election for the first time since 1927.
- There were about 160 instances where Fine Gael transfers happened in that election and in most cases a further Fine Gael candidate was available. While the internal transfer rate ranged from 22% to 90% (both in Donegal), the typical rates were in the 50%-59% range and the low 50%'s was probably the average rate. This was ahead of any other party, excepting Sinn Féin (who had relatively few examples of internal transfers).
- Labour did relatively well on Fine Gael transfers where they were in contention and account for a significant portion of the leakage.
- There were relatively few cases where no Fine Gael candidate remained to receive a transfer.

Labour

- Labour did well in the 2009 local elections, achieving over 130 seats.
- Transfers between Labour candidates, where they had more than one candidate, were comparatively good in 2009. In many urban LEAs Labour had a second candidate and like Fianna Fáil, transfer levels between them were broadly in the range 40% to 59%, with an average somewhere slightly short of 50%.
- It was somewhat less usual for Labour to have more than one candidate in rural Ireland and there levels of transfers between Labour candidates were somewhat poorer, averaging about 40%. This is perhaps due to the fact that the Labour party having two candidates was generally somewhat unusual and party supporters were not quite used to the discipline.
- Notwithstanding the occasional two candidate phenomenon, there were many instances in 2009 where Labour did not have another candidate available to take transfers, when a Labour candidate was eliminated. In those instances the major beneficiary was Fine Gael, often at rates in the 40% - 50% bracket. There were also instances where another left party was the beneficiary.
- Generally Fine Gael did well on a Labour party elimination, irrespective as to whether Labour had a continuing candidate or not. It was comparatively standard that Fine Gael benefitted at rates in excess of 20%, particularly outside the major urban areas.

Sinn Féin

- There were almost 100 occasions on which Sinn Féin votes were transferred in the 2009 local elections. This was therefore probably the first occasion on which there was a large sample of Sinn Féin transfers to consider.
- The vast majority of the transfers from Sinn Féin arose on an elimination, as it was quite unusual in 2009 for a Sinn Féin candidate to have a surplus.
- It was comparatively unusual in 2009 that another Sinn Féin candidate was available to take transfers from a fellow candidate. The average rate of transfers on the few occasions it happened was about 55%, which seems to be a decline on 2004 levels.

- In the vast majority of cases in 2009, no other Sinn Féin candidate was continuing, when a Sinn Féin elimination took place. Perception would normally be that in such a case there would be a large volume of non-transferable votes. However there are only 13 cases in about 100 examples of such transfers where the non transferable votes exceeded 40%, with twice as many at 20% or less. As discussed below many other parties got substantial Sinn Féin transfers.
- The Labour Party were comparatively quite popular in 2009 and there are quite a number of instances where the Labour party took a sizeable number of transfers from Sinn Féin, of the order of 30% or more, ranging as high as 45% in Cork City North West LEA.
- Other Left parties were occasionally the beneficiaries of high Sinn Féin transfers in 2009[9]
- There is quite a clear trend of independents being substantial beneficiaries of Sinn Féin transfers in 2009.[10]
- Even Fine Gael and Fianna Fáil got substantial transfers from Sinn Féin in 2009, although this seemed to be related to geographical loyalties in rural areas. More commonly they got transfers in the single figure percentages, with Fianna Fáil perhaps being marginally more attractive than Fine Gael.

Green Party
- The Green Party did poorly in the 2009 local elections. It was at the time the minority party in an unpopular government and was reduced to three seats in local government at county level.
- There were many instances in which Green transfers became available. The party most favoured was the Labour Party. It usually got over 30% of Green transfers and there were cases where rates were in the 40% and indeed 50% range.
- Fine Gael was also quite a strong beneficiary of Green transfers, often benefitting at rates in the region of 20%.
- Other left parties benefitted to a lesser extent than Labour or Fine Gael. The rate tended to be of the order of 10%. There was no great evidence however of significant vote transfer to Sinn Féin.
- Despite the fact that the Greens were in coalition with Fianna Fáil, there was little evidence of a material Green transfer to Fianna Fáil.

- there were two instances in Howth Malahide LEA (Fingal) and Drogheda East LEA (Louth) of a transfer between two Green candidates. This was at a rate of 42% and 38% respectively.

Independents and Smaller parties
- There was quite a lot of evidence of a propensity for independent candidates to transfer to each other in the 2009 local elections. The average rate appears to be of the order of 30%. However the vast majority of cases involved small numbers of transfers and these often were at rates of higher than 30%, thus distorting the average upwards. In practice the high rate of transfers generally did not produce seats for independents that would have not have been won anyhow.
- The vast majority of transfers by smaller parties came from parties of the left such as the Socialists and the Workers Party. There was a tendency for about 60% of those to go to other left candidates. The Labour Party seemed to be preferred, at rates of an average of about 28%. Other left parties and Sinn Féin averaged in the high teens. There are some isolated examples of a small left party running two candidates in the same LEA with transfer rates for them ranging from 27% for the Socialists in Swords LEA (Fingal) to 67% for the Socialists in Mulhuddart LEA, also in Fingal.

Non-transferable votes
Generally the level of non transferable votes in the 2009 local elections was around 10% or less. However greater levels were incurred as follows

Party	Circumstance
Fianna Fáil	Usually over 10%. At average effective 45% where no FF candidate remained
Fine Gael	As high as an effective 60% where no Fine Gael or Labour candidate remain
Sinn Féin	High level where only Fianna Fáil/Fine Gael remain
Other Left	Sometimes in 20-30% range

Local Elections 2014

It should be noted that the 2014 local elections were very unusual in that in most places there was either a dramatic increase in number of seats (largely on the east coast but also Cork County, Donegal, Galway and Kerry) or a significant decline in the number of seats (elsewhere). This arose because of a decision to try and make the size of each local authority broadly proportionate to population (with some floors and caps) and a decision to unify the counties of Limerick, Tipperary and Waterford in one authority. Generally therefore with the exception of Cork City and Mayo, there were significantly more or less seats than incumbent councillors.

There were some quite interesting transfer patterns which began to emerge in these elections, evident from a general analysis of transfers

- the only party to achieve significant coherence in internal transfers between two or more candidates was Sinn Féin, which achieved internal transfers at a level over 50% in about five sixths of cases
- for the two major parties, Fine Gael achieved an internal transfer rate which could be estimated in the high 40%s, whereas the typical Fianna Fáil rate was more like the low 40%s. This is a reverse of the historic pattern and occurred despite the fact that Fine Gael was perceived to have fared worse in the 2014 elections
- the pattern for Labour internal transfers was exceptionally poor, although they did relatively well where Fine Gael transfers were available with no remaining Fine Gael candidate
- there was a stronger pattern of transfers independent to independent. However the aggregate effectiveness of all that is dubious
- there were a significant number of instances where another party got a larger percentage share of transfers than fellow candidates of the transferring candidate
- the 2014 local elections saw the amalgamation of many existing areas into very big unwieldy districts. Very poor levels of internal party transfers characterised many of these areas including (North) Carlow, South and West Kerry, Kilkenny East, West Mayo, Roscommon and Ballymote-Tobercurry (Sligo) LEAs.

Fianna Fáil

- While Fianna Fáil got the highest percentage of first preference votes in the 2014 election and was seen to have done relatively well, the level of internal transfers between Fianna Fáil candidates, when one had a surplus or was eliminated, was relatively low by comparison with the past. This has to be a worrying issue for Fianna Fáil. The review of all transfers suggested that rates were on average in the 40% range, but in about two fifths of cases, it was less than that. Only about one quarter of cases resulted in an inter Fianna Fáil transfer of more than 50%. It would be reasonable to conclude that a typical Fianna Fáil level of transfer based on 2014 would be at a rate of about 43%, so that a Fianna Fáil candidate with 100 votes would transfer 43 to another Fianna Fáil candidate. Quite a number of Fianna Fáil candidates had surpluses on the first count and the transfer rates in those cases to other Fianna Fáil candidates , was even lower than the average pattern. It is also notable that on many Fianna Fáil transfers, even with other Fianna Fáil candidates available, the percentage of non transferable votes was in double digits.

- In a number of instances Fianna Fáil transfers were available with no continuing Fianna Fáil candidate; in most of those cases close to half the vote became non transferable with the rest scattering over the remaining candidates with no discernable pattern. There was a perceptible trend of Fine Gael doing quite well from Fianna Fáil transfers even when a Fianna Fáil candidate was in contention, with many transfers at over a 20% level. This is probably related to local patterns and the high number of Fine Gael candidates.

Fine Gael

- While Fine Gael did relatively poorly in the 2014 local elections, the internal transfer pattern as between Fine Gael candidates held up reasonably. Again the largest numbers were in the 40% range, but notably two fifths were in the 50% plus bracket, with less than a third in the 20% and 30% range. It would be reasonable to conclude that a typical inter Fine Gael transfer in 2014 would be at a rate of about 47%, so that a Fine Gael candidate with 100 votes would transfer 47 to fellow party candidates. Relatively few Fine Gael candidates exceeded the quota on the first count, but unlike Fianna Fáil, their transfers seem to stay loyal to the party in similar proportions on transfers at a later stage. On occasions Fianna Fáil got a substantial Fine Gael transfer.

231

- Labour do not appear to have benefitted much from Fine Gael transfers where another Fine Gael candidate was in contention. However there was a significant flow of transfers to Labour in circumstances where there was no continuing Fine Gael candidate, often at rates in the 40%s and 50%s. In the case of Killiney-Shankill LEA (Dún Laoghaire) the rate was 71%, a transfer which proved relevant to Labour retaining a second seat in that LEA, one of its few second seats in 2014. These transfer rates are significantly better than was achieved between Labour candidates.

Labour
- Labour did very poorly in the 2014 local elections being reduced to just over 50 seats. The level of internal Labour transfers in 2014 was quite poor and no doubt contributed to the huge loss of seats. Almost two fifths of internal transfers were in the 10%/20% range, with only slightly more than one tenth of cases producing a transfer at more than 50%. The prevailing rate could be estimated at around 33%, so that a typical Labour candidate with 100 votes would deliver 33 to a running mate.
- It was quite common in cases where there was a Labour candidate still in contention at the time of a Labour elimination, that another party or group got more transfers than remained within Labour. This happened on about a third of such occasions, with each of Fine Gael, Fianna Fáil, Sinn Féin and independents being beneficiaries. Indeed on the elimination of John Kennedy, the Thurles based Labour candidate in Templemore-Thurles LEA (Tipperary) more transfers accrued to each of Fianna Fáil, Sinn Féin and the remaining independent candidates than to Shane Lee, the other Roscrea based Labour candidate, possibly due to the fact that the other parties' candidates were all in or near Thurles.
- In many cases Labour candidates were eliminated with no other Labour candidate remaining. The principal beneficiary in these cases was Fine Gael, in some cases getting transfers of the order of 40% to 50%, a rate that Labour struggled to manage between its own candidates.

Sinn Féin
- The 2014 local elections were perhaps the first elections where there were substantial Sinn Féin transfers to other Sinn Féin candidates, as in 2009 that was very much a minor feature. The ability in 2014 of Sinn

Féin to achieve transfers between Sinn Féin candidates routinely at a level of over 50% is quite remarkable. In Dublin, where Sinn Féin did exceptionally well, transfer rates within Sinn Féin were generally close to the 70% level. The level of transfers was a significant improvement on the 2009 position.

- In 2014, most Sinn Féin transfers arose on account of surpluses, most usually on the first count, given that so many of their candidates exceeded quota.
- In many rural areas Sinn Féin took a conservative approach and had surpluses with no candidate available to take them. As first count surpluses do not produce non transferable votes, other left parties and independents picked up the lion's share of these surpluses with relatively little accruing to the three established parties, frequently 10% or less.
- In 2014, Sinn Féin supporters clearly had little time for the three other established parties. They transferred poorly to them, with Fianna Fáil doing best followed by Fine Gael and Labour third. This undoubtedly reflected outright opposition to Fine Gael and Labour the two government partners and a relative dislike for Fianna Fáil. This was quite different from the 2009 local elections when Labour often got a good transfer and Fianna Fáil and Fine Gael picked up some too.

Green Party

- The Green Party continued to do poorly in the 2014 local elections. They ran comparatively few candidates and seemed to be targetting particular areas. They were quite successful in picking up seats in some of those areas (south Dublin, Fingal and north Louth).
- There were relatively few instances in which Green transfers became available. The party most favoured was the Labour Party. It usually got about 25% of Green transfers and there was one case, Killiney-Shankill LEA (Dún Laoghaire-Rathdown) where the rate was in the 40% range and Labour won two seats.
- Fine Gael was also a beneficiary of Green transfers, often benefitting at percentage rates in the low teens.
- The benefit level of both Labour and Fine Gael from Green transfers was significantly down on the comparable position in 2009.
- Other left parties and independents benefitted from Green transfers to

a lesser extent than Labour but greater than Fine Gael. The rate tended to be of the order of 18% and was rather better than in 2009. There is no great evidence however of significant vote transfers from Green to Sinn Féin.

- Despite the fact that Fianna Fáil were the party with most first preference votes in 2014, there was little evidence of a material Green transfers to Fianna Fáil.

Independents
- In the 2014 local elections, there was a tendency for independent candidates, when eliminated, to transfer more strongly to other independents than to party candidates. Rates were probably somewhat higher than in 2009. Rates at 40% to 50% for lower placed independents transferring to other independents seemed to be quite common. However frequently there were so many independents that the votes still got quite scattered.
It is very difficult to draw any clear pattern on transfers of the independent vote. A number of examples suffice to show a mixed pattern.
- There were two high polling independents in rural Cork, O'Shea (Kanturk-Mallow LEA) and Collins (West Cork LEA) with respectively 4, 374 and 3,409 first preferences. Their transfer rates to other independents were respectively 26% and 19%, which were not very high rates given the circumstances.
- In Ballincollig-Carrigaline LEA (Cork) two independents were successful out of a field of six. The four eliminated independents (including CPPC) had an aggregate first preference vote of 1,832 and the two successful independents accrued 988 transfers from them, an aggregate of 54%. One of the independents Joe Harris came from outside the "leaders' enclosure" to win a seat, undoubtedly helped by quite coherent transfers from other independents.
- In Ballymun LEA in Dublin City there were six independents, of which the leading one was Geraldine Gough with 607 first preferences. There was the usual pattern of higher inter independent transfers when independent 6 (the lowest) is eliminated and lower when independent 2 is eliminated. In the event Gough had reached 1,113 when the last other independent was eliminated. 142 of her transfers had come from other

party sources, meaning that she was the beneficiary of 364 transfers from other independent sources. Às the other 5 independents started with an aggregate of 1,528 first preferences, that is an effective rate of just under 24%.[11]

- The above examples are probably representative of the high and low points of the aggregate effect of transfers between independents. The prevailing trend for individual transfers from one independent to other remaining independents seemed to be in the 30% region.

  The cumulative effect of some votes being non transferable and the scattering of preferences is that independents catch up on other candidates, but perhaps generally not quite enough to displace them. The conclusion to be drawn from the 2014 local elections is that independents did tend to transfer to other independents, but the cumulative effect was perhaps less than the effect of transfers within the established parties. In the 2014 local elections Fine Gael and Labour were very much out of favour and the response to Fianna Fáil was somewhat muted. Given the established pattern of inter independent transfer and that 2014 was probably a good year for independents, it seems reasonable to conclude that a large and fragmented aggregate independent vote will not necessarily translate into seats; it is a completely different matter if a small number of independents are well placed after the first count.

Smaller parties

- There was a clear pattern in the 2014 local elections of quite high transfers within smaller left parties in the few cases where they ran two candidates.
- Generally where smaller parties were eliminated, there were no other candidates of the same party to receive transfers. There was a tendency to deliver significant transfers to other parties of the radical left and to independents. Generally Sinn Féin did less well from smaller party candidates where there was another radical left party in the race.
- Transfers to the three established parties from smaller parties of the left were in all cases quite low.

Non-transferable votes

Generally the level of non transferable votes in the 2014 local elections was around the mid teens. However greater levels were incurred as follows:

Party	Circumstance
Fianna Fáil	At average effective 50% where no FF candidate remained
Labour	About 20% where no Labour candidate remained
Sinn Féin	Very high level where no Sinn Féin candidate available, particularly where only Fianna Fáil/Fine Gael/Labour remain[12]
Green	Usually in 20-30% range[13]
Independents	Usually 20% or above for higher polling independents

Transferring at better levels to other parties

- Possibly for the first time in elections, there is a pattern in the 2014 local elections, in the case of all three established parties, that transfers sometimes went in greater measure by percentage to another party than within the party.
- This type of leakage happened to the greatest extent to the Labour Party, but also happened about 20 times to both Fianna Fáil and Fine Gael (representing about one tenth of the times Fine Gael candidates were eliminated or had surpluses and about one seventh of Fianna Fáil eliminations/surpluses)
- The most spectacular examples of failure of transfers between party candidates occurred in the Ballymote-Tobercurry LEA (8 seats) in Sligo where Fianna Fáil gained five seats and Fine Gael one. This was assisted greatly by three Fine Gael transfers at ratios of respectively 45:48, 35:56 and 26:53 in favour of Fianna Fáil. In each case the main beneficiary of a Fine Gael elimination in Ballymote, Tobercurry and Dromore West respectively was a local Fianna Fáil candidate in the same town or area. Indeed Joe Queenan of Fianna Fáil obtained +524 (41%) on the elimination of Blair Feeney of Fine Gael, an accrual of votes scarcely matched on any other transfer in the entire country. Ballymote-Tobercurry was an amalgamation of three existing LEA's and thus was a prime example of poor transfer cohesion in the unwieldy electoral areas created by the boundary review prior to the 2014 election. Many of the cases where internal Fine Gael transfers were at lesser percentage rates than transfers to another party were in the north west (Mayo to Donegal), contributing to a very poor Fine Gael performance in that area.

Conclusions that can be drawn from recent transfer patterns with reference to the future

There is a rather inconsistent pattern of transfers over the last five national elections since 2007. These are the only elections considered reasonable to look at, in terms of forming a view as to the future. Internal rates of transfer will remain important to Fianna Fáil, Fine Gael and Sinn Féin. They may occasionally be so for Labour. It is doubtful that any other party will become so well established in the short term that this will be relevant. There is some evidence to suggest that there will be internal patterns within Fianna Fáil, Fine Gael and Sinn Féin of transfers to other party candidates in the 50%+ (perhaps 70%+ for Sinn Féin) bracket on average for general elections. It seems possible that Sinn Féin will do best, followed by Fine Gael and then Fianna Fáil. The order of the latter two parties may to some extent depend on whether they are doing well or badly in the particular election. A similar pattern but perhaps in the 40% to 50% range is to be expected for local elections. It seems more likely that Sinn Féin can approach general election levels of loyalty in local elections. To the extent that Labour have two or more candidates, there will be internal transfers but at a rate less than the other parties, perhaps by as much as 15% less.

There may well be a decline, at least in general elections, in the numbers of candidates reaching quota on the first count. It seems all parties now accept that this is wasteful of the party votes. The phenomenon of frequent first count surpluses may also be connected with a party getting in the region of 40% or more of the first preference votes, a feature which is likely to disappear. Given that the distribution of second preferences deriving from a first count surplus is time consuming, this should help to speed up counts.

There are established patterns of transfers between Fine Gael and Labour, transfers between Labour and other left parties (but not Sinn Féin) and transfers between other left parties. This seems likely to continue, with a possible question as to the Fine Gael/Labour transfer pattern. Further where Fine Gael are in competition with the other left parties for Labour transfers, the other left parties may do marginally better. There is also the factor of Fine Gael having a better rate of transfer from Labour than Labour can manage internally. Because a lot of these transfers seem to be at rates in the low 30%s and there appear to be a spread towards other parties, it is questionable whether this level of transfers will enable the beneficiaries to catch up, except in situations where the gap is narrow.

There is a long established pattern of transfers from the Greens to Labour and to a slightly lesser extent to Fine Gael. As these patterns seem to have endured through good and bad elections for both Labour and Fine Gael, it seems highly possible that they should continue. As the Greens might well have 3% to 4% of the national vote in future general elections and as little of that may be required to elect candidates, the votes available for transfer will be quite a material part of the transfer pool and will be important.

There appears to be a pattern on individual transfers of relatively few votes being non transferable. However there is also some evidence of an unwillingness of the left (other than Labour) to transfer to either Fianna Fáil or Fine Gael (and probably vice versa), although there are few examples to date. This will probably mean the accrual of a large number of non transferable votes on the elimination of the last candidate from either side of the left/right divide. This pattern can be seen in the Carlow Kilkenny bye-election 2015 moving left to right with the elimination of Funchion (Sinn Féin) and the Dublin South West bye-election 2014 moving right to left with the elimination of Cait Keane (Fine Gael). Bye-elections probably exaggerate the phenomenon, but it is likely to be there. More interesting will be the tendency of Fianna Fáil voters to produce non-transferable votes where no Fianna Fáil candidate is left (and to a lesser extent with Fine Gael supporters); this seems to be reducing, but the evidence is somewhat unreliable. Any cohesion in transfers between Fianna Fáil and Fine Gael as seemed to be emerging in 2016 will have an impact on the significance of transfers.

There is also a wholly imponderable issue of transfers between independents and a further issue as to whether smaller parties will be included to a material extent in any such transfers from independents. If ultimately there is a pattern of transfers in the 30% range between such candidates, that may be unlikely to enable an independent to catch up. The fragmentation of votes across a range of independents and smaller parties may mean that most of them are not in the first three to five (or three to ten in the case of local elections) leaders' enclosure and the usual problem of catching up will arise.

References in Chapter 16

[1]   In the 2007 general election for example in Carlow Kilkenny, the transfers of Fergal Browne only accrued at 50% to Fine Gael but 21% of his vote leaked to Labour and in Kerry South 48% of Cosai Fitzgerald's transfers went to Fine Gael with almost 20% leaking to Labour.

[2]   The highest level of non transferability of Sinn Féin votes in the 2007 general election was in Dublin Central where the votes of Mary Lou McDonald were 34% non transferable on her elimination. It is possible of course that a lot of these Sinn Féin votes transferred to other left and independents and ended up being non transferable because of their earlier elimination.

[3]   In two cases in 2011 Terence Flanagan in Dublin North East and Martin Heydon in Kildare South, no other Fine Gael candidate was available, resulting in a near 60% benefit for Labour and independents respectively.

[4]   For example in the general election of 2011, Dylan Haskins (1,928 votes) in Dublin South East transferred to the remaining independent at 20%, Sean Canney (6,431 votes) in Galway East did so at 11% and Tom Welby (3,504 votes) in Galway West did so at 17%. Even in the Kerry South constituency which elected two independents, the strongest other independent, Michael Gleeson (7,037 votes), transferred to other independents on his elimination at 37%.

[5]   In the 2016 general election, poorer levels of inter Fianna Fáil transfers were seen in two county or big constituencies such as Kerry, Longford-Westmeath, Sligo-Leitrim and Tipperary. The highest level seen was almost 84%, being the transfer of a McSharry surplus in Sligo Leitrim, derived from another Fianna Fáil candidate.

[6]   In the 2016 general election, as with Fianna Fáil, there were poorer levels of Fine Gael internal transfers in two county or divided constituencies such as Cork East, Longford-Westmeath and Tipperary (where it surprisingly failed to win a seat). The highest level seen was 87%, being the transfer of a John Paul Phelan surplus in Carlow Kilkenny, derived from another Fine Gael candidate. .

[7]   There were only three instances in the 2016 general election where the rate of transfer from Labour to Fine Gael (with no continuing Labour candidate) fell below 45%, Dublin Central (42%), Dublin Mid West (36%) and Wicklow (42%).

[8]   The most notable left beneficiaries of Sinn Féin transfers in the 2016 general election, all of whom were elected, were People before Profit in Dublin Mid West (54%) and Dún Laoghaire (69%),the Greens in the neighbouring Dublin Rathdown (42%), Joan Collins and Brid Smith in Dublin South Central (almost 90% in aggregate) and Seamus Healy (WUAG) in Tipperary (46%).

[9]   Cases of other left parties benefitting from Sinn Féin transfers in the 2009 local elections included People before Profit (39.04% Crumlin Kimmage LEA

in Dublin City, 50.1% Ballybrack LEA in Dún Laoghaire), the Greens (18.44% in Glencullen-Sandyford LEA in Dún Laoghaire, 28.29% in Castleknock LEA in Fingal, 18.24% in Dundalk South LEA in Louth), the Socialists (21.97% and 22.05% respectively in Balbriggan LEA and Howth-Malahide LEA in Fingal and the Workers Party (45.63% in Cork City North East LEA, 30.84% in Waterford City East LEA). These probably reflect most of the cases where these parties had higher votes than Sinn Féin.

10 The cases where independents benefitted from Sinn Féin transfers in the 2009 local election included places such as Clontarf LEA in Dublin City (39.15%), Blarney LEA in Cork (53.38%), Donegal LEA (36.52%), Conamara LEA in Galway (44.2%), Dundalk South LEA in Louth (34.46%), Clones LEA in Monaghan (51.1%), Enniscorthy LEA in Wexford (40.19%) and Baltinglass LEA (39.73%) and Bray LEA in Wicklow (39.2%).

11 In Kilkenny City East LEA, another example of an independent coming from outside the leaders' enclosure, a successful independent candidate picked up 179 transfers from five eliminated independents. As these 5 collectively had 740 votes, the rate of transfer was 24%, very similar to Ballymun LEA.

12 The level of Sinn Féin non transferable votes was high even where other left and independent candidates remained in the contest. This would suggest that those candidates got a significant bonus when Sinn Féin had a surplus on the first count with no other Sinn Féin candidates, as in those cases, votes with no further preferences indicated are ignored.

13 The greater rate of non transferability of Green votes in the 2014 local elections probably reflects the fact that both Fine Gael and Labour were highly unpopular at that time.

PART 4

Different Sized Constituencies and Lea's

CHAPTER 17

Issues regarding respective size
of Constituencies and LEAs

All modern general elections in Ireland have been fought in constituencies, which have a minimum of three seats and a maximum of five seats. Equally local elections have generally been fought in LEAs which had between three and seven seats. However in the 2014 local elections, the range for LEAs was fixed at six to ten seats, with a few minor exceptions in Cork City. The Irish position is quite different from many other democracies, which tend to have constituencies which elect a single member, at least at parliamentary level. As the following chapters will show, different result patterns, not always fully appreciated, emerge in constituencies and LEAs of different sizes. There is often a perception that different sizes of constituencies or LEAs are advantageous to some parties or tend to a particular result; these perceptions are largely unfounded. However there are patterns, particularly those associated with constituencies and LEAs with even numbers of seats, that are very important but little appreciated. Part 4 of this work explores these issues in detail.

How does constituency/LEA have the number of seats assigned to it?

This is a really important issue, given that constituency or LEA size in terms of numbers of seats has a significant impact on the result. In all cases the number of seats correlates to the population in the constituency or LEA. It can be somewhat of a fluke as to what size constituency covers a particular area. However the predominant determining factor is the population of the county concerned in the case of a constituency and population of a town's hinterland in case of a LEA.

There is a very loose and perhaps now historic practice in general elections, of larger sized constituencies being used in big urban areas and of smaller constituencies being used in rural areas. The urban area criterion was a feature of the terms of reference for the first constituency commission when the current constituencies were being drawn up prior to the 1981 general election. It resulted in five five seat constituencies in Dublin, two in Cork City and one in each of Limerick and Galway cities. However the pattern has now become so varied that even that is an unsafe assumption.

Usually the terms of reference for the relevant boundary committee, sets out base criteria. For example the local electoral area boundary committee which drew up the boundaries for the 2014 local elections was instructed that the number of seats should "typically be seven"[1] and "not more than ten or less than six". The terms of reference on which the 2016 general election boundaries were drawn up provided that "each constituency shall return 3, 4 or 5 members".

As is seen elsewhere (chapter 4), representation in Dáil elections must be proportionate to population. In framing Dáil constituencies, the basic building block in deciding numbers of seats has tended to be the respective populations of counties, of which there are 26. The commission tends to look at the population of individual counties or groups of counties and each of them is then allocated seats according to population. If the populations of counties do not justify a full seat, the commission then looks at possible boundary breaches.

In the case of ten counties, their population has been so small that they (excepting Kilkenny and Westmeath) are not sufficient for a three seat constituency by themselves. Therefore there is a requirement to put two counties together, resulting in the traditional two county, predominantly midland, constituencies of Carlow Kilkenny, Cavan-Monaghan, Laois-Offaly, Longford-Westmeath and Sligo-Leitrim. A further six counties Clare, Louth, Roscommon, Waterford, Wexford and Wicklow have tended to be stand alone county constituencies. Eight counties, Donegal, Galway, Kerry, Kildare, Limerick, Mayo, Meath and Tipperary have at most times had too great a population for a single five seat constituencies and have been divided into two parts, with some room for debate around the internal boundaries. Only Cork and Dublin counties have the population to require extensive subdivision and give rise to possible internal mixtures of three, four or five seat constituencies. In practice therefore, only two of the 26 counties give much scope for choice as to subdivision into three, four or five seats; the allocation of seats to the rest is largely driven by county population. Over the period 1981 to 2016, there has been a tendency for the number of three seat constituencies to rise, accompanied by a corresponding fall in the number of five seat constituencies.

In practice in local elections, LEAs have been drawn up based on the significant towns and their natural hinterlands. Once these areas are mapped, it is then a question of apportioning the seats allocated to the county in accordance with the respective populations of the sub-areas. A good example is Wexford, where four electoral areas focus on the large towns of Enniscorthy, Gorey, New Ross and Wexford, with more seats allocated to the Wexford town area as it is more populous. Many other counties follow a similar pattern. In many counties, large towns have had to be artificially divided, given the maximum limit imposed up to 2009 of seven seats, but this problem was somewhat lessened in 2014.

Approaching different constituency/LEA sizes

There is a broad awareness in political circles that different electoral approaches are required when addressing a constituency or LEA with a particular number of seats. For example the thinking behind the failed "Tullymander" in 1974, discussed in Chapter 4 "Fixing the Constituencies", was that Fianna Fáil would struggle to get two seats in three seat constituencies and that therefore an electoral map consisting substantially of three seat constituencies would probably not produce a Fianna Fáil majority. Of course it achieved the exact opposite in the ensuing 1977 general election. There is a view among minor parties that they simply do not win seats in three and four seat constituencies and LEAs and that therefore they should lobby hard for terms of reference promoting the creation of areas at the five seat level in case of constituencies and six/seven seats in case of LEAs. However as will be seen in the subsequent chapters of this section, a lot of the views are questionable and it is perhaps the case that many parties are not as well informed as to the issues which arise in particular types of areas as they should be. This Part attempts to identify these patterns.

The following is the mix of types of constituencies over eleven general elections:

Election	No of 3 seat constituencies	No of 4 seat constituencies	No of 5 seat constituencies
1981	13	13	15
1982 (Feb)	13	13	15
1982 (Nov)	13	13	15
1987	13	13	15
1989	13	13	15
1992	12	15	14
1997	12	15	14
2002	16	12	14
2007	18	13	12
2011	17	15	11
2016	13	16	11
Totals	153	151	151

As can be seen the number of three and four seat constituencies has tended to increase over time with a corresponding reduction in the number of five seat constituencies.

The following is the mix of types of LEAs over six local elections:

NUMBER OF LEAS							
No of seats	1985	1991	1999	2004	2009	2014	Total
3	12	13	28	28	3	nil	84
4	49	48	43	43	57	2	242
5	66	65	53	53	49	2	288
6	29	30	30	30	33	67	219
7	21	21	26	26	29	24	147
8					2014 only	23	
9					2014 only	13	
10					2014 only	6	

As can be clearly seen, over both types of elections, there is a sample of approximately 400 cases in which 4 and 5 seat areas have been fought, over 200 cases where 3 and 6 seats have been fought and a smaller sample for areas from 7 to 10 seats. A detailed comparison of these areas with one another in the aggregate is instructive. There are however different patterns between general elections and local elections. Therefore it is best to compare the two types separately. This is generally the approach adopted.

How many candidates typically contest constituencies or LEAs?

In general, the larger the constituency or LEA, the more candidates are likely to contest. The following is the general election pattern. The trend has been broadly upwards towards 2016.

No of seats	Average Number per Election	Minimum number	Maximum number
3 [2]	5.8 to 10.6	4 (6 occasions, 4 in Limerick W)	15 (Dublin Central 2016)
4 [3]	9.3 to 14.25	7 (4 occasions all 1982)	21 (Dublin S Central 1997)
5 [4]	10.8 to 17.5	8 (Kildare Feb 1982)	24 (Wicklow 2011)

The following is the local election pattern. The trend is more mixed and the number of candidates on average has not varied that much from 1985 to 2014.

No of seats	Average Number per Election	Minimum number	Maximum number
3 [5]	7 to 9.4	4 (5 occasions, three in Drumlish LEA, Longford)	15 (Cabra LEA Dublin 1991)
4 [6]	8.67 to 9.85	5 (3 occasions)	17 (Finglas LEA Dublin 1985 and 1991)

5 [7]	10.5 to 11.3	6 (Rathkeale LEA Limerick 1999)	20 (Dublin South Inner City LEA 1985)
6 [8]	11.5 to 13	7 (Ballinamore LEA, Leitrim 1991 and 2004)	20 (Wicklow LEA 2014)
7 [9]	13.65 to 15	10 (all local elections bar 1991)	21 (Athlone LEA Westmeath 1991)
8 [10]	17.26	12 (Clondalkin LEA, S Dublin, Enniscorthy LEA Wexford)	27 (Ennis LEA, Clare)
9 [10]	18.23	14 (Tralee LEA, Kerry)	26 (Swords LEA, Fingal)
10 [10]	21.5	20 (Carlow LEA)	23 (Sligo LEA)

Continuity of Representation by Party – Local elections

It is somewhat difficult to measure the change in party representation election to election between LEAs as their location keeps changing. However the LEAs fought in the 1985 and 1991 elections were the same (apart from two LEAs in Longford where allocation of seats changed) and equally there were no changes in the LEAs between 1999 and 2004. Some LEAs also continued into the 1999 local election in a form similar to 1991 and into the 2009 local election in a form similar to 2004, so it is possible to measure whether representation changed in those areas too. There was virtually no continuity in 2014, so that is not considered.

The following is the approximate level of change encountered between successive local elections where no revision of boundaries took place. For example between 1985 and 1991, there was a change in parties represented in 10 of the 12 three seat LEAs which continued, hence an 83% rate of change.

No of seats in LEA	Change 1985/1991	Change 1999/2004
3	83%	82%
4	66%	72%
5	70%	62%
6	65%	90%
7	70%	85%

There were extensive local boundary changes between 1991 and 1999 and between 2004 and 2009. However quite a number of LEAs survived without material change. The following is the approximate level of change between those elections with the number of unchanged areas denoted in brackets.

No of seats in LEA	Change 1991/1999	Change 2004/2009
3	33% (3)	33% (3)
4	77% (22)	61% (23)
5	72% (33)	65% (21)
6	75% (13)	80% (11)
7	75% (12)	90% (16)

Thus it can be seen that a change tends to occur in more than two thirds of LEAs between two successive elections, with the figure rising to 80/90% change in larger areas. There is no comparator as yet for the 8 to 10 seat LEAs as they were only fought in 2014.

It is in particular relatively uncommon that the same people are elected in successive elections in the same LEA, to such an extent that this is noted as an exceptional position in any of the detailed works on a particular election. For example 48 four seat LEAs continued between the 1985 and 1991 local elections. Only four of these returned the same four people as elected in 1985. Similarly between 1999 and 2004, 43 four seat LEAs continued. Only three of these returned the same four people as elected in 1999 [11]. By contrast the number of areas which remained unchanged as to party representation were 16 (1985/91) and 12 (1999/2004). The difference is explained by changes of personnel due to death, resignations and retirement and change of party personnel in the later election. This pattern is very typical of all LEAs and is explored in this book with four seat LEAs as an example for illustration.

What vote (in quotas) is required to win?

Candidates often ask what number of votes they require to win. This is difficult to answer in terms of numbers of votes, as turnout affects this. However there are some principles which can be expressed in terms of quotas.

In general elections, it is comparatively rare for a candidate to get more than 0.6 quotas and not to win. It is also comparatively rare for a candidate to get less than 0.5 quotas and win. There are as always exceptions. Unsuccessful candidates with very high votes include Michael Smith of Fianna Fáil (Tipperary North November 1982 with 0.97 quotas, John Ellis of Fianna Fáil (Sligo Leitrim November 1982) with 0.92 quotas, Candidates with low first preference votes who won seats in general elections are noted elsewhere in this work.

In local elections, relatively few candidates get 0.67 quotas or over and fail to get elected. There were only 5 such candidates in 2014, although there were somewhat more in previous elections, there being 24 in 2009. Generally local elections up to 2009 averaged about 60 candidates with 0.6 quotas or more who did not get elected. However there were also many candidates who got elected from such a position. The most unfortunate candidates included Vinnie Munnelly of Fine Gael in Killala LEA (Mayo) in 1991 (0.87 quotas), Tom Connolly of Fine Gael in Claremorris LEA (Mayo) in 1999 (0.82 quotas) and Charlie Hopkins of Fine Gael in Boyle LEA (Roscommon) in 2009 (0.85 quotas), but it is quite exceptional to get 0.8 quotas and not win.

It should also be noted that quite a number of successful candidates in every local election got a first preference vote of less than half a quota. In the 2009 local elections, 41 candidates succeeded from such a base vote and this increased to 78 candidates in the 2014 local elections [12]. While in previous elections, more candidates were unsuccessful from a base of

0.6 quotas than were successful from below 0.5 quotas (the numbers in 2009 were 64:41), this pattern was completely reversed in 2014 when the numbers were 33:78. This is likely due to the 6 to 10 seat allocations per LEA in 2014 as opposed to the earlier 3 to 7 seat allocations.

Percentage votes required in each type of constituency or LEA

The following chapters of this Part 4 attempt to analyse in the aggregate the outturns in a particular type of seat. In particular it is of interest to see the minimum percentage of first preference votes which has achieved a seat in each type of area, the minimum level of first preference votes with which a party has won two or more seats and circumstances where, despite obtaining the required numbers of quotas, a party has failed to translate that into the equivalent level of seats.

The following table shows the lowest percentage of votes (and quotas it represents) ever encountered in winning a given number of seats in constituencies of various sizes

Type of constituency	Number of seats won			
	4 seats	3 seats	2 seats	1 seat
Three seat	-	-	34.35	8.4
			(1.37Q)	(0.34Q)
Four seat	-	47.11	24.22	6.6
		(2.36Q)	(1.21Q)	(0.33Q)
Five seat	64.96	35.53	19.58	6.63
	(3.9Q)	(2.13Q)	(1.17Q)	(0.4Q)

The following table shows the lowest percentage of votes (and quotas it represents) ever encountered in winning a given number of seats in LEAs of various sizes [13]. They are usually a little lower than the equivalent for a general election.

Type of area	Number of seats won				
	5 seats	4 seats	3 seats	2 seats	1 seat
Three seat	-	-	-	35.82	11.23
				(1.43Q)	(0.45Q)
Four seat	-	-	46.7	21.24	6.99
			(2.33Q)	(1.06Q)	(0.35Q)
Five seat	-	52.4	32.57	17.13	5.47
		(3.14Q)	(1.95Q)	(1.03Q)	(0.33Q)
Six seat	-	44.73	31.15	16.16	4.81
		(3.13Q)	(2.18Q)	(1.13Q)	(0.34Q)
Seven seat	56.39	35.42	23.73	14.66	3.74
	(4.51Q)	(2.83Q)	(1.9Q)	(1.17Q)	(0.3Q)
Eight seat	38.42	30.95	26.15	13.6	3.02
	(3.46Q)	(2.78Q)	(2.35Q)	(1.22Q)	(0.27Q)
Nine seat	-	35.21	24.06	16.14	3.85
	-	(3.52Q)	(2.41Q)	(1.61Q)	(0.38Q)
Ten seat	-	38.96	21.73	12.11	3.01
		(4.29Q)	(2.39Q)	(1.33Q)	(0.33Q)

As bigger parties can anticipate getting between 20% and 40% of the vote in many areas, it is particularly relevant to appreciate the possibilities with that level of vote.

It is notable that a first preference vote in the 20%-29% range is sufficient in quota terms for

Quotas	Possible higher end
one seat in a three seat area (25%),	
one seat in a four seat area (20%),	
one seat in a five seat area (16.66%),	2 seats
two seats in a six seat area (28.57%),	
two seats in a seven seat area (25%),	
two seats in an eight seat area (22.22%),	3 seats
two seats in a nine seat area (20%); and	3 seats
three seats in a ten seat area (27.27%).	

In practice first preference votes at the higher end of the 20%-29% range are also potentially sufficient for two in five, three in eight and three in nine.

A first preference percentage vote in the 30%-39% range is sufficient in quota terms for

Quotas	Possible higher end
one seat in a three seat area (25%),	2 seats
one seat in a four seat area (20%),	2 seats
two seats in a five seat area (33.33%),	3 seats
two seats in a six seat area (28.57%),	3 seats
three seats in a seven seat area (37.5%),	
three seats in an eight seat area (33.33%),	4 seats
three seats in a nine seat area (30%); and	4 seats
four seats in a ten seat area (36.36%)	5 seats

In practice first preference votes at the higher end of this range are potentially sufficient for two in three, two in four, three in five, three in six, four in eight, four in nine and five in ten. Thus nearly every type of constituency or LEA gives scope to win an extra seat if a party has a first preference vote in the 30% to 39% range, particularly where there is an even number of seats. Frequently the bigger parties are trying to reach the potential of these areas by achieving that level and organizing their votes accordingly.

Not converting quotas to seats

A clear feature to be seen from a full analysis of all the three to five seat constituencies is that there is only one   example in a modern general election where a party achieved "x" quotas in first preference votes, but did not achieve at least "x" seats. That was in the three seat Limerick West in 1987. [14] There are however a significant number of near misses, a number of which should have been converted to the higher number of seats and some of which were clearly very relevant to the outturn of a tight general election.

By contrast in local elections, it is shockingly common that a party will achieve "x" quotas in first preference votes, but achieve "x - 1" seats. This seems to be a particularly common feat in 4 and 6 seat LEAs. It is somewhat less common in 3, 5 and 7 seat LEAs. Where instances of obtaining near (and not converting) a quota are noted in this work, they are generally confined to 0.8 or more of a "spare" quota. Further if a party gets 1.9 quotas and the other party gets 3.1 quotas in a four seat LEA, the failure to convert the 0.9 to a seat is not inappropriate, so these are generally ignored.

It should be mentioned that there were two instances in the very tight 1973 general election where Fianna Fáil got more than 50% of the vote in a three seat constituency but only won one seat. In Mayo West they got 50.59% and in Sligo-Leitrim they got 50.62%, but in both cases Fine Gael got two seats, the second of which in Mayo was taken by Henry Kenny, father of the later Taoiseach. As the National Coalition won 73 seats in that election as opposed to 69 for Fianna Fáil, those two debacles were very costly.

The different chapters following note "super performances" such as 3 out of 4 seats, 4 out of 5 seats, 4 out of 6 seats and 5 out of 7 seats and the circumstances in which such a result was achieved. These "super performances" are achieved from time to time and are quite instructive, as they often display features such as good vote management and exploitation of local geography, which are both key components of "super performance".

References in Chapter 17

[1]   The boundary committee largely ignored the "typically seven" term of reference. Only 24 of the 137 LEAs created had seven seats. The terms of reference were not well thought out; for example a county with 18 seats could not possibly mathematically have a seven seat area.

[2]   The average number of candidates contesting a three seat constituency was around 6 for the 1981 to 1989 elections (1989 5.8), around 8 from 1992 to 2002 and then increasing rapidly in 2007 to 2016 (10.6). The maximum number of candidates seen up to 2016 was thirteen and this was a feature of Cork South West, Meath West and Sligo-North Leitrim in the 2011 general election. The 2016 general election featured fifteen candidates in Dublin Central, a record, with Cork North West producing thirteen.

[3]   The average number of candidates contesting a four seat constituency was around 10 in the general elections 1981 to 1982 (February 1982 9.3) and in 1989. In all other elections, the average moved to about 12.5, but this increased further to 14.25 in 2016. After the 21 candidates who contested the Dublin South Central constituency in 1997, the next highest number was 18 in both Longford-Westmeath and Sligo-Leitrim in the 2016 general election. It is therefore no wonder that the Longford-Westmeath took until the following Thursday to complete. The Dublin South Central race in 1997 was the most competitive ever with 5.25 candidates per available seat.

[4]   The average number of candidates contesting a five seat constituency averaged around 11 for the general elections 1981 to 1982 (November 1982 10.8) and in 1989. For 1987 and elections from 1992 to 2007, it averaged around 14. The average increased dramatically in the 2011 general election to 17.5. It dropped back slightly to 16.8 in 2016. On one occasion, Kildare in February 1982, only eight candidates contested a five seat constituency, but there are quite a number of examples of nine. The 24 candidates who contested Wicklow in 2011 is also a general election record. This resulted in a ballot paper of two halves left and right, which was somewhat unsatisfactory. The gang of 24 included 2 Fianna Fáil, 3 Fine Gael, 3 Labour, 1 Sinn Féin, 1 Green, 2 Fis Nua and 12 independents. Other instances with more than 20 candidates included Dublin West (20) as early as 1987, Laois Offaly (21) in 2011, Dublin Bay North and Galway West (both 20) in 2016 and Dublin South West (21) in 2016.

[5]   The average number of candidates contesting a three seat LEA was around 9 for the 1985 (9.4) and 1991 elections and around 7 for the three subsequent elections. On one occasion, in Granard LEA in Longford in 1991, there were only three candidates and no election was required. The maximum number of candidates seen was fifteen in Cabra LEA in Dublin City in 1991 (curiously the constituency in which it is located, Dublin Central set the general election record in 2016).

[6]   While 17 candidates contested Finglas LEA (Dublin) in both the 1985 and 1991

local elections, curiously for the following two elections enthusiasm waned and only 10 candidates contested the Finglas LEA. The Kilbeggan LEA was not contested at all in 1999 and therefore four is the lowest number. There were 5 candidates in Athlone LEA (Roscommon) in 1991, Claremorris LEA (Mayo) in 1999 and Castleblayney LEA (Monaghan) in 2009.

[7]   There is a clear pattern over local elections 1991, 1999, 2009 and 2014 of an average of about 10.5 candidates in a five seat LEA. The two other elections in 1985 and 2004 show averages of 11.3. While the lowest was the 6 who contested Rathkeale LEA (Limerick) in 1999, it is not unusual to see a contest of 7. The highly competitive races tend to be in urban areas.

[8]   The average number of candidates contesting a six seat LEA has been pretty consistent, being around 12 for elections from 1985 to 2009 (11.5 in 1985). The average rose slightly to about 13 for the 2014 local elections, in which there were far more six seat LEAs.. While the minimum is 7, there have been a number of contests with 8 candidates in an LEA. While the maximum is 20, there were 19 candidates in Edenderry LEA (Offaly) in 2009 and Wexford LEA in 1985.

[9]   There is a clear pattern over local elections from 1985 to 2009 of an average of between 13.65 and 14.76 candidates in a seven seat LEA, so about two candidates per available seat. The election in 2014 showed an increased average of almost 15. Cavan LEA was contested by 10 candidates in each of 1985, 2004 and 2009. The highly competitive races tend to be in urban areas.

[10] There were a very large number of candidates in each of these large LEAs. Ennis LEA with 27 candidates, necessitating 20 counts to reach a final result. Swords LEA (Fingal) had one less on 26. The 27 candidates in Ennis was the largest number ever encountered in a modern election.

[11] The 4 seat Milford LEA (Donegal), Dundrum LEA (Dún Laoghaire), Tobercurry LEA (Sligo) and Coole LEA (Westmeath) returned the same candidates in 1985 and 1991. , The 4 seat Leixlip LEA (Kildare), Ferbane LEA (Offaly) and Mullingar East LEA (Westmeath) returned the same candidates in 1999 and 2004. Indeed in the case of Leixlip there was a change of party as Catherine Murphy, one of the successful candidates had switched party.

[12] Many of the candidates who succeeded form a starting position of less than 0.5 quotas had the benefit of transfers from a party running mate. Some works which assess the number of candidates who succeeded from such a low base, do not take those candidates into account. Of the 78 candidates who succeeded from a base of less than 0.5 quotas in 2014, 16 of them were in the 0.3 quotas range (2009 comparative figure 6) and 4 were less than 0.3 quotas (three of those being in Mulhuddart LEA in Fingal)

[13] The figures below for 8, 9 and 10 seat LEAs are based on a limited sample, as LEAs of this size were only in place for the 2014 elections. If they are used in the future, lower percentages are liable to win a given number of seats.

[14] Fine Gael did not achieve a seat in Limerick West, despite having 27.8% of the vote (1.11 quotas), spread across three candidates. See chapter 28.

CHAPTER 18

Three seat Dáil constituencies and electoral areas

The Irish constitution, in Article 16.2.6 states that three persons is the minimum number of members for any Dáil constituency. It is also the smallest size found in practice for a local authority or county borough electoral area, but has never proved very popular in those elections. The three seat constituency or LEA has been quite controversial, because of a perception that it militates against any party, other than the two traditional large parties, getting a seat. On the basis that the tradition of two large parties may be a thing of the past, the objection may have become obsolete. Theoretically getting a seat in a three seat constituency or LEA requires obtaining the quota of 25% of the first preference vote, so there is an incorrect perception that less than 20%, which minor parties are accustomed to, just won't do the business. Because three seat LEAs are quite uncommon and effectively became obsolete after 2004, it has been decided to deal with constituencies and LEAs of this size together in this chapter.

The following are the key messages to be drawn from the history of 237 contests in three seat constituencies and LEAs.

- It is not uncommon that a single party wins two of the three seats and this can be achieved with a share of the first preference vote of anything from about 35% upwards.
- A single seat has been won in a three seat constituency or LEA on quite a number of occasions, with a first preference vote of around 15%. The lowest up to 2016 included two wins by Labour's Joan Burton respectively in Mulhuddart LEA (Fingal) 12.94% and Dublin West constituency 12.71%, Paul Gogarty for the Greens in 2002 in Dublin Mid West on 12.33 % and the win by Martin Coughlan of Labour in Macroom LEA (Cork) in 2004 with 11.23%. In the 2016 general election however, Catherine

257

Martin of the Greens won a seat in Dublin Rathdown with 10.03% of the first preference vote and Maureen O'Sullivan, Independent won a seat in Dublin Central with 8.4% of the first preference vote.

- There may be a view that three seat constituencies and LEAs are unfavourable to smaller parties; this does not appear to be borne out by experience, but they do appear to be Labour hostile.

Where are three seat constituencies used for Dáil purposes?

Three seat constituencies have been commonly used in bigger counties where the population is somewhat too large to allow for a five seat constituency. Thus in the period from 1980 to date, there have frequently been two three seat constituencies in each of Donegal, Kerry, Kildare, Mayo, Meath and Tipperary and in most elections, this has accounted for the largest share of the three seat constituencies. The relative proportionate decline in population, when compared with other areas, in each of Donegal, Kerry, Mayo and Tipperary resulted in each of them becoming single constituencies for 2016. Indeed in the case of Mayo the change occurred in 1997 and for 2016, it controversially became a four seat constituency. Conversely Kildare has become so large in population terms than one of its three seat constituencies has acquired a fourth seat and the 2017 boundary commission has recommended that the other also have four seats .

The three seat constituency has been a consistent feature of the counties containing the three largest urban areas outside Dublin, counties Cork, Galway and Limerick. This has resulted in the three seat constituencies of Cork North West, Cork South West, Galway East and Limerick West (now Limerick County) being pretty well permanent features of the landscape (apart from the last few elections before 2016 where Galway East became a four seat constituency).

Three seat constituencies have been used infrequently for single counties, because virtually none of them have had the required population. The three counties of Longford, Roscommon and Westmeath have traditionally been allocated seven seats, divided four and three. Up to 1989 Roscommon was a three seat constituency by itself. From 1992 to 2002, Westmeath was a three seat constituency. In each case Longford was associated with the other of them. By 2007 population trends in the area were such that the adjacent Sligo-Leitrim could not sustain 4 seats. This resulted in Longford Westmeath being reconstituted and the splitting of Leitrim in two, roughly at Lough Allen, with the northern half being added to Sligo and the southern half being added to Roscommon, in each case forming a three seat constituency. The 2016 election saw the re-emergence of Roscommon as the core of a three seat constituency and also the addition of two new three seat constituencies, Laois and Offaly, now recommended to be rejoined by the 2017 boundary commission.

One of the unsatisfactory features of each of the counties which became a "stand alone" three seater is that in nearly all cases, surgery has been required to add a bit of another county. Roscommon has generally required a little bit of north east Galway or half of Leitrim. For 2016 it required a substantial chunk of east Galway, including the town of Ballinasloe. Sligo has required the northern half of Leitrim. Laois requires that part of Kildare around Monasterevin. Offaly requires the Borrisokane area of north Tipperary. Westmeath on the other hand has always required the loss of that part of the county around Delvin, which has always been part of a Meath constituency.

The final area of use of three seat constituencies has been Dublin. In the Dublin county area there have been at various times three 3-seat constituencies, Dublin North, Dublin West and Dublin Mid West. On account of increasing population these have all at some point become four seat areas. By contrast declining population relative to other areas on the north side of Dublin city has resulted in traditional four seat constituencies in Dublin Central, Dublin North Central, Dublin North East and Dublin North West being reduced to three seats each for some or all of the 21st century elections and now the amalgamation of North Central and North East into one five seat constituency. Election 2016 also saw a debut for the new three seat constituency of Dublin Rathdown, following the dismemberment of the volatile five seat Dublin South constituency to follow rather illogical county boundaries within Dublin (which boundary committees are expressly mandated to ignore in their terms of reference).

Over the five general elections in the period 1981 to 1989 there were 13 three seat constituencies. For 1992 and 1997, there were 12. The last three general elections before 2016 saw an increase to 16, 18 and 17 respectively, so that they have become much more prevalent. The number reduced to 13 for the 2016 election. Over eleven elections, three seat constituencies have been fought on 153 occasions, an average of 14 per election.

Where are three seat LEAs used for local election purposes?

Three seat LEAs have never been prevalent for local authority purposes. In the 1985 and 1991 local elections there were only 12 of them (a technical increase to 13 in 1991). For the 1999 and 2004 local elections, their number increased to 28. Largely on account of the perceived problems with them, the committee reviewing the boundaries for the 2009 local elections was instructed to use them only in exceptional circumstances. This resulted in three surviving Bandon LEA in Cork, Dingle LEA in Kerry and Baltinglass LEA in west Wicklow. As the terms of reference for the 2014 local elections boundary committee stipulated a minimum of six seats, no three seat LEA was contested in that election.

Three seat LEAs were quite common in Dublin city and county[1]. Outside of Dublin three seat LEAs were usually created for comparatively large rural districts with a relatively small principal town or towns[2]. There were a number of three seat LEAs in more populous areas, such as Carlow Town No 1, Bandon (Cork), Macroom (Cork), Galway City South, Athy (Kildare) and Celbridge (Kildare), presumably because they plugged gaps in an otherwise logical allocation of seats around bigger towns and areas.

In total three seat LEAs have been fought on 84 occasions, an average of 14 per election.

Continuity of representation in three seat constituencies

The longest period of continuity of the same three seat constituencies was the five elections from 1981 to 1989 and since then there has been significantly less continuity. There have been 121 occasions on which a three seat constituency was contested that was substantively the same as the previous election. Only 50 of those elections (41%) resulted in a change in the mixture of parties holding the seats, a relatively high rate of continuity, which contrasts with pretty well every other type of constituency/LEA. Every three seat constituency which survived from 2007 to the general election of 2011 saw a change in party representation, meaning that the prior nine elections saw relatively little change in three seat constituencies. There was also quite significant change in the surviving three seat constituencies between 2011 and 2016. The most volatile three seat constituencies have been Kerry South, Limerick County and Tipperary North, each of which have seen five changes in party representation from election to election. Of course aside from the 50 cases which saw a change in parties represented, there have been quite a number of further changes in the person representing a party.

What percentage is required to win two seats and one seat in a three seat constituency/LEA?

Two seats

It goes without saying that achieving 50% of the first preference vote should secure two seats. However this does not always happen. In the 1999 local elections, in the Drumlish LEA in north Longford, Fianna Fáil had 50.96% (2.03 quotas) of the first preference vote, but still lost the last seat by 10 votes to a Republican Sinn Féin representative. Further Fianna Fáil on numerous occasions, were quite close to 50%, but failed to take two seats, most notably in both the Kerry South and the Tipperary North Dáil constituencies in February 1982 where three candidates on 49.2% failed to deliver the second seat. In Ballinrobe LEA (Mayo) in 2004, Fine Gael had 47.17% of the first preference vote, but only won one seat.

However two seats have been delivered on 13 occasions in general elections on percentages of first preference votes in the 30's. Examples include the 1981 general election win by Fine Gael in Dublin North constituency with a vote share of 37.65% (1.51 quotas), the spectacular 1997 general election win by Fine Gael of two seats in Limerick West constituency based on a vote share of 37.19% (1.49 quotas), the regaining by Fine Gael of the second seat in Cork South West constituency in 2007 with 36% (1.44 quotas) of the first preference vote, the Labour win in Dublin North East in 2011 with 34.35% (1.37 quotas), the re-gaining by Fianna Fáil of two seats in Cork North West in 2016 on 34.62% (1.38 quotas) of the first preference vote and the retention of two seats by Fine Gael in Meath East in 2016 on 34.76% (1.39 quotas)of the first preference vote. In all these cases there were two candidates, although the vote was not always split evenly between them. So it seems that 35% of the first preference vote (about 1.4 quotas) is about the minimum required for a chance of two seats in a general election. Fine Gael won two of three contested seats in Dún Laoghaire (4 seats with Ceann Comhairle) in 2016 with 35.97% of the vote.

In local elections, there are fewer examples of wins from a percentage in the 30s. Key examples are:

Election	Party	LEA	Percentage of vote	No of candidates
1999	FG	Ballinrobe (Mayo)	39.63	2
2009	FG	Dingle (Kerry)	38.94	2
1991	FF	Cabra (Dublin)	38.88	3
1985	FF	Baltinglass (Wicklow)	37.94	2
1999	FG	Suir (Waterford)	35.82	2

The candidates were generally not split evenly on first preference votes obtained.

It has been pretty common that a single party takes two seats in a three seat constituency and this has happened on over 60% of occasions. It is somewhat less common in local elections at about 50%. By definition all of the other cases are 1:1:1.

One seat

The percentage of first preference votes required to win one seat in a three seat constituency/LEA can slip to quite a low level. One of the more spectacular feats was Finian McGrath, Independent, winning a seat in the 2007 general election in Dublin North Central with a first preference vote of 14.19%, comprehensively defeating outgoing Fianna Fáil TD Ivor Callely, by hoovering up 82% of preferences delivered as between the two of them. This was a very small field of 7 candidates, which certainly aided McGrath in getting high numbers of preferences from Labour, Green and Sinn Féin. It's not unusual that a seat is won, with a party base of about 15% of the first preference votes[3]. Perhaps however the most spectacular feats are the wins by Catherine Martin of the Greens in Dublin Rathdown in 2016, with a first preference vote of 10.02% (0.4 quotas), and Maureen O'Sullivan, Independent in Dublin Central in 2016 with 8.4% (0.34 quotas) or 1,990 first preferences and Carol Nolan, Sinn Féin in Offaly in 2016 with 10.91% (0.44 quotas).This suggests that a seat can be won in a three seat constituency/LEA with a first preference vote of about half a quota, particularly by minor parties. The 2016 experience suggests that the possibilities may be trending even lower.

Of course conversely it is possible to not win a single seat and have above or close to 25% of the first preference vote. The only modern example of a general election failure was the performance of Fine Gael in Limerick West in 1987 where it failed to win a seat (with three candidates) despite having over 27% (1.11 quotas) of the first preference vote. The most spectacular local election failure was in Kilmacthomas LEA in Waterford in 1999 where Fine Gael had almost 32% (1.29 quotas) (split evenly between two candidates) and failed to take a seat. In the disastrous 2011 general election, Fianna Fáil managed to win no seat with quite high first preference votes in Cork South West (23.63%), Donegal South West (22.53%) and Sligo-North Leitrim (21.85%), while retaining a seat in Kildare South (albeit with two candidates) and Limerick County on lesser percentage votes. The distinguishing issue was that two candidates were run in the first three with poor rates of internal transfers from one Fianna Fáil candidate to the other (Cork South West 57%, Donegal South West 55% and Sligo-North Leitrim

48%). By contrast in the 2016 general election, Fianna Fáil comfortably won a seat in Cork South West on a reduced first preference vote of 19.61%.

The 50/25/25 pattern

A number of Dáil three seat constituencies showed at times when things were competitive a broad 50% Fianna Fáil, 25% Fine Gael and 25% Labour pattern. This included Kerry North (with SF replacing Labour in 2002, although by then Fianna Fáil were well off 50%), Kerry South, Tipperary North and Westmeath. With very tight margins between Fianna Fáil and the rest, the destiny of the final seat was crucial. These seats were sometimes marked by high transfers between Labour and Fine Gael, which often tipped the balance.

Tight transfer patterns

Voters in three seat constituencies seem to have been acutely aware of the need for exceptionally high transfers between the non Fianna Fáil parties. In both Cork North West and Cork South West, Labour and later Progressive Democrat transfers to Fine Gael helped consolidate the two Fine Gael seats, with rates as high as 75% from Labour in Cork North West in 1981 and as high as 71% from the Progressive Democrats in Cork South West in 1987. This pattern resumed in 2007 when Fine Gael regained its second seat in Cork South West on 66% Labour transfers. Where either Labour or Fine Gael fell slightly adrift of 25% of the first preferences in Kerry South, Tipperary North or Westmeath at times they were "bellweather" constituencies, small surpluses were usually available from the other to help out. For example in the general election of November 1982, John Ryan's vote (Labour) fell a bit in Tipperary North but he was assisted to win a vital seat by an 86% transfer of a small Fine Gael surplus.

Good and bad tactical approaches for three seat constituencies/LEAs

While tactical approaches are dealt with in Part 5, some specific considerations apply where there are three seats. The most obvious tactical approach is to keep the candidates fairly level on first preferences, if a party is attempting to win two seats. For example Fine Gael in winning two seats in the Cork North West and Cork South West constituencies over 6 general elections from 1981 to 1992 usually managed to keep the two candidates fairly level. In the very bad 2002 general election for Fine Gael, it managed to keep its two outgoing TD's in Limerick West within a few votes of each other on first preferences, the resulting margin at the end of proceedings being 1, but failed to retain the two seats for simple lack of votes. On the occasions when Fianna Fáil succeeded or nearly succeeded in the Tipperary North constituency, it usually involved keeping the two candidates level. Of course having candidates with an even number of first preferences is not always a virtue, notably when struggling for a quota.

In 2016, the winning of two seats in each of Cork North West (FF), Kildare South (FF), Limerick County (FG) and Meath East (FG) was based on relatively level votes as between two candidates, as was the win of two seats by Fine Gael in Dún Laoghaire, effectively a three seat constituency due to the outgoing Ceann Comhairle, Sean Barrett, being automatically returned.

Where two seats are being sought with significantly less than two quotas and the two candidates are uneven in first preference votes, it is likely that the party will fail. This is accentuated if the lead candidate is better placed to pick up transfers. In the two west Cork three seat constituencies, the Fianna Fáil performance in 1981 was indisciplined, making it easier for Fine Gael to pick up the seats, although they probably would have done so anyhow. In Cork North West one Fianna Fáil candidate exceeded the quota in 1981, whereas the other was 300 adrift of the second Fine Gael candidate. A more even balance between the candidates might have put Fianna Fáil close to the two seats. In Baltinglass LEA (Wicklow) in 1985, Fine Gael had 40% as opposed to Fianna Fáil's 38%, but Fine Gael only secured one seat. This was because one Fine Gael candidate vastly outpolled the others.

A tactical approach that seems uniformly bad in a three seat constituency or LEA is to have more candidates than the number of seats targeted and particularly to have two more candidates than expected seats. This is usually done for geographic reasons. Fianna Fáil failed to take two seats in Tipperary North in 1981 and February 1982, probably not assisted by the adoption of a three candidate strategy. In the 1981 general election in Dublin North, Nora Owen of Fine Gael, then virtually unknown, polled 3,540 first preference votes as against a combined Labour total of 4,317 across three candidates. When the last surviving Labour candidate was eliminated, he had amassed an aggregate 3,779 votes on a not unimpressive internal transfer from other Labour candidates of about 66%. It took Labour until 1989, with one candidate, to secure a foothold in Dublin North. The Fine Gael debacle in Kilmacthomas LEA (Waterford) in 1999 was facilitated by having two candidates almost evenly matched who secured about 0.65 of a quota each and transferred at the rate of 42% between themselves. In Borris LEA (Carlow) in 2004, Fianna Fáil on 23.28% failed to take a seat with two candidates virtually even on first preferences. Fianna Fáil ran two candidates in Cork South West in 2011, got 23.63% of the vote but failed to win a seat; in 2016 they comfortably won a seat with a single candidate on 19.61% of the first preference vote.

It is very difficult to identify situations where additional candidates have been useful in a 3 seat constituency or LEA. One possible example is the Cork North West general election in 2007 where Fianna Fáil retained two seats with three candidates (one based in Ballincollig, the only large urban area in the constituency, which had recently been transferred in). They did however have 53% of the vote. Fine Gael in regaining the second seat in that constituency in 2011 adopted the same approach.

Are three seat constituencies/LEAs damaging to the interests of minor parties?

There is, as pointed out above, the view that three seat constituencies and LEAs are hostile to minor parties (i.e. parties other than Fianna Fáil and Fine Gael). This thinking has clearly influenced the bias against creating three seat LEAs in local elections. It also influences a bias against them for general elections, but population constraints make them impossible to avoid there.

But is this true? The answer to this question seems to be no. In assessing this issue it is useful to categorize three seat constituencies and LEAs into those in urban Ireland and those in predominantly rural constituencies. In practice minor parties tend not to win seats in rural constituencies and areas, irrespective of the number of seats and tend to win seats in urban constituencies and areas. A majority of three seat constituencies are rural.

In predominantly rural constituencies, the minor parties have tended not to be strong, no matter what the size of the constituency/LEA. For example when Mayo became a five seat constituency in 1997 from its previous form of two three seat constituencies, the minor party vote was still negligible, although it is true that Dr Gerry Cowley, Independent, managed to take a seat in 2002. Before Meath was split into 2 three seat constituencies, the old five seat constituency generally had negligible minor party presence. The trend has therefore been in rural areas that the two traditional largest parties share out the seats, although there are notable exceptions such as Baltinglass LEA Wicklow (1991 to 2009), Borris LEA Carlow (1999 and 2004) and Milford LEA Donegal 2004 where the largest parties only got one seat between them. By contrast in 2014 when Baltinglass LEA and Borris LEA were subsumed into larger areas, the two main parties dominated.

In urban three seat areas however, it is the norm that at least one seat goes to a party other than Fianna Fáil and Fine Gael. Indeed in Ballyfermot LEA (Dublin City) in 2004 and Dublin North West in 2011, neither of the two got a seat. The exceptions where the two main parties got three seats in urban areas are few[4].

Labour has tended to do poorly in three seat constituencies and LEAs. It has won a seat in less than 30% of such areas in general elections between 1981 and 2016. However other minor parties apart from Labour and independents have done quite well. In the aggregate slightly more than 50% of such areas have delivered a seat to a party other than the two traditional large parties ("major" below).

The following chart shows the trends:

Year of election	3 to major parties	2 to major parties	1 to major parties	none to major parties
(number of areas in brackets)				
1981(13)	9	4		
Feb 1982 (13)	9	4		
Nov 1982 (13)	9	4		
locals 1985 urban (8)	7	-	1	
locals 1985 rural (4)	3	1		
1987 (13)	10	3		
1989 (13)	8	5		
Locals 1991 urban (8)	1	4	3	
Locals 1991 rural (5)	3	1	1	
1992 (12)	7	5		
1997 (12)	3	8	1	
locals 1999 urban (11)	3	5	3	
locals 1999 rural (17)	11	4	2	
2002 (16)	4	9	3	
locals 2004 urban (11)	2	4	4	1
locals 2004 rural (17)	8	6	3	
2007 (18)	10	8		
locals 2009 rural (3)	2	-	1	
2011 (17)	2	7	7	1
2016 (13)	4	5	4	
Totals	**115**	**87**	**33**	**2**

A factor that has been very material to this in recent years, is a greater tendency for parties of the left to transfer at better percentage rates between themselves. Up to about 1991 the left was very incohesive and this showed in results. For example in Clondalkin LEA (South Dublin) in 1985, Fine Gael on 17.27% of the first preferences beat an amalgam of five left candidates including three Labour candidates.. But even in 1985 there was evidence of some co-operation with good transfers winning Pat Rabbitte, then of the Workers Party, a seat in Tallaght Rathcoole LEA (South Dublin) with a first preference vote of 14.33%. By 1991, left transfers were electing Joan Burton Labour in Mulhuddart LEA (Fingal) with a first preference base of 12.94%, despite Fine Gael having 17.79%. The high point of this trend is probably the 2007 re-election of Finian McGrath to the Dáil from Dublin North Central discussed above and the elections of Catherine Martin and Maureen O'Sullivan in 2016.

Conclusion

- While in theory it is necessary to win 50% of the vote to win a seat in a three seat constituency or LEA and 25% to win one, in practice a lesser vote can often suffice. The lesser vote can be as low as 35% for two seats and about 12% for a single seat (perhaps trending even lower if the pattern shown in 2016 is to become the norm). Electoral tactics are particularly relevant to achieving two seats from a low base.
- While there is a view that three seat constituencies are hostile to parties other than Fianna Fáil and Fine Gael, this seems to be a myth. Generally in urban areas, a party other than the traditional big two wins at least one seat. In rural areas, the two larger parties have predominated, but they tend to do so in those areas in constituencies and LEAs of a much larger size too.
- Generally there is less change in party representation from one general election to the next, this happening in 41% of cases, so three seat constituencies are a lot less volatile than those comprised of four or five seats. However three seat LEAs appear to be highly volatile.

References in Chapter 18

[1] Three seat LEAs were used in Dublin for clearly defined county areas such as Howth, Mulhuddart (both Fingal), Clondalkin, various parts of Tallaght (all South Dublin), Clonskeagh, Glencullen and Stillorgan (all Dún Laoghaire-Rathdown) and for city areas such as Ballyfermot, Ballymun-Whitehall, Cabra, Pembroke, South East Inner City, and South West Inner City. Many of these LEAs represented a fairly well recognized community and were far more satisfactory for local authority purposes. Many of these areas had by 2014 been subsumed into much larger LEAs, often quite illogically. For example South East Inner City LEA has become part of a much larger Pembroke South Dock LEA and has lost its identity. Some, such as Mulhuddart LEA and Clondalkin LEA, by sheer growth of population, have survived much as they were but with far more seats.

[2] Rural three seat LEAs were Borris (Carlow), Scarriff (Clare), Milford;Stranorlar (Donegal), Dingle (Kerry), Callan (Kilkenny), Ballinalee; Drumlish; Granard (Longford), Carlingford (Louth), Ballinrobe (Mayo), Castlerea (Roscommon), Dromore (Sligo), Borrisokane (Tipperary), Kilmacthomas; Suir (Waterford), Coole (Westmeath) and Baltinglass (all elections to 2009) (Wicklow).

All of these areas, except Stranorlar, were subsumed into much larger areas by 2014 and have lost their separate identity, a regrettable step.

[3] Examples where a single seat has been won in a 3 seat constituency or LEA with a vote of less than 15% include Pat Rabbitte (WP Tallaght Rathcoole LEA South Dublin 1985 14.53%, 0.58 quotas), the late Jim Mitchell (Fine Gael Cabra LEA Dublin city 1991 14.2%, 0.57 quotas), Joan Burton (Labour Mulhuddart LEA Fingal 1991 12.94%, 0.52 quotas), the aptly named Richard Greene for the Green party (Clonskeagh LEA Dún Laoghaire 1991 14.9%, 0.6 quotas). Pat Rabbitte (WP) and Breda Cass (PD) (Tallaght-Oldbawn LEA South Dublin 1991 13.46%, 0.54 quotas and 12.67%, 0.51 quotas respectively), Fiona O'Malley (PD Stillorgan LEA Dún Laoghaire-Rathdown 1999 13.43%, 0.54 quotas), Paul Gogarty (Green Dublin Mid West 2002 12.33%, 0.49 quotas), Joan Burton again (Labour Dublin West 2002 12.71%, 0.51 quotas), Martin Coughlan (Labour Macroom LEA Cork 2004 11.23%, 0.45 quotas), David Healy (Green Howth LEA Fingal 2004 12.26%, 0.49 quotas), Katie Ridge (Fine Gael Celbridge LEA Kildare 2004 12.6%, 0.5 quotas), Michael Colreavy (Sinn Féin Sligo-North Leitrim 2011 13.3%, 0.53 quotas), Noel Rock (Fine Gael, Dublin North West 2016, 12.54%, 0.5 quotas) and Paschal Donohoe (Fine Gael, Dublin Central 2016 13.62%, 0.54 quotas). Some of these are well known politicians.

[4] Urban constituencies and LEAs where the two traditional large parties took all three seats were the Dublin North constituency 1981-87, most of the few urban LEAs in 1985 (but all bar Cabra (Dublin city) were lost in 1991), Carlow No 1, Glencullen LEA (Dún Laoghaire) and Howth LEA (Fingal) in 1999 and Carlow No 1 and Athy LEA (Kildare) in 2004.

CHAPTER 19

Four seat Dáil constituencies

The four seat constituency has been a standard feature of Dáil politics in the last 35 years. Over 11 elections, a four seat constituency has been fought on 151 occasions, giving an average of 13.7 per election. The numbers range from a low of 12 in the general election of 2002 to 15 in the general elections of 1992, 1997 and 2011. The number increased by 1 to 16 for the general election of 2016.

The following are key messages to be drawn from the last 36 years:
- It is incredibly difficult to win three seats in a four seat constituency and the last time it happened (properly) was 20 years ago in 1997.
- By contrast it is quite easy to get two seats, even with a very low base of first preference votes. This feature makes four seat constituencies very attractive to large parties. In the vast majority of the 151 contests, two seats was won by one of the parties and indeed there are 30 instances (mainly historic) where two parties, usually Fianna Fáil and Fine Gael, have split the seats evenly, two each.
- Because it is relatively easy for one of the parties to get two seats, it follows that it is somewhat unusual to have four representatives, each representing a different party. This has happened 24 times, with nearly all instances being in a Dublin constituency, where there is a of course a much more varied market of parties.

In theory the following percentages of first preferences are required to win seats in a four seat constituency:

one seat	20%
two seats	40%
three seats	60%

In practice however seats are often won with less.

Where are the four seat constituencies located?

The four seat constituency is a common feature in Dublin and probably can be said to be the dominant form of constituency used in Dublin. Indeed at some point over the past 35 years every voter in Dublin (apart from those living in the former Dublin South constituency) has been resident in one. Dublin South East has been a perennial four seat constituency throughout that period. The general elections of 1992 and 1997 saw eight of them in Dublin. Probably on average in every general election, 40% of the four seat constituencies are in Dublin and they have historically typically produced a 2 Fianna Fáil:1 Fine Gael:1 other result.

Clare, Cork East and Waterford have also been consistent members of the four seat club, with very little adjustment to their boundaries, as has Longford Westmeath, when it existed as a constituency. Louth had always been a four seat constituency until the 2011 election, when it was increased to five. This increase was largely to deal with a population problem in Meath, most easily resolved by the Louth constituency spilling over into that county to the south of Drogheda.

Occasional members of the four seat club have been Cavan-Monaghan, Cork North Central, Cork South Central, Galway East, Kildare North, Limerick City, Longford Roscommon, Mayo, Sligo-Leitrim, Tipperary South and Wicklow, generally falling in or out on account of sluggish or very rapid population growth.

Continuity of representation

The longest period of continuity was the five elections from 1981 to 1989 and since then there has been significantly less continuity. As noted above, Clare, Cork East, Dublin South East and Waterford have remained in place throughout the period and continued to do so for the 2016 general election. There have been 119 occasions on which a four seat constituency was contested that was substantively the same as the previous election. 83 of those elections (69.7%) resulted in a change in the mix of parties holding the seats, a relatively low rate of continuity. Every four seat constituency which survived from 2007 to the general election of 2011 saw a change in party representation and all bar one saw a change in representation between 2011 and 2016. The most volatile four seat constituency has been Dublin South East (now Bay South) which has seen a change on nine of ten elections (the only exception being November 1982 where there was a change of personnel on the Fine Gael side with Joe Doyle replacing Alexis Fitzgerald). The Sligo-Leitrim constituency while it existed saw a change at every election. High volatility was also a feature of Clare, Cork East, Waterford and both Dublin North and Galway East (in their four seat form). Of course aside from the 83 cases which saw a change in parties represented, there have been quite a number of further changes in the person representing a party.

Do they achieve minor party representation?

The answer to this question seems to be yes. As noted below Labour have achieved a seat in a four seat constituency on 52% of the occasions they have been contested. This compares favourably with their rate of success (54%) in five seat constituencies. Sinn Féin won a seat in just more than half of the four seat constituencies in 2016. Other minor parties and independents have also often won seats. There are only 27 occasions where the two traditional large parties have monopolized all of the seats.

Winning three seats in a four seat constituency

This has historically proved to be a very difficult task. It has however happened 8 times (5% of cases), in all cases for Fianna Fáil. A failure to achieve three of four was probably a material contributor to the failure of Fianna Fáil to obtain an overall majority on several occasions. It has really only been on the horizon in two bastions of Fianna Fáil theology, the bailiwicks of de Valera in Clare and Charles J Haughey in Dublin North Central. The other areas it has happened tend to be the two county constituencies of Sligo Leitrim where it has happened twice and Longford Westmeath, where it has happened once. The only other true instance is in Louth in the February 1982 election. In the 2016 general election Fine Gael technically achieved three of the four seats in Dún Laoghaire; however the Ceann Comhairle, Sean Barrett, a Fine Gael T.D., was automatically returned, with Fine Gael filling two of the remaining three. It should also be noted however that in the 2002 general election, the five seat Carlow Kilkenny was contested as a 4 seat constituency, as the outgoing Ceann Comhairle was located there and on that occasion Fianna Fáil won three of the four seats (similarly in Cavan-Monaghan in 1987).

The sagas of the quest for three seats in four can be best be explored in the constituencies of Clare and Dublin North Central.

In Clare, Fianna Fáil had started brightly in both the June 1981 and February 1982 general elections with a handy three seats. Indeed this had so enthused the masses that for the November 1982 election, the chair of the Fianna Fáil convention, seemingly unidentified, had enthused at convention that there was an outside chance of all four. This was in response to consistent muttering from Fine Gael that Clare was marginal and indeed that in the hallowed halls of the late President, the outcome could well be the heretical outcome of two Fianna Fáil and two Fine Gael. Indeed this heresy was to come to pass in November 1982 and it has proved very resistant since then, having been repeated 5 times. The sole occasion where Fianna Fáil managed to get back to three seats in Clare was the general election of 1997. This was an important gain in beating the outgoing Fine Gael coalition government led by John Bruton.

In Dublin North Central, the bastion of sometime Taoiseach Charles J Haughey, it was a crowning ambition of his to secure three seats. However throughout the increasingly fractious 1980's elections this prize kept slipping away. It was always a given that Fianna Fáil would win two seats and Fine Gael one. It seems also to have been a given, that enormously high personal votes were required to satisfy the ego of the great man. The corollary of this, as is often the case in Irish politics, was a series of running mates, who could probably be fairly considered as low profile. In 1981, the obstacle to the fourth seat was the formidable veteran deputy and former Minister, Dr Noel Browne TD, who won the seat handily. However happily Dr Browne decided to retire in February 1982 to leave triumph for the great hero within sight in a snap election caused by a budgetary difficulty with children's shoes. However in a dastardly move, the sitting Fine Gael deputy, George Birmingham was joined on the ticket by a newcomer, Richard Bruton, brother of John, then 28 and the pair managed to steal the prize of 2 seats off a base of 32.65% of the first preference vote. This state of affairs was repeated in November 1982. The next election in 1987 saw Fine Gael in deep decline and there was a clear opportunity there. However in an infamous triumph, the dastardly duo of Birmingham and Bruton managed to hold their two seats off the low position of 24.22% of the first preference vote, perhaps the most remarkable triumph ever in a four seater. The two managed to get almost exactly 5,200 first preferences vote each (with 5 votes separating them) and were well clear, at the death, of Ivor Callely, the third Fianna Fáil man. This had the side effect of contributing to Mr Haughey, who at that point was becoming Taoiseach again, leading from a minority government position. However finally in 1989, on the last ever electoral outing for the Boss, the three seats were achieved. The Boss' own vote fell to 9,105, still a handy 1,500 votes ahead of quota. The other two candidates Vincent Brady and Ivor Callely were placed almost equally at 5,320 and 5,340 votes respectively and the Fine Gael hex was broken, with George Birmingham, the unfortunate loser, being despatched back to the Law Library. And all of this with 51.64% of the first preference vote, a vote not dissimilar to the four previous occasions where the prize slipped from the grasp.

The other constituencies which tend to produce three seats for one party outcomes are the two county constituencies. In all of these cases, a significant factor is the disparity in population between the two counties. The current ratio of population (census 2016) between Longford and Westmeath is 34:66 and the current ratio of population between Sligo and Leitrim is 67:33 and this is broadly reflective of how it has been through the current political era. There is a tendency for voters to vote within their county. This leaves open the possibility that the smaller county will only have one seat, held by the dominant party. If the dominant party can then get a majority of the votes in the larger county by population, it should be able to win two of the three that will be there, thus getting the magic three in four. This is exactly what panned out in Sligo-Leitrim in both February 1982 and 1987 and in Longford Westmeath in 1987. Good discipline across the party vote in the larger county is also essential for this. It is also a feature underpinning the Fianna Fáil three out of four in 2002 in Carlow Kilkenny, when that was effectively a four seater, due to the Ceann Comhairle being automatically returned. Notably three seats were never obtained in the elections between 1992 and 2002 when Longford-Roscommon (about 2:3 ratio) was a four seat constituency, but the margin against it happening in 2002 was a mere 55 votes. Louth, the other constituency where this has happened has a sharp Drogheda/Dundalk divide which undoubtedly contributed to it happening there.

Where three seats have been secured, it has often been with a first preference vote in the mid to high fifties. The three in Louth in February 1982 were however achieved with a base of 47.11% (2.36 quotas). There are quite a number of instances where votes for Fianna Fáil in the mid to high fifties did not achieve three seats.[1] It is notable that the very narrow failure of Fianna Fáil to obtain three seats in Longford-Roscommon in 2002 was with a first preference vote marginally over 40% or two quotas, suggesting that three seats can be obtained with a vote as low as that. The comparative low base for three seats out of four in an LEA is 46.7% (2.33 quotas), a little lower than in a general election.

It is reasonable to speculate whether we will ever again see the securing of three seats in a four seat constituency (apart from the technical circumstances of Dún Laoghaire in 2016). With the fragmentation of votes across parties, it is difficult to see this happening much, if at all, in the future and therefore it is probably an historical curiosity. An interesting case was the effort by Fine Gael to defend three seats in the now four seat Mayo constituency in the 2016 general election. As the three candidates were based in the three key urban centres, the geography was quite good for a repeat. However the vote management proved impossible and despite obtaining 50.96% of the vote, the third Fine Gael candidate, Michelle Mulherin fell short by over 2,000 votes.

Securing two seats in a four seat constituency

It is clear from looking at the 151 contests held in four seat constituencies that on 84%+ of the occasions, one party has held at least 2 seats. So the predominant life form of the four seat constituency is 2:1:1. On 30 occasions, the constituencies have split 2:2, nearly always as between Fianna Fáil and Fine Gael but latterly between Fine Gael and Labour.

It is comparatively easy to get two seats with a first preference vote in the 30%+ range, even where that figure is 31 or 32. Some discipline between the candidates is required so that votes are split evenly. It's a little more difficult to do it with first preference figures in the 20's but it has been done.[2] Realistically one needs to be looking at a prospective first preference percentage vote in the low thirties to have serious aspirations to take two seats however. Fine Gael nearly managed to take two seats in Longford Westmeath in 2016 with 23.82% (1.19 quotas), their second candidate, James Bannon being eliminated by 6 votes, although it is not certain that he would have won the seat had the elimination gone the other way.

There is no case where a party has secured 40% or more of the first preference votes and failed to get two seats. However as a corollary to the relative ease of getting two seats with a low 30's percentage of first preference votes, there are quite a few examples of failure to do so with percentages of first preference votes in the high thirties.[3] The 1.99 quotas obtained in Cork East in February 1982 seems to be the highest ever quotas obtained in a modern general election without a matching number of seats.

The most notorious example of all was that of Fianna Fáil in Dublin Central in the 1992 general election. Fianna Fáil had 14,299 first preferences or 39.28% (1.96 quotas) of the vote. However 11,374 of those were secured by Bertie Ahern and the two other candidates had approximately 1,800 and 1,000 votes respectively. On the distribution of Ahern's surplus over 1,200 votes leaked to rival candidates and in the end the second Fianna Fáil candidate was not even remotely close to success. This example is analysed in Chapter 14 "Managing a large surplus".

The 2016 election showed a pattern where only half of the four seat constituencies delivered two seats for a single party. This suggests that the pattern for the future may be much lower and that a 1:1:1:1 outcome may be more prevalent. However eight constituencies did deliver two or more seats for a party in circumstances where both Fine Gael's and Fianna Fáil's national vote share was about 25%.

Securing a single seat in a four seat constituency

There are obviously plenty of examples of single seats being secured in four seat constituencies. Where the party is targeting a single seat, this is often secured with a percentage first preference vote in the mid to late teens. There appear to be relatively few examples of seats being secured off very low bases, which suggests that the dynamics of a four seat constituency does not as easily leave itself open to this. This is probably a corollary to the ease with which two in four is obtained.[4]

The most spectacular success was that of Derek McDowell of Labour in Dublin North Central in the 1997 general election. The 1992 general election had seen a big surge for Labour, the so called "Spring tide", but the tide was going out fast for Labour in 1997. Standing on the shores of Dublin Bay in Clontarf in 1997 was Derek McDowell who had come home spectacularly in 1992 in the Spring tide. However in the 1997 general election, with the tide vastly disappearing on the horizon at Dollymount Strand, Mr McDowell got a lowly 6.6% (0.33 quotas) of the first preference vote. By contrast Fianna Fáil had 46.44%. He struggled manfully however, picking up transfers from all quarters and finally crept home into the last seat by a margin of almost 400 votes over that old veteran of the unlikely victory, Sean Dublin Bay Loftus. Fianna Fáil really should have won three seats on that occasion. However there was a giant competition going on between Ivor Callely and Sean Haughey for "top dog" position and the third candidate local councillor, Ita Green really did not feature, being eliminated at the last count. It should be noted that the comparative "low base" for four seat electoral areas is 6.99% of the first preference vote, more than the McDowell vote in the 1997 general election.

Labour have done surprisingly well in four seat constituencies, perhaps aided by the tendency for about 40% of them to be in Dublin. They have won a seat on 78 occasions they have been contested or about 52% of the time. In both surge Labour elections 1992 and 2011, they have got 2 seats in a four seat constituency and in both those elections, they secured representation in every four seat constituency (bar Roscommon Longford in 1992, a constituency where they would not have had real prospects of success).

As one would expect, it is eminently possible not to win a seat at all in a four seat constituency on a percentage close to 20%. Most of the examples of this are in the Fianna Fáil wipe out of 2011, most notably Cork East on 16.94%. However in most cases where high votes have not secured a seat, it is stronger performances by others that have caused the problem.

There have been some interesting races where candidate A is on 15% and candidate B is on 12% but B has won. Usually these are explained by transfer patterns, which are predictable, rather than poor strategy.

Conclusions

- It is relatively easy to secure two seats in a four seat constituency. It has been achieved with first preference votes of as low as 24% and is a realistic objective of a major party. However the message of general election 2016 is that it may become more difficult for a party to secure two seats.
- While there are historic examples of a party achieving three seats in a four seat constituency, this seems unlikely to be achieved in a future election, not least because it likely requires a first preference vote in the mid 50 percent range.
- The Labour party has done almost as well in four seat constituencies as in five seat constituencies. They have not been quite as favourable for other minor parties.
- It seems to be more difficult to achieve a seat in a four seat constituency off a low first preference vote. The record is that of Derek McDowell in Dublin North Central in 1997 at 6.6%, interestingly almost a percentage point lower than the equivalent low point for a five seat constituency up to the 2016 election and equivalent to the new record low for a five seat constituency.
- Generally there is a change in representation by party from one election to the next, this happening in almost 70% of cases.

References in Chapter 19

[1]   Examples where 3 seats were not achieved with almost three quotas include Clare (November 1982 56.15% (2.81 quotas)), 1989, 55.18% (2.76 quotas)), Longford Westmeath (November 1982, 52.98% (2.65 quotas)), 1989 54.24% (2.71 quotas)), Longford Roscommon (1992, 52.28% (2.61 quotas)) and Sligo Leitrim (November 1982, 52.6% (2.65 quotas)).

[2]   Taking two seats on less than 30% of the vote has most often been achieved by Fine Gael for example in Clare 1987 (28.02%, 1.4 quotas) and 2016 (25.8%, 1.29 quotas), Dublin North Central 1987 (24.22%, 1.21 quotas- discussed above) and Dublin South East 1989 (27.66%,1.38 quotas). Fianna Fáil has done so in Dublin South Central 1992 (29.56%, 1.48 quotas), Kildare North 2016 (28.2%. 1.41 quotas) and Mayo 2016 (27.7%,1.39 quotas). Labour achieved it in 2011 in Dublin South East with 25.36%. These cases are generally characterized by good discipline as between the candidates' votes and often there are only two candidates (three in Clare 2016 and Dublin South Central).

[3]   The phenomenon of one seat in four with almost 40% of the vote particularly affected Fianna Fáil in the early 80's in the geographically adjacent constituencies of Cork East (see Chapter 28 for a detailed discussion) and Waterford. Only one seat was obtained with 38.1%, 1.9 quotas (Cork East 1981), 39.82%, 1.99 quotas (Cork East again February 1982) and 39.56%, 1.98 quotas (Waterford February 1982) of the first preference votes. This was largely due to an incoherent electoral strategy, resulting in each case in the election of a strong SFWP (later Workers Party) candidate. Both issues were nailed in the November 1982 election with a disciplined ticket. These failures proved to be quite costly in an environment with a very small Dáil margin between government and opposition blocks. The course of history would probably have been quite different, if Fianna Fáil had secured two seats in each of Cork East and Waterford in February 1982. Other notable failures (always with surplus candidates) to gain 2 seats in a four seat constituency were Fine Gael in Dublin South West in 1981 at 38.21%, 1.91 quotas, Fine Gael in Sligo Leitrim in February 1982 at 37.47%, 1.85 quotas, Fianna Fáil in Wicklow in both 1982 general elections at 36.49 and 35.68% respectively, about 1.8 quotas and Fianna Fáil 1992 in Dublin North at 36.51%, 1.83 quotas.

[4]   Examples of achieving a seat in a four seat constituency with a low first preference percentage include the colourful independent Sean Dublin Bay Loftus in Dublin North East in 1981 with 2,395 first preference votes (7.39%, 0.37 quotas), Pat McCartan of the Workers Party with 8.61%, 0.43 quotas in the same constituency in 1987, Trevor Sargent for the Greens in Dublin North in 1992 with 8.77%, 0.44 quotas and Willie Penrose of Labour in Longford-Westmeath in 2016 with 8.72%, 0.44 quotas.

CHAPTER 20

Four seat electoral areas

Over the six local elections reviewed in this book, four seat LEAs were contested on 242 occasions being:

1985	49
1991	48 (Drumlish LEA in Longford adjusted to 3)
1999	43
2004	43
2009	57
2014	2 [1]

Many of the 57 LEAs, which were 4 seat LEAs in 2009, were amalgamated for 2014 to form much larger districts.[2] This seems to have lost the identity of the smaller towns and villages and it is not clear what benefit has resulted. There was certainly a significant drop in turnout from 2009 to 2014, although this was a general feature of the 2014 local elections. Hopefully a future boundary commission will be able to re-instate these areas as separate council entities, as this seems the better arrangement.

As noted elsewhere in the context of constituencies, theoretically 60% of the vote is required to win three seats, 40% to win two seats and 20% to win one seat. However it is eminently possible to win seats from lower percentages. There are also a few instances of parties not getting the relevant numbers of seats despite having the percentage first preference vote.

Where are 4 seat LEAs located?
4 seat LEAs have been used predominantly in the big urban centres and in forming an area based on a smaller town within a county to give it a separate identity.

Thus four seat LEAs have been found in Dublin city, all of the counties of Dublin, Cork city, Limerick city, Galway city and Waterford city in the elections up to 2009.

These types of electoral areas were used for a smaller town and its hinterland (or at least relatively smaller for the county). [3]

Very occasionally they have been used to deal with a large urban areas requiring more seats than the maximum (historically seven but increased to ten for 2014) allowed for in the terms of reference for the boundary review and they have been used in this regard for Carlow, Drogheda, Ennis, Kilkenny, Mullingar and Tralee.

The only counties where they have never featured are Cavan and Leitrim.

Do four seat LEAs give minority representation?

In all elections at least two thirds of the four seat LEAs elect at least one candidate from a party other than Fianna Fáil or Fine Gael. The percentage ranges from 65% in 1985 to 88% in 2009. The two LEAs contested as four seat areas in 2014 both returned other representation. Therefore it is clear, despite the theoretical need to get 20% of the vote to obtain a seat, that minor parties and independents can secure representation in this size of LEA.

The Labour party have done reasonably well in four seat LEAs winning seats in 35% in 1985, 48% in 1991, 42% in 1999, 56% in 2004 and 58% in 2009. Therefore on average Labour take a seat in about 50% of these areas.

Winning three seats in a four seat LEA

As with Dáil constituencies, it is comparatively rare that a party wins three seats in a four seat LEA. It has happened 15 times out of 242 contests. This is a slightly greater incidence than in four seat Dáil constituencies. Fianna Fáil have managed it ten times and Fine Gael five times. [4]

This has sometimes been achieved with a relatively low first preference vote including Westport LEA in 1999 Fianna Fáil (46.7%, 2.33 quotas) and Ballymote LEA in 2009 Fine Gael (48.52%, 2.43 quotas). The Westport LEA Fianna Fáil triumph in 1999 was notable in that Fine Gael got 44.2% of the vote, less than 3% behind Fianna Fáil, but still only ended up with one seat. This debacle was concocted up out of a huge vote for sitting Fine Gael deputy Michael Ring followed by a 35% internal Fine Gael transfer from him to the other Fine Gael candidate (see chapter 28). It is unusual that three seats are achieved in circumstances where the first preference vote is in excess of 60%. The record was Coole LEA (Westmeath) in 1985 where Fianna Fáil got 65.51% of the vote.

It is of course possible not to get three seats with a first preference vote in the mid-50's. This usually arose because the other parties are actually nearer or over the required quotas, but sometimes is a as a result of a tactical mess.[5]

Occasionally three seats of the four in an LEA are won by a collection of minor parties and independents, usually in Dublin.

Winning two seats in a four seat LEA

As with four seat Dáil constituencies, the predominant form of result in a four seat LEA is that one party wins two or more seats. This has happened about 180 times or in 75% of the contests, not quite as prevalent though as in general elections. In the earlier local elections it was more common that Fianna Fáil and Fine Gael won two seats each; however this has become an unusual feature in the twenty first century. Both the Labour party and Sinn Féin have also managed to get two seats in a four seat LEA, this happening in the case of Sinn Féin in the Cork North West City LEA in 2014.

Generally where two seats in a LEA are obtained with below 40% of the first preference vote, it is based on a first preference vote in the 30% + range. However there are some instances below 30%.[6] The most spectacular performance was that by Labour in Artane LEA (Dublin) winning two seats with 21.24% of the first preference vote.

Winning a single seat

There are of course many examples where a party or an independent has won a single seat in a 4 seat LEA, generally with first preference votes in excess of about 14%. There are comparatively few examples of winning from a first preference vote of less than 10%. This is mainly done by minor parties and independents, the lowest example being 6.99% in Tralee LEA in1991.[7]

Failing to take seats represented by available quotas

Local elections throw up a number of examples of failure by a party to gain seats in a four seat LEA despite having the requisite quotas (14 cases) or almost the quotas so to do.[8]

Election	Party (and seats won)	Percentage obtained (quotas)	Candidates
1985 Limerick City area 1	Fine Gael (1)	41.09 (2.05)	4
1985 Ballaghadereen (Ros)	Fine Gael (1)	42.76 (2.14)	3
1985 Mullingar (Lough Owel) (Westmeath)	Fine Gael (-)	26.47 (1.32)	4
1991 Castlerea (Ros)	Fianna Fáil (-)	23.57 (1.18)	3
1999 Limerick 3	Labour (-)	23.26 (1.16)	5
1999 Kilmallock (Lim)	Fianna Fáil (1)	41.79 (2.09)	4
1999 Westport (Mayo)	Fine Gael (1)	44.2 (2.21)	2
1999 Lismore (Wat)	Fianna Fáil (2)	60.6 (3.03)	3
2004 Balbriggan (Fingal)	Fianna Fáil (-)	20.02 (1.00)	3
2004 Ballaghadereen (Ros)	Fianna Fáil (-)	22.65 (1.13)	3
2004 Gorey (Wex)	Fine Gael (1)	45.09 (2.25) (discussed ch 28)	5
2009 Luggacurren (Laois)	Fianna Fáil(1)	40.75 (2.04)	3
2009 Castleblayney (Mon)	Fianna Fáil (1)	40.5 (2.02)	2
2009 Lismore (Wat)	Fianna Fáil (1)	40.36 (2.02)	3

The reasons for the failures are many, ranging from a lead candidate being too far ahead, to poor transfers between candidates, to too many candidates.

Conclusion

- It is comparatively easy for a party to take two seats in a four seat LEA and consequently this is a realistic objective for a major party. This can be achieved with as low as 21% of the first preference vote, although realistically 30% is required.

- There are a number of examples where three seats have been won in a four seat LEA, typically requiring 50% of the first preference votes.

- It is possible to win a seat with a relatively low base of first preferences. The record low is 6.99%.

- Generally where areas are continuous from election to election, two thirds change in terms of party representation.

- There is a strong track record of parties failing to get a number of seats equal to the quotas obtained. This has happened 14 times or about one in every twenty times a four seat LEA is fought.

References in Chapter 20

[1] The reduction to 2 in the 2014 local elections was as a result of the terms of reference of the then boundary commission, which was instructed to provide a minimum of six seats in each LEA. However the boundary committee was not asked to review Cork City; there were two existing 4 seat areas in Cork city and these remained.

[2] Thus the mergers of Borris/Bagenalstown (Carlow), Blarney/Macroom (Cork), Ballyfermot/Crumlin Kimmage/South West Inner City (Dublin), Emo/Luggacurren (Laois), Drumlish/Granard (Longford), Belmullet/Westport (Mayo), part Castleblayney/Clones (Monaghan), Birr/Ferbane (Offaly), Ballymote/Dromore/Tobercurry (Sligo) and Coole/Mullingar East (Westmeath).

[3] Four seat LEAs were found in Bagenalstown; Borris; Tullow (Carlow), Killaloe (Clare), Blarney; Fermoy; Kanturk; Macroom; Mallow (Cork), Milford (Donegal), Oranmore (Galway), Athy; Clane; Leixlip (Kildare), Callan; Thomastown; Tullaroan (Kilkenny), Emo; Luggacurren and Tinnahinch (Mountmellick) (the colourful names given respectively to north east, south east and north west Laois), Kilmallock; Rathkeale (Limerick), Ballinalee; Drumlish; Granard (Longford), Belmullet; Claremorris; Swinford; Westport (Mayo), Trim (Meath), Castleblayney; Clones (Monaghan), Birr; Ferbane (Offaly), Ballaghadereen; Boyle; Castlerea; Strokestown (Roscommon), Ballymote; Dromore; Tobercurry (Sligo), Borrisokane; Cahir; Cashel (Tipperary), Lismore (Waterford), Coole; Kilbeggan (Westmeath), Gorey; New Ross (Wexford) and Greystones (Wicklow)

[4] Three seats of four were obtained in the following LEAs (Fianna Fáil unless otherwise stated)
Luggacurren, Mountmellick x2 (Laois)
Rathkeale (Fine Gael) (Limerick)
Westport x 2 (Fine Gael once) (Mayo)
Strokestown (Roscommon)
Ballymote (Fine Gael) (Sligo)
Borrisokane x 2, Cahir, Cashel (Fine Gael) (Tipperary)
Coole x 2 (Westmeath)
Greystones (Fine Gael) (Wicklow)

[5] Examples of a failure to take three seats with a first preference vote in the mid 50's or higher include
Killala LEA (Mayo) in 1985 (Fianna Fáil 56.2%, 2.8 quotas),
Swinford LEA (also Mayo) in 1985 (Fianna Fáil 57.58%, 2.88 quotas),
Dromore LEA (Sligo) in 1991 (Fianna Fáil 58.5%, 2.92 quotas),
Lismore LEA (Waterford) in 1999 (Fianna Fáil 60.6%, 3.03 quotas) and
Boyle LEA (Roscommon) in 2009 (Fine Gael 53.43%, 2.67 quotas).

6   Examples of 2 seats in 4 gained with low (below 30%) first preferences include **Artane LEA (Dublin) in 1991 (Labour 21.24%, 1.06 quotas)**, Tralee LEA (Kerry) in 1991 (Fianna Fáil 28.38%, 1.42 quotas), Rathfarnham LEA (South Dublin) in 1991 (Fine Gael 28.28%, 1.41 quotas) Galway No 3 in 1999 (Progressive Democrats 29.36%, 1.47 quotas) Limerick City 3 LEA in 1999 (Fine Gael 29.3%, 1.46 quotas), Lismore LEA (Waterford) in 1999 (Fine Gael 29.93%, 1.5 quotas), Fermoy LEA (Cork) in 2004 (Fine Gael 29.15%, 1.45 quotas), Rathmines LEA (Dublin) in 2004 (Labour 29.32%, 1.47 quotas), Galway City 2 LEA in 2004 (Labour 25.59%, 1.28 quotas), Emo LEA (Laois) in 2009 (Fine Gael 28.2%, 1.41 quotas), Thomastown LEA(Kilkenny) in 2009 (Labour 26.73%, 1.34 quotas), Tobercurry LEA(Sligo) in 2009 (Fine Gael 28.19%, 1.41 quotas) and New Ross LEA (Wexford) in 2009 (Fine Gael 29.72%, 1.49 quotas). In all bar one of these (Emo LEA 2009) the successful party had two candidates and both polled relatively equally, with both picking up transfers as counts progressed.

7   Examples of winning a single seat with under 10% include Frank Buckley for Labour in Dundrum LEA (Dún Laoghaire) in 1985 (9.86%), John Blennerhassett Independent in Tralee LEA (Kerry) in 1985 (8.98%) Frank McIntyre Independent Mullingar Urban LEA(Westmeath) in 1985 (9.16%), Sheila O'Sullivan for Labour in Cork North in 1991 (9.85%) Claire Wheeler for the Greens in Pembroke LEA(Dublin) in 1991 (7.80%), Betty Reeves for the Greens in Blackrock LEA (Dún Laoghaire) in 1991 (9.88%), **Tommy Foley Independent in Tralee LEA (Kerry) in 1991 (6.99%),** Nuala Ahern for the Greens in Greystones LEA (Wicklow) in 1991 (9.48%), Victor Boyhan for the Progressive Democrats in Blackrock LEA (Dún Laoghaire) in 1999 (8.84%), Veronica O'Reilly Independent in Greystones LEA (Wicklow) in 1999 (8.59%), May McKeon Independent in Balbriggan LEA(Fingal) in 2004 (7.70%), Lily Wallace Independent in Limerick area 3 LEA in 2004 (7.33% or 331 first preferences), Jim Long Independent in Limerick City 4 LEA in 2004 (7.60%), Seanie Lonergan for Labour in Cahir LEA (South Tipperary) in 2004 (9.15%), Brian Meaney for the Greens in Ennis West LEA(Clare) in 2009 (9.44%), Ted Tynan for the Workers Party in Cork City North East LEA in 2009 (8.93%) and Marion O'Sullivan for the Anti Austerity Alliance in Cork City North West LEA in 2014 (9.35%). The lowest of these was Tommy Foley with almost 7%. Rather surprisingly, quite a few of these candidates managed to hold their seats in the subsequent election. It is notable that some areas feature twice in this list, suggesting they have some characteristic that favours candidates with low percentages of first preferences.

[8]   Further examples (11) of failure to gain seats despite having near the relevant quotas (see also footnote 5) include:

Election	party and seats won	percentage obtained (quotas)	candidates
1985 Athlone (Ros)	Fine Gael (1)	37.83 (1.89)	3
1985 Swinford (Mayo)	Fianna Fáil (2)	57.58 (2.88)	3
1991 Rathmines (Dublin)	Fine Gael (-)	18.37 (0.92)	3
1991 Clane (Kildare)	Labour (-)	18.61 (0.93)	2
1991 Limerick City area 4	Fianna Fáil (-)	19.63 (0.98)	3
1999 Ballaghadereen (Ros)	Fianna Fáil (1)	38.79 (1.94)	3
1999 Tobercurry (Sligo)	Fianna Fáil (1)	38.99 (1.95)	4
2004 Balbriggan	Fine Gael (-)	16.73 (0.84)	2
2009 Borris (Carlow)	Fianna Fáil (-)	19.57 (0.98)	2
2009 Oranmore (Galway)	Labour (-)	18.33 (0.92)	2
2009 Swinford (Mayo)	Fianna Fáil (1)	39.12 (1.96)	3

There are other examples of an unconverted quota of 0.8 to 0.9, including Strokestown LEA (Roscommon) and Kilbeggan LEA (Westmeath) in 1991.

In 2004, with Leo Varadkar as sole candidate, Fine Gael got 1.91 quotas in Castleknock LEA (Fingal).

CHAPTER 21
Five seat Dáil constituencies

The five seat constituency is the largest form of constituency fought in Irish general elections. The five seat Dáil constituency also tends to be the most watched aspect of Irish general elections. This is because it is perceived that they give the best chance for parties other than the main two parties an opportunity to win a seat. It is also perceived as the most likely vehicle for smaller parties such as Democratic Left, the Greens, People before Profit, the Progressive Democrats and the Social Democrats to win seats and of course for an independent or two as well. Over the election cycle dealt with in this book, the following has been the pattern with 5 seat constituencies. An issue of particular interest in five seat constituencies is whether all the seats are monopolised by Fianna Fáil and Fine Gael or whether Labour or other parties and independents win seat. As can be seen from the chart below, there is a trend away from a Fianna Fáil/Fine Gael monopoly and a trend towards smaller parties and independents.

Election	No of 5 seat Constituencies	All seats won by FF/FG	Labour seat (number)	Other seats (number)
1981	15	3	9 (60%)	3
Feb 1982	15	6	8 (53%)	3
Nov 1982	15	5	8 (53%)	3
1987	15	3	7 (47%)	13
1989	15	3	6 (40%)	11
1992	14	1	14*(93%)	12
1997	14	5	4 (29%)	9
2002	14	1	8 (57%)	14
2007	12	1	7 (58%)	7
2011	11	1	9* (73%)	9
2016	11	-	3 (27%)	24

Labour won two seats in a constituency, Dublin South West and Dublin South Central respectively and the percentage represents the percentage of five seat constituencies in which it got a seat.

Technically the quotas required to win seats in 5 seat constituencies are as follows:

One seat	16.66%
Two seats	33.33%
Three seats	50%
Four seats	66.66%

In practice seats can be won with levels of vote which fall short of the quotas required.

It can be seen that the number of 5 seat constituencies is on a declining path and this pattern continued into the general election of 2016 with 11 five seat constituencies (Donegal, Dublin Bay North, Dublin Fingal, Kerry and Tipperary being new to the 5 seat club, but with Cavan/Monaghan, Mayo and Laois/Offaly dropping out due to declining (or in the case of Laois/Offaly increasing) population.

Where are 5 seat constituencies located?

Traditionally five seat constituencies have been located in three types of areas

Urban areas such as Dublin, Cork City, Limerick City and Galway City. Over time with a relative decline in urban population, Limerick and both the north and south side of Cork city reduced to 4. Dublin used to have five 5 seat constituencies but this had reduced to two by 2011, increasing to three in 2016.

The two county constituency. Consistent examples are Carlow Kilkenny, Cavan-Monaghan and Laois-Offaly. The latter two dropped out of the five seat category in 2016 due to population trends. Indeed Laois-Offaly had been a five seat constituency since 1922, so perished at the ripe old age of 94. Both are to be re-instated as part of the 2017 boundary review.

The single county. Wexford has been a 5 seat constituency since the pre 1981 reforms and has been joined over time by Louth, Mayo and Wicklow. Kildare and Meath started the modern cycle as five seat constituencies, but have since been divided because of increasing population. For the 2016 election, Donegal, Kerry and Tipperary joined the club. In a number of cases surgery involving adjacent counties is done to fit a single county into the five seat range, so that for 2016 only Kerry and Wexford were integral five seat constituencies, wholly composed of the county of that name.[1]

Continuity of representation

The longest period of continuity was the five elections from 1981 to 1989 and since then there has been significantly less continuity. There have been 125 occasions on which a five seat constituency was contested that was substantively the same as the previous election. 81 of those elections (64%) resulted in a change in the mix of parties holding the seats, a relatively low rate of continuity. Every five seat constituency which survived from 2007 to the general election of 2011, excepting Cork South Central, saw a change in party representation. Between 2011 and 2016 only Wexford of the five surviving constituencies produced no change in party terms in representation. The most volatile five seat constituencies have been Dublin South and Dún Laoghaire, each of which has seen seven changes in representation by party. Notably the most volatile four seat constituency is the adjacent constituency of Dublin South East. Dublin Central and Mayo saw a change on every occasion they were contested as five seat constituencies and Dublin Central has remained volatile in its four seat form. Of course aside from the 81 cases which saw a change in parties represented, there have been quite a number of further changes in the person representing a party.

Do they achieve minor party representation?

Five seat constituencies have been fought in general elections on 151 occasions (so that 755 seats were available). Seats have been won by parties outside the two traditional large parties as follows

Labour	83	Progressive Democrat	33
Green	7	Sinn Féin (including H Block seat won in 1981)	19
Democratic Left/Workers Party	11	Independents/other parties	38

It is probably true to conclude that for the Greens, Progressive Democrats and Workers Party/Democratic Left, five seat constituencies were an important factor for getting a foothold in the Dáil. They have probably been less relevant for both Sinn Féin and the independents.

The performance of the Labour Party is broadly similar, irrespective of whether a constituency is a four or five seat constituency. The pattern for Labour in three seat constituencies is less favourable, but this has more to do with their predominantly rural location than any inherent lack of favourability to Labour.

The total seats in five seat constituencies won by minor parties and independents are 191 (or 25.3% of the seats available); this of course leaves a staggering 564 seats gained by the two traditional large parties. It is highly unusual (but less so in 2016) that one of the two traditional large parties does not get at least two seats. This has only happened twelve times.[2] The Dún Laoghaire and Wicklow contests in 1992 were the only two contests prior to 2016, where 5 separate political groupings were represented after the general election. This position became much more prevalent in 2016.

It is relatively unusual also that the two traditional large parties do not gain at least a seat in a five seat constituency. This did happen to Fine Gael in Dublin Central in 1987, Dublin South West in 1992, Dún Laoghaire in 2002 and Tipperary in 2016. It only happened to Fianna Fáil in a general election for the first time in 2011, arising in Dublin South, Dublin South Central and Wicklow. Indeed prior to 2011 there were only 11 occasions where Fianna Fáil gained less than two seats in a five seat constituency.

Winning four seats in a 5 seat constituency

This has been achieved only once, the Mayo result for Fine Gael in the 2011 general election. This was achieved with a first preference vote (48,170 votes, a record) across four candidates of 64.96%, which was very close to four quotas. A key background factor was that Enda Kenny, the then likely incoming Taoiseach was the leading Fine Gael candidate in the constituency. There was a candidate in the three large urban centres of Ballina, Castlebar and Westport, which would have helped to capture the urban vote and a fourth candidate covering the smaller towns in the eastern end of the county. It seems highly unlikely that this feat could ever be repeated.

Winning three seats in a 5 seat constituency

This is not uncommon (31% of such areas contested) and has happened as follows:

Election	No of times	Percent of constituencies
1981	4	26.7
Feb 1982	8	53.3
Nov 1982	6	40
1987	4	26.7
1989	4	26.7
1992	3	21.4
1997	5	35.7
2002	5	35.7
2007	4	33.3
2011	4	36.4
2016	nil	0

It has happened in 15 five seat constituencies.[3] No party other than Fianna Fáil or Fine Gael has achieved this. It is comparatively as common as achieving three of five seats in a five seat LEA.

It is quite noticeable that three seats are often achieved with a first preference vote of less than 50%. Indeed since 1997, it is exceptional that it is achieved with a vote in excess of 50%. There are quite a number of examples of percentages of first preference votes below 43% (which is about 2.6 quotas) securing three seats

Election	Constituency	Party	Percentage (quotas)	Candidates
2011	Carlow Kilkenny	FG	39.22 (2.35)	3
2007	Cavan Monaghan	FF	37.77 (1.89)	2
(but Ceann Comhairle automatically elected)				
2011	Cavan Monaghan	FG	39.56 (2.37)	4
1997	Cork North Central	FF	**35.53 (2.13)**	3
2002	Cork North Central	FF	41.48 (2.49)	3
1997	Cork South Central	FF	42.61 (2.56)	3
1987	Dublin Central	FF	42.13 (2.53)	3
2011	Dublin South	FG	36.35 (2.18)	3
1981	Dublin West	FG	42.09 (2.52)	3
1982 Feb	Dublin West	FG	42.47 (2.55)	3
1997	Meath	FF	41.88 (2.51)	3
1982 Nov	Wexford	FG	41.42 (2.50)	3
2011	Wicklow	FG	39.61 (2.38)	3

It is notable that in all of these cases, apart from Cavan Monaghan in 2011, the successful party ran three candidates. In many cases the successful three candidates were closely bunched together. For example in Cavan Monaghan in 2011, 469 votes separated the three successful Fine Gael candidates.

Winning two seats in a 5 seat constituency

As noted already, it is almost always the case historically that a party has won at least two seats in a five seat constituency. Of the 151 contests in five seat Dáil constituencies, 144 have resulted in at least one of the parties holding two or more seats. With the increasing fragmentation in the system, it is possibly less likely that this will happen. Five of the 11 five seat constituencies contested in the 2016 general election produced representation for five groups.

In addition to the two main parties, Labour (Dublin South West 1992, Dublin South Central 2011), the Progressive Democrats (Limerick East 1987, 1989 and 1992) and Sinn Féin (Louth 2016) have won two seats in a five seat constituency.

While in theory it is necessary to have 33.33% of the vote to be assured of two seats, the feat is often achieved with a base of 26% (approx 1.55 quotas) or less of the first preference votes. The following table details fourteen cases where two seats were achieved from a lower base of first preference votes.

Election	Constituency	Party	Percentage (quotas)	Candidates
1987	Cork North Central	FG	26.24 (1.57)	2
1992	Cork North Central	FG	22.74 (1.36)	2
1989	Dublin West	FG	24.58 (1.47)	2
1997	Dún Laoghaire	FF	25.83 (1.55)	2
2016	Galway West	FG	24.02 (1.44)	3
1987	Kildare	FG	26.30 (1.58)	2
1992	Kildare	FG	22.44 (1.35)	2
2011	Laois Offaly	FF	26.78 (1.61)	3
1992	Limerick East	PD	26.14 (1.57)	2
2007	Limerick East	FG	25.52 (1.53)	2
2016	Louth	FG	**19.58 (1.17)**	2
1987	Meath	FG	25.68 (1.54)	3
2016	Wexford	FG	23.32 (1.40)	3
2007	Wicklow	FG	23.15 (1.39)	2

It is generally notable in these cases that two candidates only were running and that the candidates polled fairly closely together in terms of first preferences. For example in Louth in 2016, the two Fine Gael candidates Fergus O'Dowd and Peter Fitzpatrick obtained 6,814 and 6,408 first preference votes respectively. This is pretty well the same pattern as is seen where three seats are won with a first preference vote below 43%. It should be noted that in local elections it has sometimes proved possible to get two seats of five with first preference votes in the high teens, probably due to less tight transfer patterns in those elections.

Winning a single seat in a five seat constituency

Theoretically a candidate or party requires 16.66% to win a seat in a five seat constituency. However there are quite a number of examples where a candidate has won a seat from a starting position of 10% or less of the first preferences, the most notable of which are

Election	Constituency	Candidate	Percentage (quota)
2007	Carlow Kilkenny	Mary White (Green)	7.96 (0.48)
2016	Dublin Bay North	Finian McGrath (Ind)	7.98 (0.48)
2016	Dublin Bay North	Tommy Broughan (Ind)	7.28 (0.44)
2016	Dublin South West	Katherine Zappone (Ind)	**6.63 (0.4)**
2007	Dún Laoghaire	Ciarán Cuffe (Green)	7.72 (0.46)
1987	Galway West	Michael D. Higgins (Lab)	7.35 (0.44)
2016	Galway West	Catherine Connolly (Ind)	7.59 (0.46)

There are 31 candidates[4], all from smaller parties, who filled seats starting from a first preference vote of less than 10%, with the 7.35% achieved by now President Michael D Higgins in 1987, being by far the lowest up to 2016, this record being broken by both Tommy Broughan and Minister Katherine Zappone in 2016. There is obviously a pattern of certain constituencies continually featuring in this list, particularly Cork South Central, Dublin South and Limerick East. It is notable that in five seat LEAs it has been possible to win a seat with a first preference vote of less than 7%. This is probably because of less tight transfer patterns in those elections.

Obtaining quotas but not related number of seats

There is no example in modern elections in a five seat Dáil constituency of a party obtaining a number of quotas not matched by at least the same number of seats. There have been a number of "near misses" though.

Election	Constituency	party(seats)	percentage (quotas)	candidates
Feb 1982	Carlow/Kilkenny	FF (2)	47.94 (2.88)	5
Feb 1982	Dún Laoghaire	FG (2)	48.2 (2.89)	3
Nov 1982	Dún Laoghaire	FF (1)	30.05 (1.8)	4
1992	Dún Laoghaire	FF (1)	31.18 (1.87)	3
2002	Dún Laoghaire	FG (-)	15.04 (0.9)	3
1981	Galway West	FG (1)	30.00 (1.8)	4
1981	Kildare	FF (2)	48.63 (2.92)	4
Feb 1982	Kildare	FG (1)	32.05 (1.92)	3
Nov 1982	Kildare	FF (2)	47.82 (2.87)	4
1989	Limerick East	FF (1)	32.43 (1.95)	3
1992	Limerick East	FF (1)	30.25 (1.81)	2
2007	Limerick East	FF (2)	48.69 (2.92)	3
Nov 1982	Meath	FF (2)	47.50 (2.85)	4
2016	Tipperary	FG (-)	16.09 (0.97)	3
1981	Wexford	FF (2)	48.23 (2.89)	4
1997	Wicklow	Lab (-)	13.8 (0.83)	2

The three Limerick East instances are instructive. In each case Willie O'Dea, the lead Fianna Fáil T.D. got a massive vote. There was however a significant leakage on transfers. In two cases there were two other candidates who polled poorly on the first count. An effort to reduce O'Dea's vote to quota level would likely have resulted in an extra seat in each of the contests. Most of these cases involve one more candidate than desirable.

Conclusion

The following conclusions can be drawn on five seat constituencies

- They have been a significant route for smaller parties, particularly the Green Party and the Progressive Democrats to obtain seats.
- There is no particular evidence that Labour does much better in five seat constituencies than it would in four seat constituencies.
- Three seats have been won from as low as 35.53% of the first preferences, with the comparative percentages for two and one seat being 19.58% and 6.63%. In all of these cases the comparative low figure in local elections has historically been a few percentage points lower.
- The four seats won by Fine Gael in Mayo in 2011 seems to be an anomaly, unlikely ever to be repeated.
- In 151 contests, there is no instance of parties getting less seats than they obtained quotas.
- It is highly likely that one party will get two seats in a five seat constituency, so this is a realistic goal for the larger parties.
- Generally there is a change in party representation from one election to the next, this happening in 64% of cases.

References in Chapter 21

[1] Following the 2016 general election, the only areas of the country that will have been comprised in a 5 seat constituency since 1981 are Carlow Kilkenny (the bit of Carlow county in the Wicklow constituency has also always been part of a 5 seat constituency), Galway West, Wexford and the Rathfarnham area of south Dublin.

[2] The twelve occasions where neither Fianna Fáil nor Fine Gael got a second seat in a five seat constituency were in Dublin Bay North 2016, Dublin Fingal 2016, Dublin South Central 2011, Dublin South West 1992 and 2016, Dún Laoghaire 1992, Kerry 2016, Limerick East 1987, 1989, 1992, Tipperary 2016 and Wicklow 1992.

[3] It has happened in each of Carlow/Kilkenny, Cavan/Monaghan, Cork North Central, Cork South Central, Dublin Central, Dublin South, Dublin West, Dún Laoghaire, Galway West, Kildare, Laois/Offaly, Mayo, Meath, Wexford and Wicklow. In fact the only regular five seat constituencies where it has not happened are Dublin South Central and Limerick East. In the case of each of Carlow/Kilkenny, Cavan/Monaghan and Wexford, both main parties have achieved three seats out of five at some point since 1981. So in Wexford, Fianna Fáil achieved three seats in the February 1982 election and Fine Gael achieved three seats in the immediately following November 1982 election.

[4] In the following cases a single seat was obtained with less than 10% of the first preference vote.

Election	Constituency	Candidate	Percentage (quota)
2007	Carlow Kilkenny	White (Green)	7.96 (0.48)
1987	Cork South Central	O'Sullivan (Lab)	8.64 (0.52)
2002	Cork South Central	Boyle (Green)	8.96 (0.54)Q
2007	Cork South Central	Lynch C (Lab)	9.25 (0.56) Q
2016	Donegal	Pringle (Ind)	8.49 (0.51)
2016	Dublin Bay North	McGrath (Ind)	7.98 (0.48)
2016	Dublin Bay North	Broughan (Ind)	7.28 (0.44)
2016	Dublin Fingal	Ryan (Lab)	9.95 (0.6)
2016	Dublin Fingal	O'Reilly (SF)	8.66 (0.52)
1989	Dublin South	Garland (Green)	8.81 (0.53)
1992	Dublin South	O'Donnell (PD)	8.66 (0.52)

Election	Constituency	Candidate	Percentage (quota)
1997	Dublin South	O'Donnell (PD)	9.39 (0,56)
2002	Dublin South	Ryan (Green)	9.45 (0.57)Q
1987	Dublin South Central	Cluskey (Lab)	9.09 (0.55)Q
1992	Dublin South West	Rabbitte (DL)	8.78 (0.53)
2016	Dublin South West	Zappone (Ind)	**6.63 (0.4)**
2002	Dún Laoghaire	Cuffe (Green)	9.33 (0.56)
2007	Dún Laoghaire	Cuffe (Green)	7.72 (0.46)Q
1987	Galway West	Higgins (Lab)	7.35 (0.44)Q
2016	Galway West	Connolly (Ind)	7.59 (0.46)
1981	Limerick East	Kemmy (Ind)	8.62 (0.52)
1997	Limerick East	O'Sullivan (Lab)	9.19 (0.55)
2002	Limerick East	O'Sullivan (Lab)	9.26 (0.55)
2002	Limerick East	O'Malley T (PD)	9.77 (0.59)
2007	Mayo	Flynn (Ind)	9.50 (0.57)
2016	Tipperary	Kelly (Lab)	9.94 (0.6)
2016	Tipperary	Healy (WUAG)	9.56 (0.57)
1987	Wexford	Howlin (Lab)	9.61 (0.58)
2002	Wexford	Twomey (Ind)	9.62 (0.58)Q
1992	Wicklow	Fox (Ind)	9.15 (0.55)
2011	Wicklow	Donnelly (Ind)	9.26 (0.56)

Most of these candidates did not reach the quota; however those denoted Q did.

CHAPTER 22

Five seat electoral areas

Five seat areas are encountered in both general and local elections. Over the six local elections 1985 to 2014, they have been contested on 288 occasions. However only 2 five seat LEAs were created for local election 2014, both in the city of Cork (which uniquely was not reviewed for that election). Consequently for each of the five elections where they were material, there was an average of 57 such areas.

The percentage of votes technically required to achieve quotas in five seat LEAs is as follows

1 seat	16.66%
2 seats	33.33%
3 seats	50%
4 seats	66.66%

The maximum number of seats that has been achieved by any single party is 4 and this has happened four times. The maximum vote achieved is the 65.16% (over 3.9 quotas) won by Fianna Fáil in Kilmacthomas LEA (Waterford) in 1985, although this percentage of votes only won three of the five seats.

Where do they occur?

Five seat LEAs are seen in most counties and covering a variety of areas, ranging from exclusively urban to exclusively rural. They have historically been quite prevalent in Dublin, in Cork City and in Waterford City. However at one time or another there has been a five seat LEA in every county. Some areas were consistently so until 2014.[1]

Do they achieve minor party representation?

The number of areas where the two traditional large parties took all of the seats in a five seat LEA has declined as follows: 19 (1985), 14 (1991), 14 (1999), 9 (2004) and 4 (2009). Thus it is clear that representation for other parties is now almost always a feature of a five seat LEA. Commensurately there is a growing trend for one of Sinn Féin, smaller parties and independents to be represented in five seat LEAs with this happening in 72% of the areas in 2004 and in 80% of the areas in 2009.

There have been quite a number of instances where one of the two traditional large parties failed to take a seat in a five seat LEA.[2] This has happened to Fine Gael in every local election and to Fianna Fáil in 1991, 2004 and 2009, predominantly in urban LEAs.

The Labour party performance in five seat LEAs has been patchy. The only local election where Labour won a seat in more than half such areas was 1991, when it scraped through 50% (33 of 65) of the 5 seat LEAs and 2009 when it took a seat in 60% of such areas. However Labour has managed to take two seats in five seat LEAs on 30 occasions. This usually has happened in Dublin but also in Bagenalstown (Carlow), Celbridge (Kildare), Thomastown (Kilkenny), Mullingar (Westmeath) and Wicklow LEAs.

Sinn Féin has taken seats in five seat LEAs in every local election. They won 8 seats in 1999, increasing to 18 in 2004 and 20 in 2009. The 2009 performance meant a seat was achieved in about 40% of those areas and about 50% of those actually contested by the party.

Winning 4 seats in a five seat LEA

This has been achieved four times. It was first achieved by Fianna Fáil in New Ross LEA (Wexford) in 1985 with a first preference vote of 63.41% (3.8 quotas) and Rathkeale LEA (Limerick) with a vote of 59.39% (3.56 quotas). It was also achieved twice in 1999. Fianna Fáil achieved it in Ballinasloe LEA (Galway) with a vote of 64.95% (3.9 quotas). More significantly Fine Gael achieved the same in 1999 in Boyle LEA (Roscommon), but with a vote of 52.4%, being 3.14 quotas. The achievement was on the basis of four strategically placed candidates, one in Boyle town and three in the north, east and south of the LEA, each of whom beat the local Fianna Fáil candidate and got significant local transfers (see chapter 27). In all four cases, the successful party had four candidates.

Winning three seats in a five seat LEA

This is quite common but has become decreasingly so over time

Election	Number of times achieved (including 4/5)	Percentage of areas
1985	35	53%
1991	18	28%
1999	17	32%
2004	11	21%
2009	10	20%
2014	nil	nil

It is usually achieved with a first preference vote for the party of over 45% and in many cases in excess of 50%. The most notable achievement was the winning of three seats by Fine Gael in Ardee LEA (Louth) in 2009 with 32.57% (1.95 quotas), but there are a number of cases where it was achieved on first preference votes of 2.5 quotas or less.[3] Half of these cases have only three candidates and sometimes they are tightly bunched together. For example in Kells LEA in 2009, there were only three Fine Gael candidates and 63 votes separated them. In the other cases there were four candidates. The equivalent achievement in a general election nearly always involves three candidates.

Winning two seats in a five seat LEA

This is a pretty common feature of local elections to the extent that it is pretty well the norm for at least one of the parties to win two seats. Indeed it is not unusual that two parties or a party and the independent groups win two seats each, leaving the last seat to another party or group. In the 1985 election one party, usually Fianna Fáil, won at least two seats in every such area; by 1991 there were 9 areas where no party won more than a single seat, all in urban Ireland. This reduced to 2 in 1999, increasing to 6 in 2004 and to 7 in 2009. Both LEAs contested as 5 seats in 2014 produced two seats for Fianna Fáil and in one case two seats for the Anti Austerity Alliance. Thus of 288 times five seat LEA's have been contested, only 24 contests (less than 10%) resulted in a 1:1:1:1:1 outcome, with in many cases a few independents rather than five separate parties. It can therefore be expected that if five seat LEAs are to feature in future local elections, a party is likely to win two seats.

All of the main parties have won two seats in five seat LEAs. Labour have done so, as noted earlier, on 30 occasions or about 10% of 5 seat LEAs contested. Sinn Féin has done so on three occasions in the adjoining areas of Carrickmacross LEA (Monaghan) and Dundalk-Carlingford LEA (Louth). The Workers Party did so in Waterford No 3 LEA in 1991.

While in theory it is necessary for a party to get 33.33% of the vote to secure two seats in a five seat LEA, there are many examples where this has been achieved on first preference votes of close to or less than 25% (which is about 1.5 quotas).[4] The most extraordinary performance is that of the Progressive Democrats in Edenderry LEA in 2004. In that case three candidates shared 17.13% of the vote or 1.03 quotas with the two successful candidates on 503 and 445 votes respectively with a quota of 1,182. The lower successful candidate was in fact seventh ranking on the first count. The internal transfers from the third candidate were not good, being at a rate of only 44% and favoured the candidate with more first preferences. The critical issue seemed to be that both candidates got excellent transfers as two lower Fine Gael candidates were eliminated, thus enabling both of them to pass out the second Fine Gael candidate, beating her by a margin of 22 votes in the end. Another relevant issue was surplus Fianna Fáil votes which favoured them over Fine Gael rivals. It is a perfect illustration of the various ways in which a vote of less than 25% can be converted to two seats in a five seat LEA.

There is no obvious pattern to cases where two seats were won on less than a quarter of the vote. There are quite a few cases where the successful party had just two candidates, managed to get them into the top five based on first preferences and got both elected. However in many cases where there were only two candidates, the vote was not extraordinarily well balanced. Notable exceptions were the success of Fine Gael in Cork City South West LEA in 1999, where the two candidates finished within 8 votes of each other, each within the top 5 and tracked each other closely as the count progressed and the success of Labour in Tallaght South LEA in 2004 where the gap between the two candidates on first preferences was 48. A surprising number of the cases however involved three candidates for the successful party and indeed the Labour success in Wicklow LEA in 1985 involved four candidates. It is also fairly clear that better transfers from other sources were an important factor. The Labour Party feature extensively in cases where two seats were obtained with 1.5 quotas or less, perhaps reflecting a better (and perhaps historic) ability to pull transfers from all sorts of different sources.

However as a broad principle, first preference votes for a party of 25% or less in a five seat LEA achieve only one seat. It is quite notable how often parties are successful with votes in the high 20's. Equally occasions where a party has 30% or more and fails to achieve two seats are very much the exception. The tipping point seems to be around 28%, which is probably the target for a party hoping to take two seats.

Winning a single seat in a five seat LEA

Theoretically 16.66% of the vote is required to achieve a seat in a five seat LEA. However there are frequent instances of seats being won with first preference votes of less than 10% which is 0.6% of a quota and there are 37 instances (representing 2.6% of the seats won in five seat LEAs)[5] where a candidate's first preference votes were at a level of less than 9%, with no party colleague to assist. Most of these candidates were independents and the others were from minor parties. The vast majority of these candidates got elected without reaching the quota, which is a likely scenario. Curiously many of them were elected in the subsequent election, in many instances without a drastic improvement in their votes. Quite a number of them did not contest the subsequent election.

The candidate who succeeded from the lowest ever percentage Sadhbh O'Neill (Green) is interesting. She was apparently on holidays throughout the campaign and therefore did no canvassing. She did not even return to vote and her final margin on the last count was two votes. An interesting route to success from less than a third of a quota. Notably she did finish in fifth position on the first count.

There are of course many other party candidates who won a seat while starting with a similar percentage level of first preferences, but they had the benefit of transfers from colleagues.

In practice the figure required to be reasonably confident of a seat is more like 12% and in most cases, candidates achieving that tend to be elected.

Obtaining quotas but not related numbers of seats

This has happened in a number of instances.

LEA	Local authority	Party	Election	Percentage (quotas)	No of seats	Candidates
Cabra-Glasnevin	Dublin City	Fianna Fáil	2009	34.21 (2.05)	1	3
Celbridge	Kildare	Labour	1985	34.00 (2.04)	1	1
Ballyragget	Kilkenny	Fianna Fáil	1985	51.18 (3.07)	2	5
Tinnahinch	Laois	Fine Gael	1985	50.03 (3)	2	5
Limerick 2	Limerick City	Fianna Fáil	1991	18.93 (1.14)	nil	4
Birr	Offaly	Fine Gael	2004	34.51 (2.07)	1	4
Roscommon	Roscommon	Fianna Fáil	1991	35.84 (2.15)	1	4
New Ross	Wexford	Fianna Fáil	2004	50.53 (3.03)	2	5
Arklow	Wicklow	Labour	2004	36.48 (2.19)	1	2
Wicklow	Wicklow	Fine Gael	1985	17.79 (1.07)	nil	3

The most evident factor in most of these ten contests was that the party failing to convert its quotas had too many candidates, usually two in excess of the number of seats it was aiming to win. The excess candidate factor was generally compounded by a poor transfer rate, once the excess candidates were eliminated and often the transfers favoured the stronger candidate rather than the one seeking the marginal seat. In two cases Cabra-Glasnevin LEA and Arklow LEA, the leading candidates, Mary Fitzpatrick and Nicky Kelly respectively exceeded the quota by a significant margin but then proceeded to transfer to other fellow party candidates at rates of 47.4% and 13.3% respectively. In the case of Celbridge LEA in 1985, Labour had just the one candidate.

There have also been quite a number of instances of failure to take a second seat with a party first preference vote of 31 or 32 percent, failure to take three seats off first preference vote percentages in the high 40s and failure to take a fourth seat with a percentage first preference vote in the mid 60s[6]. These and other instances of under performance are generally due to imbalance in the vote between candidates or too many candidates, coupled with poor transfers.

Conclusion

The following broad conclusions can be reached about five seat LEAs (to the extent they become a feature of future local elections)

- While historically the two traditional large parties probably got between 3 and 4 seats between them in these areas, this has probably now adjusted to a possibility of three between them.
- It is highly likely that a five seat LEA will return at least one independent or very minor party candidate.
- as electoral patterns are evolving, it is likely that Sinn Féin will tend to get at least one seat in most of these areas.
- the Labour party performance in these types of areas is mixed but generally they tend to have a seat in at best about half of them. The likely level of success will vary according to the "mood music" around Labour at a particular election.
- generally if a party is aiming to take a number of seats in a five seat

LEA, it is necessary to have the appropriate quotas. However 4 seats have been obtained on 52.4% (3.14 quotas) , three seats on as little as 32.57% (1.95 quotas), two seats on as little as 17.13% (1.03 quotas) and one seat on as little as 5.47% (0.33 quotas).

- typically there is about a 70% level of change where an LEA survives broadly intact between elections.

- there are a few examples in these types of LEAs of underperforming by reference to quotas achieved, so electoral discipline is important in these areas.

- historically the best outcome achieved in these areas was 4 seats. The 2014 local election suggests however that the likely realistic maximum target for the future is two and it probably requires around a minimum 28% of the vote to achieve this.

References in Chapter 22

[1]   The following LEAs have always had 5 seats until their effective abolition in 2014: Belturbet (Cavan), Cork City NC; Cork City SC (Cork City), Bantry/Schull (Cork), Clontarf (Dublin City), Ballinasloe (Galway), Ballyragget (Kilkenny), Dromahaire; Manorhamilton (Leitrim), Ardee (Louth), Carrickmacross (Monaghan), Roscommon, Templemore (Tipperary North), Tipperary (Tipperary South), Enniscorthy (Wexford) and Wicklow LEAs.

[2]   The following (mainly urban) five seat areas have had no representation for a major party

Cork City NC	2014 Fine Gael
Cork City SC	2014 Fine Gael
Donaghmede (Dublin)	1991 Fine Gael
North Inner City (Dublin)	1991, 1999 and 2004 Fine Gael
South Inner City (Dublin)	1991 Fine Gael
Ballybrack (Dún Laoghaire)	2009 Fianna Fáil
Balbriggan (Fingal)	2009 Fianna Fáil
Lucan (S Dublin)	2009 Fianna Fáil
Tallaght South (S Dublin)	1999 and 2004 Fine Gael
Limerick No 2	1991 Fianna Fáil
Thurles (Tipperary N)	2009 Fine Gael
Clonmel (Tipperary S)	1991 Fine Gael

Waterford City 2	1991 Fine Gael; 2004 Fianna Fáil
Waterford City 3	1985 Fine Gael
Waterford City South	2009 Fianna Fáil
Wicklow	1985 and 1991 Fine Gael

3   Three seats in five in an LEA were achieved with a relatively low vote in:

Year	LEA	Local authority	Party	Percentage (quotas)	Candidates
2009	Ballyragget	Kilkenny	Fine Gael	41.7 (2.5)	3
2004	Newcastle	Limerick	Fine Gael	42.02 (2.52)	4
2004	Granard	Longford	Fine Gael	42.27 (2.53)	3
1999	Ardee	Louth	Fianna Fáil	40.77 (2.45)	4
2009	**Ardee**	**Louth**	**Fine Gael**	**32.57 (1.95)**	**4**
2009	Kells	Meath	Fine Gael	37.99 (2.28)	3
2004	Ballymote	Sligo	Fine Gael	40.09 (2.40)	4
1991	Cashel	Tipperary South	Fine Gael	42.06 (2.52)	4
1985	Tipperary	Tipperary South	Fianna Fáil	36.96 (2.22)	3
2009	Enniscorthy	Wexford	Fine Gael	40.32 (2.42)	3

4   Two seats in five in an LEA were achieved with a relatively low vote in:

LEA	Local authority	Party	Election	Percentage (quotas)	Candidates
Cork SC	Cork City	Fianna Fáil	2014	22.8 (1.37)	2
Cork SW	Cork City	Fine Gael	1999	20.36 (1.22)	2
Clontarf	Dublin City	Fine Gael	1985	25.44 (1.53)	3
Clontarf	Dublin City	Fine Gael	2004	25.36 (1.52)	2
North Inner City	Dublin City	Fianna Fáil	1999	24.84 (1.49)	3
North Inner City	Dublin City	Labour	2004	25.66 (1.54)	2
Howth-Malahide	Fingal	Fine Gael	2009	22.97 (1.38)	2
Swords	Fingal	Labour	2004	24.56 (1.47)	3
Swords	Fingal	Labour	2009	25.37 (1.52)	3
Lucan	South Dublin	Labour	2009	17.21 (1.03)	2

LEA	Local authority	Party	Election	Percentage (quotas)	Candidates
Tallaght Central	South Dublin	Labour	1999	21.87 (1.31)	3
Tallaght South	South Dublin	Labour	1999	23.17 (1.39)	2
Tallaght South	South Dublin	Labour	2004	19.22 (1.15)	2
Terenure	South Dublin	Labour	1991	23.68 (1.42)	2
Celbridge	Kildare	Fine Gael	1985	24.61 (1.48)	3
Thomastown	Kilkenny	Labour	2004	21.19 (1.27)	2
Dundalk-Carlingford	Louth	Sinn Féin	2009	24.81 (1.49)	2
Dunshaughlin	Meath	Fine Gael	1991	24.39 (1.46)	2
Edenderry	**Offaly**	**Progressive Dem**	**2004**	**17.13 (1.03)**	**3**
Waterford 2	Waterford City	Fine Gael	1985	23.36 (1.40)	2
Waterford 2	Waterford City	Fianna Fáil	1999	19.33 (1.16)	2
Waterford 2	Waterford City	Fine Gael	2004	23.73 (1.42)	3
Mullingar West	Westmeath	Fianna Fáil	2004	25.66 (1.54)	3
New Ross	Wexford	Fine Gael	1991	21.48 (1.29)	2
New Ross	Wexford	Fine Gael	1999	24.11 (1.45)	2
Arklow	Wicklow	Fine Gael	1999	24.92 (1.49)	3
Arklow	Wicklow	Fine Gael	2004	25.24 (1.51)	3
Wicklow	Wicklow	Labour	1985	24.77 (1.49)	4

It is notable that three excellent Fine Gael performances in Arklow from 1991 to 2004 (1991 was in a six seat LEA) followed a 1.85 quota performance in 1985, which delivered only a seat in a then six seat LEA.

5   One seat in 5 in an LEA with a relatively low vote were achieved in:

LEA	Local Authority	Candidate (and party)	Election	Percentage (quotas)
Donaghmede	Dublin City	Sadhbh O'Neill (G)	1991	**5.47 (0.33)**
Cork SC	Cork City	Kathleen Lynch (WP)	1985	6.06 (0.36)
Dundalk Urban	Louth	Martin Bellew	1991	6.11 (0.37)
Clontarf	Dublin City	Derek McDowell (Lab)	1991	6.60 (0.40)
Thurles	Tipperary North	Martin Kennedy (Lab)	1991	6.71 (0.40)

LEA	Local Authority	Candidate (and party)	Election	Percentage (quotas)
Tipperary	Tipperary South	Denis Leahy	2009	6.87 (0.41)
Balbriggan	Fingal	May McKeon	2009	6.99 (0.42)
Terenure	South Dublin	Seamus Ashe	1985	7.17 (0.43)
Clontarf	Dublin City	Bronwen Maher (G)	2004	7.65 (0.46)
Waterford S	Waterford City	Cha O'Neill	2009	7.69 (0.46)
North Inner	Dublin	Christy Burke (SF)	1985	7.76 (0.47)
Cork NC	Cork City	Thomas Gould (SF)	2009	7.8 (0.47)
Naas	Kildare	Tim Conway (PD)	1999	7.99 (0.48)
Connemara	Galway	Peadar Ó'Tuathail	1991	8.01Q(0.48)
Thurles	Tipperary North	Billy Clancy	2009	8.01 (0.48)
Slane	Meath	Jimmy Cudden	1985	8.13 (0.49)
Cork NW	Cork City	Don O'Leary (SF)	1999	8.21 (0.49)
Slane	Meath	Dominic Hannigan	2004	8.35 (0.50)
Waterford 1	Waterford City	Martin Cullen (PD)	1991	8.38 (0.50)
Drumcliff	Sligo	Michael Carroll	1991	8.44Q(0.51)
Dundalk Urban	Louth	Neil McCann	1985	8.45 (0.51)
Sligo	Sligo	Tommy Higgins (Lab)	1985	8.45 (0.51)
Shannon	Clare	Bridget Makowski	1991	8.5 (0.51)
Naas	Kildare	JJ Power (G)	2004	8.52 (0.51)
Cork SC	Cork City	Paudie Dineen	2014	8.54Q(0.51)
Naas	Kildare	Mary Glennon	2004	8.6Q (0.52)
Killorglin	Kerry	Michael Healy-Rae	1999	8.64 (0.52)
North Inner	Dublin City	Joe Costello	1991	8.67Q(0.52)
North Inner	Dublin City	Mick Rafferty	2004	8.68 (0.52)
Connemara	Galway	Peadar Ó'Tuathail	1985	8.71 (0.52)
Slane	Meath	Tom Kelly(G)	2004	8.73* (0.52)
Belturbet	Cavan	Damien Brady	2009	8.74 (0.52)
Letterkenny	Donegal	Dessie Larkin	1999	8.77 (0.53)
Celbridge	Kildare	Colm Purcell (WP)	1985	8.82Q(0.53)
Cork NE	Cork City	Annette Spillane (SF)	2004	8.88 (0.53)
Drumcliff	Sligo	Michael Carroll	1985	8.96 (0.54)
Enniscorthy	Wexford	Sean Doyle	2004	8.98Q(0.54

Q denotes reached the quota at or before the final count

* the 8.73% represents the aggregate votes of Mr Kelly and a party colleague. The internal transfers from the party colleague to Mr Kelly were at 42%, so Mr Kelly's starting position was effectively 6.81%.

6   The following serious underperformances occurred in 5 seat LEAs

Fianna Fáil failed to take four seats in Kilmacthomas LEA (Waterford) in 1985 despite having 65.16%, 3.91 quotas of the first preference vote.

Fianna Fáil failed to take three seats in Dromahair LEA (Leitrim) in 1985 despite taking 49.13%, 2.95 quotas of the first preference vote.

Fine Gael failed to take two seats in Roscommon LEA in 1985 despite having 32.85%, 1.97 quotas of the first preference vote.

Fianna Fáil failed to take a seat in Limerick No 4 in 1991 with 19.63%, 0.98 quotas of the first preference vote.

Fine Gael failed to take three seats in Templemore LEA (Tipperary) with 47.07%, 2.82 quotas and 48.23%, 2.89 quotas of first preferences respectively in 1991 and 1999, despite outpolling Fianna Fáil on each occasion.

Labour failed to take a second seat in Tipperary LEA in 1991 despite polling 32.4%, 1.94 quotas of the first preferences, significantly more than the other two parties.

As can be expected with Labour, they failed to gain a seat in Gorey LEA (Wexford) in 1991 with 15.67%, 0.94 quotas of the first preferences but spread over two candidates.

Labour failed to take three seats in Mullingar West LEA (Westmeath) in 1999 despite taking 49.19%, 2.95 quotas of the first preferences, but only running two candidates.

Fianna Fáil (with four candidates) failed to take a second seat in Carrickmacross LEA (Monaghan) in 2004 on a first preference vote of 33.22%, 10 votes short of two quotas, missing the last seat by 222 votes.

It should also be noted that the extraordinary performance of the Progressive Democrats in taking two seats in Edenderry LEA (Offaly) in 2004 was matched by poor Fianna Fáil and Fine Gael performances (47.47% first preferences for two seats and 29.3% first preferences for one seat respectively). There are many other examples of underperformance with 0.85 quotas and above wasted including Cork City SW, Kildare, Kilmallock (Limerick), Castlebar (Mayo), Slane (Meath) and Boyle (Roscommon) LEAs in 1991.

CHAPTER 23
Six seat electoral areas

Six seat areas are only encountered in local elections. Over the six local elections 1985 to 2014, they have been contested on 219 occasions. The five local elections from 1985 to 2009 had an average of 30 areas each. However the minimum level for the number of seats per LEA was set at six for the boundary review preceding the 2014 local election. In fact the number of six seat areas increased in that election to 67.

The percentage of first preference votes technically required to achieve quotas in six seat areas is as follows

1 seat	14.28%
2 seats	28.57%
3 seats	42.86%
4 seats	57.14%

The maximum that has been achieved by any single party is 4 seats and the maximum first preference vote achieved is the 64.47% recorded by Fianna Fáil in the Castleconnell LEA in Limerick County in 1985.

Where do they occur?

Six seat LEAs have been a feature in nearly every county at one time or another. In 2014 they featured in every local authority apart from Carlow, Dublin Fingal, Kerry, Mayo, Sligo and Wexford. In particular six of the eight local authorities which consist of the minimum 18 seats were divided entirely into six seat LEAs in 2014. Only Carlow and Dublin Fingal have never had a six seat LEA.

Do they achieve minor party representation?

It is pretty standard that candidates for parties outside of Fianna Fáil and Fine Gael are elected in six seat LEAs. There have been twenty three occasions where the two major parties won all of the seats, but most of these occurred in the pre 2000 elections. In the 2014 election, the only six seat LEA to return a clean sweep for the two established parties was Granard LEA (Longford) where the seats divided 3 : 3 between the two main parties. It is in fact now surprisingly common that these LEAs return at least one candidate outside the four larger parties. This happened in all but 14 LEAs in the 2014 local elections and in three of those areas, only the established four parties contested the election.

There have indeed been nine instances where one or both of the two traditional large parties have failed to take a seat in a six seat area, including the failure of both to take a seat in Tallaght South in 2014.[1]

Minor party representation has often been measured by reference to whether the Labour party achieves representation. The only election where Labour succeeded in more than 50% of the six seat LEAs was the local election in 2009, where they won seats in 22 of the 33 electoral areas of that size. There is thus no greater pattern of Labour success in LEAs of this size than in smaller LEAs; it can however be noted that such areas can be prevalent in counties where Labour are traditionally quite weak; indeed of the 11 LEAs "missed" in 2009, they did not even contest four of them.

Sinn Féin became a significant feature of the electoral landscape in the 2009 and 2014 elections. In 2009, it won seats in a third of the six seat LEAs; by 2014 this had increased to winning seats in five/sixths of those areas (with the six seat LEAs where Sinn Féin did not take a seat concentrated in the south east quarter of Dublin, Longford and Roscommon). Thus it is now predictable that Sinn Féin will secure a seat in a six seat LEA. Indeed they hold two or more seats in 14 of them. The Workers Party took two seats in Waterford Area 3 in 1999.

Winning four seats in a six seat LEA

As noted above, this theoretically requires over 57% of the vote. Four seats of six have been achieved 21 times (or about 10% of contests) 15 times by

Fianna Fáil and 6 times by Fine Gael.[2] The technical required level of 57% was only exceeded in 6 cases.

The most notable performances were the ones in Arklow LEA (FF) in 1985 achieved on first preferences of 48.68%, Dundalk Carlingford LEA (FF) in 1999 achieved on 47.34%, Ballina LEA (FG) 2004 achieved on 47.41%, Borris in Ossory LEA (FG) in 2009 achieved on 47.1% and Inishowen LEA (FF) 2004 achieved on 44.73%. Notably these cases did not show particularly good electoral discipline and there were five candidates in two of them. Generally however four seats have been won on foot of a first preference vote in excess of 50%. Another notable performance is the taking of four seats in Donegal LEA by Fianna Fáil in three successive elections. It should be noted that despite the significant increase in the number of such LEAs in 2014, no party won four seats in any six seat LEA in 2014. This is perhaps suggestive of the fact that it may be unlikely to recur in an environment with numerous parties.

Winning three seats in a six seat LEA

This has been achieved quite frequently by each of Fianna Fáil and Fine Gael and also by each of Labour and Sinn Féin. There are also some instances where three seats are held by independents and others outside the major parties. The incidence of holding three seats of six is however reducing with only 19 such instances occurring for the four main parties in the local election of 2014. In the elections in the 20th century, it was the norm that one of the parties would take at least three seats in six seat LEA.

While in theory it is necessary to get almost 43% of the first preference vote to secure three seats, it has often been achieved on percentages close to or below a third of the vote or 2.33 quotas with the gain of three seats in Trim LEA (Meath) by Fine Gael on 31.15% (2.18 quotas) in 2014 being the lowest.[3] Pretty well all of these cases are characterized by having three candidates and in some cases they polled close to one another in first preference terms.

Winning two seats in a six seat LEA

This is a pretty common feature of all local elections. Before 2000 all contests resulted in at least one party holding two seats or more, with the exception of Cork City South East and Wexford in 1991. The prevalent pattern until then was that at least two parties held two or more seats. Since 2000, a pattern where six separate entities win seats is a little more common. Thus in the 2014 local elections, six separate entities (counting independents as separate) were elected in Donegal, Templeogue-Terenure (South Dublin), Galway City East, Galway City West, Limerick City North, Tramore/Waterford City West and Waterford City East LEAs. The prevailing pattern in the 2014 local elections was that the two biggest parties get an average three seats between them, with the balance being shared by other parties and independents.

While in theory it is necessary to get over 28% of the vote to secure two seats, they have been secured on percentages of around or less than 22% or about 1.5 quotas.[4] The most extreme example is the achievement by Labour in 2009 of two seats in Dún Laoghaire LEA with a first preference vote of a mere 16.16% or 1.13 quotas and three candidates.[5]

There is no very clear pattern to how two seats are generally achieved. Exactly half of the 22% or less cases involved just two candidates who sometimes polled very closely together. However others seem to involve a very ragged discipline such as the Fine Gael success in Edenderry LEA (Offaly) in 2009, achieved with four candidates and with the successful pair Nichola Hogan and Liam Quinn taking the fourth and fifth seats with a margin of 350 votes over the "last man standing" and the Fine Gael success in the adjacent Kildare LEA in 2004.

It should be said that it is far more common that two seats are obtained with a percentage more that the 28.57% representing two quotas. The situations where two are obtained from below quota are rather less common.

Winning a single seat in a six seat LEA

While the theory is that over 14% of the vote is necessary to get a single seat, there are quite a number of examples where a seat has been obtained with a party/independent vote in the 6% or below range[6], with the most extreme example being independent Alan Grehan in Dundalk South (Louth) in 2009 with 4.81% (0.34 quotas). It seems however that this has become more difficult in the later elections where generally a vote heading towards 10% is the minimum requirement.

It is notable that this nearly always benefits independents, who are prone to pick up transfers. It is rare that parties pick up a single seat with percentages of first preference votes of less than around 10%.[7]

Obtaining quotas but not related numbers of seats

This is surprisingly common in six seat LEAs and has happened in 11 contests (over one twentieth of the areas contested). Six seat LEAs where one seat less than quotas were obtained were

Area	Year	Party	Percentage	Seats (Candidates)
Killaloe (Clare)	1985	FF	57.43 (4.01)	3 (5)
Likely Reason for failure	*too many candidates*			
Ballyjamesduff (Cavan)	1991	FF	43.08 (3.01)	2 (4)
Likely Reason for failure	*candidates too close together on first preferences range 633-690 and poor transfers toward lowest*			
South Cork	1991	FF	43.76 (3.06)	2 (4)
Likely Reason for failure	*two candidates too far ahead and lowest two with similar low votes*			
Glenties (Donegal)	1991	FF	31.18 (2.18)	1 (4)
Likely Reason for failure	*too many candidates and poor transfers*			
Ballinamore (Leitrim)	1999	FF	42.98 (3.01)	2 (3)
Likely Reason for failure	*Fianna Fáil had one candidate too far ahead*			
Carrick/Shannon (Leitrim)	1999	FG	36.16 (2.53)	1 (4)
Likely Reason for failure	*FG had 2.53 quotas spread over 4 candidates and poor transfers*			
Midleton (Cork)	2009	FF	15.2 (1.06)	0 (3)
Likely Reason for failure	*candidates with 24% and 26% transfer rate respectively. Better transfers to other Cobh and Youghal candidates*			
Ballina (Mayo)	2009	FF	29.98 (2.09)	1 (3)
Likely Reason for failure	*three FF candidates with lower two almost equal. Transfers skewed significantly to lead candidate. Final margin of 19 votes*			

Area	Year	Party	Percentage	Seats (Candidates)
Claremorris (Mayo)	2009	FF	28.66 (2.01)	1 (4)
Likely Reason for failure	*candidates with transfers in the 40% bracket.*			
Tallaght South (South Dublin)	**2014**	**SF**	**51.26 (3.59)**	**2 (2)**
Likely Reason for failure	*Sinn Féin only ran two candidates so not in a position to benefit from over 3.5 quotas*			
Carrickmacross/ Castleblayney (Monaghan)	2014	FG	28.6 (2)	1 (3)
Likely Reason for failure	*Poor vote spread. FF with three candidates got two seats comfortably on 26.99%*			

The Carrick on Shannon LEA example is arguably the worst failure ever across all types of LEAs with 2.53 quotas being converted to one seat, a loss of 1.53 quotas in value. While there are higher losses, they are all cases with insufficient candidates.

There are a number of other examples not shown above where a party was much nearer the next highest quota but failed to get that number of seats such that it affects about one eighth of the areas contested.[8] This illustrates that this is a particular hazard of the six seat LEA.

As can be seen from the brief explanations, there are a variety of reasons why it is particularly common not to get the number of seats indicated by the quotas obtained in a six seat LEA. Because a bigger party is typically aiming for two or three seats, there are tactical issues as to whether to run the exact number of candidates or to have one or indeed two more. It is impossible to conclude which is the better option as often extra candidates are needed to deal with the geography of an area. There is some suggestion that minimalist candidate strategies are best, but circumstances will vary from one LEA to the next. With a large range of candidates, there is greater scope for transfers to leak outside the party or not to go to the candidate who needs them.

There can be an imbalance with one candidate getting too many votes and consequent leakage of a surplus, often dictated by the geography of the area. For example if the quota is 2,000 and it is known that there are likely to be 3,000 party votes in an area covered by one candidate, there is a possibility that that candidate will get 3,000 votes and will generate a surplus of 1,000, many of which will leak to rival party candidates in that area. Possible steps to combat this would include a second local candidate or persuading strong party supporters to vote for a candidate located elsewhere.

Conclusions

The following broad conclusions can be reached about six seat LEAs:

* While historically the two main parties probably got between 4 and 5 seats between them in six seat LEAs, this has probably now adjusted to a likelihood of three between them
* It is now highly likely that a six seat LEA will return at least one independent or very minor party candidate. Indeed two such persons are becoming quite normal
* as electoral patterns are evolving, it is likely that Sinn Féin will tend to get at least one seat in most of these areas
* the Labour party performance in these types of areas is mixed but generally they tend to have a seat in at best about half of them. The likely level of success will vary according to the mood music around Labour at a particular election
* generally if a party is aiming to win a number of seats in an LEA, it is necessary to have the appropriate quotas. However four seats have been obtained on as little as 44.73%, three seats on as little as 31.15%, two seats on as little as 16.16% and one seat on as little as 4.81%
* there are numerous examples in these types of areas of underperforming by reference to quotas achieved, so electoral discipline is a particular necessity in these areas
* Generally where areas are comparable, there have been changes in personnel each election as between parties in most areas
* historically the best outcome by party achieved in these areas was four seats. The 2014 election suggests however that the likely realistic best target for the future is three and it probably requires around 40% of the vote to achieve this.

References in Chapter 23

[1] No candidate was elected for one of the two traditional large parties in the following six seat LEAs:

Midleton (Cork)	2009 Fianna Fáil
Ballyfermot Drimnagh (Dublin)	2014 Fine Gael
Crumlin Kimmage (Dublin)	2014 Fine Gael
Dublin North Inner City	2009 Fianna Fáil
Tallaght Central (South Dublin)	2014 Fine Gael
Tallaght South (South Dublin)	2014 Fianna Fáil and Fine Gael
Killarney (Kerry)	1999 Fine Gael
Limerick City North	2009 Fianna Fáil
Thurles (Tipperary)	2004 Fine Gael

[2] Four candidates were elected for one of the two traditional large parties in the following six seat LEAs

Fianna Fáil	
LEA and percentage	Number of candidates
Ennistimon (Clare) 1999 62.3%	5
Kilrush (Clare) 1991 60.21%	5
Kanturk (Cork) 1985 52.84%	5
Donegal 1985, 1991, 1999 51.96%, 51.96% and 54.01%	4,5 and 5
Inishowen (Donegal) 2004 44.73%	**5**
Galway Rural 1985 57.5%	4
Killarney (Kerry) 1985 55.53%	4
Carrick on Shannon (Leitrim) 1999 49.86%	4
Castleconnell (Limerick) 1985 64.47%	5
Newcastle West (Limerick) 1985 57.53%	4
Dundalk Carlingford (Louth)1999 47.34%	4
Kells (Meath) 1999 57.9%	4
Arklow (Wicklow) 1985 48.68%	5

Fine Gael	
Borris in Ossory (Laois) 2009 47.1%	4
Ballymahon (Longford) 1999 55.94%, 2004 55.01%	4 and 4
Ballina (Mayo) 2004 47.41%, 2009 52.54%	5 and 4
Claremorris (Mayo) 2009 51.65%	4

3   Three candidates were elected with a low base vote for one of the parties in the following six seat LEAs

LEA, percentage and quotas	Number of candidates
Pembroke Rathmines (Dublin) 2009 (Labour 31.95% 2.24q)	3
Tallaght Central (South Dublin) 2009 (Labour 34.07% 2.38q)	3
Killorglin (Kerry) 1985 and 1991 (Fine Gael 31.19% 2.18q and 34.88% 2.44q)	3 and 3
Granard (Longford) 2014 (Fianna Fáil 33.04% 2.31q)	4
Trim (Meath) 2014 (Fine Gael 31.15% 2.18q)	**3**
Thurles (Tipperary N) 1999 (Fianna Fáil 33.7% 2.36q)	3
Comeragh (Waterford) 2014 (Fianna Fáil 34.61% 2.42q)	3

4   Two candidates were elected with a low base vote for one of the parties in the following other six seat LEAs

LEA, percentage and quotas	Number of candidates
South Cork 1991, Fine Gael 22.5% (1.57q)	4
Cork City South West 2009, Labour 21.46% (1.5q)	2
Donegal 2004, Fine Gael 21.64% (1.51q)	3
Ballybrack (Dún Laoghaire) 1999, Labour 19.68% (1.38q)	2
Killiney Shankill (Dún Laoghaire) 2014, Labour 18.57% (1.3q)	2
Dundrum (Dún Laoghaire) 2004, Fine Gael 19.06% (1.33q)	2
Stillorgan (Dún Laoghaire) 2014, Fianna Fáil 22.25%(1.56q)	2
Clondalkin (South Dublin) 2009, Fine Gael 21.11% (1.48q)	2

Tallaght Central (South Dublin) 2014, AAA 22.39% (1.57q)	3
Galway City Central 2014, Fine Gael 18.94% (1.32q)	2
Galway City East 2009, Labour 22.09% (1.55q)	3
Ballinasloe (Galway) 2014, Fine Gael 20.99% (1.47q)	3
Kildare 2004, Fine Gael 20.72% (1.45q)	4
Castleconnell (Limerick) 1991, Fine Gael 21.81% (1.53q)	2
Ashbourne (Meath) 2014, Fine Gael 21.28% (1.49q)	3
Edenderry (Offaly) 2009, Fine Gael 20.46% (1.43q)	4
Arklow (Wicklow) 1991, Fine Gael 18.79% (1.31q)	2

5   In Dún Laoghaire LEA in 2009, both Stephen Fitzpatrick 1,154 first preference votes and the long serving Jane Dillon Byrne 974 first preference votes got elected for Labour, with Fitzpatrick nearly reaching the quota of 2,563 on the last count and Dillon Byrne having a margin of 145 votes over the "last man standing". Their life was further complicated by a running mate who secured 771 votes. And all this was despite Dillon Byrne finishing ninth on the first count. A significant contributor to the success was a surplus of over 1,500 held by the People Before Profit candidate Richard Boyd Barrett, which transferred better to Labour than to others and indeed brought Dillon Byrne into seventh position on the second count.

6   A candidate was elected with a low base vote in the following six seat LEAs

LEA	Year	Candidate	Party	Percentage (quotas)
Carrigaline (Cork)	2009	David Boyle	Independent	5.08 (0.36)
Midleton (Cork)	1991	John Mulvihill	Labour	6.46 (0.45)
Ballymahon (Longford)	1991	John Nolan	Independent	6.81 (0.48)
Ardee (Louth)	2014	Jim Tenanty	Independent	4.84 (0.34)
Dundalk South (Louth)	1999	Mary Grehan	Independent	6.94 (0.49)
Dundalk South	**2009**	**Alan Grehan**	**Independent**	**4.81 (0.34)**
Dunshaughlin (Meath)	2004	Joe Bonner	Independent	6.10 (0.43)
Tullamore (Offaly)	1985	Thomas Dolan	Independent	6.52 (0.46)
Waterford City 3	2004	Mary O'Halloran	Fine Gael	6.61 (0.46)

Waterford City East	2009	Mary Roche	Independent	6.93 (0.48)
Tramore (Waterford)	1999	Betty Twomey	Independent	6.85 (0.48)
Arklow (Wicklow)	2014	Miriam Murphy	Independent	6.31 (0.44)
Wicklow	2014	Pat Kavanagh	Independent	5.19 (0.36)

[7] In some circumstances, parties took a single seat with a low base vote in a six seat LEA. Prior to 2014, the only occasion for Sinn Féin gaining a single seat with less than 9% was the gain of a seat in Nenagh LEA (Tipperary) in 2009 with 8.69% (0.61 quotas). However in the 2014 local elections, Sinn Féin gained a single seat in 12 six seat LEAs with first preference percentages in the 7%– 9% range, in some cases with the aid of significant transfers from other left wing parties.

Until 2014 Fianna Fáil had never gained a seat in a six seat LEA with a percentage of first preferences of less than 10%, but they achieved seats in that election with 8.74%(0.61 quotas) in Ballyfermot Drimnagh LEA (Dublin) and with 9.64% (0.67 quotas) in Waterford City South. It is similarly rare for Fine Gael to get a seat in a six seat LEA on less than 10%, the exception (apart from Waterford noted in footnote 6) being the gain by Ray McAdam in Dublin North Inner City LEA in 2009 with 7.82% (0.55 quotas), a seat retained in 2014 in an eight seat LEA on an even lower percentage of 5.88% (0.53 quotas).

[8] Parties obtained almost full quotas but not related seats in the following six seat LEAs

Area	Year	Party	Percentage	Seats (Candidates)
Kanturk (Cork)	1985	FG	42.28 (2.96)	2(4)
Likely Reason for failure	*one candidate too far ahead and too many candidates*			
Killorglin (Kerry)	1985	FF	41.71 (2.92)	2 (4)
Likely Reason for failure	*one candidate too far ahead and poor transfers to weaker candidate*			
Ballina (Mayo)	1985	FF	56.66 (3.97)	3 (4)
Likely Reason for failure	*FG had just more than 3 quotas*			
Tullamore (Offaly)	1985	Labour	10.85 (0.76)	0 (5)
Likely Reason for failure	*five candidates with poor transfers*			
Arklow (Wicklow)	1985	FG	26.42 (1.85)	1 (5)
Likely Reason for failure	*five candidates, four with low votes*			

Area	Year	Party	Percentage	Seats (Candidates)
Ballinamore (Leitrim)	1991	FF	42.08 (2.94)	2 (3)
Likely Reason for failure	*Third FF candidate too far behind. FG had better vote management on slightly fewer votes*			
Ballymahon (Longford)	1991	FG	55.58 (3.89)	3 (4)
Likely Reason for failure	*Poor FG vote discipline with 4 candidates allowed Independent with 6.81% to be elected*			
Fethard (Tipperary S)	1991	FF	40.7 (2.85)	2 (4)
Likely Reason for failure	*Three lowest candidates poll evenly. FG and Labour with two candidates each got two seats each*			
Ballyjamesduff (Cavan)	1999	FF	41.83 (2.93)	2 (4)
Likely Reason for failure	*Lower two candidates split quota evenly between them. Sinn Féin elected on 8.9%*			
Sligo Drumcliff	1999	FG	42.52 (2.97)	2 (3)
Likely Reason for failure	*Nearly 50% of FG lead candidate's transfers went to FF*			
Ennistimon (Clare)	2004	FF	56.77 (3.97)	3 (5)
Likely Reason for failure	*too many candidates*			
Inishowen (Donegal)	2004	FG	26.47 (1.85)	1 (3)
Likely Reason for failure	*too many candidates*			
Ballina (Mayo)	2004	FF	39.48 (2.76)	2 (4)
Likely Reason for failure	*too many candidates FG got 4 seats on 47.41% with a 28 vote margin at the end*			
Killaloe (Clare)	2009	FG	39.88 (2.79)	2 (3)
Likely Reason for failure	*Joe Cooney lead candidate got too many votes and only transferred 12% to third candidate*			
Borris in Ossory (Laois)	2009	FF	39.55 (2.77)	2 (3)
Likely Reason for failure	*FG got 4 on 47.1%. Only 3 FF candidates but one had a big surplus and transferred less to weaker candidate*			
Nenagh (Tipperary)	2009	FF	27.98 (1.96)	1 (4)
Likely Reason for failure	*four FF candidates with 25% transfer at critical stage; lead candidate too far ahead*			
Killaloe (Clare)	2014	FG	39.87 (2.79)	2 (3)
Likely Reason for failure	*as in 2009, leading FG candidate Joe Cooney got too many votes allowing FF to take three seats with 38.1%*			
Ballinamore (Leitrim)	2014	FG	28.04 (1.96)	1 (3)
Likely Reason for failure	*FG third candidate transferred locally. Sinn Féin got two seats on less first preference votes*			

CHAPTER 24

Seven seat electoral areas

Like six seat LEAs, seven seat LEAs are only encountered in local elections. Over the six local elections from 1985 to 2014, they have been contested on 147 occasions, so are somewhat less common than six seat LEAs. The number of seven seat LEAs in local elections has ranged from 21 (in 1985 and 1991) to 29 (in 2009) so has been relatively consistent over the cycle. Seven seats was the maximum permissible number of seats per LEA for all local elections up to 2014.

The percentage of first preference votes technically required to achieve quotas in seven seat areas is as follows

1 seat	12.5%
2 seats	25%
3 seats	37.5%
4 seats	50%
5 seats	62.5%

The maximum that has been achieved by any single party is 5 seats and the maximum first preference vote achieved is the 59.79% (4.78 quotas) recorded by Fianna Fáil in the Bailieborough LEA in Cavan in 1985, although this only achieved four seats. The better performances in the earlier elections were generally a party winning four or five seats; in later elections this has changed to winning two or three seats with much less than 2 or 3 quotas.

It should be noted that in Dáil elections up to 1944 there were several seven seat constituencies. These included Dublin South, Kerry, Limerick, Leitrim -Sligo and Tipperary. The seats obtained by parties in each case closely followed the quotas obtained. It should be noted that post 1932, Fianna Fáil took five of the seven seats in the Kerry constituency, achieving over 67% of the vote in the 1933 election.

Where do they occur?

There has been a tendency for seven seat LEAs to occur in rural counties where there is a large town. The LEA is usually made up of the town and the immediate hinterland. Seven seat LEAs have been relatively uncommon in large urban areas, being only encountered consistently in east Galway city. However they have been used quite frequently in suburban areas adjacent to larger urban areas.[1]

Their other use is across relatively large districts with a number of smaller towns. Examples include Bailieborough (east Cavan), Kilrush (west Clare), Bandon (Cork), Skibbereen (west Cork), Inishowen (north Donegal), Conamara (Galway), Loughrea (south Galway), Listowel (north Kerry), Borris in Ossory (west Laois), Claremorris (south Mayo), West Mayo, Kells (north Meath), Castlerea (west Roscommon) and Cashel/Tipperary.

The 2014 election saw much greater use of seven seat LEAs in large cities with one in Cork city, five in Dublin and one in Limerick city.

Do they achieve minor party representation?

In the earlier local elections in the period, there were a few elections where the entire representation elected in a seven seat LEA came from Fianna Fáil and Fine Gael. There were 4 such cases in 1985, two in 1991 and two in 1999. It has however happened only once in the 21st century, Athlone (Westmeath) in 2004, so it is probably safe to assume that there will always be representation outside the two traditional large parties in seven seat LEAs. Indeed in the 2014 elections, where both of the two traditional large parties performed moderately well, only 6 of the then 24 seven seat LEAs contested produced an aggregate five seats for the two traditional established parties and indeed Fine Gael failed to gain a seat in the seven seat Cabra-Finglas LEA in Dublin city. Fianna Fáil had also failed to gain a seat in the Limerick City South LEA in 2009.

In the 2014 local elections Sinn Féin won at least one seat in every seven seat LEA. This contrasts with a previous pattern of gaining seats in 4, 8 and 11 of those areas, showing the growing presence of Sinn Féin over a number of local elections.

Independents and/or very small parties (such as the Greens, Progressive Democrats and Workers Party) have generally achieved representation in seven seat LEAs. In the elections in the 21st century they had representation in most of them, such that for example, they are represented in all but three of the 24 seven seat LEAs contested in 2014.

The results of the Labour party as usual have been far more mixed and there is no pattern of better Labour representation in larger LEAs of this size.[2]

Winning five seats in a seven seat LEA

This has happened on only two occasions Kells LEA (Meath) in 1985 and Athlone LEA (Westmeath) in 1999. In both cases it was achieved with a first preference vote of 56% (roughly 4.5 quotas) and in both cases by Fianna Fáil. In each case there were six candidates and a reasonably high level of transfers from candidate six when he was eliminated. By way of contrast, while the Kells LEA produced five seats for Fianna Fáil in 1985, the adjacent Bailieborough LEA (Cavan) with almost 60% of the vote produced a mere four, with just five candidates; the issue seems to be down to fairly random factors such as the positioning of candidates, the availability of more Fine Gael transfers for an independent in Bailieborough LEA and there appears to be no particular message for strategy.

Winning four seats in a seven seat LEA

In the earlier part of the period being considered by this work, this was a surprisingly common achievement. In theory this requires 50% of the first preference vote. There are 30 such instances, which is slightly over 20% of the times a seven seat LEA has been contested. It has been achieved 21 times by Fianna Fáil and nine times by Fine Gael. Only nine instances (all Fianna Fáil) involved a first preference vote of more than 50%.[3] It should also be noted that there was only one occasion in 2014 where four seats were won in a seven seat LEA and that was with a first preference vote of 2.83 quotas, which was slightly short of what would theoretically be required to win three seats, not to mention four.

It is worth noting those performances where four seats were achieved, based on a first preference vote of 43% (about 3.4 quotas) or below being Kilrush LEA 42.87% FF, Bailieborough LEA 42.83% FG, Ballymote LEA 40.41% FG, Skibbereen LEA 40.23% FG, Limerick City South LEA 39.22% FG, Loughrea LEA 38.73% FG and Tullamore LEA 35.42% FF. In all of the cases, bar one, no successful candidate for that party exceeded the quota on the first count. In four of the seven cases, only four candidates were run by the successful party to get four seats.

Winning three seats in a seven seat LEA

It is again quite common that a party would win three seats or more in a seven seat electoral area. In the last century elections, this was the norm and only a few areas did not return three or more seats for at least one of the two major parties. The incidence of this dropped a little bit in 2004 and 2009. However there was a major change in 2014. In that election only 8 of the 24 seven seat LEAs returned three or more candidates for one of the two traditional large parties and Sinn Féin returned three candidates in two more.

Labour has never achieved three seats in a seven seat LEA (although they have managed the more difficult feat of three in a six seat LEA on a few occasions). Sinn Féin has achieved this in Cabra Finglas LEA (Dublin), Dundalk South LEA (Louth) and Monaghan LEA. Independents and smaller parties have achieved three seats collectively in a number of such LEAs in the 21st century elections.

There are thirteen instances[4] where three seats have been achieved on a first preference vote near to or below 30% (about 2.4 quotas), including two, Carrick on Shannon LEA (Leitrim) 2009 (24.53%, 1.96q) and Ratoath LEA (Meath) 2014 (23.73% 1.9q) where the party (FG) vote was less than two quotas. In a bare majority of these contests the successful party had just three candidates and in general no candidate from that party exceeded the quota on the first count.

Winning two seats in a seven seat LEA

It is absolutely standard that at least one party wins at least two seats in a seven seat LEA and there is only a single instance where this has not happened, Celbridge Leixlip LEA (Kildare) in 2014. Indeed the prevailing pattern is that at least two parties each achieve at least two seats. So in 2014, two separate parties won at least two seats in 16 of the 24 (two thirds) seven seat LEAs. Two seats have been won in seven seat areas by all the major parties on quite a number of occasions.

Generally first preference votes of 20% plus will secure two seats, but there are quite a number of instances where it was achieved on 20% (about 1.6 quotas) or below.[5] These include the following exceptional performances below 18%

LEA	Party	Year (and percentage/quotas)
Ballymun (Dublin)	**Lab**	**2014 (14.66% 1.17q)**
Killarney (Kerry)	FG	2009 (17.2% 1.38q)
Clonmel (S Tipperary)	FG	1999 (14.78% 1.18q)

There are a number of consistent features where two seats are achieved with 20% or less. A number of the cases have only two candidates for the successful party, although over a half of the cases involve a third candidate. Often the two successful candidates are close together in terms of first preference votes and usually they are in the top seven on the first count. The transfer of the third candidate's votes, where there was one, usually worked out in a favourable way.

Winning a single seat in a seven seat LEA

While theoretically 12.5% of the first preference votes are required to secure a seat in a seven seat LEA, there are quite a number of examples where seats have been achieved with less than 7% (about 0.55% of a quota) of the first preference votes.[6] These included the following exceptional performances below 6%, less than half a quota.

LEA	Election	Candidate (party)	Percentage of votes (quotas)
Tralee (Kerry)	1999	Billy Leen (Ind)	5.66 (0.45)
Inishowen (Donegal)	2009	Martin Farren (Lab)	5.48 (0,44)
Adare (Limerick)	2009	Pat Fitzgerald (Ind)	5.12 (0.41)
Galway E & N	1985	Brendan Holland (Ind)	4.8 (0.38)
Laytown-Bettystown (Meath)	2014	Tom Kelly (Ind)	4.81 (0.38)
Ballymun (Dublin)	**2014**	**Andrew Keegan (PBPA)**	**3.74 (0.3)**

Again there is a clear pattern of this being confined to independents and minor parties, although the Labour Party are represented on a few occasions.

Obtaining quotas but not related number of seats

As with other multi seat areas, there are examples where parties have achieved quotas or virtually a full quota in a seven seat LEA, without obtaining the appropriate number of seats.[7] The cases where a full quota (or virtually full) was achieved are

LEA	Year	Party(seats obtained)	Percentage of votes (quotas)
Bailieborough (Cavan)	2009	Fianna Fáil (2)	41.4 (3.31)
Skibbereen (Cork)	1985	Fianna Fáil (3)	49.41* (3.95)
Letterkenny (Donegal)	2009	Fine Gael (1)	24.72* (1.98)
Loughrea (Galway)	2004	Fianna Fáil (2)	38.98 (3.12)
Borris in Ossory (Laois)	1985	Fianna Fáil (3)	50.17 (4.01)
Longford	1999	Fianna Fáil (3)	49.78* (3.98)
Sligo-Strandhill	2009	Fine Gael (2)	37.91 (3.03)
Dungarvan (Waterford)	2004	Fianna Fáil (1)	27.8 (2.22)

*denotes areas where just short of the relevant number of quotas obtained

As can be seen, some LEAs appearing in this category gave rise to the problem in more than one election and in some cases related to the same party, indicating that particular difficulties arise in those areas with conversion of quotas to seats. There are however only 5 instances in 147 contests where quotas were not converted to seats or 3.4% of cases, so making a mess of a seven seat LEA seems significantly less prevalent than encountering problems in LEAs with a lesser number of seats, particularly 4 or 6.

The five cases where less seats than full quotas were obtained are instructive. Each involved a lead candidate who was far too far clear of the field. In the four cases involving Fianna Fáil, there were far too many candidates respectively five in Bailieborough LEA (2009) and Dungarvan LEA, six in Loughrea LEA and a staggering seven in Borris in Ossory LEA. In those cases the second, third or fourth candidate was often eliminated prior to the end or was just not competitive. The Sligo-Strandhill LEA case involving Fine Gael is a classic example of a very lopsided vote with the lead candidate Tony McLoughlin having almost 66% of the vote between three candidates. Generally the unsuccessful party having too many candidates is a feature of most of these electoral contests.

Conclusions

The following broad conclusions can be reached about seven seat LEAs

- While historically the two traditional large parties probably got between 4 and 5 seats between them in these areas, this has probably now adjusted to a likelihood of four between them.
- It is now quite likely that a seven seat LEA will return at least two independents or very minor party candidate. Indeed three such persons are occasionally seen.
- as electoral patterns are evolving, it is likely that Sinn Féin will tend to get at least one seat in all of these areas, as it did in the 2014 local elections.
- the Labour party performance in these types of areas is mixed but generally they tend to have a seat in about half of them in their better elections. The likely level of success will vary according to the mood music around Labour at a particular election.
- generally if a party is aiming for a number of seats in a five seat LEA, it

is necessary to have close to the appropriate quotas. However 5 seats have been obtained on as little as 56%, 4 seats have been obtained on as little as 35.42%, three seats on as little as 23.73%, two seats on as little as 14.66% and one seat on as little as 3.74%.

- there are some examples in these types of areas of underperforming by reference to quotas achieved, so electoral discipline is a necessity in these areas.

- historically the best outcome achieved in these areas was 5 seats. The 2014 election suggests however that the likely realistic high target for the future is three and it probably requires around 30% of the vote to achieve this.

- there is nearly always a change in party representation between elections where there are comparable positions.

References in Chapter 24

[1]   Larger towns where 7 seat areas have been encountered are Carlow, Cavan, Ennis (Clare), Mallow (Cork), Letterkenny (Donegal), Tuam (Galway), Killarney (Kerry), Tralee (Kerry), Naas (Kildare), Kilkenny (city), Portlaoise (Laois), Longford, Dundalk (Louth), Castlebar (Mayo), Navan (Meath), Monaghan, Tullamore (Offaly), Nenagh (North Tipperary), Clonmel (South Tipperary), Dungarvan (Waterford), Tramore (Waterford), Athlone (Westmeath), Wexford and Bray (Wicklow). Suburban areas where they are encountered are Piltown (South Kilkenny), Ballymote/Sligo Strandhill (Sligo), Cobh (Cork), Carrigaline (south Cork city), Athenry/Oranmore (Galway), Bruff/Adare (Limerick), Castleconnell (or Cappamore-Kilmallock) (both adjacent to Limerick city) Celbridge/Leixlip (Kildare) and Dunshaughlin / Ratoath (south Meath).

[2]   Labour's respective percentages of seven seat LEAs where they won a seat is 28.5% in 1985, 48% in 1991, 46% in 1999, 50% in 2004, 55% in 2009 and 37.5% in 2014. This is despite the fact that many of these LEAs are based on larger towns or are in areas adjacent to cities.

[3]   Parties obtained four seats in a seven seat LEA as follows

Fianna Fáil		
LEA	Percentage	Number of candidates
Bailieborough (Cavan)	1985 (59.79%); 1999 (43.4%)	5 and 5
Cavan	1985 (51.01%); 1999 (45.19%)	5 and 4
Ennis (Clare)	1999 (48%)	5
Kilrush (Clare)	1999 (51.64%); 2004 (42.87%)	6 and 5
Mallow (Cork)	1985 (46.67%)	5
Loughrea (Galway)	1985 (57.65%); 1991 (49.91%); 1999 (46.14%)	6, 6 and 5
Borris in Ossory (Laois)	1999 (53.7%)	4
Bruff (Limerick)	1999 (47.64%)	5
Kells (Meath)	1991 (51.3%)	6
Navan (Meath)	1985 (52.06%)	5
Tullamore (Offaly)	**2014 (35.42%)**	**4**
Nenagh (Tipperary N)	1999 (54.19%); 2004 (46.97%)	6 and 5
Athlone (Westmeath)	1985 (48.96%); 1991 (45.21%); 2004 (50.21%)	5, 6 and 6

Fine Gael		
LEA	Percentage	Number of candidates
Bailieborough (Cavan)	2009 (42.83%)	5
Cavan	2009 (46.67%)	4
Bandon (Cork)	1985 (49.73%); 1991 (48.52%)	4 and 4
Skibbereen (Cork)	2004 (40.23%)	5
Loughrea (Galway)	2009 (38.73%)	4
Limerick City South	2009 (39.22%)	4
Castleconnell (Limerick)	2009 (43.3%)	4
Ballymote (Sligo)	1991 (40.41%)	4

[4] Parties won three seats in a seven seat LEA with a low base vote in the following cases

LEA	Percentage and Quotas	Number of candidates
Fianna Fáil		
Skibbereen (Cork)	1991 (30.62% 2.45q)	3
Portlaoise (Laois)	2014 (30.4% 2.43q)	4
Fine Gael		
Carlow	1985 (29.07% 2.32q)	4
Tuam (Galway)	1991 (30.32% 2.42q); 2004 (29.84% 2.39q)	3 and 3
Listowel (Kerry)	2014 (29.21% 2.34q)	4
Kilkenny	2009 (29.16% 2.33q)	3
Carrick on Shannon (Leit)	2009 (24.53% 1.96q)	3
Longford	2004 (27.87% 2.23q)	3
Navan (Meath)	1999 (29.87% 2.39q); 2004 (28.86% 2.31q)	4 and 4
Ratoath (Meath)	**2014 (23.73% 1.9q)**	**3**
Wexford	2009 (28.49% 2.28q)	4

5   Parties won two seats in a seven seat LEA with a low base vote in

LEA	Party	Year (and percentage/quotas)	Candidates
Cork City SE	SF	2014 (18.93% 1.51q)	2
Letterkenny (Donegal)	FG	1991 (19.21% 1.54q)	3
Ballymun (Dublin)	**Lab**	**2014 (14.66% 1.17q)**	**2**
Castleknock (Fingal)	FG	2014 (19.47% 1.56q)	3
Terenure Rathfarnham (South Dublin)	Lab	2004 (18.42% 1.47q)	3
Galway No 1	FG	1991 (19.8% 1.58q)	3
Galway No 1	FG	1999 (20.6% 1.65q)	3
Killarney (Kerry)	FG	2009 (17.2% 1.38q)	2
Listowel (Kerry)	FF	2014 (19.77% 1.58q)	2
Tralee (Kerry)	FG	2004 (19.1% 1.53q)	3
Tralee	FG	2009 (19.83% 1.59q)	2
Naas (Kildare)	FG	1985 (20.65% 1.65q)	4
Naas	FG	1991 (20.34% 1.63q)	3
Tullamore (Offaly)	FG	1999 (18.33% 1.47q)	3
Nenagh (N Tipperary)	FG	2004 (18.07% 1.45q)	2
Clonmel (S Tipperary)	FG	1999 (14.78% 1.18q)	2
Clonmel	FG	2004 (18.21% 1.46q)	3
Bray (Wicklow)	FG	2009 (19.11% 1.53q)	3
Bray	Lab	2009 (19.4% 1.55q)	2

6   Candidates won one seat in a seven seat LEA with a low base vote in

LEA	Election	Candidate (party)	Percentage of votes (quotas)
Carrigaline (Cork)	1999	Kelly (PD)	6.66 (0.53)
Carrigaline (Cork)	2004	Desmond (Lab)	6.12 (0.49)
Inishowen (Donegal)	2009	Farren (Lab)	5.48 (0,44)
Ballymun (Dublin)	**2014**	**A. Keegan (PBPA)**	**3.74 (0.3)**
Cabra-Finglas (Dublin)	2014	T. Keegan (Ind)	6.74 (0.54)
Glencullen-S'ford (DúnL)	2014	McGovern (Ind)	6.15 (0.49)

LEA	Election	Candidate (party)	Percentage of votes (quotas)
Galway E & N	1985	Holland (Ind)	4.8 (0.38)
Galway E & N	1985	Hackett (WP)	6.23 (0.5)
Conamara (Galway)	2009	Ó'Cuaig (Ind)	Q6.92 (0.55)
Tralee (Kerry)	1999	Leen (Ind)	5.66 (0.45)
Celbridge-Leixlip (Kildare)	2014	Young (Ind)	6.23 (0.5)
Naas (Kildare)	1991	English (G)	6.67* (0.53)
Kilkenny	1999	Mullen (Ind)	6.00 (0.48)
Portlaoise (Laois)	2014	Tuohy (Lab)	6.59 (0.53)
Adare (Limerick)	2009	Fitzgerald (Ind)	5.12 (0.41)
Limerick City W	2014	Loftus (AAA)	6.63 (0.53)
Kells (Meath)	1991	Fitzsimons (Ind)	6.58 (0.53)
Laytown-Bettystown (Meath)	2014	Kelly (Ind)	4.81 (0.38)
Navan (Meath)	1991	Hegarty (Ind)	Q6.76 (0.54)
Tullamore (Offaly)	1999	Buckley (Ind)	6.37 (0.51)
Tullamore (Offaly)	1999	Dolan (Ind)	6.76 (0.54)
Tullamore (Offaly)	2009	Butterfield (Ind)	6.59 (0.53)
Athlone (Westmeath)	2014	O'Brien (Ind)	6.85 (0.55)
Bray (Wicklow)	1999	de Burca (Green)	6.69 (0.53)

* two candidates for the party so vote aggregated
Q reached quota by end of count
Many of these candidates did not contest or lost the ensuing election.

[7]   The following are cases of numbers of seats gained less than quotas (or failure close to quota *) in seven seat LEAs

LEA	Year	Party (seats obtained)	Percentage of votes (quotas)	Candidates
Bailieborough (Cavan)	1985	Fianna Fáil (4)	59.79* (4.78)	5
	2009	Fianna Fáil (2)	41.4 (3.31)	5
Cavan	1999	Fine Gael (2)	35.01* (2.8)	4
Skibbereen (Cork)	1985	Fianna Fáil (3)	49.41* (3.95)	4

LEA	Year	Party (seats obtained)	Percentage of votes (quotas)	Candidates
Letterkenny (Donegal)	2009	Fine Gael (1)	24.72* (1.98)	4
Glencullen-S'ford (Dun L)	2014	Fine Gael (1)	23.53* (1.88)	4
Loughrea (Galway)	1999	Fine Gael (2)	35.37* (2.83)	4
	2004	Fianna Fáil (2)	38.98 (3.12)	6
Tralee (Kerry)	1999	Labour (1)	22.33* (1.79)	2
Naas (Kildare)	1991	Labour (-)	10.3* (0.82)	3
Piltown (Kilkenny)	1985	Fianna Fáil (3)	47.28* (3.78)	5
Borris in Ossory (Laois)	1985	Fianna Fáil (3)	50.17 (4.01)	7
	1991	Fianna Fáil (3)	47.23* (3.77)	5
Longford	1999	Fianna Fáil (3)	49.78* (3.98)	5
Claremorris (Mayo)	1985	Fianna Fáil (3)	48.04* (3.84)	6
Navan (Meath)	1991	Fianna Fáil (2)	34.87* (2.79)	5
Ratoath (Meath)	2014	Fianna Fáil (1)	23.63* (1.89)	4
Monaghan	2009	Fine Gael (1)	22.15* (1.77)	3
Tullamore (Offaly)	2014	Sinn Féin (1)	22.8* (1.82)	1
Ballymote (Sligo)	1991	Fianna Fáil (3)	47.27* (3.78)	6
Sligo-Strandhill	2004	Fine Gael (2)	34.65* (2.77)	3
	2009	Fine Gael (2)	37.91 (3.03)	3
Nenagh (Tipperary N)	1985	Fianna Fáil (3)	47.05* (3.76)	6
Dungarvan (Waterford)	1999	Fine Gael (2)	34.69* (2.77)	4
	2004	Fianna Fáil (1)	27.8 (2.22)	5
Wexford	1999	Labour (1)	22.06* (1.76)	2
	2004	Fianna Fáil (1)	23.39* (1.87)	4

CHAPTER 25
Large electoral areas

The large LEA consisting of between eight and ten seats was an innovation of the 2014 local elections. The boundary review for that election created 42 such areas, being respectively

8 seat LEAs	23
9 seat LEAs	13
10 seat LEAs	6

Prior to 1935, there were eight or nine seat Dáil constituencies in Donegal (8), Dublin County (8), Dublin North (8) and Galway (9), which returned candidates broadly in line with quotas of votes obtained. Fianna Fáil won six seats in Galway in 1933, the highest ever.

The only prior recent experience of these types of areas were the traditional town councils abolished in 2014, which usually consisted of nine seats, elected as one elected area, although some of the larger towns such as Clonmel, Kilkenny, Tralee and Wexford elected 12 from a single electoral district. The experience with the town councils was that a lot of independents were elected and therefore this could be anticipated as a possible result in the larger LEAs. The 2014 election did indeed show the following pattern in these large LEAs

Party	No of candidates elected	Percentage
Fianna Fáil	98	27
Fine Gael	86	24
Sinn Féin	49	14
Labour	21	6
Other left	19	5
Independents	88	24
Total	**361**	

One very obvious feature is how close the percentage of seats obtained is to the national vote obtained by each party. So the overall effect of these areas seemed to be to produce seats proportionate to national vote. That however is not to say there is a radically different pattern in smaller LEAs.

While the rationale for creating such large LEAs was not fully explained, the intention seemed to be to create municipal districts around large urban centres. Unofficially it was also suggested that the intention was to assist the Labour Party, then a part of the government, on the premise that they would obtain at least one and possibly two seats in such LEAs. In the event they only obtained a seat in 19 of the large LEAs (less than 50%) and achieved two seats in only two, Drogheda LEA (Louth) and Tralee LEA (Kerry). Indeed the two traditional large parties each failed to take a seat in one such area, Dublin North Inner City LEA in the case of Fianna Fáil and Swords LEA (Fingal) in the case of Fine Gael. By contrast a candidate labelled as an independent took a seat in every single one of the large LEAs excepting Limerick City East. Indeed independents took four seats in each of Letterkenny LEA (Donegal), Inner City North LEA (Dublin), Swords LEA (Fingal), Tuam LEA (Galway), Killarney LEA (Kerry), and Clonmel LEA (Tipperary)

As is usual for local elections, generally the candidates finishing in the first 8, 9 or 10 places respectively on the first count were elected. However in 60% of the contests one (or sometimes two) of the leading candidates was displaced by transfers, perhaps a greater level of displacement than is normal. In practice however, transfers were much less important that getting candidates on the right first preferences on the first count. As was also predictable, candidates with very low percentages of the first preference vote were elected in these large areas. Large LEAs (number of seats in brackets) were to be found in 16 counties.[1]

Percentages required to obtain seats

The percentage theoretically required to obtain a seat were respectively

8 seat LEA	11.11%
9 seat LEA	10.00%
10 seat LEA	9.09%

In general the parties got what their percentages in each LEA merited, although in many instances seats were obtained with less than the percentage technically required. Notable exceptions affecting 17 LEAs of over (marked *) and under performance included:

LEA (number of seats)	Seats
Bagenalstown* (8)	Fine Gael got 4 seats on 2.78 quotas (half the seats; 31% of the votes)
Ennis* (8)	Fianna Fáil got 3 seats on 2.4 quotas
West Clare (8)	Fine Gael got 2 seats on 2.94 quotas
West Cork (8)	Fine Gael got 2 seats (6 candidates) on 2.91 quotas
Letterkenny* (10)	Sinn Féin got 2 seats on 1.33 quotas
North Inner City (8)	Labour got no seat with 0.87 quotas
Dún Laoghaire* (8)	PBP got 2 seats on 1.34 quotas
Clondalkin (8)	Sinn Féin with only 2 candidates had 3.38 quotas
Clondalkin* (8)	Fine Gael got 2 seats on 1.41 quotas
Mulhuddart (8)	Sinn Féin with only 2 candidates had 2.72 quotas
Killarney* (8)	Fine Gael got 2 seats on 1.22 quotas
S/W Kerry* (9)	Sinn Féin got a seat with 0.59 quotas
Tralee (9)	Sinn Féin with only 2 candidates had 3.0 quotas
Maynooth* (9)	Fianna Fáil got 3 seats on 2.41 quotas
Drogheda* (10)	Fine Gael got 3 seats on 2.49 quotas
Castlebar* (8)	Fine Gael got 2 seats on 2.9 quotas Fianna Fáil got 3 seats on 2.35 quotas
Ballymote-*	Fianna Fáil got 5 seats on 3.46 quotas
Tobercurry(8)	Fine Gael got 1 seat on 2.43 quotas
Sligo* (10)	Fianna Fáil got 3 seats on 2.39 quotas

The most notable aberration was in the west Sligo area of Ballymote-Tobercurry LEA. This was an amalgam of three former LEAs, the third being Dromore LEA, which previously had 12 seats in aggregate. Transfer patterns and local voting issues which affected this are discussed in chapters 16 and 27 respectively.

Generally the level of under and over performance did not seem to vary much from patterns usually observed. It is however notable that the over and under performances are particularly concentrated in the eight seat LEAs, suggesting that they could be particularly tactically treacherous. There are 7 examples above of poor performance in 8 seat LEAs, way ahead of the rate of problems in any other type of area. However the sample size is very small. Apart from this, there is no reason to conclude, based on one election, that very large LEAs lead to anomalous results in terms of over or underperformance.

Obtaining seats on very small percentage votes

It was quite likely with the advent of LEAs requiring very low percentages for a quota that some candidates would succeed in getting elected with a very low percentage of the first preferences. In the 2009 local elections, where the maximum seat number was 7, only two candidates who got less than 5% of the first preference vote were elected and a similar pattern is seen in earlier elections.

However in 2014 in large electoral areas, there were 36 successful candidates who got less than 5% of the first preference vote, representing about 10% of the successful candidates in the large LEAs. In quite a number of these cases there were running mates, so a supply of "friendly" transfers was available. Of the significant number of successful candidates[2] who obtained below 5% of the first preference vote, the most notable were

Candidate and party	Votes	LEA	Percentage
Hubert Keaney FG	618	Sligo	3.69
Kenneth Flood SF	502	Drogheda (Louth)	3.62
Lorna Nolan Ind	355	Mulhuddart (Fingal)	3.02
Joe Harris Ind	702	Ballincollig-Carrigaline (Cork)	3.01
Edmond Lukusa SF	353	Mulhuddart (Fingal)	3.01
Annette Hughes AAA	215	Mulhuddart (Fingal)	1.83

1.83% is the lowest percentage first preference vote ever obtained by a successful candidate, although the 2.71% obtained by Cyprian Brady, successful Dáil candidate for Fianna Fáil in Dublin Central in 2007 is perhaps a comparator.

A seat was won on less than 5% of the first preference vote in every nine and ten seat LEA (bar five of the nine seat LEAs) and in 40% of the eight seat LEAs. Three or more seats were won from below 5% of the first preference vote in Ballincollig-Carrigaline (10), Mulhuddart (9), Swords (9) and Wexford (10) LEAs.

By contrast it was rare to be able to obtain a seat in a six or seven seat LEA in 2014 with less than 5% of the first preference vote).[3]

Conclusion

- Large LEAs were an innovation of the 2014 elections and it is hard to make a judgment on them based on a single election. They will not be continued for the 2019 local elections.
- There is some evidence of anomalous results by reference to quotas obtained, most notably in eight seat LEAs where there were a lot of poor performances.
- Given that the quota in such areas is very low in percentage terms, predictably candidates obtained seats with record low percentages of the first preference vote. Around 10% of the candidates elected from those areas got less than 5% of the first preference vote. The record low in any election was the 1.83% first preferences achieved by Annette Hughes of the Anti Austerity Alliance in Mulhuddart LEA (Fingal).

References in Chapter 25

[1] The following were the large LEAs (number of seats in brackets)

Carlow - Bagenalstown (8), Carlow (10); *Clare* - Ennis (8), West Clare (8);*Cork* - Ballincollig Carrigaline (10), West Cork (8); *Donegal* - Inishowen (9), Letterkenny (10); *Dublin* - Beaumont-Donaghmede (9), Inner City North (8), Pembroke South Dock (8), Clondalkin (8), Lucan (8), Dún Laoghaire (8), Balbriggan (8), Howth-Malahide (8), Mulhuddart (8), Swords (9);

Galway - Conamara (9), Loughrea (8), Tuam (9); *Kerry* - Killarney (8), South/West Kerry (9), Tralee (9); *Kildare* - Kildare-Newbridge (9), Maynooth (9), Naas (9); *Limerick* - Limerick City East (8); *Louth* - Drogheda (10); *Mayo* - Ballina (8), Castlebar (8); *Sligo* - Ballymote-Tobercurry (8), Sligo (10); *Tipperary* - Clonmel (9), Nenagh (9), Templemore-Thurles (9); *Waterford* - Dungarvan-Lismore (8); *Wexford* - Enniscorthy (8), Gorey (8), New Ross (8), Wexford (10); *Wicklow* - Bray (8)

[2] Other successful candidates with less than 5% of the first preference vote (although in some cases with running mates) were

Candidate and party	Votes	LEA	Percentage
John F Flynn FF	1,036	South/West Kerry	4.98
Keith Doyle FF	660	Enniscorthy (Wexford)	4.96
Mary McCamley Lab	582	Mulhuddart (Fingal)	4.96
Séamus Kilgannon FF	823	Sligo	4.91
Paul Mulville Ind	682	Swords (Fingal)	4.85
Francis Timmons Ind	682	Clondalkin (S Dublin)	4.83
Shaun Cunniffe Ind	900	Tuam (Galway)	4.83
Mike Roche SF	763	Wexford	4.78
Jimmy Kavanagh FG	896	Letterkenny (Donegal)	4.74
Richie Molloy Ind	739	Clonmel (Tipperary)	4.72
Anne Devitt Ind	663	Swords (Fingal)	4.72
John Ryan FG	590	Bray (Wicklow)	4.71
Fergal Browne FG	544	Carlow	4.64
Joe Bourke FG	856	Templemore-Thurles (Tipperary)	4.57
Tom Healy SF	768	Conamara (Galway)	4.56

Clare Colleran-Molloy FF	584	Ennis (Clare)	4.54
JP Browne FG	742	Balbriggan (Fingal)	4.53
Mary Fayne FG	677	Dún Laoghaire	4,52
Paul Keller AAA	540	Limerick City East	4.52
Michael Merrigan Ind	666	Dún Laoghaire	4.45
Duncan Smith Lab	618	Swords (Fingal)	4.4
Mary Desmond FF	1,019	Ballincollig-Carrigaline (Cork)	4.36
Niall Kelleher FF	771	Killarney (Kerry)	4.21
Peter Keaveney FG	780	Tuam (Galway)	4.19
Michael O'Brien AAA	906	Beaumont Donaghmede (Dub)	4.15
Alison Gilliland Lab	873	Beaumont Donaghmede (Dub)	4.0
Michael Murphy SF	914	Ballincollig-Carrigaline (Cork)	3.91
Willie Crowley Ind	552	Kildare-Newbridge	3.85
David Hynes Ind	614	Wexford	3.85
Deidre Wadding PBP	599	Wexford	3.76

[3]   A rare exception was Ardee LEA (Louth) where two candidates with less than 5% of the first preference votes won seats.

CHAPTER 26

Different sized constituencies and LEAs – the Future

The earlier chapters of this Part have reviewed the outcome of elections in constituencies and LEAs of different sizes. There remains however the general implications of this for the future. Irish politics has possibly become so fragmented that it may be difficult for any party to get much in excess of 30% of the vote nationally in any election. The question is how a vote of that magnitude will impact on constituencies and LEAs of different sizes. It is likely that a party seeking to get close to a majority in Dáil Eireann or a council will focus on getting half the seats in a constituency or LEA with an even number of seats and two of five, three of seven and four of nine in a constituency or LEA with an odd number of seats. A bonus would be the occasional two in three. The following are some themes that will need to be considered for the future.

Constituencies/LEAs with even numbers of seats

This should be a key focus for larger parties. One of the features of the Irish system is that in constituencies or LEAs with even numbers of seats, half the seats can be won with considerably less than half of the vote. In theory 40% of the first preference vote is required to secure this in a four seat constituency/LEA, 42.86% in a six seat LEA, 44.44% in an eight seat LEA and 45.45% in a ten seat LEA. However experience has shown that a first preference vote of 5 or 6 percentage points less than that level, if properly managed, can usually secure half of the seats. This level of vote is well within the reach of a party which is registering nationally in the 25% to 30% range of first preference votes. Therefore parties aspiring to take significant numbers of seats will look very closely at the 4/6/8/10 seat constituencies and LEAs on offer and try to formulate a strategy to take half of those seats.

While it is becoming somewhat more difficult to get half the seats, Fianna Fáil and Fine Gael managed it on nine occasions in the 2016 general election out of 16 four seat constituencies, in an election where they got scarcely more than half the aggregate vote and about a quarter each. This was generally based on a level of first preference votes in the 30% to 39% range (many close to 30) and in only two cases the relevant party exceeded 40% of the first preference vote.

In the 67 LEAs fought as six seat areas in the 2014 local elections, a party got three seats on nineteen occasions, but in no case with more than 50% of the votes. About half of these were won with a first preference vote of 30%-39%, although there were rather more cases when the number of quotas technically required was exceeded, as compared with four seat constituencies. Three of the 23 LEAs fought as eight seat areas produced four or more seats for a party, in each case secured with between 30% and 40% of the vote.

There are only six examples of ten seat areas from the 2014 local elections and in no case has five seats been achieved. They are likely to be confined to large urban areas and given the range of parties available to vote for in those areas, five seats is difficult to achieve.[1] There does appear to be a gradually declining trend by size of area of getting half the seats (probably because the technical percentage required is getting higher, with this being most likely in a four seat area and least likely where there are ten seats. Of course in approaching LEAs with an even number of seats, regard has to be had to the established pattern of underperformance in 4, 6 and 8 seat LEAs.

Winning a majority of the seats

It seems in practice highly unlikely in the future that any party will be able to obtain a majority of the seats in a four, six, eight or ten seat constituency or LEA. The only examples in the recent cycle of elections are the three seats of four obtained by Fine Gael in Dún Laoghaire in the 2016 general election, but one of those seats represented the automatic return of the Ceann Comhairle and the five of eight gained by Fianna Fáil in Ballymote-Tobercurry LEA in Sligo in the 2014 local elections. It can therefore be concluded that getting a majority of the seats in an area with an even number of seats will be exceptional. This has implications for obtaining overall majorities either at national or county level, as clearly the likely best outcome in "even number" seat areas is 50:50.

Obviously a different dynamic obtains in constituencies and LEAs with an odd number of seats, 3, 5, 7 and 9. However it is also becoming difficult to get a majority of the seats in these areas. The main remaining exception to this is three seat constituencies/LEAs. In the 2016 general election, there were thirteen three seat constituencies and a party obtained two seats on four occasions, in each case with a first preference vote in the mid- thirty percent range. There is no example in the 2016 general election of three seats being obtained in a five seat constituency, but this may be related to the quarter share of the national vote obtained by each of the two traditional large parties.

There was only one example in the 2014 local elections of a majority of the seats in any five, seven or nine seat LEA being taken by a single party. This arose in the seven seat Tullamore LEA in Offaly where Fianna Fáil got four of the seven seats with a first preference vote of 35.42%. Indeed in the 13 nine seat LEAs, four seats were obtained on only one occasion, by Fianna Fáil in Templemore-Thurles LEA (Tipperary). Generally recent patterns would suggest that it will be difficult in the future to get a majority of the seats in areas with an odd number of seats, with the exception of three seat areas. It is assumed that in the future only constituencies will be capable of having three seats and that no LEA will be formed with three seats, given the historic bias against these in formulating LEAs.

A likely reason why it is difficult to get a majority or indeed half of the seats in the larger LEAs is the sheer challenge of managing three or more candidates in an electorally efficient way. The more candidates needed, the more difficult it is to get them evenly matched in the right geographic locations and operating as a team. This seems to be a likely reason why there is a greater tendency for anomalous results in LEAs with six and to some extent seven seats (the experience with 8 to 10 seats is too limited to judge).

Obtaining two seats in a five seat constituency

This is also a realistic goal for a party which can get in the range of 25% to 30% of the national vote. It is therefore to be anticipated that parties with aspirations to lead government will be quite focussed on how this might be achieved in a five seat constituency.

In the 2016 general election, there were eleven constituencies with five seats. There were eight instances in which a party achieved two seats, with each of Fine Gael, Fianna Fáil and Sinn Féin achieving this. In two constituencies Carlow Kilkenny and Louth, two parties achieved this. It is therefore something that is eminently achievable. In all circumstances where this was achieved by both Fine Gael and Sinn Féin, it was achieved with first preference votes in the 19% to 29% range and is thus well within the reach of major parties in current electoral conditions.

Local elections 2009 were the last time there was a material number of five seat LEAs and the strong prevailing pattern was that two seats or more were achieved by at least one party in most of those areas. Therefore to the extent that five seat LEAs were to be re-instated for local elections, there is a realistic prospect that two seats (or 40% of the seats) can be obtained by a party.

Obtaining a single seat in a constituency/LEA

This is likely to be the goal of most parties outside Fine Gael and Fianna Fáil. Indeed in some cases, particularly in Dublin, this is also likely to be the goal of both Fianna Fáil and Fine Gael. To some extent, particularly in local elections, Sinn Féin will also be focussed on obtaining more than one seat. It will be recalled that the minimum first preference vote historically needed by a party/independent to win a single seat was as follows:

Size of constituency/ LEA	General election	Local election
Three seats	8.4% (2016)	11.23% (2004)
Four seats	6.6% (1997)	6.99% (1991)
Five seats	6.63% (2016)	5.47% (1991)
Six seats	-	4.81% (2009)
Seven seats	-	3.74% (2014)
Eight seats	-	3.02% (2014)
Nine seats	-	3.85% (2014)
Ten seats	-	3.01% (2014)

The above chart does not completely reflect trends, as there has been a tendency in more recent elections for persons, particularly independents, to get elected with low percentages of first preferences. Depending on the circumstances in a particular area, percentages of first preferences a few points in excess of these minima, may be sufficient for a party or independent to achieve a seat. However the minimum percentage needed for a more established party such as Fine Gael, Fianna Fáil, Labour or Sinn Féin is probably a little greater, as these parties are less transfer friendly.

Splitting votes evenly

It is clear from looking at local election results in particular, that virtually all candidates who get 0.7 of a quota or upwards secure election. In the 2014 local elections for example only two candidates in the entire country, both for Fianna Fáil, secured over 0.7 of a quota in Ballyjamesduff (Cavan) and Ballymahon (Longford) respectively but failed to be elected. Even in 2009 when LEAs were smaller (3 to 7 seats), only 12 candidates got 0.7 quotas or more and failed to be elected. It seems to follow that if a party has 2.1 quotas in a bigger area and can split it exactly, they should get three seats and if a party has 2.8 quotas, they can get four seats. The practical reality however is that parties find it very difficult to manage votes with such a level of precision and while this level of vote is often obtained the usual outcome is 2 seats for 2.1 quotas and 3 seats for 2.8 quotas (indeed sometimes the outcome is 2). It is also noteworthy in this respect that in the 2014 local elections, candidates with more than 0.6 quotas usually were elected and therefore splitting 2.4 quotas with each candidate over 0.6 also has a good likelihood theoretically of success, but probably not achieving peace and harmony between the candidates.

Realistic targets for a large party – general election

In a general election, it seems realistic that a party aspiring to lead government would set out to get two seats in both four and five seat constituencies. If the Dáil as elected in 2016 can be taken as generally indicative, about one third of three seat constituencies will return two seats to a party. A possible bonus is 3 of 5 in a few of the five seat constituencies, let us say two for illustration. If the 2016 split of constituencies is representative of the future this produces the following numbers of seats

Three seat (13)	17	(13+4)
Four seats (16)	32	
Five seats (11)	24	(22+2)
Total seats	73	

This is six seats short of a majority in a 158 member Dáil and assumes a second seat is obtained in every four and five seat constituency and a single seat in every three seat constituency.[2] This illustrates the difficulty in any party aspiring to anywhere near to a majority of the seats in Dáil Eireann in the current political climate.

References in Chapter 26

[1]   It should be noted that Fianna Fáil did get 4 seats in the ten seat Carlow LEA in 2014, but they had in excess of four quotas (and indeed only four candidates)

[2]   There is no general election since 1981 where a party got two seats in every four seat constituency. The best performances in 1981, 1987 and 2002 involved Fianna Fáil missing this target in one four seat constituency (Cork East in 1981, Dublin South East in 1987 and 2002). In the earlier two elections, the occasional 3 in 4 compensated.

PART 5
Tactics

CHAPTER 27

Good electoral tactics

It is notable from a review of all elections since 1981 that there are a number of very good vote management techniques used by parties to maximise seats. Many of these are related to one another and by far the most significant is vote management, designed to get candidates relatively level on first preference votes. The key factors in vote management are competition between candidates and/or factors related to geography. In some cases these factors are supplemented by efforts by a party to have its supporters vote for or transfer to a particular candidate. In Part 4 of this book, spectacular over-performance by a party by reference to quotas received is noted. In many of these cases the factors discussed in this chapter are relevant.

Managing candidates' votes so that they are relatively equal

This is by far the most significant technique that has been used often with great success. It is usually referred to as "vote management". Often balancing of the party vote has happened merely because of a mixture of competition between two or three candidates and geography. However in some instances it has undoubtedly been assisted by some vote management at local level. The raw results, as published, when taken together with knowledge of the local geography, tell little as to how relevant vote management was, so any evidence on this tends to be anecdotal. Classic vote management involves a party being short of "x" quotas, but getting "x" seats by virtue of the successful candidates being relatively level on the first count, each with a significant part of a quota.

Fine Gael seem to have been pioneers over 30 years ago of this form of vote management. This undoubtedly arose because Fine Gael were usually critically short of 40% of the votes in four seat constituencies and LEAs and needed a plan to win two seats in a four seat constituency from a base in the low 30's. Occasionally Fine Gael were competitive for two in a three seat constituency/LEA or three in a five seat constituency/LEA and the technique would also have been relevant. By contrast Fianna Fáil generally tended to have the first preference votes for two seats in a four seat area, often with three competing candidates, so the technique was less important. There is however some evidence of both parties focussing on this issue in three and five seat areas, on the basis of being a bit short of the 50% required for a majority of the seats..

There is a perception that Fianna Fáil became "transfer friendly" from about 1997. While there are some moves in transfer patterns, most notably Progressive Democrat pacts, which broadly helped Fianna Fáil from 1997 onwards, this is overstated, as discussed in chapter 13. However what is evident from 1997 to 2007 is that Fianna Fáil established a mastery in keeping two or three candidates relatively even in first preference terms. This may have been prompted by declining levels of transfers between Fianna Fáil candidates. It was an exceptionally effective technique in a fragmented market. Fine Gael used the technique extensively in 2011 and this perhaps was the greatest factor in its enormous seat bonus.

Notable events in the early Fine Gael evolution of this form of management were the winning of two seats for the first time in Clare in November 1982 and the retention of two seats in Dublin North Central and Cork North Central in 1987. In Clare, the two successful candidates Madeleine Taylor-Quinn and Donal Carey got 7,553 and 6,339 first preferences respectively. In Dublin North Central, while the initial gain of two seats was based on an unequal vote, the surprise retention of the two seats in 1987 was achieved on an almost perfect first preference split of 5,201 votes for George Birmingham and 5,196 votes for Richard Bruton, with an aggregate vote of 24.22%. The Magill guide to the 1987 election (at page 74) recites that it was not all sweetness and light. "But this time, with the polls showing a decline in the Fine Gael vote it was every man for himself. Bruton produced personal literature and Birmingham retaliated with leaflets made to look like official Fine Gael documents but subsequently disowned by the party, claiming that there was an agreement that Fine Gael voters should give him their number ones". ...."By the accident of their competition, Fine Gael managed to produce the kind of spread of their vote between the two candidates which they had previously planned with meticulous care". In Cork North Central, Fine Gael were not quite as precise with Bernard Allen getting 5,934 first preferences and Liam Burke getting 5,438 first preferences, a total of 26.24% in a five seat constituency.

Fianna Fáil showed some evidence of this type of vote management in November 1982 in Meath (3 candidates with first preferences from 7,133 to 6,133 and a sweeper too), Sligo-Leitrim (3 candidates with first preferences from 8,552 to 7,897), Tipperary North (two candidates with first preferences of 7,945 and 7,843) and Wexford (three candidates with first preferences from 6,492 to 5,891 and a sweeper) but in each case were unsuccessful.

Vote management became a very significant feature in the tight 1997 general election, in which both Fianna Fáil and Fine Gael improved their numbers of seats. Examples include:

Constituency	Successful candidates and first preference votes	
Clare	Killeen 8,169, de Valera 8,025, Daly 7,420	Fianna Fáil
Cork East	Bradford 7,859, Stanton 5,117	Fine Gael
Cork North Central	Kelleher 5,419, Wallace 5,273, O'Flynn 4,943	Fianna Fáil
Cork North West	M Moynihan 8,299, D Moynihan 7,867	Fianna Fáil
Cork South West	Sheehan 8,008, O'Keeffe 7,454	Fine Gael
Dublin South	Mitchell 8,775, Shatter 8,094	Fine Gael
Dublin South Central	Briscoe 4,762, Ardagh 4,634 Mulcahy 4,574	Fianna Fáil (two seats)
Galway East[1]	Burke 6,931, Connaughton 6,445	Fine Gael
Laois Offaly	Enright 8,375, Flanagan 8,104	Fine Gael
Meath	Dempsey 8,701, Wallace 7,669 Brady 7,372	Fianna Fáil

Sligo-Leitrim	Reynolds 6,743, Perry 5,786 Leonard 4,016	Fine Gael (two seats)
Wicklow	Jacob 6,150, Roche 6,104, Lawlor 3,368	Fianna Fáil (two seats)

In pretty well all of these cases, the party concerned had less quotas than the seats they obtained. On the face of it the Bradford and Stanton split in Cork East does not seem that clever. However as Labour were likely to fare badly in that election and as the Labour candidate was in Stanton's part of the constituency, the split suited the way transfers were likely to fall. There was a more remote possibility there that the Democratic Left candidate Joe Sherlock would have been eliminated, in which event Stanton would not have succeeded, but the gamble proved correct.

The 2002 and 2007 general elections showed quite a number of very fine splits, although not all successful.[2] Key examples included:

Constituency	Candidates	
Dublin South West 2002	O'Connor 7,155, Lenihan 7,080	Fianna Fáil - successful
Galway East 2002	Callanan 7,898, Treacy 7,765, Kitt 7,454	Fianna Fáil - unsuccessful
Limerick West 2002	Neville 7,446, Finucane 7,410	Fine Gael - unsuccessful
Longford-Roscommon 2002	Kelly P 7,319, Finneran 6,502, Kelly G 6,430	Fianna Fáil - unsuccessful (by 55 votes)
Sligo-Leitrim 2002	Ellis 6,434, Scanlon 6,345, Devins 6,307	Fianna Fáil - unsuccessful
Tipperary North 2002	Hoctor 8,949, Smith 8,526	Fianna Fáil - successful
Cork South West 2007	Sheehan 7,739, O'Keeffe 7,560	Fine Gael - successful

Dublin North East 2007	Woods 7,003, Brady 6,861	Fianna Fáil - unsuccessful
Kildare South 2007	O'Fearghail 8,731, Power 8,694	Fianna Fáil - successful
Rosc- S Leitrim 2007	Feighan 9,103, Naughten 8,928	Fine Gael - successful

Fine Gael continued the pattern into 2011, most notably in the four constituencies where it obtained three seats:

Constituency	Percent	Candidates (all Fine Gael)
Carlow Kilkenny	39.22	Phelan 10,929, Hogan 10,525, Deering 7,470
Cavan-Monaghan	39.56	O'Reilly 8,333, Humphreys 8,144 Conlan 7,864 (there was a fourth candidate)
Dublin South	36.35	Mitchell 9,635, Mathews 9,053, Shatter 7,716
Wicklow	39.61	Doyle 10,035, Timmins 9,165, Harris 8,726

Fine Gael took 12 of the 20 (60%) seats on offer in those constituencies with an aggregate vote of less than 40% in each case, a significant contribution to its seat bonus. It wasn't that far short of the same in Wexford, where its three candidates were also closely matched.

There were also a number of tight performances by Fine Gael to win two seats, most notably Meath East where Regina Doherty had 8,677 first preferences and the late Shane McEntee had 8,794 first preferences, a gap of 117. This performance certainly involved some vote management between north and south of the constituency.

Labour has won two seats in a number of constituencies, most notably in 1992 and 2011. This however has never been based on a balanced vote. If anything their successes are despite a wholly unbalanced vote.

In the 2016 general election, it was a major challenge for any party to win two seats, given the fragmentation in the system. Vote management was therefore critical to many of the cases where two seats were obtained often from significantly less than two quotas

Constituency	Candidates	
Clare	Pat Breen 6,583, Joe Carey 6,071 Howard 2,053	Fine Gael (1.29 quotas)
Cork NW	Aindrias Moynihan 8,924, Michael Moynihan 7,332	Fianna Fáil (1.38 quotas)
Cork SC	Michael McGrath 11,795, Micheal Martin 11,346	Fianna Fáil (2.08 quotas)
Donegal	Charlie McConologue 12,533, Pat The Cope Gallagher 10,198	Fianna Fáil (1.86 quotas)
Dublin Bay South	Eoghan Murphy 6,567, Kate O'Connell 5,399	Fine Gael (1.51 quotas)
Dún Laoghaire	Mary Mitchell O'Connor 10,817, Maria Bailey 10,489	Fine Gael (1.44 quotas)
Kildare N	James Lawless 7,461, Frank O'Rourke 6,341	Fianna Fáil (1.41 quotas)
Kildare S	Fiona O'Loughlin 6,906, Séan Ó'Fearghaíl 6,469	Fianna Fáil (1.45 quotas)
Limerick Co	Patrick O'Donovan 8,479, Tom Neville 8,013	Fine Gael (1.49 quotas)
Louth	Gerry Adams 10,661, Imelda Munster 8,829	Sinn Féin (1.73 quotas)
	Fergus O'Dowd 6,814, Peter Fitzpatrick 6,408	**Fine Gael (1.17 quotas)**
Mayo	Dara Calleary 9,402, Lisa Chambers 8,231	Fianna Fáil (1.39 quotas)
Meath E	Helen McEntee 7,556, Regina Doherty 6,.830	Fine Gael (1.39 quotas)
Wexford	Michael D'Arcy 7,798, Paul Kehoe 7,696, Hogan 1,214	Fine Gael (1.4 quotas)

These fourteen cases represent the majority of the twenty one cases where a party managed to win two seats in the 2016 general election campaign.

Some failures of the 2016 general election illustrate exactly the reverse including

Constituency	Candidates	
Cavan-Monaghan	Humphreys 12,391, O'Reilly 6,566 (FG one seat)	1.59 quotas
Clare	Dooley 10,215, 2 others 7,365 (FF one seat)	1.54 quotas
Donegal	P Doherty 10,300, 2 others 9,878 (SF one seat)	1.65 quotas
Longford-Westmeath	Troy 11,655, Gerety-Quinn 3,944 (FF one seat)	1.41 quotas
Offaly	Cowen 12,366, Fitzpatrick 3,394 (FF one seat)	1.43 quotas

There are many similar examples of even performance in local elections. There is probably little point in listing them out as they re-inforce the same point. However one very notable feature of the local elections of 2014 is the relatively indisciplined performance by nearly every party in keeping its candidates balanced as to their respective votes. In the relatively few cases (6) where Labour won two seats, this was despite an imbalance in the vote between the candidates. Even Sinn Féin with its excellent performance found it difficult to balance the vote as between its candidates, with performances such as keeping three candidates in Cabra-Finglas LEA (Dublin) within 355 votes of each other on the first count and of keeping two candidates in Kells LEA (Meath) on 1,599 and 1,562 first preferences respectively very much more the exception than the rule. The level of indiscipline with the two major parties is also notable. A notable exception is the gaining of three seats by Fine Gael in Ratoath LEA (Meath) with Maria Murphy at 933, Gerry O'Connor at 861 and Gillian Toole at 793 first preferences, all succeeding against a quota of 1,363. The gaining of five seats by Fianna Fáil in Ballymote-

Tobercurry LEA wasn't wholly disciplined as the lead candidate was over 300 votes ahead. However a performance of Joe Queenan 1,117, Paul Taylor 1,107, Eamon Scanlon 1,106 and Jerry Lundy 1,032 first preferences is impressive with 11 first preferences separating the middle three candidates and a gap of 85 covering the group.

Sometimes balancing the vote involves ensuring that candidates come in with unequal first preferences, in the knowledge that the lower candidate is more likely to pick up transfers. An excellent example is in the Arklow LEA in Wicklow in the 1991 local elections. In that LEA Vincent Blake of Fine Gael got 1,020 first preferences and Tom Honan got 671 first preferences. This was an aggregate 1.31 quotas. However Blake was located in Tinahely at the rural end of the LEA and unlikely to gain many transfers. On the last count Honan had reached 1,176 votes and Blake had reached 1,140 votes and both were elected, 50 votes clear of a Fianna Fáil challenger. By contrast Fianna Fáil in the same election also got two seats but with 2.8 quotas, more than double the Fine Gael vote. This type of vote balancing was repeated in all subsequent elections until the district was radically changed in 2014, although the later elections featured two urban based candidates.[3]

It seems clear that with the diminishing vote share of all parties, this type of planning will become critical, particularly if parties are to win two seats in a constituency or to win three or four seats in some of the larger local authority areas.

It should be noted that there is one circumstance where a balanced vote is a problem rather than a positive. This is where a party has about a quota of votes and the two or indeed three candidates are evenly balanced. In those circumstances, poor transfers from one to the other usually result in there being no seat. This is discussed in chapter 28.

Running candidate numbers equal to likely seats

It has been evident for some time that all parties' preferred position for general elections is to run a number of candidates equal to the number of seats they realistically could aspire to win. This is the predominant reason that parties outside of Fianna Fáil and Fine Gael generally run one candidate only. The 2007 elections, in which both of Fianna Fáil and Fine Gael did well, illustrate the point for those two parties. In that case Fianna Fáil ran the minimum number of candidates in 28 constituencies and Fine Gael ran the minimum number of candidates in 25 constituencies.[4] There was a total of 43 constituencies. If one looked at elections in the early 80's the corresponding numbers were less than half of that and there were a considerable number of sweeper candidates. Further in 2007 there were only six constituencies where both parties each ran one more candidate than any realistic target. In Dublin South, Galway East, Louth and Waterford, they each ran three (four in the case of Fine Gael in Galway East), where the maximum seats each could expect was two (accepting that that was rather an outside possibility for Fine Gael in Waterford). The two other constituencies affected were geographically large constituencies Laois-Offaly and Mayo where it is customary to run candidates to cover each area. The trend in 2011 was continued by Fine Gael, but perhaps broke down a bit with Fianna Fáil due to the extraordinary collapse in their vote. The 2016 general election saw a resumption of this strategy by the two main parties, although the need to meet gender quotas led to some additional candidates. It is predictable that this minimalist trend will continue to dominate. Its attraction is that it should avoid loss of votes on transfer and it maximises the chances of being able to elect candidates who poll evenly.

This trend is also present in local elections although there is a greater trend in those to run extra candidates.

Marking and beating candidates of other parties in geographical areas

Where a party is extraordinarily successful in a local election, it is often on the basis that it has a candidate in each geographical area of a LEA, who then goes on to beat the local rival from the other major party in his or her district. While it is difficult to get precise details on the location of candidates in past local elections, this is almost certainly the key factor where a party gets 4 of 5, 4 of 6 and 5 of 8 as has happened in a small number of local election LEAs. Two examples Boyle LEA (Roscommon) in 1999 and Ballymote-Tobercurry LEA (Sligo) in 2014 will illustrate the point.

In Boyle LEA in 1999, Fine Gael took four of the five seats.[5] The following seems to be the first preference vote of the candidates in each local area in the LEA (the location of some Fianna Fáil candidates is guessed from transfers)

Area	Fine Gael candidate	Fianna Fáil candidate
Boyle town	Frank Feighan 1,090	John Cummins 526
Carrick area	Gerry Garvey 546	Tommie Bourke 153
South of Boyle	Kitty Duignan 577	none
Arigna area	Charlie Hopkins 669	Michael Gaffney 426
uncertain		Padraig McWeeney 275

The key seems to be finishing ahead of the local candidate for the other party and then taking a significant number of his or her transfers. This seems to have happened directly with Bourke with transfers to Garvey and indirectly with McWeeney with transfers to Duignan and Garvey via an independent. Co-incidentally they were the two weakest Fine Gael candidates and Fianna Fáil local transfers favoured them over Gaffney, the "last man standing", who lost by 90 votes.

The picture in Ballymote-Tobercurry LEA is much easier to work out as the location of candidates is readily ascertainable in electronic media. Fianna Fáil won five seats and Fine Gael one in an eight seat LEA. The following are the local "matches" with first preferences and transfers from the local "match"

Area	Fianna Fáil candidate	Transfer ex FG	Fine Gael candidate
Tobercurry	Jerry Lundy 1,032	+270	Michael Fleming 573
Ballymote	Eamon Scanlon 1,106	+162	Pat McGrath 450
Enniscrone/ Dromore	Joe Queenan 1,117	+524	Blair Feeney 1,068
Gorteen	Paul Taylor 1,107	+104	also ex Fleming

The strongest Fianna Fáil candidate Martin Baker, based in the east, got 1,454 first preferences and got elected, largely without material transfers from any source. His local rival was the Fine Gael "last man standing" whom he beat. The key to success was beating the Fine Gael man in your own locality and then benefitting to a significant extent from his transfers, based on the local area needing a councillor.

This local transfer factor is not really an issue in general elections in terms of gaining seats, with one exception. This arises in the two county constituencies where there is an imbalance in population, working against the smaller county. This arises in Carlow Kilkenny, Longford-Westmeath and Sligo-Leitrim, where in each case the smaller county, respectively Carlow, Longford and Leitrim have a tendency to be only able to secure one seat. There can be a tendency for local transfers to accrue behind the lead candidate in the small county to such an extent as to elect him or her. The phenomenon is most obvious in Carlow where the election of Michael Nolan in 2007 and Pat Deering in 2011 is heavily influenced by cross party transfers in Carlow. In 2011 Pat Deering had 7,470 first preferences. He picked up a total of 2,313 cross party Carlow transfers from Greens, Labour, Sinn Féin and Fianna Fáil Carlow candidates, considerably more than one might normally have expected. While he probably would have won the seat anyhow, the high levels of cross party support in Carlow was important.

Trying to control accumulation of excessive first count surpluses

This is discussed in detail in chapter 28, "Bad Electoral Tactics", with particular reference to efforts made by Dr Garret Fitzgerald in Dublin South East and Ray McSharry in Sligo-Leitrim to deal with this. Chapter 14 also deals with the leakage arising from first count surpluses. It is uncommon to find measures taken to tackle this. Indeed one frequently hears the argument from self assumed knowledgeable sources that the best way to elect Ms Y is for Mr X to get an enormous vote and bring Y in on his surplus. Curiously X is invariably male.

Trying to direct transfers

This is really only relevant where there are three or more candidates for a party, so it really has only affected Fianna Fáil and Fine Gael. This is very difficult to do unless in some way geography helps to have transfers delivered to the weaker candidate. Occasionally one will see a leaflet from a political party asking that voters in an area, if voting number 1 for A, give their number 2 vote to B and vice versa. It is really quite difficult to know whether this has worked as it requires quite skilled people seeing the boxes from the affected polling stations and being able to assess the level of transfers that seem to follow the request. Anecdotally it is suggested that it has been seen to work in the very few cases it is done.

It is often quite obvious (but perhaps not to C) that C will be the weakest of three candidates and by reason of geography will likely transfer substantially to B. It therefore makes sense to try and organize that A does rather better than B, so that the effect of the transfer is to bring A and B to a relatively even number of votes. This is exceedingly difficult to achieve, as usually C does not accept that they are the weakest and therefore any divvying up between A and B is problematic. Further it is often the case that A is geographically in the middle so getting transfers to leap from C to B is tricky.

While this isn't really a tactic as such, it is sometimes predictable, generally based on geography, that elimination of minor candidates will likely favour candidate A over B. Thus B needs to be ahead of A, if the candidates are to be level after the elimination of the minor candidates. This in practice can happen in constituencies or LEAs which have a clearly defined lesser populated part, such as Leitrim in Sligo-Leitrim, the northern ends of both Cork East and Cork North West and the rural end of Arklow LEA (Wicklow). Generally most of the eliminations are at the populous end of those constituencies and LEAs, so usually the candidate at the other end needs a cushion.

Getting candidates into "leaders' enclosure"

As discussed at length in chapters 11 and 12, there is a clear pattern that candidates who are in the top 3, 4 or 5 in respectively 3, 4 or 5 seat constituencies are relatively unlikely to be displaced. This is largely the reason why the "Managing candidates' votes so that they are relatively equal" strategy, discussed earlier in this chapter works, as usually the effect of that is to get those candidates into the leaders' enclosure. Polls are frequently conducted by parties during campaigns and any adjustments that take place to strategy as a result of polls are usually aimed at that objective.

Appreciating the population distribution in a constituency/LEA

There is a tendency for voters to vote for local candidates where they can, which is obviously particularly prevalent in local elections. If the distribution of population in a constituency or LEA starts to change radically, it is important to have candidates in the area where there is growth and frequently candidates in areas where the relative level of population is in decline start to struggle. For example in Laois, there has been a major increase in the percentage of the population living in both Portlaoise and Portarlington, leading to it being desirable to have strong candidates in those towns. Parties are often not very live to these trends and it can be difficult to recruit suitable candidates in growing areas and to "restrain" existing representatives in declining areas.

A key issue for every party is to appreciate population movements as each census is completed and react accordingly. The 2016 census for example shows quite significant population movements within constituencies and LEAs. Because the 2016 election took place a short time before the census, this would have been reflected in the results. Parties aspiring to multiple seats do however need to consider the changes in the context of the 2019 local elections. For example in the Graiguecullen-Portarlington LEA in Laois, the population has increased by 1,333 between 2011 and 2016. However of the 33 DEDs that make up this LEA, there has been a population increase in 21 and a decrease in 12. Further over 1,000 of the increase is in the three biggest urban areas in the LEA, so that they now represent just short of 50% of the population. A coherent strategy to maximise performance in this LEA needs to have regard to the shift in population, although bearing in mind a likely lesser turnout in urban areas.

References in Chapter 27

[1] The two candidate strategy in Galway East was known as the railway line strategy. Voters were asked to vote for a particular Fine Gael candidate depending on whether they lived to the north or south of the Dublin-Galway railway line.

[2] These were the cases where in the 2002 and 2007 general elections, careful splits in party votes either paid or nearly paid off

Constituency	Candidates	
Clare 2002	Killeen 8,130, de Valera 7,755, Daly 6,717 -	Fianna Fáil – unsuccessful
Cork East 2002	Bradford 7.053, Stanton 6,269 –	Fine Gael unsuccessful
Cork South Central 2002	Clune 5,535, Coveney 5,183	Fine Gael – unsuccessful
Cork South West 2002	O'Donovan 7,695, Walsh 7,187	Fianna Fáil – successful
Dublin North 2002	Glennon 5,892, Wright 5,658, Kennedy 5,253	Fianna Fáil – successful 2 seats
Dublin South 2002	Mitchell 5,568, Shatter 5,363	Fine Gael – unsuccessful
Dublin South West 2002	O'Connor 7,155, Lenihan 7,080	Fianna Fáil – successful
Galway East 2002	Callanan 7,898, Treacy 7,765, Kitt 7,454	Fianna Fáil – unsuccessful
Kildare South 2002	Power 7,782, O'Fearghail 7,370	Fianna Fáil - successful
Limerick West 2002	Neville 7,446, Finucane 7,410	Fine Gael – unsuccessful
Long-Roscommon 2002	Kelly P 7,319, Finneran 6,502, Kelly G 6,430	Fianna Fáil – unsuccessful (by 55 votes)
Sligo-Leitrim 2002	Ellis 6,434, Scanlon 6,345, Devins 6,307	Fianna Fáil – unsuccessful
Tipperary North 2002	Hoctor 8,949, Smith 8,526	Fianna Fáil – successful
Carlow Kilkenny 2007	McGuinness 11,635, Aylward 11,600 Nolan 9,037	Fianna Fáil – successful
Cork East 2007	Bradford 8,916, Stanton 7,686	Fine Gael – unsuccessful

Cork South West 2007	Sheehan 7,739, O'Keeffe 7,560	Fine Gael – successful
Dublin North East 2007	Woods 7,003, Brady 6,861	Fianna Fáil – unsuccessful
Dublin North West 2007	Ahern 7,913, Carey 7,211	Fianna Fáil – successful
Dublin South Central 2007	Ardagh 8,286, Mulcahy 7,439	Fianna Fáil – successful
Dublin South West 2007	Lenihan 8,542, O'Connor 7,813	Fianna Fáil – successful
Kildare South 2007	O'Fearghail 8,731, Power 8,694	Fianna Fáil - successful
Laois-Offaly 2007	Flanagan 9,067, Enright 8,297, Buckley 2,196	Fine Gael – successful (two seats)
Roscommon – S Leitrim 2007	Feighan 9,103, Naughten 8,928	Fine Gael – successful
Tipperary North 2007	Smith 7,871, Hoctor 7,374	Fianna Fáil – unsuccessful
Wicklow 2007	Timmins 8,072, Doyle 6,961	Fine Gael – successful

3   Similar discipline can be seen in Northern Ireland in the Assembly elections. In the 2016 election in the six seat Lagan Valley constituency (the area centered on Lisburn), the four Democratic Unionist candidates registered 5,364, 4,638, 4,236 and 4,087 votes respectively although this was not quite enough to retain four seats. The failure was probably due to the Ulster Unionists being able to balance their two candidates at respectively 4,376 and 3,871 votes and then benefit from better transfers. The balancing in the vote probably reflected a postering campaign, which made it clear which party candidate local supporters were requested to support.

4   It is not always clear what number of seats a party might realistically aspire to in certain constituencies, so these numbers are estimates, although certainly broadly indicative of the position. 2007 is chosen, as it is probably the last election where the parties' vote shares were predictable well in advance of the election.

5   Coincidentally in 1991 in the previous local election in Boyle LEA, Fine Gael had only taken two seats on 47.98% or 2.88 quotas. A small rise to 3.14 quotas doubled the number of seats.

CHAPTER 28

Bad electoral tactics

A number of features are regularly encountered which can be classified as bad electoral tactics. If one looks at the examples, outlined elsewhere in this work, of failure to convert quotas or virtual quotas to seats, these features are often prevalent in those cases. Some of them, such as too many candidates or two candidates evenly balanced when seeking one seat, are well understood by parties and rarely arise. Issues around first preference imbalance or transfer imbalance are surprisingly common and often do not seem to be or simply cannot be addressed. Part 4 of this book notes spectacular underperformance by parties by reference to quotas received. In many of these cases, the factors discussed in this chapter are relevant.

It is of course easy in this work to point out bad results, given the vote share of a party, with the benefit of hindsight. Features such as too many candidates and imbalance in votes between candidates are very difficult to control. Party conventions can select the "wrong" candidates and this often leads to candidate numbers in excess of what is appropriate. Nearly always incumbents have to be allowed to run and this can result in extra candidates.

Party's expectations as to votes not met

For larger parties, the process for selecting general and local election candidates usually starts about one year before the actual election. The optimum number of candidates per constituency or LEA is critically influenced by the national level of vote the party enjoys at the time of the election. A view needs to be taken during the selection process as to what this vote share is likely to be at election time. If this is significantly over estimated, the party is likely to have too many candidates and will under perform even its lower actual vote, largely for the reasons set out below. In practice the larger parties will take views on these issues at a central level. This is fundamentally what the senior officers are paid to do; they do however occasionally get it badly wrong.

By contrast if a party under estimates its position, it is likely to have too few candidates and to end up with unused quotas of votes in terms of potentially electing candidates. This happened to the Labour Party in the 1992 general election (but notably not in 2011) and to Sinn Féin in some urban areas in the 2014 local elections. This problem is somewhat easier to address very close to election day, by adding candidates. For example in the 2011 general election, Fine Gael, anticipating a good election, added candidates in both Cavan-Monaghan and Dublin South, both of whom won a third seat for the party on polling day. In the 2016 general election, Fianna Fáil exceeded quota with one candidate in seven constituencies and there is a perception that it left seats "on the table". There is no substance to this perception as it is unlikely a second candidate could have been competitive in any of those constituencies.

Two obvious cases where a party suffered for over estimating its vote are Fine Gael in the 2002 general election and Fianna Fáil in the 2011 general election. In both cases a bit of wishful thinking was probably involved. The polls for many months out hinted at the 22% and 17% respectively won by Fine Gael and Fianna Fáil in those elections. However a failure to heed the warning signs led to an excessive number of candidates for some constituencies and an exceptionally poor result, even when compared with the percentage vote obtained. The problem was exacerbated by having too many outgoing TDs. In general it is unusual that incumbent TDs and councillors are not allowed run and this is a well understood complication when vote share is on the slide.

The most critical bad tactical issue therefore, is a poor judgment on this fundamental question.

Too many candidates

It would be the author's view that the classic reason for a party failing to take a number of seats reflecting the quotas obtained, is having too many candidates for the number of seats targeted. Of course sometimes the number of seats targeted may not be entirely clear, even in the mind of the party involved. Generally the critical errors happen where a party has two more candidates than the number of seats it is likely to obtain.

Generally having two candidates for one seat, three candidates for two or four candidates for three is not in itself a bad idea. Often with excessive candidates, there is vote leakage above a desirable rate. Of course it is always difficult to tell whether the party vote would have been much less without the "extra" candidates anyhow. There are numerous examples, but the following situations are very good examples of excessive candidates.

Fine Gael	Limerick West 1987
Fianna Fáil	Cork East 1981 and February 1982
Fine Gael	Gorey LEA, Wexford 2004

Fine Gael – Limerick West 1987

This is the most spectacular general election example of failure to convert quotas to seats. In 1987 long serving Fine Gael TD, Willie O'Brien retired in a very stable constituency and the decision was taken to allow three candidates have a shot at succession. No one seemed to have spotted the Progressive Democrats as a threat, despite the party leader Des O'Malley having a substantial association with Limerick.

The first count produced the following first preferences

John Mc Coy (PD)	6,580
James Houlihan (FG)	3,352 (35.4% of the FG vote)
Michael Finucane (FG)	3,218 (34%)
Dan Neville (FG)	2,894 (30.6%)

The total Fine Gael first preference vote was 9,464 or 1.11 quotas, almost 3,000 in the aggregate ahead of John McCoy. However McCoy won the seat with a margin of 1,980 votes with the surviving Fine Gael candidate ending up with just 75% of the aggregate Fine Gael vote and failing to be elected.

Fianna Fáil-Cork East 1981/82

In the early 1980's elections Fianna Fáil failed to pick up a second seat (representing a realistic target) in the Cork East constituency in a number of very tight elections. This cost them dearly, because of the tight overall position in Dáil numbers. The constituency stretched from Youghal, Midleton and Cobh in the south to Mallow and Fermoy in the north and traditionally divides south and north with regional voting patterns. A key issue in this constituency is whether the candidates are geographically located north (N) or south (S). In each of the two elections it was clear that Fine Gael were going to get two seats, so they are ignored for illustration.

In 1981 the key players in the battle for the two other seats were as follows (quota is 8,573)

Candidate	First pref	Minor transfers	FG third candidate (direct/indirect)	Mortell	Dowling
Sherlock SFWP (N)	6,241	+308 6,549	+917 7,466	+627 8,093	+319 8,412
Joyce FF (N)	5,661	+87 5,748	+247 5,995	+1,540 7,535	+754 8,289
Brosnan FF (S)	4,401	+103 4,504	+58 4,562	+548 5,110	+2,465 7,575
Dowling FF (S)	3,489	+54 3,543	+42 3,585	+194 3,779	ELIM (241NT)
Mortell FF (N)	2,773	+24 2,797	+342 3,139	ELIM (230NT)	

The Fianna Fáil vote here was 16,324 first preferences or 38.09%. The SFWP vote is 14.56% of the first preferences so is a long distance from a quota. However at the end Joe Sherlock, who was Mallow based at the northern end, was over 800 votes ahead of the second FF candidate. The key problem here is that Fianna Fáil should probably only have had two candidates, Carey Joyce and John Brosnan. The Fianna Fáil north candidates, Fermoy based Joyce and Mortell (probably Mallow based) had an aggregate 8,434 votes. The Fianna Fáil south candidates had 7,890 votes. In each case that considerably exceeds Sherlock's total of 6,241. It is highly possible if they had opted for just Joyce and John Brosnan, that they would have secured two seats. The internal transfers between Fianna Fáil candidates were actually quite good at 73% and 85% respectively.

A further issue was leakage of votes from the fourth Fianna Fáil candidate to Sherlock. 627 of the 3,139 Mortell votes leak, virtually 20%. Subsidiary problems here included stronger other and Fine Gael transfers to the SFWP candidate.

In February 1982, there was an apparent determination to deal with the problem, with the number of candidates being reduced to three. It still didn't work, although the gap had reduced.

Quota 8,243 (valid votes 41,213). Two Fine Gael candidates were elected on the first count.

Candidate	First pref	Minor transfer	Cronin	FG surplus	FF surplus
Ahern FF (S)	7,011	+138 7,149	+1,681 8,830	ELECTED	
Sherlock SFWP (N)	6,677	+523 7,200	+474 7,674	+428 8,102	+35 8,137
Joyce FF (N)	5,601	+58 5,659	+1,598 7,257	+199 7,456	+552 8,008
Cronin FF (N)	3,799	+46 3,845	ELIM (NT 92)		

As can be seen, Fianna Fáil had 16,411 first preference votes or 39.82%. They were 75 votes short of two quotas. Despite this they were beaten by a man who was 1,566 votes short of the quota. Their internal transfer rates from Cronin's votes were a respectable 85% and 94%. The first transfer however split slightly in favour of the south candidate, despite those transfers being of northern origin.

The problem was nailed in November 1982, an election otherwise going nationally in the wrong direction for Fianna Fáil. This time they were down to two candidates on respectively 8,324 and 8,061 votes (against a quota of 8,314). Sherlock polled a respectable 6,186 but was well beaten at the end.

Fine Gael - Gorey LEA 2004

Another classic example of too many candidates was the Fine Gael debacle of five candidates in the 4 seat Gorey LEA (Wexford) in 2004. The realistic Fine Gael target was probably two seats. The Gorey Guardian in its report on the convention held in February 2004 stated that there were "raised eyebrows", as indeed there should have been. Indeed despite the subsequent withdrawal of a selected candidate, that candidate was replaced, leaving the team at 5. The party had 5,649 first preferences or 45.09% of the vote (2.25 quotas) but still managed to win only one seat. The following is a summary of the relevant contenders' votes at critical counts.

Quota 2,506					
Candidate	First pref	O'Gorman transfers	Webb transfers	Kinsella transfers	Final position
Darcy FG	1,952	+107 2,091	+258 2,459	ELECTED	
Fleming SF	1,479	+35 1,594	+134 1,876	+125 2,116	2,148
Earle FG	1,130	+53 1,219	+129 1,416	+456 2,012	2,069
Kinsella FG	1,121	+72 1,213	+156 1,429	ELIM (1,532)	
Webb FG	838	+171 1,038	ELIM (1,153)		
O'Gorman FG	608	ELIM (621)			

The internal transfer rates were respectively 65% (O'Gorman), 47% (Webb) and 30% (Kinsella). The Sinn Féin candidate Fleming, who the second Fine Gael candidate was trying to catch, picked up 294 (almost 9%) of the available Fine Gael transfers, presumably partly based on geographical factors. There were 569 non transferable Fine Gael votes. This debacle was a heady mixture of too many candidates and poor internal transfer rates, with Darcy, the lead Fine Gael candidate, picking up transfers he didn't really need.

Other failed four for two strategies include Fianna Fáil in Cork North Central in the general election in 1992. In the same election Fine Gael took two seats (with a margin of 25 votes) with less first preference votes but significantly better balanced. Similarly four for two failed for Fianna Fáil in Dublin South West in 1992. One would wonder why a four for two strategy was sensible in an urban constituency. In a rural constituency, it can be driven by a desire to have a candidate located in every part of the constituency, but this is a lesser concern in an urban area.

A prominent failed three for one strategy was that of the Labour party in the 1981 general election, where three candidates ultimately in aggregate outpolled Nora Owen of Fine Gael, the successful third placed candidate, but where the last one was eliminated to result in her election.

Another bizarre Labour strategy was seen in the Limerick City No 3 LEA in 1999. Labour had won two seats in this four seat LEA in 1991. Since then Democratic Left had merged with Labour. They took the rather bizarre decision to run five candidates, likely having something to do with keeping each of the merged contingents happy. The quota was 822 and the candidates scored respectively 316, 246, 227, 83 and 83 first preferences or a total of 955 votes (1.16 quotas). The last of the 5 was 158 votes adrift at the last count. Indeed the gap at the start was 195 votes, so the transfers of four running mates hardly dented the gap. As Sean Donnelly so rightly concluded. "The Labour party cause wasn't helped by the decision to run five candidates in a 5 seater area and with just over one quota spread so wide their chance of even one seat was remote. Not a good result for the new party with two of their candidates losing their deposits" (at page 405 Elections '99 – All Kinds of Everything)

It was common in local elections particularly in 1985 to 1999 for a bigger party to have five, six and even seven candidates. A glance at all of those cases shows a common theme of underperforming quotas obtained, with the cases of overperformance somewhat an exception. The cases where a party with such a high number of candidates gets more seats than its votes expressed in quotas to 2 decimal places is at best about 1 in every 5 cases.

Can too many candidates be advantageous?

The view that too many candidates is always a bad thing would not be universally accepted. Sometimes parties deliberately run three or four candidates with a view respectively to one or two seats. It is generally the case that the aggregate party vote at the end hasn't improved much. What is impossible to tell though is whether the party would have had a lot less first preference votes if it had just run two or one. This is the key to the issue. Some pundits and commentators would be of the view that the vote is maximised and that the loss of vote on transfers is tolerable. Others would see that the loss of vote is excessive. Two examples suffice, both from the constituency of Galway West. It can be readily seen that the number of transfers within the party on elimination is rather less than the first preference vote of the eliminated candidate. Arguably both these strategies were poor, but escaped criticism because the end result was fine.

Progressive Democrats 2002

Bobby Molloy retired as Galway West TD shortly before the 2002 election and the Progressive Democrats ran three candidates to succeed him. Their challenger was Margaret Cox, the third Fianna Fáil candidate.

The following were the material events in the count:

First preferences		Elimination of McDonnell	Elimination of Lyons	Final position
Cox FF	3,269	+69 3,870	+309 4,623	5,906
Grealish PD	2,735	+245 3,121	+1,221 4,544	6,215
Lyons PD	1,995	+477 2,545	ELIM 2,798	
McDonnell PD	1,462	ELIM 1,506		

The aggregate PD vote after the lower two were eliminated was 4,544 out of a total 6,192 first preferences or 73% of the initial vote. This seems an excessive level of leakage, bearing in mind that there are also other transfers in the 4,544. It seemed like awfully hard work given their lead over Cox in terms of first preferences. Of course Cox would likely have won, if Fianna Fáil had itself done a small amount of vote management.

Fine Gael 2011

Fine Gael ran four candidates in Galway West in 2011 with the objective of securing two seats. They just about got there, with a winning margin of 17 over Connolly the Independent candidate. The following were the material events in the count.

First preferences		Elimination of Naughten	Elimination of Healy Eames	Final position
Walsh FG	5,425	+1,044 7,008	+2,707 10,277	10,105
Kyne FG	4,550	+729 6,470	+1,946 9,020	9,112
Connolly Ind	4,766	260 6,148	+708 9,083	9,095
Healy-Eames FG	5,046	+1,055 6,542	ELIM 7,020	
Naughton FG	3,606	ELIM 3,993		

The aggregate Fine Gael vote at the end was 19,217. This compared to 18,627 at the start so there was a gain of 590 votes. This seems like a very poor gain, in what was a very good election for Fine Gael.

There are some other cases where success was achieved with what seemed like too many candidates, including the Fine Gael "four for two" performances in Clare and Galway East of 2007. Notably in both those cases the aggregate Fine Gael vote when the field reduced to two was not materially ahead of the starting point. Further Fine Gael commonly had four candidates in Cavan-Monaghan, two in each county and this generally delivered two seats. Probably the truth of the matter is that it can be a good tactic in unusual circumstances, but that broadly having too many candidates is a bad idea.

Too many votes for the lead candidate

It is often the case that the lead candidate for a party polls too strongly and it is impossible for other candidates to then win a further seat. There have been some very noted attempts by leading political figures to depress their personal vote to try and address the issue. An hypothetical solution to this problem in the case of Fianna Fáil in Dublin Central in 1992 is set out in chapter 14 "Managing a large surplus", a solution which also has application to other vote imbalances.

It was particularly common that party leaders gave rise to this problem and very few attempts have been made to address this. The notable exception is the successful effort made by Charlie Haughey of Fianna Fáil in Dublin North Central in 1989, finally achieving a coveted third seat for his party. It is probably quite difficult for party leaders to address this, as everyone tends to want to vote for them. They also have a tendency in some cases to have less than spectacular running mates. Even when they do have a strong running mate, imbalance can still be a problem. This is amply shown by the Dublin South East election in 1981 where Dr Garret FitzGerald, leader of Fine Gael got 13,794 first preferences, with former Finance Minister Richie Ryan achieving 1,722 first preferences. It is not always the case that a party missed a seat gain because the leader outperformed. For example Richie Ryan was also elected in 1981; however seats have been missed in these circumstances.

A few examples will suffice.[1]

Fine Gael - Westport LEA
In the 1999 local elections Fine Gael got 3,349 first preference votes in the Westport LEA (Mayo) representing 44.21% of the vote and 2.21 quotas. Yet they failed to win two seats. Why? The first count to the extent material was

Quota	1,516
Ring FG	2,694
Sweeney FF	1,304
Chambers FF	1,171
Adams FF	1,063
McManamon FG	655

The problem here was that Michael Ring had over 80% of the Fine Gael vote and there was a gap of over 400 votes to be closed on his transfers. Thus of 1,178 votes to be transferred, Peter McManamon needed 408 or 34.6% to close the gap and this would be on the basis that Margaret Adams, also Westport based would get no transfers from Michael Ring, also Westport based. In fact transfers were as follows:

Sweeney	+128	1,432
Chambers	+107	1,278
Adams	+274	1,337
McManamon	+418	1,073

Thus Mr McManamon only got 35% of the votes available for transfer, whereas the three Fianna Fáil candidates got over 43% between them. The 418 transfers received by McManamon implied that he received about 955 second preferences from Ring. If even 400 of those people had been persuaded to give their number 1 to McManamon instead, that would likely have caused McManamon to pass out Chambers given the other patterns evident in the transfers. That could possibly have been achieved by a letter to a part of the LEA from Michael Ring, asking them to give their first preference to the other candidate.

Fianna Fáil - Limerick East
In the 2007 general election, Fianna Fáil got over 24,000 votes (or 48.69%) in this five seat constituency, but only won two seats. The votes were split Willie O'Dea 19,092, Peter Power 3,569 and Noreen Ryan 1,391. As Kieran O'Donnell of Fine Gael managed to get elected on 5,094 first preferences and a final total of 6,966 votes, there is little doubt that about 7,500 votes appropriately redistributed from O'Dea would have likely given Fianna Fáil three seats, rather than the two they won. This type of imbalance is a regular problem with O'Dea, as it also happened in 1992.

Fine Gael - Dublin South East
A very extreme approach to addressing the problem was seen in the 1989 general election. In the general election of 1987, despite a significant defeat for Fine Gael, the outgoing Taoiseach, Dr Garret Fitzgerald obtained 8,068

votes or a surplus over quota of 413. His party colleague Joe Doyle TD obtained 3,323 votes, but failed to be elected. In the 1989 election with the national fortunes of Fine Gael improving slightly, Fitzgerald set his mind to delivering two seats. He decided to ask pretty well all of his voters in the constituency to give their number 1 vote to Doyle instead, with a very small area of Ballsbridge not being addressed in this way. The first count outcome was thus

| Doyle | 5,235 |
| Fitzgerald | 3,865 |

One of the problems FitzGerald then had was that the combined Fianna Fáil vote behind him was 5,491. However two more "friendly" candidates, John Gormley of the Greens and Michael McDowell of the Progressive Democrats were also behind him and despite strong Fianna Fáil internal transfers, he held his seat, as intended, on the basis of strong transfers from the others in the field, winning at the end by about 850 votes.

Fianna Fáil - Sligo-Leitrim

Another example of depressing the vote of a lead vote getter was that of Ray McSharry in Sligo-Leitrim (4 seats or 20% quota). In the 1980's elections, McSharry started in 1981 with 10,818 votes or 22.68% of the vote. This declined in February 1982 to 9,214 (20.16%) and in November 1982 to 7,897 (17%). In the last case the desired objective of retaining three seats was not achieved despite the three Fianna Fáil candidates being respectively 18.42%, 17.59% and 17%. However McSharry went perilously close to not being elected himself. The coveted goal of three seats was achieved in 1987, albeit against a background of a recovery in the McSharry personal vote to 9,521 (20.83%).

General imbalance in vote

While this cannot be criticised fairly in the same way as the enormous imbalance towards one candidate, it is evident that in many elections, the balance between two candidates could have been refined. This is of course a phenomenon easy to identify with the benefit of hindsight, but much more difficult to spot in advance of an election. In this light it is debatable as to whether it can be described as a bad tactic.

In the general election of 1992 in Waterford, there were two Fianna Fáil candidates. Brendan Kenneally, city based had 6,793 first preference votes. Jackie Fahey, who was west Waterford based, got 5,410 first preference votes. Fahey for location reasons was less likely to attract transfers. In the event Martin Cullen surprisingly took the last seat for the Progressive Democrats. A better balance between the two Fianna Fáil candidates would probably have delivered two seats. 500 extra votes in mid Waterford diverted from Kenneally to Fahey would probably have achieved that, although that would have put Kenneally only narrowly ahead of Fahey.

Also in the general election of 1992, this time in Wicklow, there were two Fianna Fáil candidates in contention, Joe Jacob with 6,475 votes and Dick Roche with 5,250 votes. As the final margin of loss for Dick Roche was 429 votes, a somewhat more even split would have likely produced two seats.

Also in the general election of 1992, Fianna Fáil were aiming for two seats in the then new constituency of Westmeath. Athlone based Mary O'Rourke got 7,396 votes and Mullingar based Henry Abbott got 6,598 votes. As Abbott only lost out by 137 votes on the last count, it is evident that had the candidates switched about 200 votes between them, Fianna Fáil would likely have shaded a second seat. In practice the electoral finesse required to have achieved that was probably unobtainable.

The above three examples from 1992 illustrate a difficulty in addressing the situation. It is evident that Kenneally, Jacob and O'Rourke were the slightly preferred Fianna Fáil candidate with party supporters. While an effort could have been made to divert a couple of hundred votes in small parts of their constituencies from each of them, the margins as shown by the actual result were already quite fine. It would likely have been very difficult to assure the candidate preferred by the party supporters that there was no threat to them in a diversion of a small number of votes. Further in some of these instances, there would have been existing intense rivalry between the two candidates, making it even more difficult to effect some vote management.

There are a number of examples of imbalance that fall somewhere between one candidate being far too far ahead and the narrower margins discussed above. Two examples from the 2007 general election will suffice.

In Kerry South, with Fianna Fáil hunting for two seats, the respective candidates and first preference votes were John O'Donoghue 9,128 and Tom Fleming 6,740. In the event Fleming lost to Independent Jackie Healy-Rae by a margin of 460 votes. A diversion of 750 votes from O'Donoghue to Fleming would have produced two Fianna Fáil seats, without threatening the leading position of O'Donoghue. An unexpected factor in that election was that Jackie Healy-Rae underperformed expectations, so Fianna Fáil might not have been live to the possibility. Much the same had transpired in 2002.

In Galway West, with Fianna Fáil hunting for three seats, the respective candidates and first preference votes were Eamon Ó'Cuív 9,645, Frank Fahey 5,854, Michael Crowe 4,969. A diversion of 1,000 votes from Ó'Cuív to each of the other two would have made Fianna Fáil competitive (although probably not quite winning it) for a third seat without threatening Ó'Cuív getting a seat.

In the 2016 general election, there are a couple of examples where Fianna Fáil might have won an extra seat with a better split of its vote, such as Clare and Offaly.

In general, it could be concluded that practical steps can usually be taken to get better balance in cases where either the lead candidate is very significantly ahead or the lead candidate has a margin of at least 3,000 votes. Cases with lower margins than that are liable to be problematic to manage.

Two candidates for one seat evenly split

While it is usually a good tactic to be able to split a vote evenly between two candidates, it does give rise to problems where the aggregate vote is about or a little more than a quota. In these instances the votes can transfer badly from the second candidate to the first and leave the lead candidate stranded. Parties are generally well aware of this, so it does not happen too often.

In the 1999 local elections, Fine Gael had two candidates in the three seat Kilmacthomas LEA in Waterford. The candidates Oliver Coffey and Eddie Rockett had respectively 493 and 476 votes, a split of 50.9:49.1. They had 32.35% of the vote or 1.29 quotas. However they failed to win a seat, with Coffey finishing almost 50 votes adrift of the third candidate.

In 1997 Fine Gael lost its Dáil seat in Dublin North West, which it finally regained in 2016. The Fine Gael candidates were local councillor Brendan Brady with 2,901 first preferences and outgoing T.D. Mary Flaherty with 2,825 first preferences, a 50.7:49.3 split and a total of 5,726. The rival for the seat was outgoing Minister, Proinsias de Rossa of Democratic Left who polled 3,701 first preferences. On the final count Brady lost by 100 votes with poor transfers from Flaherty. The danger of the two candidate strategy was well anticipated in advance.

In the 2011 general election, Fianna Fáil managed this feat in eight cases.[2] In many of these constituencies, a successful candidate from another party was within range with any reasonable aggregation of the vote. In two of the cases both unsuccessful candidates were outgoing Oireachtas members and obviously there would have been an issue with leaving one of them on the sidelines.[3]

Of course an even worse tactic is to have three, four or five candidates where one seat is the likely outcome. The 1987 debacle for Fine Gael in Limerick West is noted above. In the 2002 general election in Dún Laoghaire, Fine Gael failed to achieve a single seat in a perceived party heartland. In that case the two lead candidates, both former deputies, were Helen Keogh on 3,229 first preferences and Liam Cosgrave on 3,135 first preferences. As a complication, there was a third candidate, John Bailey, with 1,705 first preferences. In the past, the Labour party quite routinely in local elections tended to have multiple candidates for a possible one seat, sometimes as many as 5.[4]

It is possible to achieve the same outcome (i.e. one seat rather than two) when seeking two seats with three equally balanced candidates, but no example readily springs to mind. A case where four Fianna Fáil candidates had three quotas was Ballyjamesduff LEA (Cavan) in 1991. The four candidates had respectively 690, 654, 647 and 633 first preferences but only secured two seats. The transfers in favour of the last man standing were poor and he lost by a margin of 65 votes.

Significantly more than one quota but only one candidate

This tends to be a Labour speciality, particularly in the Spring tide of 1992. In that election Seán Ryan in Dublin North with 1.7 quotas and Eithne Fitzgerald in Dublin South with 1.74 quotas could both have delivered a second seat with a second candidate. Probably the success of Labour at this level was unanticipated and hence they can be excused. In some areas of Dublin in the 2014 local elections, Sinn Féin had insufficient candidates and this benefitted other left candidates. While Fine Gael managed this a couple of times in the 2011 general election, the partial quota is unlikely to have delivered a seat and the same applies to Fianna Fáil in the 2016 general election.

Candidates over quota

While it may be gratifying to an individual candidate to get over the quota on the first count, it is not an efficient use of party votes. Chapter 14 outlines high levels of immediate "leakage" on transfers, which reduce the party's aggregate votes at the start. It is also quite notable that in cases where a party gets significantly more seats than its vote represents in quotas, it is rare that an individual candidate has exceeded the quota. This is a very difficult problem to manage.

Poor split of a transfer

Cases are seen from time to time where two candidates are as between themselves quite well balanced to take two seats. However there is a third candidate, whose votes are almost certainly going to split in a way that will destroy the balance. In these circumstances the original balance is dubious.

In the general election of 1997 in Louth, two Fine Gael candidates, Fergus O'Dowd from Drogheda (south) and Brendan McGahon from Dundalk (north) were brilliantly matched at 4,486 and 4,346 first preferences respectively. The problem was that the third candidate, Terry Brennan (also north), who had 3,723 first preferences was liable to split decisively in favour of McGahon for reasons of geography. This is indeed what happened in a 2:1 ratio. In the event O'Dowd lost to Labour by about 400 votes. The practicalities of management were virtually impossible here as the competition between the two northern candidates would make it nigh impossible to designate parts of mid-Louth as being "south".

In the general election of 2007 in Tipperary South, Fianna Fáil narrowly and unexpectedly took two seats. However the first preference vote split Mattie McGrath 7,608, Martin Mansergh 6,110 and Siobhán Ambrose 4,286. A more even split between McGrath and Mansergh would have made it obvious from the start that they would take two seats. In the event the key factor was that the Ambrose transfers split 20:16 in favour of Mansergh, giving him a very narrow win. The opposite split would likely have produced a different result.

References in Chapter 28

[1]   Bertie Ahern was a serial offender on having excessive votes in Dublin Central. Other offenders include David Andrews (Fianna Fáil) in Dún Laoghaire in 1992, Ivor Callely and Sean Haughey (both Fianna Fáil) in Dublin North Central in 1997, Frank Fahey and Eamon Ó'Cuív (both Fianna Fáil) in Galway West in 1997 and 2002, Micheál Martin and Michael McGrath (both Fianna Fáil) in Cork South Central in 2007, Charlie McCreevy (Fianna Fáil) in Kildare North in 2002, Michael Noonan (Fine Gael) in Limerick East in 1997 and 2002 and Emmet Stagg (Labour) in Kildare in 1992. In all of these cases, better balance would seem likely to have delivered an extra seat. It should be noted that some of these cases involve two "big beasts" slugging it out with each other, leaving a third candidate very far behind. The Callely/Haughey case in 1997 was the case where Derek McDowell of Labour retained his seat despite a very poor first preference vote of 2,848, a record percentage low for an elected candidate. In many of these cases, it is eminently foreseeable before the election that the lead candidate will run away with the contest.

[2]   The cases were Cork East (O'Keeffe 5,024, Ahern 4,618), Cork South West (O'Donovan 5,984, O'Sullivan 4,803), Donegal South West (Coughlan 4,956, Ó'Dómhnaill 4,789), Dublin North (O'Brien 4,115, Kennedy 3,519), Dún Laoghaire (Hanafin 5,090, Andrews 3,542), Louth (Carroll 5,681, Breathnach 5,177), Meath West (Brady 3,789, Cassells 3,496) and Sligo-North Leitrim (Scanlon 5,075, MacSharry 4,633). Of course given the poor transfer rates, it is debatable whether a single candidate could have done rather better. There are certainly a number of instances in 2011 of single Fianna Fáil candidates who were equally unsuccessful and one case Kildare South, where a seat was obtained, despite there being two candidates. A single candidate would certainly have focussed minds on the problem.

[3]   Another example is in the 1991 local elections in Dún Laoghaire LEA, the Green Party had two candidates, Vincent McDowell who got 700 votes and Jane Sexton who got 611 votes. Their aggregate vote, amounting to 0.69 quotas, was more than 150 votes ahead of Jane Dillon Byrne, the sole Labour candidate. In the event Dillon Byrne won the last seat with a margin of 29 votes, even though the Greens in general were more transfer friendly.

[4]   Examples of excessive Labour candidates include Cork NE LEA (Cork City) in 1985 (3 candidates), Limerick Area 3 LEA in 1999 (5 candidates), Tullamore LEA (Offaly) in 1985 and 1991(5 and 4 candidates respectively), Terenure LEA (South Dublin) in 1985 (3 candidates) and Athlone LEA (Westmeath) in both 1985 and 1991 (4 and 3 candidates respectively).

CHAPTER 29
Electoral Anomalies

There are a number of features of the Irish electoral system, which are perhaps best described as "anomalous". This chapter discusses several such issues.

Candidate tops the poll but fails to be elected

There are several examples of this phenomenon:

In Sligo-Leitrim in November 1982, outgoing TD John Ellis based in mid Leitrim topped the poll with 8,552 votes, 735 votes short of quota. He then picked up a mere 239 transfers (2.5%) out of 9,531 votes transferred, transfers being from Sligo based candidates. One of his problems was that the votes of Tom Lavin, a South Sligo Fine Gael candidate were looked at three times, firstly on his elimination, secondly by looking at the 2,213 votes transferred by Lavin to McCartin, also Fine Gael and thirdly by looking at the 1,353 votes transferred from Lavin via McCartin to Nealon, the third Fine Gael candidate.

In the 2004 local elections, Matthew Coogan of Sinn Féin was the poll topper in Drogheda West LEA in Louth with 853 votes. Despite picking up 237 transfers, he was beaten for the final seat by Gerald Nash of Labour by almost 100 votes. He does not seem to have featured as a Sinn Féin candidate since.

It's also not wholly unknown for a candidate who finishes in second place on the first count to be overhauled. This happens relatively frequently in three seat constituencies and LEAs and occasionally in four seat constituencies/LEAs. For example in the 1991 local elections Vinnie Munnelly of Fine Gael finished second in the four seat Killala LEA (Mayo) but lost out in the end by 35 votes and in the 2016 general election, Gerry Reynolds finished second on the first count in Sligo-Leitrim, but failed to be elected..

Candidate finishing bottom of the poll and being elected

This has also happened. In the five seat Ballinasloe LEA (Galway) in the 1991 local elections, Pat O'Sullivan of Fianna Fáil finished bottom of a field of seven candidates with 799 first preferences, 85 votes adrift of the sixth placed candidate. However fortuitously one of his colleagues Michael Kitt had a first count surplus of 668 votes and the transfers from this took him ahead of an independent on the second count. After a further Fianna Fáil surplus widened the gap, the independent was eliminated. However at that point, O'Sullivan was still 133 votes adrift of a rival Fianna Fáil candidate and outgoing councillor, James Joyce. However, as so often happens in these cases, the pattern of transfers from the independent favoured O'Sullivan and put him 13 votes clear of his colleague and residual Fine Gael surpluses then increased his margin to 38 votes. While both Mr Joyce and Mr O'Sullivan took seats in 1999, the tables were turned in 2004 and Mr O'Sullivan lost his seat.

Again it is not wholly unusual for a candidate to be close to the bottom on the first count and to be elected. In the six seat Cork City South West LEA in 2014, P J Hourican of Fine Gael finished ninth of ten (only four votes ahead of another Fine Gael candidate) but was elected. The key was a large first count surplus for another Fine Gael candidate, John Buttimer.[1]

Transferring the same vote several times over

Under the rules of alternative voting, where a candidate reaches a quota on a count subsequent to count 1, only those votes which take the candidate over quota are examined in distributing the surplus. If this in turn produces surpluses for other candidates, effectively the same votes are looked at over and over again. An interesting example is the Dublin South East count in the 1997 general election. It will be recollected that John Gormley famously won the last seat with a margin of 27 votes over Michael McDowell with a recount going on for many days. Joe Doyle of Fine Gael was eliminated with 4,886 votes, the vast majority of which were his 4,541 first preferences. The elimination gave 3,814 votes to his running mate Frances Fitzgerald, presumably mainly number 2's and she was elected. These 3,814 votes then had to be looked at to decide where Fitzgerald's 2,232 surplus went to. Of these 1,791, presumably in the main third preferences, went to Ruairi Quinn of Labour resulting in him having a surplus of 1,708. This meant that the 1,791 votes, largely Doyle first preferences, had to be examined for preferences as between Gormley and McDowell. In fact only 1,131 of those voters gave a preference to Gormley or McDowell, but crucially many more of them preferred Gormley to McDowell, giving Gormley a narrow victory margin. So effectively a bundle of votes for Joe Doyle, which mainly went 1 Doyle, 2 Fitzgerald, 3 Quinn and then favoured Gormley over McDowell were the key ingredient in a very tight battle. The Sunday Tribune Guide to Politics rightly commented "An interesting feature of the count was the way Doyle's votes elected three TDs. Firstly, his elimination put Fitzgerald over the quota. Then the Doyle votes from Fitzgerald's surplus elected Quinn. Quinn then had a surplus which was taken from the last parcel of votes obtained by him which, of course, came from Doyle, by way of Fitzgerald. The Doyle votes that made up the Quinn surplus finally put Gormley in ahead of McDowell. A fascinating example of the operation of our system of PR." (at page 93).[2]

Very tight finishes

An occupational hazard of any parliamentary democracy with individual seats is that there is always a seat or two won on a tight margin. It is thus usual for example in the United Kingdom that a couple of the 650 seats have a parliamentary majority of less than 100 votes. This also happens in Ireland. There are quite a number of cases in general elections where there has been a seat won on a very small margin. This is something that is almost impossible to predict on the basis of scrutiny of transfers. In some cases the contest is between candidates of the same party. In the February 1982 general election, Sean French beat his party colleague Dan Wallace by 5 votes in Cork North Central. In Roscommon in the 1987 general election, the perennial internal Fine Gael battle John Connor v Liam Naughten was won by Naughten on a margin of 18 votes. In 2002, the equally enduring Limerick West internal Fine Gael battle between Dan Neville and Michael Finucane was won by Neville on a margin of one vote.

More importantly, some of these battles have been between candidates who are likely to be on opposing sides in Dáil Eireann following the election. The battle in Dublin South Central in the 1992 general election between Ben Briscoe of Fianna Fáil and Eric Byrne of Democratic Left was decided by five votes. In the 1987 general election, Dick Spring, then leader of Labour and Tanaiste, famously won the last seat in Kerry North by a margin of four votes over Tom McEllistrim of Fianna Fáil. The most famous battle of them all between John Gormley of the Greens and Michael McDowell of the Progressive Democrats happened in Dublin South East in the 1997 general election. This resulted in a margin of victory of 27 votes for John Gormley. All of these contests were against a background of tight Dáil numbers, so that the outcome was material. In the 2016 general election Paul Kehoe of Fine Gael won the last seat in Wexford by a margin of 52 votes over Johnny Mythen of Sinn Féin, Brid Smith won the last seat in Dublin South Central over Fianna Fáil by a margin of 35 votes and Tom Pringle, Independent won the last seat in Donegal over Sinn Féin by a margin of 36 votes.

The Gormley/McDowell battle involved a very protracted recount which went on for seven days. Initially the margin began to narrow substantially in favour of McDowell, but as heavier guns were deployed for the Greens, the margin widened again. The process encountered relatively numerous errors (recorded to a pro-forma sheet), but as can be expected, they tended to cancel each other out. In the event the margin widened in favour of Gormley, but at some point a decision was taken to withdraw a challenge to the initial result and therefore that result stood.

Given that numbers of votes in local elections tend to be a lot smaller, it is obvious that there will be local elections where the winning margin is less than 10 votes.[3] The most significant of the lot is the Bonham Fine Gael v Kavanagh, Labour battle in Borris in Ossory LEA (Laois) in 1999 with a final margin of zero. In that case Bonham won the seat, because he had 49 more first preference votes. The rules determined that in the event of a tie, the candidate with more first preferences won. This was an election where an election petition inevitably followed, entailing a minute examination of 21 disputed papers, discussed in Chapter 9. Tight finishes with a margin of 50 votes or less are quite common in local elections, happening in about 20 to 25% of LEAs in each election.[4]

There is a quite obvious pattern in a number of these local electoral battles of a poor transfer rate from a fellow party candidate afflicting the loser.

In the Carroll v O'Rourke battle in Oranmore LEA in 2009, Liam Carroll was a mere 26 votes ahead on the first count and Enda O'Rourke had the advantage of 838 Labour votes to be eliminated behind him. Carroll had a larger number of Fine Gael votes behind him, but transfers had to be shared with another Fine Gael candidate. The level of Labour transfers in the event was poor at 30%.

Of course there are also often circumstances where an elimination takes place with a small margin between two candidates. It is difficult to see many examples where much has turned on this, as the continuing candidate is usually the next to be eliminated. A possible exceptional case is the elimination of outgoing TD James Bannon of Fine Gael in Longford-Westmeath in 2016 by a margin of 6 votes behind Labour. If Labour had been eliminated instead, it seems likely that their transfers would have closed the gap of 300 between Mr Bannon and a Sinn Féin candidate and elected Mr Bannon.

It is commonly the case when a margin is so narrow, that long and careful recounts are required. In the 2014 battle in Listowel LEA, a court challenge was mounted by Dan Kiely, Independent candidate after the final result was confirmed. The key issue in the court challenge seemed to be the treatment of the mixed preferences across European and local election ballots. Curiously the senior counsel who represented Mr Kiely was apparently Michael McDowell, no stranger himself to tight losing margins.

Candidates finishing level during a count

The rules which determine how this is dealt with are discussed at length in Chapter 1, as are some examples where this happened in practice.

No Election required

It is sometimes the case that the number of nominations received is equal to the number of seats. In these circumstances, no election is required. An example of where this happened is the Granard LEA in Longford in 1991. The lucky trio were Fintan Flood and Brian Lynch of Fianna Fáil and Maura Kilbride-Harkin of Fine Gael. Two other areas in the same county only had four candidates for three seats in that local election. The lack of competition didn't do much for the Fianna Fáil duo. At the subsequent election in an enlarged Granard area, Flood finished bottom of the poll and was eliminated on the second count, whereas Lynch took the last seat. The feat was repeated in Kilbeggan LEA (Westmeath) in 1999 and in that case three of the four lucky councillors were returned in 2004. It is highly unlikely that this will happen in a future election, given the sheer number of smaller parties and independents available to contest.

Everyone elected on the first count

In the November 1982 general election each of the three successful candidates in Donegal South West were elected on the first count in an uncompetitive race, with the two other candidates trailing far behind. A similar situation arose in Donegal North East in the February 1982 general election. However in Donegal North East, the returning officer had to conduct two further counts. This was because two of the three lowest candidates Joachim Loughrey of Fine Gael and Ian McGarvey of Fianna Fáil, could possibly reach 8.33% of the vote (a third of the quota, adjusted to one quarter in 1992) if the three surpluses were distributed and thus save their deposits. This exercise required almost 17,500 first preferences to be examined, likely at a far greater cost to the taxpayer than giving the candidates the money back. However both gentlemen did in fact save their deposit.[5]

Candidates winning seats with very low numbers of first preference votes

This is quite common. In general elections quite a number of candidates with less than 4,000 first preference votes have been elected and there are instances of this in every general election since 1981. This has become somewhat less of a feature in recent elections, primarily because the number of votes cast keeps going up and also because transfers are less reliable. Many candidates elected from a base of 4,000 votes or less received a substantial number of transfers from a fellow party candidate, often more than their first preference vote. General election examples of this include Liam Fitzgerald (Fianna Fáil, Dublin North East 1981 and November 1982) and Richie Ryan (Fine Gael, Dublin South East 1981).

The lowest modern performance was the 939 votes recorded by Cyprian Brady (Fianna Fáil) in Dublin Central in the 2007 general election representing 0.136% of a quota. Other notable examples are the 1,722 first preferences recorded by Richie Ryan (Fine Gael) in Dublin South East in the 1981 general election, the 1,818 first preferences recorded by Vincent Brady (Fianna Fáil) also in 1981 and the 1,990 first preferences recorded by Maureen O'Sullivan (Independent) in Dublin Central in the 2016 general election.

Similarly in all local elections since 1985, there have been candidates elected with 400 votes or less, this being particularly prevalent in the counties with small populations. There is a lessening tendency for this over time. The lowest ever seen in recent elections was Des Coleman, a Labour candidate in Mullingar Urban LEA in 1991, who received 190 first preference votes. This also represented 0.22% of a quota, the lowest performance ever seen up to 2014.[6]

Candidates polling low numbers of votes

It is a common enough feature of both general and local elections that there are a number of candidates who poll a very low level of first preference votes. Until 2002 this was a hazardous enough undertaking in a general election as a deposit of £300 (about €400) was payable under section 47 of the Electoral Act 1992 and would be forfeit if the candidate failed to achieve a quarter of a quota. Further if a candidate contested more than one constituency, all additional deposits would be forfeit. This all changed following a court case in July 2001 entitled Redmond v Minister for the Environment. In that case an unemployed Wexford builder, Thomas Redmond claimed in the High Court that the requirement to pay deposits was unconstitutional. He claimed he would have run in the 1992 and 1994 general and European elections, but for the unfair requirement to come up with a deposit. His case was upheld and indeed subsequently Mr Redmond was awarded nominal damages of €130 for the breach of his rights.

Even though a deposit was required up until 2002, a surprising number of candidates contested general elections prior to then and received 100 or less first preference votes. The 1981/82 elections only averaged 7 such candidates. However the number increased to over 20 in the 1987 and 1997 elections. Since 2002 there have been respectively 11, 17, 20 and 17 in the four general elections, so the trend is broadly upwards. The lowest vote attained in the 2011 general election was the 18 votes recorded by Peadar Ó'Ceallaigh (subsequently Fis Nua) in Dublin South East. This was despite attractive policies being proposed by him on debt repudiation and a parallel currency. Rather impressively, he more than doubled his vote to 40 in the Dublin West bye-election later in 2011. The position improved somewhat in the 2016 general election with Patrick Feeney at 22 votes in Galway West being the lowest polling candidate. The only lesser general election performance was that by Maria McCool in 1997 in Dublin North West with an impressive 13 votes.

Some of the low vote candidates never seem to be deterred. Ireland doesn't seem to have someone as colourful as Lord Sutch and the Monster Raving Loonies. Regular candidates have included Barbara Hyland, a justice campaigner who has achieved low votes in many Dublin constituencies and in Wicklow, Noel O'Gara who has unsuccessfully contested Dublin South East, Laois Offaly, Longford Westmeath and Roscommon South Leitrim, John Keigher in Dublin Bay South, a man in Wicklow with an enormous beard called Charlie Keddy and the Christian Solidarity Party candidate, Colm Callanan who has contested Dublin South Central and various electoral areas in Laois and Offaly with spectacularly poor results such as 14, 11, 9 , 8 and 6 in the five electoral areas of Laois. By far the most prominent was Arklow's Jim Tallon, President of the Independent Republic of Glasnost, who unfortunately passed away in March 2015, having unsuccessfully contested Meath, Wexford and Wicklow in various elections from 1981 to 2011. Some of the low scoring candidates have unfortunate names such as Brian Lenihan (presumably a different one), the Christian Solidarity candidate who scored 80 in Longford Roscommon in 2002, Nora Ann Luck who had no luck with 85 votes in Cork South Central in 1992 and the "Wise duo" of Damon and Karen with respectively 27 and 6 votes in Shannon LEA (Clare) in 2004.

Most of the low scoring candidates are independents, but the Christian Solidarity Party and Fis Nua seems to feature prominently in the below 100 club. In 2014, virtually the entire slate of Fis Nua candidates achieved less than 100 first preference votes, regrettably broken by a respectable performance of 731 votes by the party's candidate in Killaloe LEA in Clare,

Niamh O'Brien. Indeed the party's Dublin Euro candidate, Damon Wise, achieved 7 votes in Ennis LEA, the lowest vote in the entire country.

Some constituencies have a fatal attraction for candidates getting very low votes. They are commonly seen in Dublin Central,, Dublin South East, Galway West and Limerick East.

It's not completely unknown that a candidate gets less than 20 first preference votes in a local election or less than 50 first preference votes in a general election. This is indeed a very poor performance. Further it is quite usual in recent general elections that (a)candidate(s) in more than half of the constituencies gets less than 200 votes.[7] By contrast in local elections, it is uncommon that many LEAs feature a candidate getting less than 100 votes, although there was a considerable increase in the number of such candidates in 2014. It is difficult to know quite why persons with such low aspirations contest local and general elections, but indeed they do.

The following charts show exceptionally low performing candidates in the last few elections. Previous performances which secured even lower votes are included in italics.

Recent general elections less than 25 first preferences (other pre 2000 lower in italics)[8]

Candidate	General election	Number of votes	Constituency
Maria McCool	*1997*	*13*	*Dublin North West*
Peadar Ó'Ceallaigh (Fis Nua)	2011	18	Dublin South East
Aidan Ryan	2002	19	Limerick East
Patrick Feeney	2016	22	Galway West
Seamus Cunningham	2007	24	Longford-Westmeath

Recent local elections - 10 first preferences or less (other pre 2000 lower in italics)[9]

Candidate	Election	Number of votes	LEA
Benny Cooney	*LE 1991*	*2*	*Mullingar Urban (Westmeath)*
Paidi Sweeney	*LE 1985*	*4*	*Waterford No 3*
Karen Wise (Fis Nua)	LE 2004	6	Shannon (Clare)
Colm Callanan (CSP)	LE 2009	6 to 30	various Laois/Offaly
Damon Wise (Fis Nua)	LE 2014	7	Ennis (Clare)
Joe Bannan	*LE 1991*	*8*	*Portlaoise (Laois)*
William Dillon	*LE 1991*	*9*	*Muinebheag (Carlow)*

References in Chapter 29

[1] Other examples of a candidate finishing second last and winning are Martin Kennedy of Labour in Thurles LEA (Tipperary) in 1991, Pat Finnegan of Fianna Fáil in Killorglin LEA (Kerry) in 1991 and Keith Doyle of Fianna Fáil in Enniscorthy LEA (Wexford) in 2014.

[2] Another example is the distribution of Shane Ross' (then Fine Gael) 4,626 votes in the 1992 general election, which directly elected his colleague Billy Timmins and Liz McManus (DL) and on transfer elected Johnny Fox (Independent).

[3] Examples of low winning margins in local elections include (winner first) McBrearty, Fianna Fáil v Carr, Fine Gael in Donegal LEA in 1985 with a margin of 3, margins of every number from 1 to 8 (bar 4) in the 1991 local elections, Hanrahan, Fianna Fáil v Meaney, Green in Ennis LEA (Clare) in 1999 with a margin of 1, Paton, Labour v O'Toole, Fine Gael in Tullow LEA (Carlow) in 2004 with a margin of 8, O'Muiri, Fine Gael v Farrell, Labour in Clontarf LEA (Dublin) in 2004 with a margin of 2, McConville, Fianna Fáil v Bell, Labour in Drogheda East LEA(Louth) in 2004 with a margin of 8, Brady, Sinn Féin v McGahern, Fianna Fáil in Belturbet LEA (Cavan) in 2009 with a margin of 1, Carroll, Fine Gael v O'Rourke, Labour in Oranmore LEA (Galway) in 2009 with a margin of 3, Fitzgerald, Independent v Sheahan, Independent in Adare LEA (Limerick) in 2009 with a margin of 4 and the original contested outcome in Kennelly, Fine Gael v Kiely, Independent in Listowel LEA, (Kerry) in 2014 with a margin of 2 (and indeed 5 votes from the next candidate).
   A key further anomaly that has an impact where there is a very narrow margin is the extra votes obtained by the two candidates from any prior surplus. If a surplus of 400 shows candidate A getting on exact mathematics 180.6 votes, candidate B getting 90.4 votes, candidate C getting 100.1 votes and candidate D getting 28.9 votes, the whole numbers only account for 398 votes and the candidates with the two highest fractional percentages (A and D) get an extra vote each to account for the 400 votes in total. If the surplus had been 399 or 401 votes, it is likely that the math would give the extra votes to different candidates. In a tight contest such as Bonham v Kavanagh, where there were six surpluses distributed, this is likely to have had cumulative significant effect on the final outcome.

[4] Thus (as shown by Seán Donnelly's excellent works) in local elections 2014 there were 31 such close results with 30 in 2009, 38 in 2004 and 40 in 1999.

[5] In the 1999 local elections and in the 2004 local elections the three successful candidates in Coole LEA (Westmeath) and Callan LEA (Kilkenny) respectively were also returned on the first count.

[6] While this work does not deal with town councils, there are examples of persons being elected to town councils with fewer than 30 first preferences. The modern record would seem to be Joseph Roche, a Fine Gael candidate elected in 1985 to Lismore Town Commission in Waterford with 18 first preference votes.

7   In the general election of 2011, there was at least one candidate in 25 of the constituencies who got less than 200 votes and this increased to 27 constituencies in the 2016 general election. Indeed five of the sixteen candidates in Mayo in 2016 attracted less than 200 first preferences as did five of the 24 in Wicklow in 2011.

8   Other low performing recent general election candidates were:

Candidate	Election	Votes	Constituency
Benny Cooney	2011	25	Dublin Central
William Gorman	2016	27	Dublin Central
Noel O'Gara	2007	27	Dublin South East
John Keigher	2011	27	Dublin South East
Patrick Mary Moore	2007	28	Limerick East
Sean Forkin	2011	29	Mayo
Maurice Fitzgerald	2007	30	Cork South Central
Peter O'Sullivan	2007	34	Dublin South East
John Dominic Keigher	2016	37	Dublin Bay South
Dermot Mulqueen	2016	39	Clare
Sean Forkin	2016	42	Mayo
Noel O'Gara	2007	45	Laois Offaly
Liam Johnston	2011	48	Dublin Central

9   Candidates with between 10 and 20 votes in a local election included:

Candidate	Election	Number of votes	LEA
Tommy Kelly	LE 2014	12	Ennis (Clare)
James Kelly	LE 2014	15	Manorhamilton (Leitrim)
Patrick Rooney	LE 2009	16	Muinebheag (Carlow)
Karen Wise (Fis Nua)	LE 2014	18	Shannon (Clare)
Errol L Farrell	LE 2009	19	Mullingar E (Westmeath)

PART 6

Other types of public elections

CHAPTER 30
Referenda

In the period under review, Ireland has had numerous referenda[1], as these are necessary to amend the constitution. In the first forty years after the constitution was adopted in 1937, there were only a handful of referenda. However since 1979, there have been 33 referenda. This is an average of nearly one a year. Mercifully, a number of them have been combined on the one day. Quite a number of them have been defeated. Referenda broadly fall under the headings

1. Social issues
2. EU required referenda
3. Institutional issues
4. Other matters

Nine referenda have been held on social issues, five on protection of the unborn, two on divorce and one each on adoption and marriage equality.

While the Irish constitution was amended in 1972 to facilitate the joining of the EU, referenda are required for any substantive changes to the EU treaties. In some cases a second referendum on the same issue has been held, because the first one was lost. This has led the "cynical" to conclude that the electorate will be asked to continue voting until they come up with the right result. There have been 8 such referenda. Issues include the Single European Act, the Amsterdam, Nice and Lisbon treaties and the Fiscal treaty. It seems to be inevitable that Ireland's relationship with the EU will be adversely affected, because a government is unable to get the electorate's assent to a particular treaty change. This is one of the many reasons why any treaty change in connection with the "Brexit" British exit is problematic.

Institutional issues addressed include the proposed abolition of the Seanad, Oireachtas enquiries, recognition of local government, cabinet confidentiality, establishment of Courts, minimum age for the President and judges' pay. These referenda have been particularly prone to rejection.

Other issues addressed include citizenship, recognition of childrens' rights, the change in the status of Northern Ireland and bail.

Turnout in referenda

The turnouts in referenda since 1979 have ranged from a low of 28.57% to a high of 68.18%. However a number of the referenda have co-incided with another political election. The highest turnout for a stand alone referendum is the 62.15% recorded for the successful divorce referendum in 1995. While there were reports of record turnouts, queues out the doors of polling stations etc for the equal marriage referendum in May 2015, in fact the turnout was just slightly in excess of 60%, still a level far in excess of what might have been anticipated. The turnout is affected to some extent by the fact that only citizens can vote; this probably means that 3% to 4% of the register cannot form part of the turnout. Nevertheless there is quite substantial non engagement.

Where referenda are run as stand alone, there are notable features of turnout, which impact on tight contests. There is a tendency for referendum turnout in Dublin and Wicklow to be ahead of the national average, particularly in middle class south Dublin. Referendum turnout also seems to be relatively high in Roscommon and Tipperary. Cork tends to be slightly ahead of the average. All of the western seaboard constituencies have significantly lower than average turnouts, becoming more pronounced as one progresses north. Donegal tends to have a figure between 7% and 10% short of the national figure and routinely has the lowest turnout in all recent referenda. It even managed to be below the average turnout for the 1998 vote on the arrangements for Northern Ireland. This broad pattern continued to be a feature in the May 2015 equal marriage referendum.

The relatively high levels of turnout in Dublin have had a material impact on two referenda which had narrow majorities, the divorce referendum of

1995 and the defeated abortion referendum of 2002, in both of which the margin was around 10,000. In the divorce referendum, Dún Laoghaire and Dublin South constituencies recorded a majority in favour of 39,638 votes. In the abortion referendum, the two constituencies were against by a 31,711 majority. Both margins were more than enough to swing the result. In both these referenda the winning side carried the Dublin constituencies, Wicklow, Kildare, Cork South Central and Limerick City and little else, but that was enough for a win. The same pattern of a relatively higher level of turnout in Dublin was evident in the equal marriage referendum. The Dublin turnout was recorded at almost 64%, a level considerably in excess of Connacht at 57% and Ulster at 54%.

The unusual significance of Dublin to the outturn of referenda can be seen by comparing the percentage which the Dublin vote represents of the total national vote in three recent elections held over a 21 month period

Election	Dublin vote	National vote	Percentage
Local elections 2014	357,974	1,698,630	21.07%
Marriage equality 2015	522,509	1,935,907	26.99%
General election 2016	529,932	2,132,925	24.84%

It should be noted that on the occasions that referenda have been run in tandem with national political elections, the turnout edge in Dublin disappears and becomes a turnout deficit. The June 1984 voting rights referendum, three November 1992 referenda on the unborn, the 1999 local government referendum, the 2004 citizenship referendum and the October 2011 referenda on Judges Pay and Oireachtas Enquiries all co-incided with political elections. Tactically in running a referendum, the government needs to be very alive to these factors, as they clearly have a potential impact on the result.

It is also notable that in the three referenda which have been run twice, the divorce referendum, the ratification of the Nice Treaty and the ratification of the Lisbon Treaty, that turnout increased substantially the second time, a factor almost certainly significant to the passing of the measure.

Spoilt votes in referenda

The level of spoilt votes in referenda seems quite high, given that all that is required of the voter is to place an "X" in one box. The range is from 7.65% in the local government referendum in 1999 representing 109,066 papers to 0.38% in the rejected Lisbon Treaty Referendum. As noted elsewhere (chapter 9) high numbers of spoilt votes are common in referenda run with political elections. This is likely explained by people being issued automatically with a referendum ballot paper as part of the package handed to them and not being interested in the referendum.

Voting trends in referenda

Given the varied nature of referenda, it is difficult to extrapolate a consistent picture. On referenda on social issues, certain Dublin constituencies have always taken a "liberal" position. Only five constituencies Dublin North East, Dublin South East, Dublin South, Dublin South West and Dún Laoghaire rejected the controversial 8th amendment inserting protection for the unborn into the constitution and the same constituencies supported divorce in the failed 1986 referendum. In later social referenda all Dublin constituencies have taken the "liberal" side. By contrast Cork North West, Limerick West and Donegal have been "conservative" on social issues, being the only constituencies to reject right to travel and right to information abortion amendments in 1992.

However Dublin constituencies have tended to be sceptical on matters of institutional reform. All Dublin constituencies rejected the abolition of the Seanad and all rejected the measures proposed for Oireachtas enquiries. Rural objection to these measures was much less. The phenomenon even goes back to Dublin scepticism in 1997 on the issue of cabinet confidentiality, as that measure was defeated in Dublin.

In the referenda of the past 20 years, Donegal has become prone to reject amendments passed in every other county or to have the lowest margin in favour. For example in the relatively innocuous referendum to enable the State cap judges pay, the vote against in Donegal was of the order of 25%, whereas nationally it was 20%. It was one of the few constituencies to reject all of the recent EU related measures. Contrary to popular belief about

Donegal, this seems to be only a feature which has crept into referenda of the 21st century. Donegal did in fact pass the amendment relating to marriage equality, although in the case of the south west constituency, the margin of victory was 33 votes.

It is also now notable, that however "innocuous" the referendum, a solid 20% can be relied upon to be against it, generally representing about 350,000 votes at least. This was the case for sanctioning the creation of a Court of Appeal, judges pay, confining citizenship to persons with an Irish parent, the abolition of the death penalty, approving the International Criminal Court and including local government in the constitution. It is again thought by many that this is a recent phenomenon. However one has to go back to the 1970's to find "innocuous" measures with minimal votes against. It is probably for example doubtful that the 1997 referendum on cabinet confidentiality passed by 52.65% to 47.35% would pass today.

References in Chapter 30

[1] It might be noted that the plural of the word referendum is itself a highly debated subject, with some opting for referenda and others for referendums. Apparently the word in its singular form is a gerund and in Latin gerunds have no plural. It was mischievously suggested in the context of the second 2015 referendum, that dealing with the issue of minimum age to contest the Presidency, that it might have been more useful to vote on what the plural was. For our purposes we are sticking with referenda.

CHAPTER 31
Bye-elections

Circumstances occur relatively frequently where a vacancy arises in the Dáil, Seanad, a local authority or the European Parliament. There are different rules set out to deal with all of these things. Obviously the greatest attention tends to be paid to Dáil bye-elections. Many a Dáil in the last 40 years has been closely balanced between government and opposition and a bye-election gives the opportunity to make significant changes to that balance.

In May 1982, Fianna Fáil were a minority government with a European Commissioner post to fill. A stratagem was arranged to appoint an opposition deputy, former Minister, the late Richard Burke of Fine Gael to that post, in the hope of filling the vacant seat with a government back bencher. At a late stage in the bye-election process, nice new trees were delivered to a number of local housing estates. However the electorate decided to return an opposition deputy, Liam Skelly of Fine Gael to fill the vacancy. Mysteriously the trees were said to have disappeared without trace a few days later.

In late 1994 there was a change of government mid-term, with John Bruton (FG) acceding to the post of Taoiseach in place of Albert Reynolds. (FF) The mathematics were greatly assisted by the fact that the opposition had picked up two seats from Fianna Fáil in bye-elections in Mayo West and Dublin South Central, thus giving it a slender majority. Indeed one of the seats picked up had been the subject of another bye-election ruse, the vacancy being left open by a Fianna Fáil led government for a very long period of time for no apparent reason. On that occasion and subsequently there were court challenges to the failure to move to fill the vacancy.

Dáil bye –elections, the legal rules
In a technical sense a vacancy in the Dáil, European Parliament or a local authority is referred to as a casual vacancy. Article 16.7 of the constitution

says that elections for membership of Dáil Eireann, including the filling of casual vacancies, shall be regulated in accordance with law. Thus it seems that there is no constitutional requirement that a vacancy in Dáil Eireann be filled by way of a special election.

In practice since the foundation of the State however, the law has provided that a Dáil vacancy be filled by a special election.[1]

Until 2011, the law did not set a timescale for the holding of a bye-election. Therefore the government of the day often delayed bye-elections to suit its purpose. This practice was challenged in a 1994 case, Dudley v An Taoiseach, brought when a 14 month period had elapsed since the resignation of John O'Connell T.D as a member for Dublin South Central. On that occasion the challenge seemed to fail on technical grounds. At September 2010, there were three vacancies.[2] A change in the party occupying these seats might well have had a material impact on the balance between government and opposition in the Dáil. In a Dáil debate in late September 2010, the Dáil declined, for the third time, a motion that these writs be moved. However in early November 2010 in a court case taken by Pearse Doherty, the prospective Sinn Féin candidate for Donegal South West (Doherty v Government of Ireland and others), the President of the High Court, Mr Justice Kearns held that the delay was unreasonable on the part of the government. He also held that the section should be interpreted as requiring the writ to be moved within a reasonable time of the vacancy occurring. In the case, unfavourable comparisons were drawn with the failure to fill parliamentary seats in Zimbabwe, due to unduly long drawn out election petitions. The court also held that the failure to hold the bye election raised issues related to the European Convention on Human Rights, which requires states to hold elections at reasonable intervals. In the court case, it was noted that the delay in the case of Donegal South West was the longest in the history of the State.

At about the same time the writ for that bye-election was moved and it was duly held on 25 November 2010. Rather churlishly the government chose a Thursday, perceived as more inconvenient for voters away from home. The equally churlish electorate chose to fill the seat with a member of the opposition. The writs for the other two bye-elections were not moved however, being overtaken by the subsequent early general election in February 2011. This matter was finally dealt with in July 2011 (the Electoral (Amendment) Act 2011) with the adoption of an amendment to section 39 of the Electoral Act 1992, directing the Ceann Comhairle to have the writ moved as soon as possible, if it is not otherwise moved in the period of six months from the date on which the vacancy occurred.

Reasons for a vacancy arising

A vacancy invariably arises because of the death or resignation of the sitting member. However there are a number of legal provisions which require a member to resign his/her position as a member of Dáil Eireann, including circumstances where a petition overturns an election (dealt with in the case of local elections in the Local Elections (Petitions and Disqualification) Act 1974) and circumstances where a member takes up another position, most notably membership of the European Parliament.

Review of Dáil bye-elections

In the period since 1981, there have been 30 Dáil bye-elections. 18 of these have been caused by the death of a sitting TD. 8 have been caused by an election of a TD to the European parliament or appointment to a European office.[3] The vast majority of the 103 bye-elections held up until 1981 arose as a result of the death of the sitting member, the most notable exception being a mass resignation causing 1925 bye-elections as a result of a protest over the handling of an army mutiny. A significant number of vacancies arose in the early 1940's but bye-elections were not held due to the then state of emergency.

Bye-elections cause massive excitement for the political classes. Usually all Oireachtas members are assigned to a patch in the constituency and the electorate are greeted in the main streets of the local towns by all the political celebrities. There is usually a lot of controversy about the level of activity of existing Oireachtas members in the constituency, to whom bye-elections are unlikely to be welcome. In one bye-election, there was a lot of comment about one of the incumbent TDs allegedly taking a holiday during the course of the campaign. Members of the parties come in and they are often great fun for the outside political activists. The local kids get an unexpected day off, as their national schools are needed for polling day. However it is clear that bye-elections are a massive turn off for the electorate. No bye-election had reached a 60% turnout since the Donegal North East bye-election in 1996, almost 20 years ago, until the Carlow Kilkenny bye-election in May 2015.[4] While it would be comforting to think that the electorate of Carlow Kilkenny were highly motivated by the contest to fill a vacancy with a maximum life span of 10 months, the more cynical would conclude that the electorate were in fact engaged to come out and vote by the equal marriage referendum held on the same day. One strongly suspects the electorate were more engaged by the prospect of tweedledum being able to marry tweedledum, than whether tweedledum or tweedledee sat in the Dáil. Half of them have seen turnouts at less than 50%, including lows of 34.13% in the Dublin South West bye-election of 2014 and a shocking 28.18% in the Dublin South Central bye-election in 1999, the lowest turnout seen in any political election in modern times. Turnout in a number of them has been at 60 - 70% of the level seen in the corresponding general election, for example Meath East 2013 38% v 66%, Dublin West 2014 46% v 69%, Meath 2005 41.5% v 59%. It is quite unusual that turnout would be at above 80% of the level experienced in the previous general election, even where the bye-election is hotly contested. There is a question as to whether the Oireachtas should exercise the power, seemingly given it under the constitution, to have vacancies filled by some form of co-option process, given the apparent public apathy about the bye-election mechanism.

Volatility

It is often said that the government hasn't won a bye-election in living memory. This is certainly largely true of Fianna Fáil, who last won a bye-election while in government in July 1982. The Fine Gael/Labour coalition elected in 2011 did however win three bye-elections during its term of office, including a gain from Fianna Fáil. Half of the thirty bye-elections since 1981 have been won by the incumbent political grouping, giving a turnover rate of 50% of the seats, a turnover rate higher than the most mould breaking general elections.

Transfers

As the leading candidate typically receives somewhat less than 50% of the first preference votes, transfers are a critical element of bye-elections. The level of non-transferable votes in bye-elections can be extremely high. In the Dublin South West bye election of 2014, 10,196 votes were cast for candidates other than the leading two candidates, the Socialist Paul Murphy and the Sinn Féin candidate Cathal King. By the end of the count, 5,460 of those votes had accumulated in the non transferable column, meaning that 53.5% of the voters for other candidates expressed no preference for either of the two lead candidates. Equally in the Longford Westmeath bye-election of 2014, 27,728 were cast for eliminated candidates and 14,364 of these accumulated to non transferable rather than in favour of Gabrielle McFadden (FG) or Aengus O'Rourke (FF), the two leading candidates, just short of 52%. Reflecting that pattern, the most recent bye-election in Carlow Kilkenny (May 2015) recorded 34,518 for the eliminated candidates of which 18,673 or 54% failed to transfer to either of the two leading candidates by the end of the count. The corollary of all of this is that in recent times, few candidates actually elected at bye-elections have reached the quota after transfers.

The poor level of transfers also gives an advantage to the candidate leading on the first count, as the second place candidate needs to be quite transfer friendly to catch up. Further candidates have been able to win off comparatively low first preference votes, as low as 18.67% in the case of Roscommon-South Leitrim.[5]

Polls

Polls have sometimes been influential in bye-elections. They often, albeit perhaps inaccurate, identify who the supposed two leading contenders are and can have the effect of causing the vote to drift in their direction, with a corresponding fall off for other candidates. They may well be conducted by companies who are not particularly well reputed for political polling. There is a stronger argument that they should be banned than would be the case for polling in a wider election. They are not conducted for every bye-election. There is no clear pattern in this; for example there was no poll in advance of the most recent bye-election, that in Carlow Kilkenny in May 2015.

Local authorities

The legal rules for a casual vacancy in a local authority are set out in section 19 of the Local Government Act 2001. Generally the vacancy is filled by way of a co-option by the local authority. Practice had evolved over many years that where a vacancy arose, the political party to which the departing member was affiliated could nominate a successor, although in some counties routinely controlled by a particular party, this was not adhered to. This practice was formally made part of the law of the land by section 19 of the Local Government Act 2001 in the case of most vacancies. The law provides that the successor must generally be nominated by the same registered political party as nominated the person who caused the vacancy.[6] In the case of an independent member, the law says that the standing orders adopted by the council should set out the process for filling a casual vacancy.[7]

The circumstances in which a vacancy arises are much the same as for Dáil vacancies. However section 18 of the Local Government Act 2001 provides that absence from attending at any meeting for six months causes the councillor to have been deemed to have resigned. If however the absence is due to illness or other good faith reason, the period for allowed absence can be extended to 18 months by resolution of the body. The resignation of Niamh Cosgrave from Dublin City Council in 2007 is reported to have been for reasons of non attendance at council meetings for six months. In September 2007, it was reported that a jailed councillor (whose conviction was subsequently reversed) had persuaded his fellow councillors that a failure to attend meetings when imprisoned amounted to a good faith reason for not being in a position to attend.

Local authority co-optees have a very mixed track record when it comes to getting re-elected. While better analysis is required, they are much less likely to get re-elected than councillors actually elected at the previous round of local elections. A factor which may influence this is that the party co-option process is often controlled by persons whose best interest may not be served by an over capable co-optee and there can therefore be a tendency to select a candidate who is unlikely to threaten the status quo. There is also a noticeable tendency to select a family member, obviously accentuated where the cause for the vacancy is a death.

European Parliament

Vacancies in the European Parliament are also dealt with by a co-option process and this has been the case since the first directly elected parliament in 1979. The European Parliament Elections Act 1997 prescribes a system where candidates have a list of substitutes nominated in advance of the election. In the case of a candidate nominated by a registered party, the party sets the list and can nominate up to four persons per candidate (so if a party has three candidates in Ireland South, it can nominate up to 12 substitutes). In the case of an individual, the person can nominate three substitutes. When vacancies have arisen in the European Parliament, they have invariably arisen because a member is elected to or appointed to another position, usually an election to Dáil Eireann. The identity of substitutes in usually determined by an internal party selection process, although defeated party candidates are usually the first substitutes. The process may contribute to a poor election track record on the part of co-optees.

European parliament co-optees have had a very poor track record of getting re-elected. The following substitutes have been appointed since 1979 and have sought re-election

Person	party	co-opted	elected at next election
Justin Keating	Lab	1984	no
Chris O'Malley	FG	1986	no
Mark Killilea	FF	1987	yes
Seán Ó'Neachtáin	FF	2002	yes
Colm Burke	FG	2007	no
Paul Murphy	Soc	2011	no
Phil Prendergast	Lab	2011	no
Emer Costello	Lab	2012	no

There was a considerable doubt around the re-election of the Galway based Ó'Neachtáin in 2004 in Ireland North West. In the event he was joined on the ticket by the Donegal based Dr James McDaid, whom he beat by a relatively small margin. As McDaid's location in Donegal was very remote, it is somewhat more doubtful as to whether Ó'Neachtáin would have survived a more centrally based challenger.

There have also been quite a number of Labour and Workers Party co-optees to the European Parliament, who have not been candidates for election in the election following their co-option. This may be because they were perceived to have a poor chance of re-election and were replaced by a candidate perceived as more electable.[8]

References in Chapter 31

1 This is provided by section 39 of the Electoral Act 1992.

2 The three Dáil vacancies in September 2010 were Donegal South West occasioned by the election of Pat The Cope Gallagher (FF) to the European Parliament effective 6 June 2009, Dublin South occasioned by the resignation of George Lee (FG) on 8 February 2010 and Waterford, occasioned by the resignation of Martin Cullen, the former Fianna Fáil Minister in March 2010.

3 The other four bye-elections were caused by the resignation of Dr John O'Connell (FF) in February 1993, the resignation of Ray Burke (FF) in 1998, the resignation of former Taoiseach John Bruton (FG) to take up an international position in 2005 and the resignation of Patrick Nulty (Ind) in 2014.

4 The following are percentage turnouts in bye-elections since 1996.

Year	bye-election	turnout	previous GE turnout
1996	Donegal NE	61.34	66 (1992)
1996	Dublin W	43.70	64 (1992)
1998	Limerick E	54.73	65 (1997)
1998	Dublin N	50.26	66 (1997)
1998	Cork SC	49.48	66 (1997)
1999	Dublin SC	28.18	61 (1997)
2000	Tipperary S	57.97	69 (1997)
2001	Tipperary S	58.91	69 (1997)
2005	Kildare N	39.22	55 (2002)
2005	Meath	41.46	59 (2002)
2009	Dublin S*	57.79	69 (2007)
2009	Dublin Central*	46.35	55 (2007)
2010	Donegal SW	56.03	66 (2007)
2011	Dublin W*	58.3	69 (2011)
2013	Meath E	38.29	66 (2011)
2014	Longford Westmeath*	57.38	68 (2011)
2014	Dublin W*	46.21	69 (2011)
2014	Roscommon S Leitrim	53.84	79 (2011)
2014	Dublin SW	34.49	67 (2011)
2015	Carlow Kilkenny*	65.34	71 (2011)

*co-incided with European and local elections (Presidential in case of Dublin West 2011, referendum in case of Carlow Kilkenny 2015), which probably aided turnout. These elections also show a greater proportion of spoilt votes, presumably voters who don't fill in the bye-election paper but deposit it blank in the ballot box.

Sometimes the turnout figure is reported differently; this seems to involve the disregarding of spoilt votes.

5   Successful bye-election candidates with low first preference votes include Bobby Aylward (FF) in Carlow Kilkenny with 27.79%, Jan O'Sullivan (Lab) in Limerick East with 24.87%, Catherine Murphy (Ind) in Kildare North with 23.64%, Maureen O'Sullivan (Ind) in Dublin Central with 26.89%, Gabrielle McFadden(FG) in Longford Westmeath with 25.23%, Paul Murphy (Soc) in Dublin South West with 27.22%, Ruth Coppinger (Soc) in Dublin West with 20.64% and Michael Fitzmaurice (Ind) in Roscommon South Leitrim with 18.67%.

6   It is not unknown that a vacancy arises after a person has switched affiliations, generally from a party to independent. In that case, it is a matter for the former party to nominate the successor. Thus in 2004, Niamh Cosgrave was elected as a Fine Gael member in Donaghmede LEA for Dublin City Council. By the time she was deemed to have resigned in September 2007 she had become an independent. However, the co-opted member had to be approved by Fine Gael and in due course Pat Crimmins, Fine Gael was co-opted to fill the vacancy.

7   For example standing order 85 of Dublin City Council (2015 version) says that in the case of an independent member, the resigning member (or in case of his death his/her nominee) nominates the successor.

8   For sake of completeness it is worth detailing how Seanad vacancies are filled. Seanad bye-elections are conducted by arranging a poll of all the members of the current Dáil and Seanad. On the basis that the government has generally had control of both of these, Seanad bye-elections are invariably won by the government parties. There is a convention that where the government is a coalition, the party whose member caused the vacancy decides who the government candidate will be. It is important that a candidate in a Seanad bye-election is duly qualified to contest the Panel in which the vacancy occurs. This was a contributory issue in the failure of the Fine Gael/Labour government to fill a vacancy in 2014. On that occasion some inappropriate steps were allegedly taken to qualify the candidate, resulting in his effective withdrawal. The Taoiseach is entitled to nominate eleven members to the Seanad and any vacancy in their case is filled by a further Taoiseach nomination. It is not unusual that the outgoing Taoiseach has a few spots to fill after a general election and this is seen as somewhat of a perk for the politically connected. While two such vacancies arose after the 2016 general election by virtue of the election of Katherine Zappone (Independent) and Hildegarde Naughton (Fine Gael) to Dáil Eireann, the acting Taoiseach chose not to fill those vacancies.

CHAPTER 32

European Elections

Elections to the European Parliament have been fought on eight occasions commencing in 1979 and thereafter on a five year cycle, with the last one held in 2014. The European Parliament elections have been fought on a mixture of three, four and five seat constituencies.

The first seven elections up to 2009 were fought on constituencies based on Dublin, the rest of Leinster, Munster and Connaught-Ulster. However over time, the Munster county of Clare and the Leinster counties of Longford and Westmeath were added to Connaught Ulster to create a reasonably level of proportionality between the constituencies as to population. Further in 2004 and 2009, the Connaught Ulster constituency became known as Ireland North West, the Leinster constituency became known as Ireland East and the Munster constituency became known as Ireland South. In 2014, the number of constituencies was reduced to three. Most of Leinster (ex Dublin) was joined to Connaught Ulster to form Ireland Midlands North West. The Leinster counties of Carlow, Kilkenny, Wexford and Wicklow were joined to Munster to form Ireland South.

For elections from 1979 to 1999, Ireland was allocated 15 seats. The EU was substantially enlarged from 2005 and this caused a reduction of Ireland's allocation to 13 seats in 2004 in anticipation of enlargement. Further enlargements involving Bulgaria, Croatia and Romania caused Ireland's allocation to fall by a further seat in each of 2009 and 2014, leaving the current representation at 11. Thus over 8 elections, 111 seats have been fought. Members of the European Parliament are colloquially referred to as MEPs.

While the 1979 election is technically outside the period covered by this work, it has been decided to include it, as it was the first direct election to the Parliament and is conveniently covered.

Method of election

Elections to the European Parliament are conducted using the same single transferable vote principle as is used in Dáil and local elections. The constituencies have usually been set by an independent committee, although generally until 2014, the provinces were kept reasonably intact. While representations have been made from time to time to create a single national constituency, it has been decided to stick with the three to five seat principle used for Dáil purposes.

Three/four and five seats

Most European elections have been fought on the basis of either three or four seats in a constituency. Three seat constituencies have featured on 16 occasions and four seat constituencies on 12 occasions. In the 1979 to 1989 elections Munster was a five seat constituency.

On 5 occasions, two seats have been won by a party in a three seat constituency, with the first preference vote going as low as 36.92% in the case of Fianna Fáil winning two seats in Leinster in 1989. On that occasion the winning margin was 10 votes, the lowest ever margin in a European election in Ireland. On all other occasions, first preferences for the successful party were in the low 40% region. The other eleven elections based on three seat constituencies resulted in a 1:1:1 outcome and Independent candidates have been elected on 7 of those occasions.

On 8 occasions, two seats have been won by a party in a four seat constituency, with the first preference vote being as low as 27.75% in the case of Fine Gael winning two seats in Ireland South in 2014. On most other occasions, first preferences for the successful party were in the 30% region, so two seats have been won with about a quota and a half of first preferences. The Dublin constituency in 1984 returned two seats for both Fianna Fáil and Fine Gael; the only other occasion this happened was in the five seat Munster in the same election. The other five elections based on four seat constituencies resulted in a 1:1:1:1 outcome. Independent and smaller party candidates have been elected on 8 occasions.

Munster was fought on three occasions 1979,1984 and 1989 as a five seat constituency. On each occasion Fianna Fáil won two seats, with independents also featuring quite strongly.

Strong performances

It is comparatively unusual that two seats are won based on a vote of more than two quotas. This has only happened four times, all in Munster in 1979, 1984, 1994 and 1999. In 1999 Fianna Fáil got 52.9% of the votes in Munster, driven by a very powerful performance by Brian Crowley. This is the only occasion in 31 contests that a party has got more than half of the vote.

Brian Crowley has been elected five times for Fianna Fáil in Ireland South/Munster and on four of those occasions obtained over 100,000 first preference votes, with an aggregate of 662,784 votes in his five elections. Mairead McGuinness of Fine Gael is the only other candidate who has got more than 100,000 votes on two separate occasions, with 114,249 and 110,366 votes respectively in Ireland East in 2004 and 2009.

Poor performances

As with other elections, European elections attract candidates who obtain very poor votes. Six candidates have obtained less than 1,000 votes.[1] Chris Morris, the lowest polling candidate ever ,was a candidate for the Community Democrats, running on the slogan "Vote No 1 Morris for the No 1 Party", a piece of advice obviously widely ignored.

Leaders' enclosure

In common with other elections it is usually the case that the three four or five candidates getting the highest first preferences succeed in three, four and five seat constituencies respectively. There are only 10 occasions out of 111 seats contested where a candidate came from outside the leading group to displace another. The largest gap made up was the 8,344 bridged by Neasa Childers, the independent candidate in Dublin in 2014. Mary Banotti of Fine Gael bridged a gap of 7,679 in Dublin in 1989, but had the assistance of 26,574 first preference votes obtained by another party candidate.

Securing one seat

There have been a number of cases where a single seat has been secured on a first preference vote of 10% or less. The most notable performance was by Pat Cox, Independent in securing a seat in Munster (4 seats) with 7.66% of the vote in 1994. In 2014 Neasa Childers, Independent secured a seat with 10.19% of the first preferences in Dublin (3 seats) and Marian Harkin secured a seat with 10.67% of the first preference vote in Ireland North West (3 seats). Generally however one seat has been secured with votes near to or exceeding the quota.

Transfers

Even though the constituencies are quite large, the rate of transfer between Fianna Fáil candidates and Fine Gael candidates is similar to that in general elections. An examination of the last five elections suggests that transfers by Fianna Fáil to other Fianna Fáil candidates averages about 55% and transfers by Fine Gael to other Fine Gael candidates averages about 57.5%. In earlier European elections, the rates of transfer for Fianna Fáil were significantly higher and the rates of transfer for Fine Gael marginally higher. Generally the Labour Party only runs one candidate in a European constituency, but on the occasions they have run two, the transfer rates have been poor and often in the 30-40% range. In some of the earlier elections Sinn Féin had multiple candidates and the transfer rates were poor. A more reliable indicator of potential Sinn Féin transfers was the 57.5% transferred between two Sinn Féin candidates in Ireland East in 2009.

Transfers from one party to another follow the usual patterns seen in general elections. There is a tendency for parties of the left to transfer left and for independents to transfer to other independents. Transfers are generally at quite low levels, which probably accounts for those in the leaders' enclosure generally winning.

Turnout

Turnout nationally has ranged from 43,96% in 1994 to 68.33% in 1989. The latter election however took place on the same day as a general election and the next highest figure was the 63.6% turnout in the inaugural 1979 elections. Turnouts in the four elections 1999 to 2014, each of which co-incided with a local election were in the 50-60% range and this appears to be the norm. The highest constituency turnout recorded was the 72.48% turnout in Connaught-Ulster in 1979. The lowest was the 36.14% turnout in Dublin in 1999. Turnout is always at its lowest in Dublin, frequently about 10% less than the other constituencies. The highest vote cast in European elections was the 1,875,920 votes cast in 2009.

Number of candidates

Each election has seen a number of candidates between 40 and 53 contesting, with the number for the last four elections settling around 40. There has been a trend for the two main parties to run the minimum number of candidates, which has contributed to a reduction in overall numbers. The lowest number of candidates contesting a constituency was 8 in the case of Leinster in 1999. The highest number contesting was 16 in Munster in 1994.

Spoilt votes

European elections always feature a high number of spoilt votes, with percentages generally in the 2% or 3% range, reaching as high as 4.78% in Leinster in 1979. It is likely that the high level of spoilt votes is related to the fact that European elections are nearly always run with another election. It is not unusual that two separate ballot papers are marked as if they were one and this can give rise to the European paper being spoilt. It is also possible that voters take two papers but decide not to mark the European ballot paper, depositing it in the ballot box unmarked. Following the 2014 election, Dan Kiely, an independent candidate in Listowel LEA in Kerry challenged the way in which certain European and local ballots were adjudged. The ruling of the Supreme Court in 2015 was to the effect that there must be an unambiguous number 1 on the ballot paper. It seems likely that this will result in a high number of spoilt ballots in future European elections.

Replacement of MEPs

This is dealt with in chapter 31.

Tactical approach

There is relatively little evidence of a sophisticated level of tactical approach by either of the main parties, Fianna Fáil or Fine Gael to European elections. This is slightly strange as presumably each party has an established vote in each county and it should be possible by appropriate postering and leafleting to divide votes equally between candidates. A difficulty which seems apparent in some cases is the presence of a "celebrity" candidate, whose vote is presumably difficult to control. Where parties have managed to obtain two seats, it is sometimes done despite a poorly balanced vote rather than on account of one.

In general in European elections, parties are realistically targeting only one seat and therefore the prime focus is to get as many number one votes for the candidate as possible. Since 2000, two seats have only been secured by a party on two occasions, both by Fine Gael and on both occasions, the level of vote was quite unbalanced. Indeed on the second occasion Ireland South in 2014, Fine Gael had three candidates, but secured two seats because the Fianna Fáil vote was exceptionally lopsided and transferred badly.

In earlier elections Fianna Fáil were quite skillful in balancing their vote in some contests. In 1999 in Leinster Jim Fitzsimons got 58,750 first preferences and Liam Hyland got 58,477 first preferences a ratio of 50.1 to 49.9. Their vote was somewhat less well balanced in the same constituency in 1989 and 1994, but was still well managed. On the two occasions that Fianna Fáil obtained two seats in Connaught Ulster, there was also a reasonable balance in their vote.

Poor balance in votes seems a more prevalent feature. In 2014 in Ireland South, Fianna Fáil had 31.99% of the first preference vote, over 4% more than Fine Gael. However it split 85.7% Crowley and 14.35% Hartley and poor transfers resulted in Hartley being 2,000 votes behind the third Fine Gael candidate at the point of his elimination. In 1999 in the Leinster constituency Avril Doyle of Fine Gael got 67,881 first preferences and Alan Gillis her party colleague and outgoing MEP got 48,729 first preferences. A better balance between them might have secured a second seat for Fine Gael.

References in Chapter 32

[1]   The six candidates polling below 1,000 votes were Chris Morris (Connaught Ulster 1979) 447, Denis Riordan (Munster 1994) 607, Paul Raymond (Connaught Ulster 1999) 840, Conor Moloney (Munster 1994) 858, Stewart Luck (Munster 1994) 890 and Kevin Clear (Dublin 1979) 915. Mr Riordan managed to stretch to 1,007 votes in the 1999 election in Munster, his highest vote in 11 different elections.

CHAPTER 33
Presidential Elections

The term of office for the President of Ireland is set at seven years under Article 12.3.1 of the Irish Constitution. While the presidency of Ireland has become vacant on a number of occasions during the period under review, there have only been three elections in 1990, 1997 and 2011. President Patrick Hillery's first term of office ended in 1983; he was however the only nominee for the position of President at that time and therefore served a second term without any requirement for an election. Similarly President Mary McAleese was the only nominee in 2004 on the expiry of her first term and she obtained a second term without need for an election.

The constitutional convention established in 2011 suggested that the term of office of a President be reduced to five years, with the intention that the elections should co-incide with elections to local authorities. However this recommendation was not proceeded with.

Nomination of candidates

The process for nomination of candidates is set out in the constitution, Article 12.4. The traditional route has been by nomination by 20 persons, each of whom is a member of the Oireachtas. All elections up to 1997 were contested on this basis, resulting in the candidates all being sponsored by one of the traditional parties. However the constitution also provides for four Councils to nominate a candidate. This has resulted in the 1997 and 2011 elections in a process where there was a degree of competition for nominations from the county councils, with a number of candidates being nominated by that route. In 1997, the parties made significant efforts to try and prevent their councillors from nominating independent candidates, but with limited success. A lot of the drama around presidential campaigns involves independent candidates trying to collect the four nominations needed by vote of a county council. The serving president (and indeed any former president) is entitled to nominate himself or herself.

Elections and transfers

The most interesting contest is perhaps that of 1990 which was contested by Brian Lenihan Snr nominated by Fianna Fáil, Mary Robinson nominate by Labour (and the Workers Party) and Austin Currie nominated by Fine Gael. On the first count Brian Lenihan obtained 694,484 votes and Mary Robinson obtained 612,265 votes, a difference of 82,219 votes. However Austin Currie, the third placed candidate had 267,902 votes and 205,565 of those transferred to Mrs Robinson, giving her a margin of victory of 86,557 votes. The rate of transfer was an impressive 76.73%. Mary Robinson was the first ever female candidate in an Irish Presidential election; this phenomenon became so popular that only one man contested the 1997 Presidential election and he finished last.

Both other contests resulted in a substantial first count lead for the successful candidate, with Mary McAleese securing 45.24% of the vote in 1997 and Michael D Higgins securing 39.57% of the vote in 2011.[1]

Two person races

While all of the contests in the period reviewed have involved more than two candidates, there has been a tendency for the voters to opt for the leading two candidates, who obtained in aggregate 83% (1990), 74.5% (1997) and 68.1% (2011) of the first preference vote respectively. In practice each of the races seems to have evolved into a choice between two persons, undoubtedly influenced by opinion polls conducted through the period of the campaign. While transfer rates have been quite high from the lower candidates, in practice, other than the 1990 election, they have not made any difference.

Non transferable votes

Presidential elections normally result in most of the votes of lower candidates being transferred to the two leading candidates, with non transferable votes being less than 25%.[2] The level of spoilt votes in Presidential elections has in the three cases been about 1% or less. Turnout has ranged from 47.6% to 64.1%.

References in Chapter 33

[1]   In 1997 the three lower candidates were all eliminated at the second count and their transfers split fairly evenly between Mary MacAleese,   the Fianna Fáil sponsored candidate and Mary Banotti, the Fine Gael sponsored candidate. In 2011, there were three successive counts, with Michael D Higgins accruing over 71% of the transfers, with just under 29% accruing to Sean Gallagher an independent candidate, perceived as being associated with Fianna Fáil.

[2]   In 1990, the 267,902 first preference votes of Austin Currie, the eliminated candidate transferred at a rate in excess of 90% to the two remaining candidates. In 1997, just under   80% of the 323,410 first preference votes of the Labour and two independent candidates transferred to the two leading candidates. In 2011 there were five other candidates (Fine Gael, Sinn Féin and three independents) with an aggregate 565,697 first preference votes and over 75% of those votes transferred to one of the two leading candidates.

SELECTED BIBLIOGRAPHY

Brennan and Murphy Brennan's Key to Local Authorities *1986 Landscape Press*

Brennan   Count, Recount and Petition, Laois County Council Local Elections 1999 *2000 Institute of Public Administration* (this is the best work for explaining in detail principles applicable to spoilt and non transferable votes)

Browne The Magill Book of Irish Politics *1981 Magill Publications Limited* (This is an excellent publication summarising all elections up to and including 1981 and containing colourful and erudite commentary from Vincent Browne).

Collins Sunday Tribune Guide to Politics *1997 Tribune Publications*

Dept of Environment Local Elections 2004 and 2009 Results, Transfer of Votes and Statistics *Stationery Office*

Donnelly Poll Position An analysis of the 1991 Local Elections *1992 Sean Donnelly*

Donnelly   Partnership The Story of the 1992 General Election *1993 Sean Donnelly*

Donnelly   Elections '99 – All Kinds of Everything *1999 Brunswick Press*

Donnelly Local Elections 2004 *Sean Donnelly*

Donnelly Local Elections 2009   *2012 Sean Donnelly*

Donnelly Local Elections 2014 *2015 Sean Donnelly*
(Mr Donnelly's work is invaluable, particularly for extensive statistical analysis)

Hogan and Whyte JM Kelly: The Irish Constitution 4th edition

Magill (elections 1982, 1983, 1987) *Magill Publications Limited*

Mc Carthy Election 2011 and the 31st Dáil (RTE The Week in Politics)

Nealon's Guide (various elections 22nd to 31st Dáil) *2011 Gill Books*

Rafter and Whelan   Malin Head to Mizen Head *1992 Blackwater Press*

Websites

Adriankavanaghelections.org
(this is the best source of contemporary political commentary)

Electionsireland.org
(an excellent source for figures but needs updating)

Irelandelection.com
(wonderful graphics showing progress of counts)

Ark.ac.uk
(this is a really good site with election data for Northern Ireland)

INDEX

M

Only candidates material to the narrative are included in this index. The party designation for a candidate is the one most recent used by the candidate in elections.